Perspectives in Law, Business and Innovation

Series Editor

Toshiyuki Kono, Professor, Graduate School of Law, Kyushu University, Fukuoka City, Japan

Over the last three decades, interconnected processes of globalization and rapid technological change — particularly, the emergence of networked technologies — have profoundly disrupted traditional models of business organization. This economic transformation has created multiple new opportunities for the emergence of alternate business forms, and disruptive innovation has become one of the major driving forces in the contemporary economy. Moreover, in the context of globalization, the innovation space increasingly takes on a global character. The main stakeholders — innovators, entrepreneurs and investors — now have an unprecedented degree of mobility in pursuing economic opportunities wherever they arise. As such, frictionless movement of goods, workers, services, and capital is becoming the "new normal".

This new economic and social reality has created multiple regulatory challenges for policymakers as they struggle to come to terms with the rapid pace of these social and economic changes. Moreover, these challenges impact across multiple fields of both public and private law. Nevertheless, existing approaches within legal science often struggle to deal with innovation and its effects.

Paralleling this shift in the economy, we can, therefore, see a similar process of disruption occurring within contemporary academia, as traditional approaches and disciplinary boundaries — both within and between disciplines — are being re-configured. Conventional notions of legal science are becoming increasingly obsolete or, at least, there is a need to develop alternative perspectives on the various regulatory challenges that are currently being created by the new innovation-driven global economy.

The aim of this series is to provide a forum for the publication of cutting-edge research in the fields of innovation and the law from a Japanese and Asian perspective. The series will cut across the traditional sub-disciplines of legal studies but will be tied together by a focus on contemporary developments in an innovation-driven economy and will deepen our understanding of the various regulatory responses to these economic and social changes.

The series editor and editorial board carefully assess each book proposal and sample chapters in terms of their relevance to law, business, and innovative technological change. Each proposal is evaluated on the basis of its academic value and distinctive contribution to the fast-moving debate in these fields.

More information about this series at http://www.springer.com/series/15440

Marcelo Corrales Compagnucci

Big Data, Databases and "Ownership" Rights in the Cloud

Springer

Marcelo Corrales Compagnucci
Centre for Advanced Studies in Biomedical
Innovation Law (CeBIL)
University of Copenhagen
Copenhagen, Denmark

ISSN 2520-1875 ISSN 2520-1883 (electronic)
Perspectives in Law, Business and Innovation
ISBN 978-981-15-0351-1 ISBN 978-981-15-0349-8 (eBook)
https://doi.org/10.1007/978-981-15-0349-8

This Springer imprint is published by the registered company Springer Nature Singapore Pte Ltd.
The registered company address is: 152 Beach Road, #21-01/04 Gateway East, Singapore 189721, Singapore

Preface

I became aware of the importance of undertaking further research in the contractual analysis of databases during a master's course in European Intellectual Property Law at Stockholm University. One of the key aspects of the LL.M. course syllabus was a focus on copyrights and database rights on the Internet. Problems can occur when companies and scientific institutions use and share "raw" data. These issues became more evident to me while working on a European Union (EU) funded project about cloud computing called OPTIMIS (Optimized Infrastructure Services) during my stay at the Institute for Legal Informatics (IRI) at the Leibniz Universität Hannover (LUH) in Germany. By a stroke of luck, I became heavily involved in the legal work that established what has turned out, for me, to be one of the most interesting topics on which to write a whole book. My personal experience of working with my colleagues from the OPTIMIS project has prompted me to pursue this field of research. I realized there was not much literature and material concerning the sui generis right as it applies to the field of cloud computing and Big Data.

In recent years, there has been an extraordinary tendency for companies and research institutions to create databases and to store them in the cloud. This new phenomenon encouraged me to further my analysis on the subject from an interdisciplinary point of view. In this process, I have utilized knowledge from the disciplines of information technology (IT), philosophy, psychology, law, and economics together. The outcome will be to take into account the fact that databases in the cloud play an important role, and that a contractual model which includes a framework for the "ownership" of data and databases is necessary for choosing an appropriate cloud provider and outsourcing data safely in an automated fashion. This paradigm is submitted as a necessary adjunct to existing models in the field of cloud computing and the Big Data movement.

In developing the concepts described in this book, I had the opportunity to learn from many people. First and foremost, I would like to thank gratefully both Prof. Toshiyuki Kono and Prof. Shinto Teramoto. They were the supervisors of my Ph.D. thesis carried out during the LL.D. program at Kyushu University in Japan. Their constant support, guidance, and recommendations were invaluable. I would also like to take this opportunity to acknowledge the Japanese Embassy in Paraguay and the Monbukagakusho-MEXT scholarship for funding my research in Fukuoka, Japan. Without the generous financial support from the Japanese government, my trip to Japan and this research work would not have been possible. I have also received additional funding from the Orin Foundation through a grant given to support my studies in Fukuoka. I owe special thanks to Date-sensei for allowing me this opportunity and for introducing me the Japanese culture.

I am also much indebted to the Max Planck Society for repeatedly awarding me a research fellowship and hosting me at both the Max Planck Institute for Comparative and International Private Law (Hamburg) and the Max Planck Institute for Innovation and Competition (Munich). Thanks to the grant I received from the Max Planck Society, I had the great opportunity to pursue part of my research endeavors and benefit from their comprehensive resources, which help greatly to generate the intellectual climate to conclude my research. I would also like to express my sincere gratitude to the EU Institute in Japan (EUIJ-Kyushu) and the selection committee for the generous grant of the "EU Research Award of Excellence" in recognition of my work. This award is a distinct honor that will be an invaluable asset to my future career as a researcher in the field of IT & IP Law.

On a personal side, I would also like to thank all my colleagues from IRI for giving me the opportunity to work with them on various cutting-edge EU funded projects such as ACGT[1] and OPTIMIS[2] throughout my academic years at IRI (LUH). I am indebted to all of them for their collective efforts in the various inspirational coffee breaks where we discussed various IT and IP Law-related issues. I have also benefited greatly from the opportunity to present lectures at the LL.M. program in IT and IP Law (EULISP) where I learnt enormously through my students. I am thankful to my colleagues from the OPTIMIS project with whom I had the chance to learn not only the legal issues involved but also all the technical complexities in cloud transformations. Special thanks are owed to Prof. Karim Djemame for helping me implement the risk assessment framework and for offering the cloud testbed of Leeds University in order to carry out the experiments showcased in Chap. 9 of this book. In this regard, I am also very thankful to Dr. George Kousiouris for helping me to translate and embed the legal issues within the SLA/XML framework of the OPTIMIS toolkit, which is part of Chap. 8 of this work. Without their technical explanations and support, this research would not contain a practical contribution to the state of the art.

Among all my mentors, it seems unfair to exempt a few for special thanks. I should heartily thank though in particular Prof. Cecilia Magnusson and Prof. Peter Wahlgren, who were my first teachers in the field of IT Law at Stockholm University in Sweden. I must also thank Katarina Renman-Claesson who was my supervisor with regard to the master's thesis about biological databases that I

[1]Advancing Clinico-Genomic Trials on Cancer (ACGT). EU funded project within the 6th Framework Program under contract IST-026996. Available at: act.ercim.eu. Accessed July 1, 2010.

[2]Optimized Infrastructure Services (OPTIMIS). EU funded project within the 7th Framework Program under contract ICT-257115. Available at: https://ec.europa.eu/digital-single-market/en/news/optimis. Accessed July 1, 2019.

submitted in 2009 and Prof. Graeme Laurie for funding a research fellowship at the SCRIPT Institute of Edinburgh University, where I also had the chance to do research on biological databases. Special thanks to Prof. Steven Van Uytsel, for the feedback provided during the Legal Research Training classes at Kyushu University and to all my mentors for the feedback provided during the various Comprehensive Research Seminars held at Kyushu University. I would also like to deeply thank Prof. Mark Fenwick, for his helpful insights with regard to the theoretical framework of this work and for kindling the interest in legal philosophy theory during the Law and Theory Colloquium at Kyushu University.

Ultimately, many thanks to Dr. Paulius Jurčys, Prof. Ryu Kojima, Prof. Nikolaus Forgó, Prof. Caslav Pejovic, Prof. Jürgen Basedow, Dr. Gintare Surblyte, and Prof. Stefan Wrbka for their support and advice in different ways. Last but not least, to my parents, friends, and relatives for their love and constant support. Thank you for always being there for me. Many other people have contributed in developing the concepts of this work in myriad ways that it makes it impossible for me to continue the list. In the hopes that they know who they are, I am sincerely thankful to all the people in my surroundings for inspiring me every day. The content of this book does not necessarily reflect the views of the aforementioned people and/or institutions. The author is solely responsible for its content.

Copenhagen, Denmark Dr. Marcelo Corrales Compagnucci

Table of Cases

Danske Dagblades Forening (DDF) v Newsbooster [2003] ECDR 5: D (City Court) (Denmark).

Radio Telefis Eireann (RTE) and Independent Television Publications Ltd (ITP) v Commission of the European Communities [the Magill case]. Competition—Abuse of dominant position—Copyright. Joined cases C-241/91 and C-242/91 P. Judgement of the Court of 6 April 1995 (France).

Le Monde v Microfor, Cass., 9 November 1983 [1984-5/1] DIT 20–23, comment Mignot (France).

Fixtures Marketing Ltd. v Oy Veikkaus AB, ECJ—Case C-46/02, 9 November 2004 (Finland).

Directmedia GmbH v Albert-Ludwig Universität Freiburg [the Directmedia case] (Germany).

HIT BILANZ IZR 290/02 Federal Supreme Court (Bundesgerichtshof), C-304/07 (21 July 2005) [the Hit Bilanz case] (Germany).

Landgericht München I (Topografische Kartenblätter), Urteil 21 0 7402/02, 9.11.2005, GRUR 2006, 225 (Germany).

Freistaat Bayern v Verlag Esterbauer GmbH., C490/14 (Germany).

Fixtures Marketing Ltd. v Organismos Prognostikon Agonon Podosfairou [the OPAP case], CJEU-Case C-444/02, 9 November 2004 (Greece).

Judgment concerning the case where the provider of the service of making it possible to acquire re-productions of broadcast programs, etc. is considered to be the party who performs reproduction (Case to seek injunction against copyright infringement, etc.), Minshu Vol. 65, No. 1, 2009 (Ju) 788, 2011.01.20 (Japan).

Decision of the Japanese Supreme Court of 31 January 2017 and the Tokyo High Court of 12 July 2016 (Japan).

Google Spain SL, Google Inc. v Agencia Española de Protección de Datos (es), Mario Costeja González, number C-131/12 (Spain).

Fixtures Marketing Ltd. v Svenska Spel AB, CJEU—Case C- 338/02, 9 November 2004 (Sweden).

NV Holdingmaatschappij de Telegraaf v Nederlandse Omroep Stichting [2002] ECDR 8 Court of Appeal of the Hague, [the Telegraaf case] (The Netherlands).

Algemeen Dagblad v Eureka Internetdiensten, ['the kranten.com' case] [2002] ECDR 1 (The Netherlands).
Innoweb BV v Wegener ICT Media BV, Wegener Mediaventions BV, Case C202/12 (The Netherlands).
Van Dale Lexicografie B.V. v Rudolf Jan Romme, Hoge Raad, Supreme Court of the Netherlands, 4 January 1991, NG 1991, 608 (The Netherlands).
Ryanair Ltd v PR Aviation BV, Case C-30/14 (The Netherlands).
Pearson Assessment and Information B.V. v Bär Software C, Court of Appeal, 22 November 2016, C/13/482409/HA ZA 11-441 (The Netherlands).
University of London Press v University Turorial Press [1916] 2 Ch 601 (United Kingdom).
Ladbroke v William Hill [1964] 1 WLR 273 (HL) (United Kingdom).
Apis-Hristovich EOOD v Lakorda AD [2009] 3 CMLR 3 (ECJ) (United Kingdom).
Exchange Communications Ltd. v Masheder [2009] CSOH 135 (United Kingdom).
The British Horseracing Board Ltd and Others v William Hill Organization Ltd., [the BHB case], CJEU, Case C-203/02, 9 November 2004 (United Kingdom).
Football Dataco and others v Yahoo and others, Case C-604/10, 1 March 2012, [hereinafter the Dataco v Yahoo case] (United Kingdom).
Football Dataco Ltd and other companies v Sportradar GMBH and another company; Football Dataco Ltd and other companies v Stan James Abingdon Ltd and other companies: Chancery Division (Mr. Justice Floyd): 8 May 2012. [the Dataco case) (United Kingdom).
Galaxy Electronics Pty Ltd v Sega Enterprises Ltd (1997), 37 IPR 462 ('Galaxy Electronics') (United Kingdom).
Mars UK Ltd v Teknowledge Ltd [1999] EWHC 226 [the Mars case] (United Kingdom).
Feist Publications v Rural Telephone Service Co. 499 U.S. 340 (1991) (United States).
New York Times Co. v. Tasini, 533 U.S. 483, 7 (2001) (United States).
Greenberg et al v. Miami Children's Hospital Research Institute Inc., 208 F. Supp 2d 918 (2002), 264 F. Supp 2d. 1064 (2003), United States District Court, S. D. F. (United States).
Schroeder v. William Morrow & Co., 566 F.2d 3 (7th Cir. 1977) (United States).
Adventures in God Eating, Inc. v. Best Places to Eat, 131 F.2d 809 (7th Cir. 1942) (United States).
Neade v. Portes, 739 N.E.2d 496 (Ill. 2000) (United States).
Jeweler's Circular Publishing Co. v. Keystone Publishing Co. v. Edward Thompson Co., 169 F. 833 (C.C.E.D.N.Y. 1909) (United States).

Contents

About the Author

Dr. Marcelo Corrales Compagnucci is Attorney-at-Law specializing in intellectual property (IP), information technology (IT), and corporate law. His research interests are the legal issues involved in disruptive innovation technologies. He is currently a Postdoctoral Researcher at the Center for Advanced Studies in Biomedical Innovation Law (CeBIL), Faculty of Law, University of Copenhagen in Denmark. His past activities have included working as a consultant and lawyer for law firms and IT companies. He was also a Research Associate with the Institute for Legal Informatics (IRI) at Leibniz Unvirsität Hannover in Germany, and a visiting research fellow in various research centers around the world, including the Max Planck Institute for Comparative and International Private Law (Hamburg), the Max Planck Institute for Innovation and Competition (Munich), the Shepherd and Wedderburn Centre for Research in Intellectual Property and Technology (SCRIPT) within the University of Edinburgh in Scotland, and the Academia Sinica in Taiwan. He has a Doctor of Laws (LL.D.) degree from Kyushu University in Japan. He also holds a Master of Laws (LL.M.) in international economics and business law from Kyushu University, and an LL.M. in law and information technology and an LL.M. in European intellectual property law, both from the University of Stockholm in Sweden. He has several publications in the field of IT & IP Law. His most recent publications include *New Technology, Big Data and the Law* (Springer, 2017); *Robotics, AI and the Future of Law* (Springer, 2018); and *Legal Tech, Smart Contracts and Blockchain* (Springer, 2019).

Acronyms

AA	Artificial Agents
ACGT	Advancing Clinico-Genomic Trials on Cancer
AI	Artificial Intelligence
AMI	Amazon Machine Image
API	Application Programming Interface
ASP	Application Service Provider Agreements
AWS	Amazon Web Services
B2B	Business-to-Business
BCE	Before Common Era
BCR	Binding Corporate Rules
BHB	British Horseracing Board
CA	Certification Authorities
CBS	Cloud Brokerage Service
CC	Creative Commons
CD-ROM	Compact Disc Read-Only Memory
CeBIL	Center for Advanced Studies in Biomedical Innovation Law
CEOs	Chief Executive Officers
CERN	European Organization for Nuclear Research
CIA	Confidentiality, Integrity and Availability
CIOs	Chief Information Officers
CJEU	Court of Justice of the European Union
CoE	Council of Europe
CPDT	Cloud Provider Description Template
CPU	Central Processing Unit
CTP	Cloud Trust Protocol
DDBJ	DNA Data Bank of Japan
DM	Data Management
DNA	Deoxyribonucleic Acid
DPD	EU Data Protection Directive
DPIA	Data Protection Impact Assessment

EBI	European Bioinformatics Institute
EC2	Elastic Compute Cloud
ECJ	European Court of Justice
EEA	European Economic Area
EEPROM	Electronically Erasable Programmable Read-Only Memory
EMBL	European Molecular Biology Laboratory
ENISA	European Network and Information Security Agency
EU	European Union
EU GDPR	European Union General Data Protection Regulation
EUIJ-Kyushu	European Union Institute in Japan-Kyushu University
EULISP	European Union Legal Informatics Study Program
FaaS	Framework as a Service
FIFA	International Federation of Association Football
GB	Gigabyte
GICTF	Global Inter-Cloud Technology Forum
GLOP	General Logic of Plans
GPS	Global Positioning System
GSM	Global System for Mobile (Communications)
GUI	Graphical User Interface
HTTP	Hypertext Transfer Protocol
IaaS	Infrastructure as a Service
ICT	Information and Communications Technologies
IDE	Integrated Development Environment
IEC	International Electrotechnical Commission
IEEE	Institute of Electrical and Electronics Engineers
IERC	IoT European Research Cluster
IHS	Information Handling Services
INFOSOC	Copyright Directive or Information Society Directive
IP	Intellectual Property
IPOs	Initial Public Offerings
IPRAT	Infrastructure Provider Risk Assessment Tool
IPRs	Intellectual Property Rights
IPs	Infrastructure Providers
IRI	Institute for Legal Informatics
ISCC	International Standard Contractual Clauses
ISO	International Standards Organization
ISP(s)	Internet Service Provider(s)
IT	Information Technology
JR	Japan Railway
LL.D.	Doctor of Laws
LL.M.	Master of Laws
LUH	Leibniz Universität Hannover
M&A	Mergers and Acquisitions
ML	Machine Learning
NCBI	National Center for Biotechnology Information

NGO	Non-governmental Organization
NIST	US National Institute of Standards and Technology
OECD	Organization for Economic Co-operation and Development
OGF	Open Grid Forum
OIRA	White House Office of Information and Regulatory Affairs
OPTIMIS	Optimized Infrastructure Services
PaaS	Platform as a Service
PbD	Privacy by Design
PIA	Privacy Impact Assessment
PIL	Private International Law
PIPA	Japan's Personal Information Protection Act (Act No. 57 of 2003)
PIPC	Personal Information Protection Commission
PM	Programing Model
PoF	Points of Failure
QoS	Quality of Service
R&D	Research and Experimental Development
RAM	Random Access Memory
RNA	Ribonucleic Acid
RWB	Reporters without Borders
SaaS	Software as a Service
SCA	Shared Cooperation Activity
SCC	Standard Contractual Clauses
SIaaS	Software Infrastructure as a Service
SLA(s)	Service Level Agreement(s)
SLO	Service Level Objectives
SLOP	Simple Logic of Planning
SMEs	Small- and Medium-sized Enterprises
SNA	Social Network Analysis
SNS	Social Networking Service
SPRAT	Service Provider Risk Assessment Tool
TCG	Trusted Computing Group
TRIPS Agreement	Agreement on Trade-related Aspects of Intellectual Property
UK	United Kingdom
UML	Unified Modeling Language
UN	United Nations
UNESCO	United Nations Educational, Scientific and Cultural Organization
URL	Uniform Resource Locator
US	United States of America
USD	United States Dollar
VM(s)	Virtual Machine(s)
VPC	Virtual Private Cloud
VW	Volkswagen
WCT	WIPO Copyright Treaty

WHO	World Health Organization
WIPO	World Intellectual Property Organization
WS-Agreement	Web Service Agreement
XML	eXtensible Markup Language
XSD	XML Schema Definition

List of Figures

List of Tables

Chapter 1
Introduction

Information technology law (or IT Law) is a new field that was practically unknown just a few decades ago. It goes back, however, to an era before the personal computer entered into mainstream markets. It was not until the mid-1990s and the rise of the Internet that the union of the fields of IT and Law into a unique system became more necessary. The legal and technological context that drives this book has taken an extraordinary upturn over the last decade in terms of opportunities for companies and organizations to store, transfer and share data and databases over the Internet.[1] However, the expansion and upsurge of pervasive technologies that provide new services on the Internet often spawn legal ambiguity and new, unprecedented legal problems for the protection of digital factual databases.[2]

According to an economic study by Yale Braunstein of the School of Information Management and Systems, at the University of California, in the majority of countries[3] databases are protected through copyrights and trademarks. Nevertheless, de facto protection through contractual agreements is also possible as the law of copyrights only provides limited protection for those creative databases which comply with the threshold of originality.[4]

Intellectual property rights (IPRs) have always been considered a powerful mechanism to recoup the investment of authors, inventors, researchers, and artists. It equips them with a limited monopoly of their works[5] and provides them with various legal tools to prevent the extraction and misappropriation of their endeavors.[6] While it

[1]Oskamp and Lodder (2006, pp. 3–4).

[2]Alikhan and Mashelkar (2009, p. 19).

[3]With the exception of Mexico and South Korea where database rights similar to the European countries also exists. See Article 108 of Mexico's Federal Law on Copyright (Ley Federal del Derecho de Autor–LFDA). For a comparative study of the sui generis right between Mexico and the EU, see De La Parra Trujillo (pp. 101–124).

[4]The work of Yale Braunstein, see Alikhan and Mashelkar (2009, p. 20).

[5]Corrales Compagnucci et al. (2010, p. 287), Guadamuz (2006, p. 321).

[6]Bainbridge (2008), Corrales Compagnucci et al. (2010, p. 287), Guadamuz (2006, p. 321).

M. Corrales Compagnucci, *Big Data, Databases and "Ownership" Rights in the Cloud*, Perspectives in Law, Business and Innovation,
https://doi.org/10.1007/978-981-15-0349-8_1

cannot be disputed that IPRs provide a strong stimulus, this does not mean that there is no room for improvement. There is an increasing wave of scholars who have argued that IPRs often create more barriers than incentives.[7]

IPRs are territorial by nature.[8] Amidst this grouping, the main legislation analyzed in this work is the European Database Directive 96/9/EC [hereinafter "the Database Directive"],[9] which entered into force in the year 1996. The Database Directive attempted to strengthen the database industry and increase the legal scope of protection for database makers. These new provisions generally created a new IPR (a "sui generis" right) based on the resources that database makers invest at the moment of creating, updating and presenting the content of databases. This directive also placed new limitations and restrictions on the extraction and re-utilization of the content of such databases. The Database Directive has been generally well-received for updating some of the rules in the previous copyright regime. However, it has also generated a lot of concerns regarding its practicality and flexibility to modern data processing technologies when using Internet services.

In August 2017, the European Commission carried out a public consultation. The aim was to gather information from various stakeholders and evaluate the impact of the Database Directive as well as to identify the possible needs of adjustment. Opinions concerning the public consultation were divided. More than 50% of respondents considered that the original objective of the Database Directive remains fit-for-purpose with the needs of the EU. However, the rest of the respondents believed that the Directive was outdated in view of the recent technological, economic and legal developments. Opinions were also split as to whether database rights achieve a good balance between database makers and users. Views were equally diverging on the impact of database rights, in particular with regard to the re-use of data.[10]

Based on the data and information collected during the public consultation, the European Commission published on April 25, 2018 the Evaluation Report on the Database Directive. The study was led by the Joint Institute for Innovation Policy and contains opinions from expert interviews and a stakeholder's workshop. The Evaluation Report suggested that some of the provisions enshrined in the Database Directive are no longer fit for the Internet era, in particular in an increasingly data-driven economy. Considerations could be given to the abolition of the sui generis rights. However, if a full repeal is not possible, the European Commission might

---

[7]See, generally, Kinsella (2008).

[8]Schiaudone (2013, p. 332).

[9]Directive 96/9/EC of the European Parliament and of the Council of 11 March 1996 on the legal protection of databases.

[10]See Digital Single Market, Summary Report of the Public Consultation on the Evaluation of Directive 96/9/EC on the Legal Protection of Databases, [online]. Available at: https://ec.europa.eu/digital-single-market/en/news/summary-report-public-consultation-legal-protection-databases. Accessed June 10, 2019.

reflect on amending some of the provisions, in particular those related to the growing importance of machine-generated data.[11]

This book reviews some of the provisions enshrined in the Database Directive with regard to various cutting-edge Internet-related technologies that are truly shaping the law. However, two distinct, but closely related, emerging trends stand out from the center of this research: cloud computing and Big Data.[12] There is no doubt that these two new technologies are changing the scope in which law is uniformly interpreted and effectively applied in a constantly evolving environment. There is, thus, a global awareness that the traditional concept and approach to legal science must be expanded to encompass new areas associated with automation and information science.

Nevertheless, it is not possible for the legislator to regulate everything on the Internet. As the constant data transfers and generation of new data are key components faced by business and science on a daily basis, it is necessary and more practical to iron out the missing legal links from a multi-disciplinary point of view. Therefore, this work reveals the dynamic nature of IT Law. It includes the sub- and related fields of e-Commerce, contract law, and IPRs. It also draws on other legal aspects including its theoretical foundations based on the theories that fall under the general headings of legal philosophy, law and economics, and behavioral law and economics.

Perhaps one the most appropriate metaphors to explain the complex phenomenon of the Internet is that of an iceberg. The average person recognizes a small fraction visible above the surface, i.e., the top 10%.[13] Underneath the waterline, however, are various layers of hidden technology,[14] leaving 90% of the mass largely unseen.[15] This is known as the Internet architecture[16] or computer "code."[17] This book is about planning and designing specific features of that hidden architecture using alternative approaches that affect the legal environment for innovation and economic growth. A good reason to focus on the architecture design is that much of the legal literature attempts to influence and amend the law. Most lawyers and legal scholars hardly discuss the implementation of embedding legal concepts into the user interface and

[11]See Study in Support of the Evaluation of Directive 96/9/EC on the Legal Protection of Databases. Available at: https://www.technopolis-group.com/wp-content/uploads/2018/07/Study-in-Support-of-th-Evaluation-of-the-Database-Directive-.pdf. Accessed June 10, 2019. In response to technological changes, the European Commission concluded the following: "(i) it is not (yet) clear how the sui generis right interacts; (ii) it could be advisable to clarify the notion of database maker; (iii) as far as possible, clarify the notions of substantial investment and substantial part including the notion of recorded and of created data; (iv) introduce a text and data mining exception; (v) as with European Commission's own conclusion to the Digital Economy Package, it is advisable to wait before proceeding to a legislative intervention in this respect." See also, Vollmer Database Directive Study: Options for Neutralising the Sui Generis Right, [online]. Available at: https://www.communia-association.org/2018/05/10/database-directive-study-options-neutralising-sui-generis-right/. Accessed June 10, 2019.

[12]Murugesan and Ananth (2016, p. 4).

[13]Muller (2015, p. 168).

[14]Horten (2016, p. 135).

[15]Lightman (2002), preface.

[16]See, generally, Van Schewick (2010).

[17]Lessig (1999), Reidenberg (1998, pp. 553–593).

related systems. Nevertheless, it is more important to focus on shaping the basic technological pillars of the Internet and injecting legal requirements into their implementation. Surely, that would represent a more effective and practical approach.[18]

The last decade has witnessed a burgeoning of the cloud computing market, which has led to an increase in the number of cloud services at the international level. The cloud shifted[19] the way computing services are managed today,[20] offering many advantages to business[21] and scientific research.[22] Part of the reason is that IT resources in the cloud are not locally stored on end-user personal devices[23] but accessed through a distributed network. This enables consumers to operate a broad spectrum of applications ranging from email and spreadsheets to more robust and reliable business software.[24] This paradigm was inspired by the central idea that computing will become a public utility, just like water, gas and electricity.[25]

Big Data is also sprawling the IT landscape and needs cloud computing power to process massive amounts of data.[26] It relies on the distributed storage of cloud services as the underlying infrastructure for smooth operation. Although there are many overlapping concepts and technologies in cloud computing and Big Data, they differ in the following major aspect: cloud computing directly transforms the IT architecture, whereas Big Data operates in the upper level and influences the analyses in the science and business decision-making processes.[27] Both cloud computing and Big Data complement each other, and are, therefore, the ideal combination that may very well disrupt the world.[28]

From a legal point of view, the implementation of cloud computing and Big Data is, however, risky.[29] It involves the processing, transferring and storing of data and databases across different jurisdictions via different cloud service providers, leaving a sense of uncertainty during the transactions. One of the recurrent aspects of human nature is having to deal with uncertainty, which may take place in the form of gains or losses. For example, when we gamble, we may earn some money. There is, however, always the prospect of losing money. Uncertainty in this context represents an undesirable aspect of human life. In the scholarship on decision-making, this observation is considered as people being "risk-averse."[30] This means that when people are confronted with two investments with similar dividends (but different

[18]See Bygrave and Bing (2009, pp. 3–4) (eds).

[19]Balasubramanyam (2013, p. 102).

[20]Srinivasan (2014, p. 5).

[21]Millham (2012, p. 2).

[22]Catlett et al. (2013) (eds.), preface.

[23]Kasemsap (2015, p. 31).

[24]Biswas (2014, p. 333).

[25]Marinescu (2013), preface.

[26]Kannan et al. (2016) (eds.), preface.

[27]Chen (2014, pp. 12–13).

[28]Mosco (2014).

[29]Lake and Drake (2014, p. 164), Iannarelly and O'Shaughnessy (2015, p. 40).

[30]Mackaay (1982, p. 173).

risks) , they will choose the one with lower risks.[31] Thus, taking risks and making decisions based upon such risks is part of human life. People usually overestimate the small and well-known risks and sometimes disregard the small risks of which they are completely unaware.[32]

Sometimes the magnitude of the risks is much higher than would be expected and we would not have taken such risks if we had known the consequences of taking such decisions deliberately. Therefore, to make a rational decision, one needs to be aware and informed about the potential risks in the first place and have some idea about its implications, such as the likelihood of the event to happen and how seriously it would affect things if a risk appeared. The same principles that apply to our daily life activities apply, generally, to our business transactions, with the only difference being that in the latter, third parties are usually involved with some commercial expectations.[33]

Entering into cloud computing contracts without being fully aware of the inherent legal risks can severely damage an organization. Thus, the potential risks involved in a cloud computing transaction should be thoroughly addressed in the service level agreements (SLAs). Broadly speaking, one of the main risks the customers—hereinafter also used interchangeably with the terms "end-user" or "consumers"[34]—face when they submit their databases and applications to the cloud is the loss of "physical control" of the data and databases. In such decision-making processes, there are many risks involved, including the risk of losing the "ownership" rights of data and databases.

The range of legal questions in cloud computing and Big Data environments is substantial. On 27 September 2012, the European Commission released a communication titled, *Unleashing the Potential of Cloud Computing in Europe*,[35] highlighting the advantages of cloud computing as a mechanism to create new job opportunities and increase productivity. The Commission realized the unprecedented degree of potential legal risks involved in the cloud, such as those related to jurisdictional issues inter alia or the applicable law when a cloud user is not a citizen of the European Union and called to take actions in elucidating the current legal framework.[36] Another major drawback is the issue of controlling where the databases are located. Servers located in different places represent the problem of dealing with different cloud service providers located in various legal jurisdictions. Therefore, issues of mutual trust and control have some legal implications. Finally, databases can be easily reproduced within virtual machines (VM) running in the cloud, and as databases

[31] See, generally, Klarman (1991).

[32] Viscusi (1998).

[33] McCormick (2010, pp. 1–2).

[34] An "end-user" is any natural or juridical person (i.e., one individual or a company) using a service deployed on a cloud. An end-user can also be a service software owner that has deployed the service on a given cloud, however, this is not the interpretation adopted in this book.

[35] COM (2012) 529, final. Unleash the Potential of Cloud Computing in Europe. Available at: http://eur-lex.europa.eu/LexUriServ/LexUriServ.do?uri=COM:2012:0529:FIN:EN:PDF. Accessed 10 July 2017.

[36] Corrales Compagnucci (2012).

play a fundamental role during the entire cloud computing life cycle, it is highly relevant to analyze in detail the provisions of database rights and how they fit into these cloud scenarios.

However, legal problems and lingering questions remain. The whole issue cries out for interpretation and clarification. Additionally, in an astonishing array of contexts, database rights are far from settled as these problems are presented more acutely in cloud computing and Big Data environments. By now, the idea of introducing database and "ownership" rights of data into the SLA negotiations is novel. Therefore, this book strives to spark further discussions and bring together different areas of work and fill the gap between the disciplines of law, economics, psychology, sociology, philosophy and information communication technologies (ICTs). It also attempts to answer some of these questions in the genuine hope that we may come to understand these challenging issues in a more meaningful, productive and pragmatic manner.

1.1 Problem Statement

"Cloud computing" and "Big Data" are amongst the most hyped-up terms and buzzwords of the moment. After decades in which individuals and companies used to host their data and applications using their own IT infrastructure, the world has seen the stunning transformation of the Internet. Major shifts occurred when these infrastructures began to be outsourced to public cloud providers to match commercial expectations.[37]

The sheer volume of data[38] generated via the cloud[39] is astonishing. Much of the information is generated in truly transnational settings. From a legal and institutional framework point of view, the main problem is what often happens in the domain of IT & IP Law with the typical shortcomings of black-letter rules. The technology has improved so exponentially that existing statutory public law, regulatory, and policy approaches face severe difficulties and limitations to keep pace with new technological changes. This problem has been exacerbated with the Big Data movement. This is due to its volatile and permeable nature, and the progress of interconnectivity among societies where data and databases move across borders in a multi-jurisdictional world.

The situation is therefore daunting, to put it mildly. It could be said that due to its global nature, the cloud is riddled with all sorts of legal concerns. Much of this legal debate has been focused on solving data protection and data security issues whereas IPR has somewhat fallen behind schedule. The difficulty is that the conventional focus of IPR has been structured in such a way as to exclude others from creating potential solutions. In my view, the actors involved in IPR need a new approach to protect their information. The focus of this book is on database rights and "ownership" rights of

[37]See, generally, Carr (2008).

[38]See, generally, McAfee and Brynjolfsson (2012).

[39]See, generally, Hashem et al. (2015, pp. 98–115).

data because there is a significant gap in the literature that has been overlooked by legal scholars in the field. Clarifying who "owns" such data on the Internet has been one of the main bottlenecks for the cloud market.[40] This means that we need a whole new framework for understanding, protecting and sharing large sets of data: a framework that is more flexible and serves as an instrument for coordination and choice.

The growing outward orientation of the law until now has shown no agreement towards a global standard that defines "ownership" rights of data. At the outset, it is important to consider this general observation in the absence of legal terminology to interpret this term more accurately. In the title of this work, and throughout the rest of the book, I have intentionally quoted the word "ownership." In so far as it refers to data, the concept of "ownership" is not a legal construct. This notion has been borrowed from tangible properties and is used as an analogy, which is extended to intangible rights such as data or information. This concept glosses over various aspects and is far from being clear. It could be said that it falls under some sort of twilight zone where neither domestic laws nor international treaties can shed light on this point. They are in a "grey area." Somewhere in between the traditional protection granted by IPR and tangible rights. Thus, "ownership" rights of data will be treated here as synonymous with the concept of owning information, and is similarly and roughly homogenous to property rights[41] in the physical form. I am fully aware of the caveat of this generalization, however, in my opinion, adequate similarities exist to justify and admit this stylization for present and practical purposes.

The second problem unfolds from the ubiquitous nature of the cloud and the territorial scope of protection of database rights, which creates legal hurdles. The European Database Directive sets up a territorial limitation regarding the person who may be subject to obtaining database rights. In principle, this right extends to only makers or rights holders who are nationals or habitual residents of an EU Member State, which includes companies or firms that have their principal place of business or central administration within the EU.[42] This is certainly a contentious and anachronistic provision in the domain of cloud computing and Big Data due to its essentially pervasive features. Since servers can be located in different countries outside of the EU, and databases can be easily reproduced in VMs, there is a risk of potential future controversies between the parties involved.

Last but not least, the third problem is the lack of a common international contractual framework to mitigate these legal risks. This leads to a lack of interoperability at the global scale that obstructs the cloud computing market from thriving. Cloud customers face difficulties in choosing the right cloud provider that best fits their

---

[40] See, generally, Al-Khouri (2012, pp. 1–8).

[41] Property rights can be categorized in different ways, most of which fall outside the scope of this book. Generally, this term can be broken down in two main areas: (i) *corporeal:* covering items which relate to an object, a thing. Something tangible that is a physical good, i.e., a car, a computer; (ii) *incorporeal:* covering items which are not visible to the human eye. Something virtual and intangible by nature, i.e., data or information. See Robson and McCowan (1998, p. 15), Corrales Compagnucci et al. (2010, pp. 293–294), Elkin-Koren and Salzberger (2013, p. 44).

[42] Article 11 paragraphs (1) and (2) of the Database Directive. See also Davison (2003, p. 97).

needs. The lack of a structure or framework supporting the clarification of such rights increases transaction costs. Ergo, it creates a tension between the stakeholders involved in cloud computing transactions. Customers using cloud computing services are no longer content to deal with these uncertainties post facto. They need clear guidelines at the time they enter into a cloud and Big Data service.

As a corollary, due to the lack of an efficient and automatic procedure for the clarification of database rights and "ownership" rights of data in the cloud, end-users must cope with the uncertainties and intricacies of decision-making. The current state of the art in the cloud market allows only for a limited category of static and non-negotiable click-through SLAs (usually ranked as gold, silver, or bronze). The manual selection of cloud providers to meet their *functional* requirements (i.e., storage capabilities, number, and size of servers, etc.) and *non-functional* capabilities (i.e., legal) has been perceived as imposing deliberation and transaction costs. End-users must go through the cumbersome procedure of manually visiting the websites of cloud providers to compare their quality of services and legal policies.[43] Put as a question, how can this quest for legal certainty be achieved? How can we satisfy the needs of cloud customers?

1.2 Summary of the Key Points Analyzed

This book advances several theoretical and practical alternatives in the field of IT & IP Law. Below some of the salient points emanating from this research are summarized:

(i) *Cloud Brokerage Services*: Standard SLAs used in the cloud are often spelled out to the advantage of cloud providers. This inequality of bargaining power creates an imbalance between contractual parties to the detriment of end-users. The figure of innovation intermediary (or "broker") as a middleman can aid to better streamline and clarify legal issues by simplifying the decision-making process;

(ii) *Automated and Flexible SLAs*: Offline negotiation and manual selection of cloud providers are imposing transaction, bargaining and deliberation costs. This has been perceived as slowing down cloud activities, which are meant to be automatic. SLAs shall provide for a more simple, efficient and flexible approach. This includes application tools that allow for an automated procedure to select and re-negotiate SLA offers;

(iii) *Plan-like Architectures*: The current architectural design of the cloud and its technical features do not allow adequate control for end-users. The Plan-like Architectures approach can be effectively implemented and more reliably enforced than legislation on a global scale. This approach will depend on how choices are framed. On this account, the technical implementation of default rules, warning signals and information disclosures are very efficient as prime nudges;

[43] See Wu et al. (2013, pp. 235–244).

(iv) *Risk Assessment and Trustworthy Framework*: Transferring data and databases to the cloud is risky. A risk assessment framework should include database rights and "ownership" rights of data. This tool ought to be implemented within the architectural design at all stages of the life cycle. This approach can be realized to reduce risks and engender greater mutual trust within cloud transactions.

1.3 The Structure of This Book

The layout of this book is separated into three main parts. The first part tackles several legal, technical and theoretical issues, which together define the background and information necessary for the preparation and proper consideration of this work. This part is drawn up in three chapters. The purpose of Chap. 2 is to lay the foundations for understanding the legal principles of the EU Database Directive 96/9/EC [hereinafter the "Database Directive"] , the reasons for its implementation in the EU and what context it is currently operating in. Very recently, the Institute of Electrical and Electronics Engineers (IEEE) Computer Society released its study "IEEE CS 2022," which revealed technologies that have the potential to change the scope for the year 2022. Among these innovative technologies are cloud computing and Big Data analysis.

Most importantly, the chapter also mentions intellectual property reform movements, which seek to enable wider access to information.[44] This chapter is therefore dedicated to providing an insight into the linkage between cloud computing, Big Data and database rights. The Database Directive proscribes, in my view, some restrictions to the extraction and re-utilization of data on a global scale, which runs afoul of the current Big Data and open data movement. Therefore, the main objectives of this chapter are to highlight the need to transcend the limitations of database rights and, consequently, to capitalize fully on a modern procedure to expedite and clarify them through and within a more flexible and automated overarching contractual framework.

Chapter 3 has cloud computing, brokerage scenarios, and databases as its overriding topics. It examines some of the technical preliminary issues useful for the discussion of this work. It also attempts to provide a comprehensive explanation of the new trends in the cloud computing market emphasizing the important role intermediaries and databases play during the entire cloud computing supply chain. As part of this description, this chapter is full of explicit examples with an eye towards the lay reader who presumably, and every so often inadvertently, uses cloud computing services in one way or another.

Chapter 4 sets the pillars for the theoretical framework of this research, which is going to be used as a methodological and analytical tool to solve some of the problems encountered throughout this work. This chapter is built upon well-established

[44] Alkhatib et al. (2014).

paradigms inspired by the general theories of law and economics as it seeks to find the best criteria for the most efficient and realistic procedure during the negotiation of SLAs. Law and economics are built upon the assumption that individuals will take the most logical or rational choice that best fits their goals. These are certainly important predisposing premises for the rational behavior of the cloud computing market. Therefore, this chapter sets out five core principles that span different levels of abstractions, which may serve as integral components of SLAs. Whilst the logical arguments and deductive reasoning methods of law and economics are always dominant and firmly established, they are also limited and need not be exclusive. Although these postulates are oftentimes borne out by reality, from the perspective of individuals, some decisions can be biased by the shortcomings and limitations of the human mind.

For this reason, in the second part, a new multidisciplinary theoretical framework was designed to underpin and reinforce this study. This part suggests going beyond the traditional premises of law and economics. It proposes, therefore, to proceed with a fresh approach that draws on a wide spectrum of social science and technology disciplines, including insights from philosophy, psychology, sociology, social capital and computer sciences. Finding a balance between law and economics and other sciences is essential to strengthen this framework and promote greater coordination and interaction among the involved parties. This second part is broken down into three chapters.

Chapter 5 captures the salient and essential features of Scott Shapiro's deliberations on "Plan Theory" and adopts Lawrence Lessig's observations with regards to the architectural design of the Internet or its "code." This new, revised theoretical framework sits in between these two theories. Plan Theory presupposes that individuals are planning creatures, ergo laws are plans. The Lessig approach conveys that other modalities impinge on the Internet and operate as a constraint. Most notably one of these forms is the web architecture and source code that can work as the main regulator. In this context, one might justifiably argue that cloud computing contracts should be framed as to what I call *Plan-like Architectures*. The choice of this label as a "legal-methodological benchmark" aims at bridging these two approaches into one coherent discourse, which can work as a heuristic mechanism.

Upon having laid down the theoretical premises, the structure of Chap. 6 follows the flow of Plan Theory and takes up how issues of trust (and distrust) can significantly affect and influence the role of any given legal regime. One of the main concerns of cloud computing end-users relates to the prevailing lack of trust. SLAs are legal instruments relying on contract law and inevitably devised based on mutual trust between the involved parties. This chapter, therefore, starts by synthesizing the meaning of trust across different disciplines and discusses its multi-layered and multi-dimensional notions that have evolved through time, which is fundamental to attract and keep customers in the cloud market. There are many factors involved in developing trust. Reasonable considerations for the development of trust may be based on track records, due diligence or assessment being carried out by trustworthy third parties, such as cloud brokers. The remainder of the chapter specifically seeks to identify the best venue for increasing the mutual trust in negotiating and concluding

SLAs, with particular emphasis given to the role of innovation intermediaries who can coordinate and reinforce dialogue between end-users and cloud providers.

Chapter 7 adopts the behavioral law and economic mode of inquiry and its philosophical foundation—also known as "libertarian paternalism"[45]—which combines economics and psychology to produce a framework based on the paradigm that end-users are influenced by the manipulation of "choice-architectures."[46] This means that within the behavioral approach designed in the contractual framework of this book, extra features are enabled to promote informed choices. A set of legal questions have been framed to influence cloud providers to take further actions, and, as a corollary, secure the smooth negotiation of SLAs. This approach will "increase welfare as measured by each individual's own preferences."[47] To elaborate this point further, this chapter submits that database and "ownership" rights of data ought to be clearly and effectively asserted through an embedded mechanism within the architectural design of the SLA framework. This chapter conceives cloud providers and brokers as main planners and choice architects that can assist with the implementation of a flexible and automated contract that can steer or nudge their customers (plan adopters) to make better decisions and at the same time respect their liberty without limiting their choices.

The third part of this book translates theory into practice. It is divided into three chapters. Chapter 8 delves into detail concerning a more flexible and consistent contractual framework between the customer and the cloud service provider and focuses on how the negotiation of the SLA fits into cloud brokerage scenarios. This chapter solidifies the theoretical framework and advocates for the establishment of clear "ownership" rights between the involved parties. It purports to extend the negotiation capabilities of cloud customers and seeks to prevent future controversies arguing that database rights and "ownership" rights of data should be clarified more effectively and included in the SLA negotiations. The SLA is expressed and organized using the form of what is known as an integrated eXtensible Markup Language (XML) schema, which is a flexible way to format information making it readable for both humans and machines. The XML schema is the key enabler for clarifying these rights on a global scale as it does not have a fixed format and anyone can use this as an adjunct to the SLAs. An extract from the description schema is appended to this chapter.

Last but not least, from the notions of trust surveyed in the social and computer sciences, it turns out that there is a continuous-combined pattern. This clear trend often regards trust as evoking more personal and emotional feelings. Some commentators conceptualize trust as the expectation or willingness to put oneself at a vulnerable state in order to avoid or reduce the risk arising from any transaction. It follows from this that one cannot increase mutual trust without properly identifying and reducing the risks involved.

---

[45]Thaler and Sunstein (2003, pp. 175–179), Sunstein and Thaler (2003, pp. 1159–1202).

[46]Thaler, Sunstein and Balz (2010).

[47]Wright and Ginsburg (2012, p. 1033).

Within this frame of mind, Chap. 9 probes, in detail, into a risk assessment model that should underpin the SLA framework. It examines a specific aspect of risk management as applied to cloud computing and Big Data. The aim is to analyze the risks regarding database rights and "ownership" rights of data and to present the requirements of an inherent legal risk inventory. Risk assessment management in cloud computing is highly intertwined with the necessity of supporting all the involved parties in making better-informed decisions concerning SLAs, which is associated with delivering the specified quality of service (QoS). This risk assessment model is a very important input to the overall SLA framework, which provides a more rational analysis and scientifically based process to cope with risks and the likelihood of its occurrence.

This book, in short, contains eight themed chapters. Each of which is preceded by a brief introduction and the literature review that contextualizes and justifies the research study. Each chapter also provides a summary at the end that recapitulates the main concepts discussed and provides a preliminary conclusion. Finally, the last chapter (Chap. 10) summarizes the key findings and conclusions derived from this research.

1.4 Methodology

This study relies upon different theories, multiple methods, and data from various sources. It aims to map in broad strokes a methodology of work that has been described as a "principle-practice" approach inspired by the "pragmatist conceptual analysis" that was articulated by Jules Coleman.[48] It includes a synthesis of the literature in each chapter, which follows a deductive method of reasoning, or "top-down" approach, building on from the more general conceptual premises to narrow it down to the more specific.

It also combines different approaches and adds new elements to construct a better and more flexible contractual framework[49] for cloud computing and Big Data transactions. More specifically, the approach of this book is manifold: (i) theoretical: as it involves the convergent analysis of different theories and principles laid down in law and economics as well as behavioral law and economics; (ii) interdisciplinary: in that it seeks to bridge the gap between the disciplines of law, economics, philosophy, sociology, psychology and IT; (iii) pragmatic: as it provides a new contractual model and XML description schema, which can be included during SLA negotiations; and (iv) risk-based: as it includes an updated and customized risk assessment methodology focused on the areas considered to present the highest risks and constraints.

Additionally, this work provides an empirical study based on a baseline survey carried out among 100 different stakeholders throughout different world regions. The objective was to collect relevant data and analyze their perceptions concerning

[48] See Coleman (2001).

[49] Trochim (2006).

database rights and "ownership" rights of data in cloud computing and Big Data transformations. The starting point of this experimental study was grounded in the evaluation and results of different surveys which were made available online. These studies included the assessment of standard contracts, which were accessible via the cloud vendors' websites. Some of these have been carried out by universities,[50] others gathered by private law firms,[51] or even by the EU Commission itself.[52] The general outcome of these works indicated user uncertainty surrounding contract terms and conditions associated with cross-border transactions.

These previous studies analyzed a variety of relevant contract terms including inter alia privacy, security, choice of law, trans-border data flow, warranties and liabilities.[53] Nevertheless, few of these studies have focused on intellectual property issues hitherto, and, if they do, some aspects of IPR are mentioned too broadly and none of them have discussed database rights or "ownership" rights of data in greater detail as part of their research. For this reason, a unique survey tailored to the needs of this research was conducted. The survey was submitted to academics and law practitioners working in the field of IT and IP Law, and, to various sectors of the IT industry such as service and infrastructure providers, software developers and datacenter provisioning services. The data collected revealed the elevated concern in this subject and suggested finding better criteria to solve these issues. It also showed a lack of awareness of database rights, as less than 40% were acquainted with the provisions of the Database Directive, especially in the IT sector. Then again, on the other hand, more than 90% of the respondents conveyed that a contract for cloud services should include language that clearly affirms and specifies "ownership" rights of data and databases.

This work attempts to raise awareness among the stakeholders involved in cloud computing transactions, showing them that potential future controversies could be solved entirely and exclusively on ex ante grounds and that the role of the intermediary in cloud brokerage scenarios is very important to reduce and mitigate the risks involved. More specifically, the aim of this research is: (i) to examine the role databases play in cloud computing transformations and to scrutinize the legal risks involved in contractual agreements; (ii) to highlight the important role of innovation intermediaries in the negotiation of contractual agreements with regard to ubiquitous services such as cloud computing and Big Data; and (iii) to elaborate a contractual model which includes database rights and "ownership" rights of data during the negotiation of the SLA's terms and conditions in the most efficient and pragmatic manner. This book concludes with a call to reform the click-through type contract to a more flexible and coordinated framework committed to the cooperation of the

[50]See Hon, Millard and Walden (2012, pp. 79–127).

[51]See Vincent, Hart and Morton (2011, pp. 1–29).

[52]COM (2012) 529 final, Commission Staff Working Document, Accompanying the document; Communication from the Commission to the European Parliament, the Council, the European Economic and Social Committee and the Committee of the Regions, Unleashing the Potential of Cloud Computing in Europe, Brussels, 27 September 2012.

[53]Vincent, Hart and Morton (2011, p. 4).

involved parties. The bottom line is: this will foster the promotion of innovation, free-flow of information, open access to data and economic growth.

As a corollary, the outcome of this work is aimed at three different types of audiences. The first are IT experts in the field of cloud computing and Big Data (service and infrastructure providers, IT managers, Chief Executive Officers (CEOs), Chief Information Officers (CIOs) and software developers). The second group is the legal community (academics, law practitioners and students) who are interested in understanding more about the attributes of managing, retrieving, sharing and using data and databases in the cloud, andthe technical and legal issues involved while drafting a contract for cloud computing and Big Data services. The third group of readers include laypersons and customers (or potential customers) alike of cloud computing services who are reluctant or even worried about losing the "ownership" rights of their data and databases when contracting with a cloud provider.

References

Alkhatib H et al (2014) IEEE CS 2022 http://www.computer.org/cms/Computer.org/ComputingNow/2022Report.pdf#page=5. Accessed 10 May 2019

Alikhan S, Mashelkar R (2009) Intellectual property and competitive strategies in the 21st century, 2nd edn. Kluwer Law International, Alphen aan den Rijn, p. 19

Al-Khouri A (2012) Data ownership: who owns "my data"? Int J Manag Inf Technol 2(2):1–8

Bainbridge D (2008) Introduction to information technology law. Person Longman, London

Balasubramanyam S (2013) Cloud-based development using classic life cycle model. In: Mahmood Z, Saqib S (eds) Software engineering frameworks for the cloud computing paradigm. Springer, London, p 102

Biswas S (2014) Relationship marketing: concepts, theories and cases, 2nd edn. Learning Private Limited, Delhi, p 333

Bygrave L, Bing J (2009) (eds) Internet governance: infrastructure and institutions. Oxford University Press, Oxford, pp 3–4

Carr N (2008) The big switch: rewiring the world: from Edison to Google. W.W. Norton & Company, New York

Catlett C et al (2013) (eds) Cloud computing and big data, preface. IOS Press, Amsterdam

Chen M et al (2014) Big data: related technologies, challenges and future prospects. Springer, Cham, pp 12–13

Coleman J (2001) The practice of principle: in defence of a pragmatist approach to legal theory. Oxford University Press, Oxford

Corrales M et al (2010) Intellectual property rights in e-health: balancing out the interest at stake–a Herculean task? Int J Private Law 3(3):287

Corrales M (2012) EU commission calls to "unleash the potential of cloud computing in Europe." Beck-Online, ZD-Aktuell, No. 03228

Davison M (2003) The legal protection of databases. Cambridge University Press, Cambridge, p 97

Elkin-Koren N, Salzberger E (2013) The law and economics of intellectual property in the digital age: the limits of analysis. Routledge, London, p 44

Guadamuz A (2006) Open science: open source licenses in scientific research. N C J Law Technol 7(2):321

Hashem A et al (2015) The rise of "big data" on cloud computing: review and open research issues. Inf Syst 47:98–115

Hon W, Millard C, Walden I (2012) Negotiating cloud contracts: looking at clouds from both sides now. Stan Tech L Rev 81 16(1):79–129

Horten M (2016) Closing of the net. Polity Press, Cambridge

Iannarelly J, O'Shaughnessy M (2015) Information governance and security: protecting and managing your company's proprietary information. Butterworth Heinemann, Oxford, p 40

Kannan R et al (2016) (eds) Managing and processing big data in cloud computing. Preface. Information Science Reference (IGI Global), Hershey

Kasemsap K (2015) The role of cloud computing adoption in global business. In: Chang V, Walters R, Wills G (eds) Delivery and adoption of cloud computing services in contemporary organizations. Information Science Reference (IGI Global), Hershey, p 31

Kinsella N (2008) Against intellectual property. Ludwig von Mises Institute, Auburn (AL)

Klarman S (1991) Margin of safety: risk-averse value investing strategies for the thoughtful investor, 1st edn. HarperCollins, New York

Lake P, Drake R (2014) Information systems management in the big data era. Springer, Cham, p 164

Lessig L (1999) Code, and other laws of cyberspace. Basic Books, New York

Lightman A (2002) Brave new unwired world: the digital big bang and the infinite internet, preface. Wiley, New York

Mackaay E (1982) Economics of information and law. Kluwer Boston Inc., Boston, p 173

Marinescu D (2013) Cloud computing: theory and practice, preface. Morgan Kaufmann, Waltham

McAfee A, Brynjolfsson E (2012) Big data: the management revolution. Harv Bus Rev. https://hbr.org/2012/10/big-data-the-management-revolution/ar. Accessed 10 May 2019

McCormick R (2010) Legal risks in the financial market, introduction, 2nd edn. Oxford University Press, Oxford, pp 1–2

Millham R (2012) Software asset re-use: migration of data-intensive legacy system to the cloud computing paradigm. In: Yang H, Liu X (eds) Software reuse in the emerging cloud computing era. Information Science Reference (IGI Global), Hershey, p 2

Mosco V (2014) To the cloud: big data in a turbulent world. Routledge, New York

Muller H (2015) The big shift in IT leadership: How great CIOs leverage the power of technology for strategic business growth in the customer-centric economy. Wiley, Hoboken, p 168

Murugesan S, Ananth A (2016) Cloud computing: an overview. In: Murugesan S, Bojanova I (eds) Encyclopedia of cloud computing. Wiley, Chichester, p 4

Oskamp A, Lodder A (2006) Introduction: Law, Information Technology and Artificial Intelligence. In: Lodder A, Oskamp A (eds) Information technology and lawyers: advanced technology in the legal domain. From challenges to daily routine. Springer, Dordrecht, pp 3–4

Reidenberg J (1998) Lex informatica: the formulation of information policy rules through technology. Tex Law Rev 71:553–593

Robson P, McCowan A (1998) Property law, Green's concise scots law, 2nd edn. Sweet & Maxwell, Edinburgh, p 15

Schiaudone R (2013) Dealing with IP matters in cross-border cases. J Intellect Prop Law Pract 8(4):332

Srinivasan S (2014) Cloud computing basics. Springer Briefs in Electrical and Computer Engineering. Springer, New York, p 5

Sunstein C, Thaler R (2003) Libertarian paternalism is not an oxymoron. Univ Chic Law Rev 70(4):1159–1202

Thaler R, Sunstein C (2003) Libertarian paternalism. Am Econ Rev 93(2):175–179

Thaler R, Sunstein C, Balz J (2010) Choice architecture http://papers.ssrn.com/sol3/papers.cfm?abstract_id=1583509. Accessed 10 May 2019

Trochim W (2006) Philosophy of research, research methods knowledge base http://www.socialresearchmethods.net/kb/philosophy.php. Accessed 10 May 2019

Van Schewick B (2010) Internet architecture and innovation. The MIT Press, Cambridge

Vincent M, Hart N, Morton K (2011) Cloud computing contracts white paper: a survey of terms and conditions. Truman Hoyle Lawyers, Sydney, Australia, pp 1–21. www.it-news.com.au/pdf/CloudComputing-Contracts-White-Paper.pdf. Accessed 10 May 2019

Viscusi W (1998) Rational risk policy: The 1996 Arne Ryde memorial lectures. Clarendon Press, Oxford

Wright J, Ginsburg D (2012) Behavioral law and economics: its origins, fatal flaws, and implications for liberty. Northwest Univ Law Rev 106(3):1033

Wu L et al (2013) Automated SLA negotiation framework for cloud computing. In: Balaji P, Epema D, Fahringer T (eds) Cluster, cloud, and grid computing, 13th IEEE/ACM International Symposium, May 13-16 2013 Delft, Netherlands. IEEE Computer Society, Los Alamitos, pp 235–244

Part I
Fundamental Legal, Theoretical and Technical Issues

Chapter 2
Database Rights in Big Data and the Cloud—Main Legal Considerations

Database Right: "*a monstrous caricature of true intellectual property laws*" (Reichman and Samuelson 1997, p. 164).

2.1 Introduction

This chapter delves into detail about the problems raised by database rights in the wake of the Internet and the Big Data era. Database rights, also known as sui generis rights, grant exclusive property protection to any creator of databases based on a qualitative or quantitative substantial investment. As there is no need for registration (contrary to patents and trademarks cases), database rights arise automatically and last for 15 years,[1] which may be extended for another period given that any substantial change has been made.[2] This means that almost any compiler of information who made a substantial investment in terms of money, human resources, technical equipment, time and/or effort, may enjoy database rights protection unless expressly excluded or waived.[3]

The sui generis right has supporters and detractors. In 1996, Mario Monti, the former EU Single Market Commissioner, said, "this innovative and comprehensive measure will ensure an appropriate level of protection for database makers and

[1]Article 10 (1) of the Database Directive.

[2]Article 10 (1) (2) and (3) of the Database Directive. Databases are dynamic works and their economic value is increased by its constant update. This means that any substantial change such as the correction, deletion or updating of the current data of a database which is considered to be substantial can enjoy another 15 years of database right protection. See Reed and Angel (2007, p. 423).

[3]Article 7 (1) and Recitals 7, 13, 14, 17 and 40 of the Database Directive; Bently and Sherman (2009, pp. 313–314).

M. Corrales Compagnucci, *Big Data, Databases and "Ownership" Rights in the Cloud*, Perspectives in Law, Business and Innovation,
https://doi.org/10.1007/978-981-15-0349-8_2

investors through the EU."[4] By contrast, for many scholars database right is considered unsuccessful.[5] According to Kingston, the Database Directive has been influenced by publisher lobbying which confers them the potential to attain a continuous monopoly on data.[6] Coining the words of Reichman and Samuelson, the database right is "one of the least balanced and most potentially anti-competitive intellectual property rights ever created,"[7] and has been characterized by them as "a monstrous caricature" of IP Law.[8] This latter statement clearly shows the negative perception among some scholars, which prompts worry about its potential negative effects.

It is not the purpose of this book to enter into such controversies. Nevertheless, I would generally agree with the idea that database rights could potentially distort the right to access information and certain issues of abuse of monopoly could emerge particularly if one looks at this problem from a global cloud computing and Big Data perspective. There are certainly flaws and limitations in the provisions enshrined in the Database Directive, especially if we consider that at the time of its creation (back in 1996), the Internet was still in its early stages. To put this into perspective, Google did not exist and less than 1% of the world's population was using the web in comparison to more than 56% in the year 2019.[9]

To start this discussion, Sect. 2.2 provides a brief analysis of the international and European legal frameworks of database rights. It illustrates the antecedents, motivations, and justifications for introducing such rights, especially in the EU. Section 2.3 examines the provisions enshrined by the Database Directive and analyzes its main features in light of the most recent case laws of the CJEU. Section 2.4 explains the problem of database rights with regards to Big Data projects. Section 2.5 poses the law of contract as an effective venue to clarify database rights. Finally, Sect. 2.6 provides a summary of the chapter, highlights the research question and the main problem raised by database rights in the cloud and Big Data transformations.

2.2 On the Legal Issues of Databases

2.2.1 International Legal Framework

The international legal framework for the protection of databases can be traced back to the Bern Convention, which protects "collections of literary or artistic works", i.e., encyclopedias and anthologies. Databases must be "intellectual creations." That is, the selection and arrangement of the content of a database must be original to

[4]Waelde and McGingley (2005, p. 78).

[5]Sundara Rajan (2011, p. 286).

[6]Kingston (2010, p. 112).

[7]Bently and Sherman (2009, pp. 310–311).

[8]Kingston (2010, p. 171).

[9]Internet Users Statistics, [online]. Available at: https://en.wikipedia.org/wiki/Global_Internet_usage. Accessed 10 May 2019.

qualify for protection. Furthermore, in accordance with the WIPO Copyright Treaty (WTC), databases are protected by the law of copyright. Article 5 of the WCT stipulates that "compilations of data or other material, in any form, which by reason of the selection or arrangement of their contents constitute intellectual creations, are protected as such…"[10] In addition, according to Article 3 of the WCT, the contracting parties shall apply, mutatis mutandis, the provisions of Article 2 to 6 of the Berne Convention in respect of the protection provided for in the WCT Treaty.[11]

Besides copyright protection, historically, there have been many attempts to introduce extra protection for databases in international fora. There seems to be a consensus in the international community that the law of copyright does not provide the right means for the protection of factual databases. The introduction of a novel right to protect such compilations was one of the points of the agenda at the Diplomatic Conference of August 1996 where a proposal was submitted. The proposal contained similar provisions to the adopted Database Directive in the EU. In this occasion, the proposal was postponed due to time constraints in the agenda, and, ever since, there have been a series of follow up discussions, though no consensus has been reached.

There appear to be different reasons for such a delay. One of them is associated with the appropriate legal framework to adopt for such protection (through the European sui generis right or under a different scheme). Another reason, inter alia, and perhaps the most important one, is grounded by the argument that a new right for factual databases, based on substantial investment, might be perhaps unbalanced with regards to access of information. Therefore, it has been suggested that a comprehensive study which involves all the stakeholders must be carried out prior to such a decision.[12]

The Agreement on Trade-related Aspects of Intellectual Property [hereinafter "TRIPS Agreement"] delineates the minimum level of intellectual property rights for the WTO members. Articles 9–14 set the criteria for the protection of copyrights including "related rights" and Article 10.2 provides copyright protection for the "compilation of data or other materials." The wordings of Article 10.2 expressly mention "machine readable" compilations, and therefore extends this to electronic databases. Compilations must be original in the way the data or other materials have been selected or arranged in order to qualify for copyright protection. This protection excludes, however, data or materials themselves.[13]

---

[10]Article 5 of the WCT. See also WIPO (2004, pp. 274, 441).

[11]Article 3 of the WCT.

[12]Reinbothe and Von Lewinski (2007, pp. 486–494), Sell (2003, p. 27).

[13]Article 10.2 TRIPS Agreement, Yamane (2011, introduction, p. 158), WIPO (2004, p. 441).

2.2.2 *Database Protection in the European Legal Framework: Justification for the Double Scheme of Protection*

In Europe, copyright protection concerning databases is regulated by both the Database Directive from 1996 and the InfoSoc Directive from 2001.[14] The Database Directive provides a double scheme of protection. The first scheme is based on copyright law; an intellectual creation based on the selection or arrangement of the content of databases with a certain degree of originality. Within this scheme, no other criteria shall be applied to determine their eligibility for such protection.[15] The second scheme is the sui generis, which protects the "investment" of databases as a compilation of data.

Before the Database Directive, copyright law with regards to the protection of databases was not harmonized in Europe and there were multiple differences among the legislation and case laws of Member States.[16] For example, in the UK and the Netherlands, databases were protected by taking into account the effort made by authors by means of the "sweat of brow doctrine" (sufficient skill, judgment and labor),[17] as will be further explained in the next section. Whereas in other European countries, such as France and Germany, they were unprotected because they did not reach the standard levels for copyright protection which was higher with regard to the "intellectual creativity" required in those countries.[18]

Such disparities and different attributes of each national legislation had a negative impact on the functioning of the internal market and could have become even more evident if Member States introduced new legislation. Therefore, this double-scheme of protection was created to remove and prevent the distorting differences in two ways[19]: (i) by raising the threshold for copyright protection in a database to a higher level of "author's own intellectual creation" and equating to the same level the domestic laws of all EU Member States in the "selection and arrangement" of the database's contents; and (ii) by introducing a new right to protect "substantial investment" made by a European database maker in obtaining, verifying and presenting the contents of the database.[20]

---

[14]Directive 2001/29/EC of the European Parliament and of the Council of 22 May 2001 on the Harmonization of Certain Aspects of Copyright and Related Rights in the Information Society [hereinafter the INFOSOC Directive].

[15]Article 3 (1) of the Database Directive; Gasaway (2006).

[16]Kroes (2010, pp. 8–9), Wery (2015, p. 1); see also Recitals 1 and 4 of the Database Directive.

[17]See *University of London Press v University Tutorial Press* [1916] 2 Ch 601. In this case, certain mathematics exam papers were regarded to be original works as they originated from the author even though there was no creativity involved but rather sufficient skill, labor, and judgment; see also Waelde et al. (2013, p. 47), *Ladbroke v William Hill* [1964] 1 WLR 273 (HL), Aplin and Davis (2013, p. 94).

[18]Derclaye (2008b, pp. 45–46), Kaye (2010).

[19]Recitals 1, 2, 3 and 4 of the Database Directive.

[20]Kaye (2010).

As a result, this would facilitate and spur the appropriate function of the European internal market, the free movement of goods and services, and the development of an information market within the European Community.[21] This approach has been emphasized in the preamble of the Database Directive as follows: "copyright remains an appropriate form of exclusive right for authors who have created databases."[22] It was also stated that in the absence of a fully harmonized system of unfair-competition rules, other measures are needed in order to avert the unauthorized extraction and/or re-utilization of the contents of a database.[23]

It is evident that the two-tier system of protection introduced by the Database Directive derives its significance from the new database right since most databases will not qualify for copyright protection, irrespective of what the threshold of creativity or originality may be. It is highly possible that both copyright and database rights will overlap. Under such circumstances, they can be exploited independently.[24]

2.2.2.1 First Scheme—Copyright Protection

A database must exhibit originality in order to be entitled to copyright protection,[25] such as innovative technical features (i.e., new search methods) or a unique structure to the contents where data is differently arranged when compared to the traditional standard methods.[26] There are different tools and applications that can help to improve the usability potential of a database and at the same time add a quota of the copyright criteria, for instance:

i. *Indexing*: there are different ways of indexing a database taking into account a range of categories, such as specific subject fields, purposes, etc.[27];
ii. *Querying systems*: there are also different ways of querying systems such as single word queries, context queries, Boolean queries, etc., which provide the database with a better layout and user-friendly interface[28];
iii. *Clustering*: another way which helps to arrange the data in different orders is by "clustering" the documents. This is done by grouping documents into different categories. For instance, a compilation of documents containing material from different subjects such as biology and medicine might be clustered in a way that all medical documents are set into one cluster and all biological documents are organized into another[29];

---

[21] Recitals 1, 2, 3 and 4 of the Database Directive.

[22] Wery (2015, p. 1); Recital 5 of the Database Directive.

[23] Kur and Dreir (2013, p. 267).

[24] Grosheide (2002, p. 39).

[25] Spinello and Bottis (2009, p. 75).

[26] Helling (2004, p. 545).

[27] Cleveland and Cleveland (2001, p. 48).

[28] Baeza-Yates and Ribeiro-Neto (1999, pp. 99–101).

[29] Grossman and Frieder (2004, p. 105).

iv. *Thesaurus*[30]: a thesaurus can be used in many ways such as in indexing, searching, or a combination of both.[31] This is used particularly in bibliographic databases,[32] such as PubMed[33] in the biological research field, or Lexis-Nexis in the legal area.

The list given above is by no means exhaustive, but is illustrative. There are a number of different tools and applications that, coupled with the creativity of the database maker, can help them comply with the creativity criteria needed to enjoy copyright protection. For example, the Swiss-Prot database[34] is copyright protected (among many others). There are no constraints on its use for non-profit organizations as long as they do not change or alter its content.[35]

Nevertheless, biological databases operate at a different level in comparison to databases from other industries. Much of the substantial value comes from an interconnected network of relational databases. Most of them keep cross-references to other databases which are mostly done by manual curation. This peculiar situation in molecular biology has led to recent efforts to standardize names for biological entities which enormously helps in the sharing and accessing of data.[36]

2.2.2.2 Second Scheme—Database Right

According to the Database Directive, the only requirement for a database to be protected by the sui generis right is the substantial investment in obtaining, verifying or presenting the content of the database to be evaluated qualitatively or quantitatively.[37] The investment refers not only to monetary terms but also to time, effort, human resources, and technical equipment.[38]

Article 7 of the Database Directive grants a right to the database maker that can prove there has been a substantial investment measured in terms of quantity and/or quality in either the obtaining, verification or presentation of the contents of the database to prevent the extraction and/or re-utilization of the whole or a substantial part of the content of the database.[39]

---

[30]The term thesaurus comes from the Greek language which means a "storehouse." The most famous thesaurus was created by Peter Mark Roget in 1852 who arranged English words and phrases not in the typical alphabetical order but in proportion to the ideas they express. See Gilchrist (1971, p. 4).

[31]Aitchison et al. (2000, p. 1).

[32]Chan and Pollard (1988).

[33]PubMed, [online]. Available at: http://www.ncbi.nlm.nih.gov/pubmed. Accessed 12 February 2019.

[34]ExPASy Bioinformatics Resource Portal, [online]. Available at: http://web.expasy.org/docs/swiss-prot_guideline.html [Accessed 12 February 2019].

[35]Markel and León (2003, p. 26).

[36]Williams et al. (2005, pp. 12–13).

[37]Article 7 of the Database Directive.

[38]Recitals 7, 40, of the Database Directive.

[39]Article 7 of the Database Directive.

What constitutes a "substantial investment" must be analyzed on a case by case basis, taking into account the following paramount aspects: use of financial resources, time expenditure, efforts made, human resources and use of technical equipment. All these aspects must always be directed at obtaining, verifying or presenting the contents of the database. Thus, substantial investment in electronic databases can be determined and broadly classified as follows:

i. *Quantitative Investment*: this refers, for example, to a substantial amount of money invested in obtaining, verification and presentation of the database;
ii. *Qualitative Investment*: this refers to the quality factor that becomes crucial in the manipulation of electronic databases. For example, this could refer to any special skills and attitudes of the person in charge of verifying the content of a database, i.e., a researcher, or "curator," in which the quality of his or her work will be brought into the database.[40]

2.2.3 The Necessity for the Legal Protection of Databases in the Cloud

Before we dive into the technicalities of the legal provisions of the EU Database Directive which provides a novel legal scheme for the protection of databases, it is important to understand the reasons why databases and, in particular, "electronic databases" deserve such protection, and the different forms this protection may take.[41]

In comparison to conventional (hard copy) databases such as printed versions of a telephone directory, databases accessible in the cloud come in an electronic format and possess different features to those which are paper-based. For example, printed versions of databases need to be stored in a physical space and therefore their access can be restricted and controlled by the owner or person who is in charge or in possession of such databases. In addition to the physical security mechanisms that the premises of an organization may have such as lockers, security codes, alarms, etc., they also enjoy protection in cases of unauthorized access to the records. These include "trespass to land and burglary" in cases of break ins and "trespass to goods and thefts" in cases where archives have been stolen. Furthermore, additional protective measures can be established in terms of a contractual agreement by restricting access to some people in the organization and implementing strict provisions on the use of the information.[42]

[40]Lesk (2008, p. 153). For example, the Universal Protein Resource (UniProt) is a compilation of data on protein and sequence which is manually annotated with information deriving from literature. See Williams et al. (2005, p. 18).

[41]Reed and Angel (2007, p. 398).

[42]Reed and Angel (2007, p. 398).

The other characteristic typical of paper-based databases is that their reproduction has to take a physical form which involves access to archives and the actual manipulation of records to make the copies, which is costly and time-consuming. However, none of these characteristics belong to electronic databases. Copying information from electronic databases can take only a few seconds and, usually, this can be done at low or no costs at all. Copying and making these copies available to the public has become very easy using new technologies and software tools to circumvent security mechanisms, and once information has been disclosed and uploaded onto the Internet, the contracts are not binding to third parties who access the information. For these reasons, and especially due to the new technological developments in the last two decades, the EU thought convenient that databases merit a special scheme of protection such as the database right[43] which is going to be explained in greater detail below.

2.2.4 Motivations for Introducing the Database Right in the EU

The origins of the database right date to the beginning of the 1990s when the idea of creating a new right for the protection of the compilation of data as a whole was born. However, after a public consultation among a circle of stakeholders, the decision was not to create a new right to protect databases. This decision was perhaps influenced by the French Supreme Court (*Cour de Cassation*) judgment in *Le Monde v Microfor*[44] that granted copyright protection to a database containing references and brief quotations.[45]

For many years copyright protection was considered to be the most appropriate mechanism for the protection of databases. However, in 1991 the Supreme Court of the Netherlands issued a first warning that copyright might not be the appropriate mechanism for database protection.[46] The European Commission had also already established that copyright protection might be inadequate for the protection of databases which do not comply with the originality criteria and that legal protection might need to be extended to databases containing material not protected by copyright.[47]

---

[43]Reed and Angel (2007, pp. 398–399).

[44]*Le Monde v Microfor*, Cass., 9 November 1983 [1984-5/1] DIT 20-23, comment Mignot.

[45]Derclaye (2008b, p. 44).

[46]*Van Dale Lexicografie B.V. v. Rudolf Jan Romme* case. In: Dommering and Hugenholtz (1991) (eds).

[47]Commission of the European Communities (1998).

This being said, the concept of protecting databases with only copyright changed radically right after a series of case laws rejecting copyright protection. In the *Van Daele v Romme*[48] ruling in the Netherlands, Van Daele could not protect the copying of its dictionary because it did not meet the threshold of originality. In the *Feist Publications v Rural Telephone Service Co.* [Feist case][49] judgment in the US, the courts decided not to grant copyright protection to a phone directory on the same grounds.[50]

These decisions represent landmarks not only because they triggered the elaboration of a new directive in Europe but also, according to Sherman and Bently, they re-started the debate on the role that "creativity" plays in modern intellectual property law and there seemed to be a revival in the interest of "creativity in copyright law."[51] Until these court decisions, unoriginal databases were protected under the scope of the "sweat of the brow" doctrine, which posits that one can obtain copyright protection in factual compilations by "dint of the effort" one makes to produce such databases.[52]

Among all the EU Member States, only a few countries, such as the United Kingdom, enjoyed adequate protection because the threshold to assess originality was lower. Only sufficient "labor, skill and judgment were necessary."[53] Consequently its protection was extended not only to the selection and arrangement of the database but to its contents as well. Having said that, one of the main reasons for introducing the *sui generis* right in Europe was that for most European countries, databases without a high level of originality were not protected. Copyright protection was given only to those databases which were structured and arranged in an original fashion and this situation represented a real problem for most of the database industry in the EU.[54]

This holds true for databases that are accessible in cloud computing and Big Data environments as database makers are presumably more interested in protecting the contents of their databases than obtaining copyright protection for the selection and arrangement of their compilations. Very recently, however, the CJEU did away with the "sweat of the brow" doctrine in *Football Dataco and others v Yahoo! UK and others*.[55] This case had been reframing the European copyright law and at the same time defying the traditional UK approach with regards to skill and labor.[56]

---

[48] *Van Dale Lexicografie B.V. v. Rudolf Jan Romme* case.

[49] *Feist Publications v Rural Telephone Service Co.* 499 U.S. 340 (1991).

[50] Derclaye (2008b, pp. 44–45).

[51] Sherman and Bently (1999, pp. 43 and 206).

[52] Radin et al. (2004, pp. 318–319). For the precedents of the "sweat of the brow" doctrine see *Schroeder v. William Morrow & Co.*, 566 F.2d 3 (7th Cir. 1977); *Adventures in God Eating, Inc. v. Best Places to Eat*, 131 F.2d 809 (7th Cir. 1942); *Jeweler's Circular Publishing Co. v. Keystone Publishing Co. v. Edward Thompson Co.*, 169 F. 833 (C.C.E.D.N.Y. 1909).

[53] Derclaye (2008b, p. 45).

[54] Derclaye (2008b, p. 45).

[55] *Football Dataco and others v Yahoo and others*, Case C-604/10, 1 March 2012, [hereinafter the Dataco v Yahoo case].

[56] Cook (2012).

The facts in the above-mentioned case concern football fixtures. Football Dataco brought legal action against Yahoo! for copyright infringement because the latter used information from Football Dataco's database.[57] Football Dataco alleged database copyright infringement in toto, taking into account the first tier of protection from the Database Directive which provides copyright protection for databases which, by virtue of the original selection or arrangement of their contents, constitute the author's own intellectual creation and the second scheme of protection, taking into account Article 7 of the Database Directive. The plaintiff (Football Dataco) argued that they undertook a substantial amount of skill and labor. The High Court and Court of Appeal of England and Wales, following Advocate General Mengozzi's opinion, accepted the fact that they were databases but denied database rights to them, taking into account the precedents rooted in the CJEU's Fixtures Marketing (C-46/02; C-338/02 and C-444/02) and BHB decisions in 2004, which will be explained below.[58]

Another important reason for databases to be more protected concerns technological development and digitization which make possible the rapid production of databases. This situation provided an immense opportunity for those seeking a free ride to circumvent database protection at no cost.[59] Finally, the database industry in the EU started to grow and compete in other markets. The "production of information" represented an innovative business which needed to be fostered within the European Community and such investment needed to be balanced. There were only two viable paths to achieve this. The first was to harmonize the EU Member State's national competition laws, which by that time seemed to be very difficult to achieve. And second was the creation of a novel "sui generis"[60] IPR.[61]

2.3 Database Rights: Legal Concepts and Main European Court Decisions

The Database Directive defines a database as, "a collection of independent works, data or other materials arranged in a systematic or methodical way and individually accessible by electronic or other means."[62] The definition provided by the Directive is rather broad and allows wide room for interpretation.[63] It could encompass practically any kind of data imaginable[64] including the following: magazines or

---

[57]Maggs (2012).

[58]Declaye (2012).

[59]Derclaye (2008b, p. 46).

[60]*Sui Generis* is a Latin moniker which means "of its own kind". *See*: Duhaime.org, Learn Law, *Dictionary of Latin Terms*, [online]. Available at: www.duhaime.org/LegalDictionary/Category/LatinLawTermsDictionary.aspx. Accessed 15 December 2018].

[61]Derclaye (2008b, p. 46).

[62]Article 1 (2) of the Database Directive.

[63]Spinello and Bottis (2009, p. 85).

[64]Bovenberg (2006, p. 175).

newspapers, encyclopedias, law reports, directories, catalogs and, depending on the circumstances, also certain web pages, textbooks containing a selection of different materials, multimedia works, a library, or geographical data.[65]

Given the proliferation of computer database software operating within a cloud computing environment, the first distinction worthy to highlight is that computer programs used for making or operating a database are not protected. However, there are some issues to clarify on this point as from the broad definition of the Database Directive it could be interpreted that the data which is stored within a computer program and "crucial to that computer program's operation" also fall under the scope of the Database Directive. This occurred in the case of *Mars UK Ltd. v Teknowledge Ltd.* [the "Mars" case],[66] where relevant data concerning the size, weight, and other dimensions were stored on the EEPROM (electronically erasable programmable read-only-memory) devices. This data was fundamental in distinguishing between "legitimate" and "illegitimate" coins. Finally, the defendants acknowledged the database rights infringement in the reproduction of data within EEPROM devices. However, according to David Davison, the solution to solve this controversy is to determine the purpose of the data inside the computer program. If the data is there to help the software to operate properly instead of instructing or informing a person, then it should not fall under the scope of the Database Directive.[67]

The word "independent" seems to be a clear term, notwithstanding this is not defined within the wordings of the Database Directive. Therefore, if we have to analyze this requirement with the rationale behind the definition of a database, then it seems logical that the intention of the drafters of the Database Directive was related to those materials which can "stand on their own, whether they are extracts or whole works."[68]

Recital 17 of the Database Directive makes clear that independent works, data or other material as such are not part of the definition but rather the "collections" of those independent works, data or other materials. This term includes collections of literature, art, music or material such as texts, sound, images, numbers, facts, and data and explicitly excludes independent works such as a recording, an audiovisual, cinematographic, literary or musical work.[69]

---

[65]C490/14, *Freistaat Bayern v Verlag Esterbauer GmbH.* On October 29, 2015, the CJEU was called upon to clarify the definition of "database" in the case between the Federal State of Bavaria and the Austrian publisher Verlag Esterbauer. In this case, the Austrian publisher has allegedly infringed database rights by scanning topographic maps from the Land of Bavaria's database. The question raised to the CJEU was whether geographic data must be regarded as falling under the definition of Article 1 (2) of the Database Directive. Not surprisingly, the Court confirmed that geographical databases fall within the scope of database rights. For a commentary of the case see Sinodinou (2015).

[66]*Mars UK Ltd. v Teknowledge Ltd.* [1999] EWHC 226 [the "Mars" case].

[67]Davison (2003, p. 71); see also Aplin (2005, pp. 45–46).

[68]Stamatoudi (2000, pp. 23–24).

[69]Recital 17 of the Database Directive.

If the Database Directive would have defined a database simply as "collection of materials...", and omitted the word "independent," any work (i.e., a song, a film, etc.) could fall under the scope of the Database Directive. Independent materials have autonomous value on their own. They carry information whose meaning makes sense regardless of another piece of information. For example, if a chapter of a book or a musical note from a symphony is taken away, these works do not make sense on their own anymore.[70]

Another relevant requirement for a database to qualify for database rights is that the data or other materials have to be "individually accessible." This seems to be linked to the first requirement of independent elements.[71] Tanya Aplin argues that the independent element must be interpreted as "conceptually or logically independent" as opposed as to the notion of "physically independent." The latter suggests the idea of being physically separated from the work, which is not the intention of the Directive. These two notions are better explained in the following two examples. This first involves multimedia encyclopedias, where elements have the same meaning if they are separated from each other.[72] For example, an entry of an animal species will still have the same meaning if it is detached from the context of the encyclopedia. The second involves multimedia video games, such as Virtua Cop[73] for example, which usually follow a sequence like a movie, and therefore if separated from its original context, do not have a meaning on their own.[74]

For this reason, unified pieces of works such as films,[75] multimedia video games, and computer programs[76] are excluded from the concept of a database because they serve their purpose as a whole and are not meant to be accessed individually. However, a list of movies, video games and computer programs can, of course, enjoy the database rights.[77] Without this test, the definition of a database would be too broad and there would be a bundle of overlapping intellectual property rights thus rendering commercial exploitation more difficult as there would be more layers of protection to be clarified.[78]

---

[70] Derclaye (2008b, p. 62).

[71] Stamatoudi (2000, p. 24).

[72] Aplin (2005, pp. 46–49).

[73] Aplin (2005, p. 48). Virtua Cop is a multimedia video game, where two cops follow a criminal band through a series of investigations where the real players have to follow a series of cues in order to achieve these objectives. This means that in order to pass to the next level certain actions and tasks have to be completed. When the followers give different responses then certain variations occur. This was the video game in the case *Galaxy Electronics Pty Ltd v Sega Enterprises Ltd* (1997), 37 IPR 462 ["Galaxy Electronics"].

[74] Aplin (2005, p. 48).

[75] Stamatoudi (2000, pp. 24–25).

[76] Aplin (2005, pp. 48–49).

[77] Stamatoudi (2000, pp. 24–25).

[78] Stamatoudi (2000, p. 25).

The Database Directive grants exclusive rights concerning the extraction of "substantial" parts from the database and the re-utilization of the extracted material. It appears that Article 7 of the Database Directive introduces a new right as the words "extraction" and "re-utilization" are not usually used in copyright law. Nevertheless, this interpretation is wrong, as will be shown below in the definitions and relevant case law in Europe. A close look at the definitions of extraction and re-utilization shows that these new terms refer to the right of reproduction that is already familiar in copyright law.[79]

Article 7 (2) (a) defines "extraction" as follows: "the permanent or temporary transfer of all or a substantial part of the contents of a database to another medium by any means or in any form."[80] In this context, the word "extraction" does not only mean the actual transfer of the content of a database from one place to another but rather the reproduction of the content in another medium. This means, for instance, that the sole purpose of looking at the content of a database and then copying substantial parts of the database in another medium would represent an infringement of the right to extraction. The same interpretation could be done in the context of electronic databases, i.e., in the cloud, where the mere act of accessing and reading the database without prior authorization of the maker of the database would also represent an infringement of such rights.[81]

This means that the extraction can be carried out directly or indirectly without the necessity of accessing the original database. The mere referral to the content of a database as a source and then copied to another means is considered to be "extraction" in the scope of the Database Directive.[82] Another key concept to support this argument is the word "temporary" which clearly alludes to the idea that temporary digital copies also fall within the concept of extraction and re-utilization of the content of the database.[83]

The real meaning of the word "extraction" has been clarified at the CJEU in the *Directmedia case*.[84] This case was about the "extraction" of substantial parts of a database with well-known poems from the year 1730 until 1930. The database was created by a German professor and his team of researchers from Freiburg University.[85] In this case, the database represented a clear substantial investment in terms of time, effort and human resources as it took two and a half years to compile 1,100 poems from a group of about 20,000 poems using different references, including

---

[79]Davison (2003, p. 87).

[80]Article 7 (2) (a) of the Database Directive.

[81]Davison (2003, p. 87).

[82]Stokes (2009, p. 62).

[83]Davison (2003, p. 87).

[84]C-304/07 *Directmedia GmbH v Albert-Ludwig Universität Freiburg* [hereinafter the Directmedia case].

[85]Barnitzke et al. (2011a, p. 140).

other publications with detailed information about the authors, title, year of publication, etc. In addition, there was a substantial investment in terms of money since the estimated cost for its compilation was of almost 35,000.[86]

Directmedia Publications (the defendant) admitted to having consulted the anthology of poems selected by the German Professor and his team of researchers but alleged that there was no direct extraction of the poems in the traditional way of copying and pasting the contents directly. As a result, Directmedia Publications obtained 856 poems from Freiburg University's database and produced a CD-ROM titled "1,000 poems everybody should have" which represented about 98% of the content of Freiburg University's compilation of selected poems.[87]

In this case, there was no doubt that this represented a substantial part of the database since 856 poems out of 1,000 represent almost the whole database. The Regional German Court decided in favor of the German professor. However, another question was raised in the second instance at the Federal Court of Justice (Bundesgerichtshof) and this was the issue of interpreting the term "extraction", taking into account that the defendant alleged that there was no direct copy of the database contents but rather a consultation where some poems were selected and others discarded. The German Federal Court decided to raise the following question to the CJEU[88]:

> can the transfer of data from a database protected in accordance with Article 7 (1) of [Directive 96/9/EC] and their incorporation in a different database constitute an extraction within the meaning of Article 7 (2) (a) of that directive even in the case where the transfer follows individual assessment resulting from consultation of the database, or does extraction within the meaning of that provision presuppose the (physical) copying of data?[89]

The CJEU, in light of Advocate General Sharpston's opinion, refused to make a limited interpretation as suggested by the German court. In their opinion, the mere act of transcribing the contents of a database is tantamount to the damage created by copying by electronic means thus prejudices the investment of the maker of the database under equal circumstances.[90]

> 'extraction' within the meaning of Article 7 (2) (a) of the Directive does not presuppose the (physical) copying of data. In order to constitute an 'extraction' within the meaning of Article 7 (2) (a) of the directive, it is immaterial whether the transfer of data from a database protected in accordance with Article 7 (1) of the Directive and their incorporation in a different database takes place following individual assessments of the data after consulting the database.[91]

---

[86]Barnitzke et al. (2011a, p. 140).

[87]Barnitzke et al. (2011a, pp. 140–141).

[88]Barnitzke et al. (2011a, pp. 140–141); see also Barnitze et al. (2011, pp. 80) et seq.

[89]C-304/07 *Directmedia GmbH v Albert-Ludwig Universität Freiburg* at [21].

[90]Barnitze et al. (2011, p. 85).

[91]C-304/07 *Directmedia GmbH v Albert-Ludwig Universität Freiburg* at [59].

It is noteworthy that the CJEU extended the interpretation of the word extraction to "on- screen consultation of the first database."[92] This is surely a correct interpretation which is going to impact the production of databases that are publicly available in the cloud. In addition, two other recent cases expanded the interpretation of the word "extraction" which echoed the view of the CJEU in construing the meaning of this word more broadly. The two cases are similar in a way that they both refer to former employees who left the company to pursue other undertakings.[93]

In *Apis-Hristovich EOOD v Lakorda AD,*[94] two former employees of Apis-Hristovich EOOD [Apis] extracted substantial parts of two modules from Apis's database. Lakorda AD [the defendants] claimed that the content of such a database was made available to the public. Thus, no database rights infringement was committed. The CJEU upheld that the public availability of the databases was essentially meaningless as long as there was a substantial investment in the creation of such a database.[95] In that order, in *Exchange Communications Ltd. v Masheder,*[96] a former employee of Exchange Communications Ltd. [Exchange] who commenced to work for a competing company, was accused of extracting parts of its former employer's database containing relevant detailed information for a potential customer. The plaintiff [Exchange] did not specify the means of the extraction and, therefore, the defendant claimed that the court ought to refuse to consider this case. Notwithstanding, the judge sent the case for substantiation, endorsing the previous CJEU interpretations that the term extraction should be widely defined.[97]

2.3.1 "Obtaining" and "Creating" Data and the "Spin-Off Doctrine" in the Eyes of the CJEU

The CJEU ruled four cases[98] in the year 2004 which represents a landmark in understanding what exactly the framers of the directive meant with the wording "obtaining" and made a distinction between the databases which "create" new data and those databases that "obtain" preexisting data. These four cases involved databases located in four different countries; England, Sweden, Finland and Greece. All four cases

[92]MacQueen et al. (2011, p. 221).

[93]MacQueen et al. (2011, pp. 221–222).

[94]*Apis-Hristovich EOOD v Lakorda AD* [2009] 3 CMLR 3 (ECJ).

[95]MacQueen et al. (2011, p. 221).

[96]*Exchange Communications Ltd. v Masheder* [2009] CSOH 135.

[97]MacQueen et al. (2011, pp. 221–222).

[98]*The British Horseracing Board Ltd and Others v William Hill Organization Ltd.* [the BHB case], ECJ, nr. C-203/02, 9 November 2004, (United Kingdom). *Fixtures Marketing Ltd. v Organismos Prognostikon Agonon Po- dosfairou* [the OPAP case], ECJ-C-444/02, 9 November 2004, (Greece). *Fixtures Marketing Ltd. v Oy Veikkaus AB*, ECJ – C-46/02, 9 November 2004, (Finland). *Fixtures Marketing Ltd. v Svenska Spel AB*, ECJ – C- 338/02, 9 November 2004, (Sweden).

shared the same commonalities, as they were all involved in the betting business. Thus, they referred to similar facts and data in the area of football and horseracing.[99]

> Finding and collecting the data which make up a football fixture list do not require any particular effort on the part of the professional leagues. Those activities are indivisibly linked to the creation of those data, in which the leagues participate directly as those responsible for the organization of football league fixtures. Obtaining the contents of a football fixture list thus does not require any investment independent of that required for the creation of data contained in that list.[100]

A good example that can be used to illustrate this is the fixtures made during the football or baseball world cups, where, similar to the four abovementioned cases submitted to the CJEU, you need to gather different groups of people (i.e., football fan associations, police authorities, etc.) during the preparation of the events and fixtures. It is also relevant to schedule those matches combining various factors, such as official holidays, weekends, and avoid overlapping of dates and matches, etc. Furthermore, a draw must be made in order to determine which countries are going to play in which group.[101] For example, South Africa, Mexico, Uruguay and France played in Group A of the 2010 Football World Cup according to the fixtures drawn by FIFA. While making these types of (fixture) databases, new data is "created" while organizing the events thus there is no "obtaining" in light of the CJEU decision.

Another important aspect which is relevant for the abovementioned discussion regarding "obtaining" and "creating" data, is the "spin-off" doctrine. "Spin-off" literally means, "any product or development derived incidentally from application or existing knowledge or enterprise."[102] In the context of databases, these are the databases created as a consequence of another business activity contrary to those created particularly for that sole purpose.[103]

It seems that this doctrine originated in Dutch jurisprudence.[104] In the *NV Holdingmaatschappij de Telegraaf v Nederlandse Omroep Stichting*,[105] the Court of Appeal of the Hague ruled: "…it must be assumed in the absence of any evidence supporting a reasonable assumption to the contrary, that the mere compilation of programmes does not entail any (separate) substantial investment…"[106] By the same token, in the *Algemeen Dagblad v Eureka Internetdiensten,*[107] inter alia, the District Court of Rotterdam rejected the database right to a list of headlines from newspapers. However, other jurisdictions have not seized the spin-off theory, such as in the *Danske*

---

[99]Barnitzke et al. (2011b, p. 86), see also Leistner (2010, p. 15), Papakonstantinou (2010, p. 494), Ito (2011, pp. 222) et seq.

[100]*Fixtures Marketing Ltd v Oy Veikkaus* decision at [44].

[101]Barnitzke et al. (2011b, p. 86); see also *Fixtures Marketing Ltd v Oy Veikkaus* decision at [10] and [11].

[102]See Collins Shorter Dictionary & Thesaurus, *"Spin-off,"* p. 705.

[103]Gaster (2005, pp. 129–135).

[104]Rowland and MacDonald (2005, p. 92).

[105]*NV Holdingmaatschappij de Telegraaf v Nederlandse Omroep Stichting* [2002] ECDR 8 Court of Appeal of The Hague, [the Telegraaf case].

[106]The Telegraaf case at [16].

[107]*Algemeen Dagblad v Eureka Internetdiensten*, [the kranten.com case] [2002] ECDR 1.

Dagblades Forening (DDF) v Newsbooster case where the Copenhagen City Court granted database protection to a constellation of headlines and articles similar to those in the kranten.com case.[108]

Neither the Database Directive nor the abovementioned CJEU decisions specifically mention this doctrine, however it can be concluded from the preamble of the Directive in Recitals 10–12, that the main purpose was to promote the investment of the formerly emerging European database industry. There is no reason to assume that the original directive's intention was to protect other databases that were "generated quasi 'automatically' as by-products of other activities."[109] Advocate General Stix-Hackl had examined this theory in *Fixtures Marketing Ltd v Organismos prognostikon agonon podosfairou AE [OPAP]* and concluded that such investment would have been carried out in any event for the purpose of organizing a betting business and not particularly for the creation of such a database.[110] The reasoning in the rationale behind this doctrine can also be tacitly concluded in the following paragraph of the BHB case[111]:

> Under the 9th, 10th and 12th recitals of the preamble to the directive, its purpose, as William Hill points out, is to promote and protect investment in data 'storage' and 'processing' systems which contribute to the development of an information market against a background of exponential growth in the amount of information generated and processed annually in all sectors of activity. It follows that the expression 'investment in…the obtaining, verification or presentation of the contents' of a database must be understood, generally, to refer to investment in the creation of that database as such.[112]

Finally, on May 12, 2012, the "spin-off" theory was rejected in the *Football Dataco v Sportradar* case.[113] To summarize this case, Dataco provided a service called "Football Live," which was employed to input live match data into a bigger football database kept by its subcontractor PA Sport UK. On the one hand, there were objective facts included in the database such as information concerning penalties, player replacements and scores which were constantly updated. On the other hand, subjective information provided by football analysts and employed by Dataco was also periodically included in the databases.[114]

Sportradar (a German and Swiss company) supplied a service to the betting industry called "Sport Live Data" which was publicly available at www.betradar.com. With respect to the football matches broadcasted live on T.V., Sportradar submitted information by his operators who were watching the games and entering data by hand. When the football matches were not broadcasted, Sportradar used information from

[108] Rowland and MacDonald (2005, pp. 89–90).

[109] Davison and Hugenholz (2005, p. 4).

[110] Rowland and MacDonald (2005, p. 92).

[111] Davison and Hugentholz (2005, p. 4).

[112] BHB Decision at [30].

[113] *Football Dataco Ltd and other companies v Sportradar GMBH and another company; Football Dataco Ltd and other companies v Stan James Abingdon Ltd and other companies: Chancery Division (Mr. Justice Floyd)*: 8 May 2012 [hereinafter the Dataco case].

[114] Alsop (2012).

different sources, including information published by PA Sport whose servers were located in Germany and Austria. Stan James was a betting company which "took a feed from Sportradar" and allowed its customers to use the data.[115]

Interestingly, this judgment discussed the difference between "created" and "obtained" data as follows: "factual data which is collected and recorded at a live event such as a football match about events outside the control of the person doing the collection and recording is not created by that person, but is obtained by him."[116] In this High Court case, the Hon Lord Justice Floyd mentions that albeit this theory is examined in the Opinion of the Advocate General in the BHB case, "it does not form part of the reasoning of the CJEU." On these grounds, Mr. Floyd cast aside this theory as it did not belong to EU law.[117]

Note that the main difference between the *BHB* and the *Dataco* case is that in the former, BHB had "control" over the data and the data was indeed created by "compiling the list itself," whereas in the latter case, the events were merely "reported" and the company had no "control" over such data.[118] The rationale behind this, in the *Dataco* case, is that anybody with the same skills and expertise could have obtained such data. To wit, any other company could have hired football consultants with the same level of expertise and create similar content equal to Dataco's database.

2.3.2 Right to Access Information and "Sole Source" Databases

Broadly speaking, it is the privilege of the owner of a copyrighted work to decide not to allow the exploitation of their rights.[119] Nevertheless, the Database Directive provides for an exception in the case of extraction for teaching and purposes of illustration. The same holds true for scientific research as long as the source has been appropriately indicated and, to an extent, justified by non-commercial activities.[120] Scientific research in the Database Directive refers to both the natural and human sciences.[121]

In this respect, the database right never aimed to create a new right to underlying single data sets.[122] Recital 45 of the Database Directive clearly expresses that "the right to prevent unauthorized extraction and/or re-utilization does not in any way constitute an extension of copyright protection to mere facts or data" and that this

[115] Alsop (2012).

[116] Dataco case, at [60].

[117] Osborne (2012).

[118] Osborne (2012).

[119] Bently and Sherman (2009, p. 258).

[120] Article 9 (c) of the Database Directive.

[121] Colston and Middleton (2005, pp. 282–283).

[122] Colston and Middleton (2005, p. 283).

right "should not give rise to the creation of a new right in the works, data or materials themselves."[123]

In this context, it can be explicitly understood that the intention of the Database Directive was to maintain the traditional copyright balance between the right to access and the protection of information.[124] A database right may be only given as an exclusive right in the database as such. It does not preclude someone from collecting the same data in order to create their own database.[125]

Nonetheless, databases that are accessible in the cloud collect data that are "unique."[126] This means that you cannot find such data elsewhere. For example, scientific data coming from a specific research project may only be collected once in a lifetime under particular circumstances, such as geological and biological data. These data sets may only be obtained under particular environmental conditions. Developments in the last decade have made databases essential for much scientific research. The emergence of this new field is expanding at a rapid pace. It thereby becomes a matter of urgency to clarify which rights are preferable in order to protect and stimulate research.[127]

On the other hand, it is also important to avoid the overprotection and restriction of research access. Access to data and the ability to extract and re-utilize data have always played an important role in scientific investigation. As always, intellectual property law raises legal questions concerning a proportionate balance between the right to access information for scientists and the adequate protection of investment for the database maker. A disproportionate balance may either hinder the proliferation of new databases which are necessary and useful to scientific research or may create a monopoly of biological data by the maker of a database. In this context two key questions might arise: (i) How can this affect scientific research? and (ii) Who "owns" the data in such collections?[128]

For this reason, databases containing data regarded to be "unique" may fall under the category of "sole source database." Therefore, if the database owner is not willing to provide access to unsubstantial parts of the database, this may be considered to be an abuse of monopoly rights and thus they can be coerced into providing access to data and are subject to competition law rules.[129] In this book, I am not going to focus on competition law rules. However, the contractual framework depicted in Chaps. 8 and 9 will also include the problem raised by scientific databases and will provide a practical, effective and automated solution to waive database rights. This will reduce the risk of a monopoly of data on a large scale.

---

[123]Recital 45 of the Database Directive.

[124]Colston and Middleton (2005, p. 283).

[125]Bovenberg (2006, p. 177).

[126]Bovenberg (2006, p. 177).

[127]Corrales Compagnucci and Frakgouli (2009).

[128]Corrales Compagnucci and Frakgouli (2009).

[129]Bovenberg (2006, p. 178).

2.3.3 Sui Generis Right Term of Protection

The Database Right subsists for 15 years, starting from the date the database was originally created.[130] Furthermore, according to Article 10 (3) of the Database Directive, any qualitatively or quantitatively substantial change to the contents of a database, including any substantial change which is produced by the accumulation of successive additions, deletions or alterations that could be considered as a new substantial investment either qualitatively or quantitatively, may qualify for database protection.[131] This means that any substantial change such as the correction, deletion or update of the content of a database that is considered to be substantial can be extended for another 15 years. For instance, if the maker of a database adds a little bit of information on a daily basis or updates a whole new section of the database with new data every month, the database right could be extended for another term of 15 years, successively. This provision is one of the most controversial as it means that databases can be overprotected for an unlimited period. As a corollary, it creates an imbalance between the protection given to the database makers and the right to access to information. This could also lead to a monopoly of information.

2.4 Big Data and the Sui Generis Right Dilemma

The term Big Data is frequently used in the literature and is commonplace in various business transactions, yet there is no consensus about an accepted universal definition.[132] Big Data can be loosely described as "data that exceeds the processing capacity of conventional database systems."[133] The size of data is so large that it surpasses the architecture of a standard database found in a conventional personal computer. Therefore, it provides an alternative to process large amounts of data.[134] Big Data has brought new and complex ways of processing and analyzing information at a larger scale.[135] In this book, the term Big Data will be used in its broadest sense as not only to a shorthand reference to a large amount of data but also include all the methods and processes that result in information that supports decision-making insights.[136] Often, Big Data is collected from different sources and is presented in a raw state. The premise is to gather as much data as possible. Then, with the use of

---

[130] Article 10 (1) of the Database Directive.

[131] Article 10 (3) of the Database Directive.

[132] Kalyvas (2015, p. 1).

[133] Dumbill (2012), loc. 30.

[134] Dumbill (2012), loc. 30.

[135] See, generally, Chen et al. (2014, p. 12); Pellegrin (2014, p. 345).

[136] Kalyvas (2015, p. 1).

data mining[137] tools, artificial intelligence (AI),[138] machine learning (ML) and analytic tools[139] from servers that can be located in different places, this data is curated, analyzed and categorized in various ways to find the answers for everyday problems.

The benefits of Big Data are astonishing. One groundbreaking example is how Google is able to track and monitor deadly viruses such as the bird flu and swine flu, which was discovered in 2009.[140] According to Google, it was possible to "predict" the spread through the Google search engine by analyzing search queries input by end-users on the Internet.[141] Typing search terms such as "medicine for cough and fever" allowed Google to track and map the location of the viruses.[142]

To date, there are many other interesting examples of Big Data. One dramatic example involves Europe's particle-physics laboratory (CERN) located in Switzerland. The famous particle-collision experiments within the Hadron Collider generate vast amounts of data. The data center stores and sends about 30 petabytes of data around the world for analysis every year.[143]

---

[137]Data mining is a fast-growing technology in the fields of knowledge discovery and decision-making processes. This technology helps to provide a more meaningful understanding of large data sets. Data mining tools can be found in various fields of computing, businesses and science such customer transactions, manufacturing, bioinformatics, geodata information services, audit systems, etc. See Adhikari and Adhikari (2015, pp. 4–5).

[138]The study of the discipline of AI started in 1956 at the Dartmouth College in Hanover, New Hampshire. Originally the concept of AI was conceived as "a set of algorithms to process symbols." This initiative led to numerous advances and applications very useful on the Internet as well as other fields of computing and electronics such as search engines, consumer electronics, automobiles, and different kinds of software, voice recognition applications. By and large, AI focuses on certain aspects or specialized "intelligent" capabilities of various computing systems which is now expanding to other areas for the study of the human brain and body and the interrelation with its environment. This is revolutionizing our way of thinking that goes beyond its original conception. For example, it provides useful information for analyzing corporations, groups of agents and network embedded systems. See Lungarella et al. (2007, p. 1); Wang and Goertzel (2007) (eds), p. 1.

[139]See Pries and Dunnigan (2015), Stimmel (2015), Loshin (2013), Bhatnagar and Srinivasa (2013) (eds).

[140]Mayer-Schoenberger and Cukier (2013, pp. 1–7, 12–18, 98–197).

[141]See Google.org Flu Trends, *How does this work?* https://www.google.org/flutrends/about/how.html. Accessed 10 November 2016.

[142]Mayer-Schoenberger and Cukier (2013, pp. 1–7, 12–18, 98–197).

[143]CERN, Computing: Experiments at CERN generate colossal amounts of data. The Data Centre stores it and sends it around the world for analysis, [online]. Available at: http://home.web.cern.ch/about/computing. Accessed 10 November 2018.

However, not only the domains of physics and astronomy are reaping the benefits of storing, processing and sharing massive amounts of information in the cloud. Today, more and more sectors of the research community,[144] as well as other industry initiatives in the private sector, are joining the Big Data club. For example, grasp projects have also started to grapple its benefits and gave generated substantial results.[145]

The problem of Big Data, such as the genetic sequence project, is that the data comes from a wide range of experiments, i.e., different databases. Some of those databases are from private institutions, such as biotech companies, and others stem from public institutions. They slice and dice information from various research projects, such as genetic sequencing, protein research or the annotations of medical records. The "complexity is daunting," affirmed Lawrence Hunter, a computational biologist at the University of Colorado-Denver. They are much more complex than those databases envisaged by the legislator of the Database Directive two decades ago.[146]

To put it into perspective, analyzing and comparing human genomes takes more computer power than the combination of a personal computer and a cloud-based file-sharing application such as Dropbox. Most Big Data technology is virtual, based on cloud computing. Many scientists access databases using software and applications directly through the cloud. For example, the European Bioinformatics Institute (EBI) has solved many of its problems associated with the storing and processing of data by hosting mirror sites at three of the many remote data centers that belong to the Amazon Web Service's Elastic Compute Cloud (EC2) infrastructure.[147]

Harnessing the benefits of Big Data seems an endearing opportunity. However, this is just one part of the story. As seen in the previous section, the CJEU denied the protection of those databases whose creator had invested only in creating the contained data.[148] In the context of Big Data, these decisions opened the door to the question of whether databases may be judged to be "creating" or "obtaining" data. In other words, the crucial element to this problem is how to define the term "obtaining" which refers to the act of collecting and gathering already existing data prior to the creation of the database in question.[149]

Interestingly, in 2005 the Landgericht (district court) of Munich[150] issued a decision in relation to geographical maps which could shed some light on our discussion. In this case, the Federal State of Bavaria was producing topographic maps of Bavaria

---

[144]For example, Big Data techniques and technologies in geoinformation. See, generally, Karimi (2014) (ed).

[145]Marx (2013, pp. 255–160).

[146]Marx (2013, pp. 255–160).

[147]Marx (2013, pp. 255–160).

[148]Davison and Hugenholtz (2005, pp. 113–118).

[149]Hugenholtz (2004).

[150]Landgericht München I, Urteil vom 9. 11. 2005 - 21 O 7402/02 [Topografische Kartenblätter], GRUR 2006, 225.

in printed form. The defendant, on the other hand, copied information from the plaintiff's maps and published it in tourist guides. As a consequence, the plaintiff argued that this was an infringement of their database right. According to the Landgericht, the investment in obtaining the relevant data through aerial photography was not considered an investment in the creation of new data, since the data already existed and anybody with certain skills and knowledge, providing a similar investment, would have come to the same results. Therefore, geographic maps are protected by the sui generis right. Since this case concerns data taken directly from nature, it could be argued, by analogy, that some databases from Big Data projects are privileged by database protection on the grounds that anybody with similar scientific skills could obtain the same biological data.[151]

The German interpretation is a good starting point to begin solving this dilemma. However, regarding biological databases, it seems more complicated to distinguish whether the data has been "obtained" or "created." This problem should be analyzed on a case by case basis since the biological data can indeed be derived from different sources. For example, data collected from other databases falls under the definition of "obtained" whereas the situation is not as clear for data coming directly from experimental work (i.e., sequencing projects).[152]

Very recently, on October 29, 2015, in a very similar case about topographic maps, the CJEU was called upon to clarify the definition of "database" in the case between the Federal State of Bavaria and the Austrian publisher Verlag Esterbauer.[153] The Land of Bavaria publishes topographic maps through its Regional Office for Surveying and Geographic Information (Landesamt für Vermessung und Geoinformation). The Austrian publisher, which publishes, amongst other things, atlases, tour books and maps for cyclists, mountain bikers and inline skaters, has allegedly infringed database rights by scanning topographic maps from the Land of Bavaria's database and reproduced the underlying data for the creation of its maps. The specific question raised to the CJEU was whether geographic data (i.e., specific points of the earth's surface) constitute "independent materials" of a database under the definition of Article 1 (2) of the Database Directive since the materials can be separated from one another without the value of their informative content being affected.[154]

Not surprisingly, given all the previous precedents,[155] the Court confirmed that geographical databases and the underlying topographic data fall under the scope of the Database Directive. The last recital of the question referred to the CJEU in the present case reads as follows:

---

[151] Corrales Compagnucci and Fragkouli (2009, pp. 6–10).

[152] Oliva and Corrales Compagnucci (2011, pp. 226–228).

[153] C490/14, *Freistaat Bayern v Verlag Esterbauer GmbH.*

[154] C490/14 at [6], [7], [8], [9] and [10].

[155] See Judgments in Fixtures Marketing, C444/02, [the OPAP case], C338/02, C46/02, The BHB case, C203/02, and also Football Dataco and Others, C604/10, [Dataco v Yahoo case].

> geographical information extracted from a topographic map by a third party so that that information may be used to produce and market another map retains, following its extraction, sufficient informative value to be classified as 'independent materials' of a 'database' within the meaning of that provision.[156]

Certainly, in this particular case, the general reasoning behind this rule is perfectly understandable and dully grounded since the "relevance" and "usefulness" of the data was direct. The topographic map in the present case was used as a basic product, then used to create sub-products (such as track maps for cyclists, mountain bikers and inline skaters) through selective extraction of geographical information from those databases.[157] Nonetheless, as discussed earlier, in the Big Data era, information is processed, mined and analyzed producing new "derivative" data through complex algorithms. In most cases, the relevance and usefulness of the data are not direct. In other words, the data is not immediately recognized since the data extracted cannot be directly used or is not "even visible" by end-users. This being said, I think that Big Data is challenging the way the EU legislature has framed the database right, and as this is a global issue, I suggest focusing on the law of contract in order to clarify this right at the international level.

2.5 Database Right and Contract Law

The ultimate rationale behind and justification of contract law is very simple and fundamental. The root cause is based on the freedom of contract and party autonomy[158] to discuss the facts of the case. The position defended in this book is that freedom of contract is one of those basic human rights[159] that makes it much easier for parties to reach an agreement based on the facts of the case. In contrast to discussing laws, regulations, principles, or directives for the purpose of convenience or easiness, it is more practical for the parties involved to discuss the elements or premises of the contract. There are an infinite number of laws and regulations and if we were to discuss the ways in which these legal principles should be employed, it would be almost impossible to persuade the other party who wants to stick to another principle. However, when we talk about a contract or the way to carry out contracts, the difference between one party and another party relates to which perspective should be emphasized, which view should be employed, or which view should be discussed temporarily. It should be much easier for the parties to agree with the contractual terms. It is not a matter of which law should be applied. It is a matter of which element should be emphasized for the purpose of solving the problem. We cannot reflect on every aspect of the facts of the contract. However, we can discuss with others about each premise or element. Moreover, even after the execution of a contract, if the

---

[156] C490/14 at [29].

[157] C490/14 at [19].

[158] See, generally, Mandery (2014); Muir (2010, pp. 250–283).

[159] Elegido (1993, p. 69).

conditions of society change, we can re-negotiate the terms and conditions. In this sense, the majority of countries with civil law permit re-negotiation of contracts if the conditions of society materially change.[160]

Contract law is a good mechanism that can be used to regulate the access and use of databases. It has many benefits such as the economic advantages of differential pricing. That is, prices can target different groups of stakeholders depending on their interests, way of exploiting the product and economic situation. For example, commercial users can be charged more than non-commercial users like universities, non-governmental organizations or any other organization working in the education sector. Whereas, competing companies can be charged more than those companies that are not using the information to compete in the same market, as long as there is always a proper balance between the prices charged in return to the investment made by the maker of the database.[161]

However, there are also several disadvantages related to the contract law regime which can affect both the owner and the user of the databases. First of all, one of the major drawbacks is that the contractual relationship is only legally binding to the parties involved in the negotiation thus this is not extended to third parties. The second main disadvantage has to do with access to the database. If anyone is able to access the database and use such information without any technical restrictions, then there is no motivation for such a person to establish a contractual relationship with the owner of the database.[162]

In these circumstances, there are two different kinds of protection. One way is through the use of technological measures such as passwords, encryption mechanisms, etc., especially in the field of cloud computing where electronic databases are involved. However, there is always the possibility of circumventing these security mechanisms, in particular, in the field of cloud computing. The other route would be by making it illegal to access the content of the database without the owner's consent. In the context of cloud computing, this can be obtained by "laws of trespass" and with electronic databases (such as the cloud accessible databases) it can be done by drafting laws with regards to technological circumvention measures.[163]

[160]Article 13 of the Database Directive confers the possibility to protect databases via contractual agreements in addition to the database right, and, Article 15 states that "any contractual provision contrary to Articles 6 (1) and 8 shall be null and void." Article 6 (1) refers to the performance by the lawful user of a database and Article 8 to the rights and obligations of lawful users.

[161]Davison (2003, p. 40).

[162]Davison (2003, p. 40).

[163]Davison (2003, p. 40).

The other major flaw of contract law, which is something that we are going to focus on in the following chapters of this book, is something that Davison has already pointed out: this involves "contracts for access databases may not in fact have the customized features"[164] and other advantages mentioned above such as the "click on" type[165] which are typical in cloud computing scenarios.

A well-known example is the recent Ryanair case[166] ruled by the CJEU in January 2015. This case involves the Irish Airline company called Ryanair[167] and the organization called PR Aviation[168] whose objective is to provide airline and air travel information, acting as a liaison between airlines and consumers as well as business-to-business (B2B). Relying on the Database Directive, Ryanair claimed that PR Aviation had allegedly infringed copyright and the database rights of its website. It sought an order against PR Aviation to stop the infringement of its rights and claimed monetary damages.[169]

In addition, Ryanair argued that PR aviation had violated the terms and conditions that had been expressly accepted by visiting Ryanair's website. PR aviation provides low fare information to its customers by gathering data using a technique called "screen scrapping," which is a software tool that extracts data from human-readable structures, i.e., websites. According to Ryanair's terms and conditions provided on its website, this technique was expressly forbidden for commercial purposes unless the involved parties entered into a written license agreement.[170]

Since 2010, this case was taken in and out of Dutch courts. According to the judgment of the court (second chamber), at the material time, access to that website presupposes that the visitor to the site accepts the general terms and conditions "by ticking a box to that effect." Those conditions included the prohibition of using the website for purposes other than private and non-commercial. It also contained an express prohibition of using automated systems or software to extract data from Ryanair's website for commercial purposes, i.e. "screen scraping."[171]

However, if one visits the website, there is no such "ticking box". Unless the website has changed since the court decision, what one can find now at the very bottom of the site and in small letters is simply a hyperlink titled "Terms of Use"[172] which indeed leads you to a Ryanair's Terms of Use site that includes the aforementioned

---

[164]Davison (2003, p. 40).

[165]Davison (2003, p. 40).

[166]*Ryanair Ltd. V PR Aviation BV,* Case C-30/14 (The Netherlands) [the Ryanair case].

[167]*Ryanair Ltd. V PR Aviation BV* at [15].

[168]PR Aviation, [online]. Available at: http://www.euronet.nl/users/rvh/PR-Aviation/PRabout.htm. Accessed 10 May 2019.

[169]*Ryanair Ltd. V PR Aviation BV* at [17].

[170]*Ryanair Ltd. V PR Aviation BV* at [16].

[171]*Ryanair Ltd. V PR Aviation BV* at [16].

[172]See Ryanair [online]. Available at: http://www.ryanair.com. Accessed 10 May 2010.

prohibition of activities such as screen scraping expressly defined in Section 3 entitled "Permitted use."[173] Finally, the CJEU, ruled that the provisions enshrined by the sui generis rights under the Database Directive[174] do not preclude the author of such database from establishing contractual constraints on its use by third parties, without prejudice to the applicable national law.[175]

The *Ryanair* case is a good example of the typical terms and conditions that one can find in various websites, including some cloud computing services sites where subtle subterfuges are usually introduced within the IP license terms, in particular by broadening their scope in terms of its use and protection. In this case, the basis for the restriction of the use of a database was not derived from the Directive as the CJEU confirmed that it was neither protected by sui generis rights nor copyrights, but by a contract.

However, in practice, it is very relevant to determine whether the mere users of the website that access its content are bound by the terms and conditions. In other words, certain websites claim to establish a contractual relationship with the users thereof, which is often not the case when these kinds of legal notices are directed to all Internet users. Some or many of these users can access the site without even having to visualize in advance these terms and conditions. The bottom line is that there is a pressing need to clarify database rights at different levels and contract law can potentially help to establish a clear and effective procedure to assert this right, but this has to come in the right format, as I will explain later in future chapters.[176]

[173]See Ryanair Terms and Conditions [online]. Available at: http://www.ryanair.com/en/terms-of-use/. Accessed 10 May 2010.

[174]Articles 6 (1), 8 and 15 of the Database Directive.

[175]*Ryanair Ltd. V PR Aviation BV* at [46].

[176]At the time of writing this book, the Court of Appeal in Amsterdam rendered its judgment on November 22, 2016 in the case of Pearson Assessment and Information against Bär Software [the "Pearson" case]. The judgement seems relevant in light of the CJEU's earlier ruling in the *Ryanair case*. In this case, Pearson published psychological information (test results, questionnaires, score form, etc.) on a database available for the benefit of research, diagnosis and medical advice. Bär software extracted and used some of these data from Pearson's database without permission. The legal dispute between Pearson and Bär was whether Pearson's database was protected by copyrights and database rights. Both the District Court and Court of Appeal ruled that Pearson's database was neither protected by copyrights nor by database rights. The most interesting part of the case concerned the contractual clauses in the users' manual. The manual contained a paragraph which prohibited the extraction and re-utilization of any part of Pearson's database without authorization. One would presume that such passage was valid given that the database did not fall under the scope of the Database Directive. However, the court ruled that it does not matter for the outcome of the case whether the passage is part of the contract since the passage does not protect the database owner either way. This decision seemed to narrow and also blurred even more the scope of protection of databases. See *Pearson Assessment and Information B.V. v Bär Software*.

2.6 Summary and Interim Remarks

This first chapter discussed the legal issues regarding the protection and clarification of database rights in the cloud and Big Data environments. It highlighted the legal constraints concerning the main features of the Database Directive and questions of "ownership" rights of data, which is still under debate. The main problem of the Database Directive is that it was quite broadly drafted. In the legal field, this usually leaves wide room for interpretation, protecting more than it should.[177] The global nature of cloud computing and Big Data pose legal quandaries with regards to territorial rights such as the sui generis right. Therefore, the overarching aim of this work is to demonstrate how these legal issues should be communicated in the Service Level Agreements (SLAs) and what sort of actions are required so as to incorporate the information about database rights and "ownership" rights of data into the data management system. An innovative theoretical and pragmatic framework will be discussed in the forthcoming chapters, keeping in mind the end goal to execute the management of these legal requirements. Certain methodologies will be examined in order to guarantee that the general objective will be addressed.

References

Adhikari A, Adhikari J (2015) Advanced in knowledge discovery in databases, intelligent systems reference library, preface, vol 79. Springer, Cham, pp 4–5

Aitchison J, Gilchrist A, Bawden D (2000) Thesaurus construction and use: a practical manual, 4th edn. Aslib IMI, London, p 1

Alsop M (2012) Data on live football was "obtained" rather than "created" and thus could be the subject of database rights, Charles Russell LLP http://www.mondaq.com/x/185708/data+protection/Data+On+Live+Football+Was+Obtained+Rather+Than+Created+And+Thus+Could+Be+The+Sub-ject+Of+Database+Rights. Accessed 10 May 2019

Aplin T (2005) Copyright law in the digital society: the challenges of multimedia. Hart Publishing, Oxford, pp 45–46

Aplin T, Davis J (2013) Intellectual property law: text, cases, and materials, 2nd edn. Oxford University Press, Oxford, p 94

Baeza-Yates R, Ribeiro-Neto B (1999) Modern information retrieval. Addison Wesley Longman, ACM Press Books, New York, pp 99–101

Barnitzke B, Corrales pagnucci M, Frakgouli A (2009) Legal issues in biological databases: a sui generis approach, paper presented at the 2nd international seminar of information law (ISIL), Corfu, Greece, 26 June 2009. In: Bottis M (ed) A world for information law, Proceedings of the 2nd ISIL 2009, Ionian University, Nomiki Vivliothiki, Corfu

Barnitzke B, Corrales Compagnucci M, Forgó N (2012) Aspectos Legales de la Computación en la Nube: Seguridad de Datos y Derechos de Propiedad sobre los mismos, locs. 637 et seq., Kindle Edition. Editorial Albremática S.A., Buenos Aires

Bently L, Sherman B (2009) Intellectual property law, 3rd edn. Oxford University Press, Oxford, p 310

Bessmer N (2013) Cloud computing for small business, loc. 24, Kindle Edition

Black N (2012) Cloud computing for lawyers. American Bar Association, Chicago, p 211

---

[177] Derclaye (2008a).

Bort J (2011) 10 technologies that will change the world in the next 10 years. NetworkWorld. http://www.networkworld.com/article/2179278/lan-wan/10-technologies-that-will-change-the-world-in-the-next-10-years.html. Accessed 10 May 2019

Butler B (2012) Cloud computing's most over-hyped terms. http://www.computerworlduk.com/indepth/cloud-computing/3376086/cloud-computings-most-over-hyped-terms/?intcmp=most_pop;cldcmptng;6. Accessed 10 May 2019

Buyya R et al (2009) Cloud computing and emerging IT platforms: vision, hype, and reality for delivering computing as the 5th utility. Futur Gener Comput Syst 25(6):599–616

Carrol C (2014) What's a cloud services broker, and why do you need one? http://www.cio.com/article/2462417/cloud-computing/cloud-computing-whats-a-cloud-services-broker-and-why-do-you-need-one.html. Accessed 10 May 2019

Cherry D (2008) Scaling the database out, not up. IT Knowledge Exchange. http://itknowledgeexchange.techtarget.com/sql-server/scaling-the-database-out-not-up/. Accessed 10 May 2019

Columbus L (2013) Top 12 sites for free cloud computing & enterprise software research. Forbes. http://www.forbes.com/sites/louiscolumbus/2013/08/25/top-12-sites-for-free-cloud-computing-enterprise-software-research/. Accessed 10 May 2019

Columbus L (2014) Roundup of cloud computing forecasts and market estimates. Forbes. http://www.forbes.com/sites/louiscolumbus/2014/03/14/roundup-of-cloud-computing-forecasts-and-market-estimates-2014/. Accessed 10 May 2019

Davison M (2003) The legal protection of databases. Cambridge University Press, Cambridge, p 71

Davison M, Hugenholtz P (2005) Football fixtures, horse races and spin-offs: the ECJ domesticates the database right. EIPR 3:4

Derclaye E (2008a) Database rights are too tough on business, says expert http://www.out-law.com/page-9406. Accessed 10 May 2019

Derclaye E (2008b) The legal protection of databases: a comparative analysis. Edward Elgar Publishing, Cheltenham, pp 45–46

Derclaye E (2012) Football Dataco: skill and labour is dead! Kluwer Copyright Blog http://kluwercopyrightblog.com/2012/03/01/football-dataco-skill-and-labour-is-dead/. Accessed 10 May 2019

Dommering E, Hugenholtz P (eds) (1991) Protecting works of fact: copyright, freedom of expression, and information law. Kluwer Law and Taxation Publishers, Boston

Dumbill E (2012) Getting up to speed with big data: what is big data? loc. 30. In: O'Reilly Media, Big data: current perspectives from O'Reilly Media. O'Reilly Media Inc., Beijing

Elegido J (1993) A basic rationale for contracts, Persona y Derecho 28:69 http://ssrn.com/abstract=2515272. Accessed 10 May 2019

Gasaway L (2006) Databases and the law, Cyberspace law course, Spring 2006. University of North Carolina, Chapel Hill

Gaster J (2005) "Obtinere" of data in the eyes of the ECJ: how to interpret the database directive after the British Horseracing Board Ltd. et al v William Hill Organization Ltd. Comput Law Rev Int 6(5):129–135

Gilchrist A (1971) The thesaurus in retrieval. Aslib IMI, London, p 4

Grosheide F (2002) Database protection—the European way. Washington University Journal of Law & Policy 8:39. In: Symposium on intellectual property, digital technology & electronic commerce. http://openscholarship.wustl.edu/law_journal_law_policy/vol8/iss1/4. Accessed 10 May 2019

Grossman D, Frieder O (2004) Information retrieval: algorithms and heuristics. The information retrieval series, vol 15, 2nd edn. Springer, Dordrecht, p 105

Helling E (2004) Retrieving the sources of legal decision-making, technical possibilities and related legal issues. In: Wahlgren P (ed) Scandinavian studies in law, vol 47. Stockholm, p 545

Hugenholzt P (2004) Abuse of database right: sole-source information banks under the EU database directive. http://www.ivir.nl/publications/hugenholtz/abuseofdatabaseright.html. Accessed 10 May 2019

Ito A (2011) Legal aspects of satellite remote sensing. Studies in space law. Martinus Nijhoff Publishers, Leiden, pp 222 et seq
Kalyvas J (2015) A big data primer for executives. In: Kalyvas J, Overly M (eds) Big data: a business and legal guide. CRC Press, Boca Ratón, p 1
Karimi H (ed) (2014) Big data: techniques and technologies in geoinformation. CRC Press, Boca Ratón
Kaye L (2010) The directive on the legal protection of databases of March 11 1996: does it have a future? http://copyright-debate.co.uk/?p=154. Accessed 10 May 2019
Kingston W (2010) Beyond intellectual property: matching information protection to innovation. Edward Elgar Publishing, Cheltenham, p 112
Kroes Q (2010) E-business law of the European Union, 2nd edn. Kluwer Law International, Alphen aan den Rijn, pp 8–9
Kur A, Dreir T (2013) European intellectual property law: text, cases & materials. Edward Elgar Publishing, Cheltenham, p 267
Leistner M (2010) Der Rechtsschutz von Datenbanken im deutschen und europäischen Recht: Eine Untersuchung zur Richtlinie 96/9/EG und zu ihrer Umsetzung in das deutsche Urheberrechtsgesetz, vol 34 de Urheberrechtliche Abhandlungen des Max-Planck-Instituts für Ausländisches und Internationales Patent-, Urheber- und Wettbewerbsrecht. Beck C. H., Munich, p 15
Lesk A (2008) Introduction to bioinformatics, 3rd edn. Oxford University Press, Oxford, p 153
Loshin D (2013) Big data analytics: from strategic planning to enterprise integration with tools, techniques, NoSQL, and graph. Elsevier, Amsterdam
Lungarella M et al (2007) AI in the 21st century—with historical reflections. In: Lungarella M et al (eds) 50 years of artificial intelligence: essays dedicated to the 50th anniversary of artificial intelligence. Springer, Berlin, p 1
MacQueen H et al (2011) Contemporary intellectual property: law and policy. 2nd edn. Oxford University Press, Oxford, p 221
Maggs A (2012) Are you creating data? Then the database directive is (probably) not for you! Cookies on the Wragge & Co website http://www.wragge-law.com/insights/are-you-creating-data-then-the-database-directive/. Accessed 10 May 2019
Mandery M (2014) Party autonomy in contractual and non-contractual obligations: a European and anglo-common law perspective on the freedom of choice of law in the Rome I regulation on the law applicable to contractual obligations and the Rome II regulation on the law applicable to non-contractual obligations, comparative and international law studies (Book 189). Peter Lang GmbH., Frankfurt am Main, pp 1–310
Markel S, León D (2003) Sequence analysis in a nutshell: a guide to common tools and databases, 1st edn. O'Reilly Media, Sebastopol, p 26
Marx V (2013) Biology: the big challenges of big data. Nature 498:255–260
Mayer-Schoenberger B, Cukier K (2013) Big data: a revolution that will transform how we live, work and think. John Murray Publishers, London, pp 1–7, 12–18, 98–197
Muir H (2010) "Party autonomy" in international contracts: from the makings of a myth to the requirements of global governance. Eur Rev Contract Law (ERCL) 6(3):250–283
Oliva M, Corrales Compagnucci M (2011) Law meets biology: are our databases eligible for legal protection? SCRIPTed 8(3):226–228
Osborne C (2012) No spin-off: database rights subsist in live football data—the high court gives its judgment in the Football Dataco v Sportradar case http://www.osborneclarke.com/connected-insights/publications/no-spin-database-rights-subsist-live-football-data/. Accessed 10 May 2019
Papakonstantinou V (2010) Intellectual property rights: the security perspective. In: Jahankhani H et al (eds) Handbook of electronic security and digital forensics. World Scientific, New Jersey, p 494
Pellegrin T (2014) Economics of big data: a value perspective on state of the art and future trends. In: Akerkar R (ed) Big data computing. CRC Press, Boca Ratón, p 345
Pries K, Dunnigan R (2015) Big data analytics: a practical guide for managers. CRC Press, Boca Ratón

Radin M, Rothchild J, Silverman G (2004) Intellectual property and the internet. Foundation Press, New York, pp 318–319

Reed C, Angel J (2007) Computer law: the law and regulation of information technology, 6th edn. Oxford University Press, Oxford, p 423

Reichman J, Samuelson P (1997) Intellectual property rights in data. Vanderbilt Law Rev 50(51):164

Reinbothe J, Von Lewinski S (2007) The WIPO Treaties 1996: the WIPO copyright treaty and the WIPO performances and phonograms treaty—commentary and legal analysis. Tottel Publishing Ltd, West Sussex, pp 486–494

Rowland D, MacDonald E (2005) Information technology law, 3rd edn. Cavendish Publishing Ltd., London, p 92

Sell S (2003) Private power, public law: the globalization of intellectual property rights. Cambridge University Press, Cambridge, p 27

Sherman B, Bently L (1999) The making of modern intellectual property law. Cambridge University Press, Cambridge, pp 43 and 206

Spinello R, Bottis M (2009) A defense of intellectual property rights. Edward Elgar Publishing, Cheltenham, p 75

Stamatoudi I (2000) To what extent are multimedia products databases? In: Stamatoudi I, Torremans P (eds) Copyright in the new digital environment: the need to redesign copyright. Perspectives on intellectual property law, vol 8. Sweet & Maxwell Ltd., London, pp 23–24

Stimmel C (2015) Big data analytics strategies for the smart grid. CRC Press, Boca Ratón

Stokes S (2009) Digital copyright: law and practice. Hart Publishing, Oxford, p 62

Sundara Rajan M (2011) Moral Rights: principles, practice and new technology. Oxford University Press, Oxford, p 286

Waelde C, MacGinley M (2005) Public domain, public interest, public funding: focusing on the three Ps in scientific research. SCRIPTed—J Law Technol Soc 2(1):78

Waelde C et al (2013) Contemporary intellectual property: law and policy, 3rd edn. Oxford University Press, Oxford, p 47

Wang P, Goertzel B (eds) (2007) Advances in artificial general intelligence: concepts, architectures and algorithms. In: Proceedings of the AGI workshop 2006. IOS Press, Amsterdam, p 1

Wery E (2015) Legal protection of databases. http://www.ulys.net/up-load/file/Database.pdf. Accessed 10 May 2019

Williams A et al (2005) Biological databases: infrastructure, content and integration. In: Azuaje F, Dopazo J (eds) Data analysis and visualization in genomics and proteomics. Wiley, Chichester, pp 12–13

WIPO (2004) WIPO intellectual property handbook: policy, law and use, 2nd edn. WIPO publication no. 489 (E), pp 274, 441

Yamane H (2011) Interpreting TRIPS: globalization of intellectual property rights and access to medicines, introduction. Hart Publishing, Oxford, p 158

Chapter 3
Brokers, Clouds and Databases—*The Good, the Bad and the Ugly*

> "*You never visit them, you never see them. But they are out there. They are in a cloud somewhere. They are in the sky, and they are always around. That's roughly the metaphor*" [Eric Schmidt (The work of Eric Schmidt, see Lindberg and Svensson 2010, p. 13)].

3.1 Introduction

This chapter examines some of the technical issues that are useful for the discussion of this book. The chapter begins with the suggestion that over recent decades, information technology in the form of the Internet is at the apex of technological development and cloud computing is going to revolutionize the Internet world as it is known today. On the one hand, it argues that cloud computing has become a widespread tool that is constantly evolving into new ways of providing services, which are present in almost every transaction that we make in our daily lives.

On the other hand, it opens a window for the future of cloud computing, which is going to take on a "brokerage form." Studies reveal that the Internet will witness a large growth of cloud brokerage in all fields, especially among cloud ecosystems. Cloud brokers could aid in the provision of new services that enable flexibility, interoperability, scalability and highly secured technologies compatible with the cloud computing models popular today on the Internet.[1] This chapter proceeds as follows: Sect. 3.2 sets out the background and technical considerations for databases. It highlights the importance of today's database industry and the current situation in cloud environments. It also provides some examples of large databases that are publicly available in the cloud in order to place them in perspective and to prepare the reader for the subsequent sections. Section 3.3 outlines a brief forecast of cloud computing and brokerage scenarios on the cloud market. It also provides a set of cloud

[1] Mukherjee and Loganathan (2014, pp. 142–143).

M. Corrales Compagnucci, *Big Data, Databases and "Ownership" Rights in the Cloud*, Perspectives in Law, Business and Innovation,
https://doi.org/10.1007/978-981-15-0349-8_3

computing definitions and analyzes the main features, advantages, disadvantages and resources available in the cloud. It demonstrates the importance of databases and the crucial role they play in cloud computing transformations. In addition, this section also attempts to provide some concrete examples of cloud services that are commonly used on the Internet.

Section 3.4 provides a taxonomy of cloud deployment models and looks at the different types, such as private, public, and community clouds, and highlights the relevance of hybrid clouds as a new type of deployment model. Section 3.5 outlines the three typical cloud service models, also known as the "cloud stack," such as Software as a Service (SaaS), Platform as a Service (PaaS), and Infrastructure as a Service (IaaS). It also introduces a relatively new concept of providing cloud services, which is seldom discussed in the literature, called Software Infrastructure as a Service (SIaaS). This novel way of providing cloud services is a mixture of SaaS and IaaS and a good example of this is given in the OPTIMIS (Optimized Infrastructure Services)[2] project, which is the software toolkit used in this work.

Section 3.6 solidifies some of the abstract concepts previously explained and showcases a cloud brokerage scenario based on the assumption that hybrid clouds are becoming the new way of deploying services, insomuch as they will become the common place of provisioning cloud services in the near future. This brokerage scenario is illustrated in Fig. 3.1 and is referred to in the next chapters of this work in order to further explain specific legal issues involved, particularly when the contractual terms of the SLA are discussed. This chapter examines the cloud computing capabilities as well as the pros and cons of using cloud computing services and attempts to introduce not only primary cloud computing terminology but also seeks to stress the role of databases and the innovation intermediaries involved in the whole life cycle of cloud computing transactions.

3.2 Databases: Background and Technical Definition

Databases have existed for centuries. They were used to store data from scientific research, historical facts and to track ledger accounts. However, it was not until the 1970s when E. F. Codd introduced the idea of a relational database model that more structured database systems started to proliferate.[3] Nowadays, databases are crucial to businesses. They are used to keep records and to provide information to customers and clients on the Internet. They are also essential for many other kinds of activities

---

[2]The OPTIMIS consortium included different European cloud providers as well as other universities and research institutions such as Atos Origin (Spain), Umea University (Sweden), The 451 Group (UK), Universität Stuttgart (Germany), ICCS (Greece), Barcelona Supercomputing Center (Spain), SAP (UK), Fraunhofer-Gesellschaft (Germany), University of Leeds (UK), Leibniz Universtät Hannover (Germany), Flexiant (UK), BT Group (UK) and City University London (UK).

[3]Paragon Corporation, *Databases: Past, Present and Future*, [online]. Available at: http://www.paragoncorporation.com/ArticleDetail.aspx?ArticleID=20. [Accessed 1 December 2018].

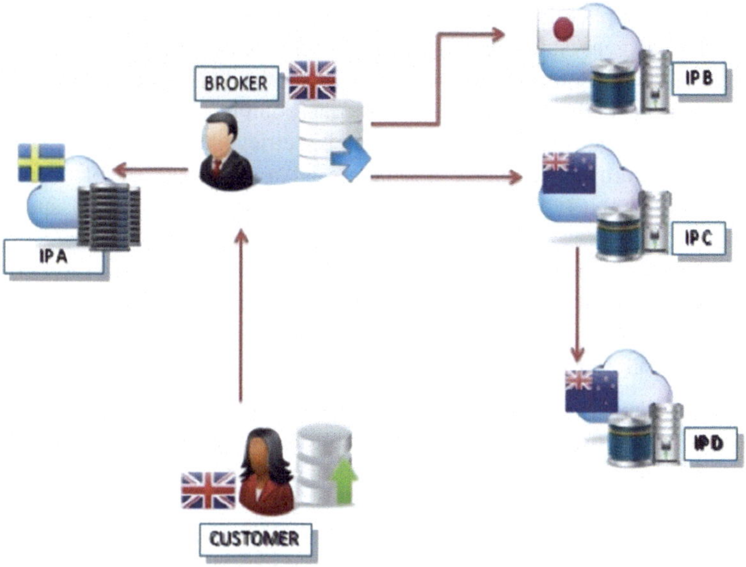

Fig. 3.1 Cloud Brokerage Scenario

and not only for commercial purposes, including genomic research, biochemistry, astronomy and many other types of scientific investigations.[4]

Defining databases is not an easy and straight forward process, particularly since technology is constantly evolving, thus the technical and legal concepts may vary from time to time. Therefore, in this section I intend to provide a set of definitions and to portray the landscape of the main characteristics that can help us to form a general concept of what a database is in the context of a computing environment. Simply stated, we could start by saying that a database is "a repository of data."[5] More precisely, a database is "a collection of data which is accessed by more than one person and/or which is used for more than one purpose."[6]

According to Frost, it is also regarded as a "set of resources" which includes the storing and maintenance of the different levels of security and privacy constraints of the database such as back-up capabilities in cases of software malfunction. In addition, a database must provide the input and output routines for the users.[7] For example, input of data simply refers to the data submitted by the customer, i.e.,

[4]Garcia-Molina et al. (2002, p. 1).

[5]Simovici and Tenney (1995, p. 1).

[6]Frost (1984, p. 3).

[7]Frost (1984, pp. 3–5). See also Papazoglou and Valder (1989, p. 2).

registration and application forms (input); whereas output of data is the result of analysis which is generated from data that was previously entered.[8]

Another technical definition which is relevant for the discussion of this work is the following: a "large body of information stored in a computer which can process it and from which particular bits of information can be retrieved as required."[9] According to the Oxford English Dictionary, a database is "a structured set of data held in computer storage and typically accessed or manipulated by means of specialized software."[10]

Databases have evolved over time and today they form one of the most complex types of computer software available and are referred to as "database management systems" or simply "database systems" in the computer science jargon. They provide users with the following capabilities[11]:

i. *Persistent Storage*: Similar to any other kind of file system, databases provide storage capabilities for large quantities of data which are independent of any processes that are using the data. Databases support not only storage but effective access to data[12];
ii. *Programming Interface*: This permits the user to access and handle data through an efficient and sophisticated query language. In contrast to a regular file system, a "database system" allows the handling of large amounts of data in complex ways[13];
iii. *Transaction Management*: This is the capability of a database to support "concurrent access to data." That is, "simultaneous access" by different kind of processes called "transactions." This capability manages the transaction in a way that avoids failures and errors when multiple transactions are executed at once.[14]

3.2.1 A Few Examples of Databases in the Cloud

Some concrete examples of databases which can be accessed in the cloud are LEXIS-NEXIS, BRS, DIALOG and WESTLAW.[15] These databases contain relevant information for legal practitioners, judges, academics and law students such as case law material, legislation, journals, articles and books. These databases are very costly

[8]Simovici and Tenney (1995, p. 2).

[9]Lloyd (2004, p. 509).

[10]Oxford English Dictionary [online]. Available at: http://www.oed.com/view/Entry/47411 [Accessed 1 December 2018].

[11]Garcia-Molina et al. (2002, p. 1).

[12]Garcia-Molina et al. (2002, p. 1).

[13]Garcia-Molina et al. (2002, p. 1).

[14]Garcia-Molina et al. (2002, p. 1).

[15]Tenopir and Soon Ro (1990, p. 1).

and the fact that they are online and/or in electronic format, makes them a potential candidate for copyright infringement.[16]

Other examples of large and complex databases, which are operated simultaneously on the Internet, are airline reservations and bank account databases.[17] Similarly, scientific databases are also good examples that best illustrate the complexities and difficulties on a large scale, both in terms of technical and legal issues. Biological databases, for instance, are increasingly transitioning from private to hybrid cloud models. Some examples of public cloud models of biological databases are the so-called "primary databases," which are those databases containing Deoxyribonucleic Acid (DNA) and Ribonucleic Acid (RNA) generic information.[18] The three largest primary databases are Genbank (USA), DNA Data Bank of Japan (DDBJ) and the European Molecular Biology Laboratory (EMBL), which is located in Germany.[19]

Another category of scientific databases belongs to the group called taxonomic databases, which contain information related to the classification of organisms. Within this group, the most relevant is the (NCBI) taxonomy database.[20] The third category belongs to the group of bibliographical databases, such as ProMED, which contain information coming from different sources such as books, journals, reports and patents.[21] Finally, there are the so-called gene databases which contain only genetic material such as DNA in contrast to biological databases which may also contain different datasets besides DNA. The definition of this last category is very broad and there are also different names used as synonyms to refer to them, such as biobanks, DNA banks and population databases.[22] These are just a few concrete examples of databases that are accessible in the cloud. Most of these belong to the category of public clouds as they can be accessed by everyone with an Internet connection. Some of them are free of charge and others need the payment of an individual or institutional fee. However, these public clouds can also be used in combination with a private cloud model, such as in the cloud brokerage scenario as depicted in the sections below.

3.3 Cloud Computing and Brokerage Scenarios

3.3.1 Literature Review and Background Considerations

One of the most profound challenges and concerns about doing research involving new technologies is to provide a body of literature which includes current knowledge.

[16]Bently and Sherman (2009, p. 310).

[17]Ullman (1988, p. 5).

[18]Valle et al. (2003, p. 13).

[19]Hansen (2004, p. 9).

[20]Williams et al. (2005, p. 17).

[21]Williams et al. (2005, p. 17).

[22]Tutton and Corrigan (2004, p. 2).

It is also imperative to provide the context which predicts how long into the future these technologies will last. This forecast is very difficult because one significant disruptive change in technology can shift the market towards a completely new direction. However, there are many indicators in the scientific field as well as in the cloud market that suggest an increase in cloud computing and that this new way of providing services will remain in the cloud market as a business model for several years. In this section, I decided to begin with a brief meta-analysis using statistical data to provide an estimated overview of the cloud computing market landscape. I also discuss the increasing role of intermediaries that will constitute a substantial portion of cloud purchases to leverage expertise and more complex services.[23]

The Information Handling Services (IHS) firm's analysis showed that business expenditures related to cloud technologies will triple from $78.2B spent in 2011 to $235.1B by 2017[24] and, according to a prediction from CISCO, by 2020 one-third of all data will be stored in or transferred through the cloud.[25] With regard to cloud models, the current states of the art indicate a transition from private clouds to hybrid cloud ecosystems (the combination of both private and public cloud services).[26]

According to a study carried out by the firm KPMG, cloud computing "is one of the most disruptive forces in business in 20 years."[27] This is in line with the predictions of the leading scientist Michio Kaku who said: "computers as we now know them will disappear; they will be everywhere and nowhere, ubiquitous yet hidden, just like electricity and running water. The cloud will follow us silently and seamlessly, carrying out our wishes anytime, anywhere."[28] It has been perceived as a new paradigm and essential need for the society that will one day be the 5th utility service after water, electricity, gas and telephony.[29] This means that the idea of the cloud is not going to disappear but rather will get stronger. What will most probably disappear are computers as they will progressively shrink to the point of reaching the size of a microchip and cost a penny.[30]

As far as the cloud brokerage market is concerned, the research firm Marketsand-Markets estimates that the cloud brokerage enablers, which are software platforms that enable such services, will grow from $225.42 million in 2013 to $2.03 billion by 2018. The general market will grow from $1.57 billion in 2013 to $10.5 billion by 2018.[31] This corresponds to a 55.3% growth per year.[32]

I have not yet found any research study that contradicts the view that the cloud computing market is thriving and that it will remain in the market for several years.

[23] See Carrol (2014).
[24] Columbus (2014).
[25] Bort (2011).
[26] Jansen (2014).
[27] Garthwaite (2014).
[28] Kaku (2013).
[29] Buyya (2009, pp. 599–616).
[30] Buyya (2009, pp. 599–616).
[31] Panettieri (2013).
[32] Linthicum (2015).

On the contrary, those authors who claim that cloud computing will disappear do not mean this in a pejorative form. They mean this in a way that cloud service offerings are just the first step towards this vast digital transformation era that will become so common in the future that all companies will embrace it. The Internet world as we know it today is transforming into "everything-as-a-service" and cloud services are the "basic ingredient" for this change to happen.[33] The sections below are a follow-up of the origins and evolution of this new paradigm. They define how this is related to the research question and limits the question to databases and its related rights, which is the main problem I have identified that needs further research.

3.3.2 The Cloud Metaphor

The term cloud computing was first coined by Eric Schmidt from Google while mentioning Software as a Service (SaaS) in 2006.[34] As a familiar cliché, it is just a metaphor for the Internet[35] which became a "hyped-up" term[36] and one of the hottest buzzwords of the moment.[37] Despite this marketing hype campaign, cloud computing is not just touted as a panacea as it provides useful resources on-demand such as servers, storage, and networking for many of the typical scaling points that a web application needs.[38]

The term cloud computing has been reproduced in various ways.[39] Every leading IT consultancy company, such as the Gartner Group, McKinsey & Co. and Forrester, including cloud service providers such as Amazon, Google and Salesforce.com, have all provided their own contribution to this concept. For example, according to a white paper published by McKinsey & Co. in the year 2009, there were already 23 definitions, including McKinsey & Co.'s.[40]

The US National Institute of Standards and Technology (NIST) provides one of the best definitions[41] as it embraces important aspects of cloud computing. The definition is meant to serve as a comparative model of the different cloud services and deployment strategies.[42]

---

[33] Soumelidis (2014).

[34] Others think that the term "cloud of computers" was first published in the New York Times in an article about Microsoft's Hailstorm. See Kingfisher (2011).

[35] Knorr and Gruman (2008).

[36] Butler (2012), Rosenberg and Mateos (2011, p. 1).

[37] Carey (2007), Rosenberg and Mateos (2011, p. 1).

[38] GoGrid, *Scaling Your Internet Business*, [online]. Available at: http://www.gogrid.com/cloud-hosting/re-sources/scaling-with-cloud-computing.php [Accessed 1 November 2013].

[39] Mosco (2014, p. 6).

[40] Lindberg and Svensson (2010, pp. 12–13).

[41] Popescu (2009).

[42] Mell and Grance (2011, p. 1).

> Cloud computing is a model for enabling convenient, on-demand network access to a shared pool of configurable computing resources (i.e., networks, servers, storage, applications, and services) that can be rapidly provisioned and released with minimal management effort or service provider interaction.[43]

A paper published at the Computer Communication Review analyses 20 different definitions. This has shed some light on the plethora of cloud computing concepts and summarized all these ideas in the following definition[44]:

> Clouds are a large pool of easily usable and accessible virtualized resources (such as hardware, development platforms and/or services). These resources can be dynamically reconfigured to adjust to a variable load (scale), allowing also for an optimum resource utilization. This pool of resources is typically exploited by a pay-per-use model in which guarantees are offered by the Infrastructure Provider by means of customized SLAs.[45]

The above definition is very useful for the purposes of this book because it also introduces the notion of a "customized SLA" offered by the infrastructure provider, which is explored in greater detail in the last part of this book.[46]

Cloud computing includes a wide scope of technologies and services and comes in different forms. A comprehensive description of the main elements of cloud computing can be found in the Report from the UC Berkeley Reliable Adaptive Distributed Systems Laboratory[47]:

> Cloud computing refers to both the applications delivered as services over the Internet and the hardware and systems software in the datacenters that provide those services. The services themselves have long been referred to as Software as a Service (SaaS). The datacenter hardware and software is what we will call a cloud. When a cloud is made available in a pay-as-you-go manner to the general public, we call it a Public Cloud; the service being sold is Utility Computing. We use the term Private Cloud to refer to internal datacenters of a business or other organization, not made available to the general public. Thus, cloud computing is the sum of SaaS and Utility Computing, but does not include Private Clouds. People can be users or providers of SaaS, or users or providers of Utility Computing.[48]

Other short and succinct definitions that might help to understand this term more easily are as follows: "cloud computing is a style of computing where computing resources are easy to obtain and access, simple to use, cheap, and just work."[49] Pew Internet, a US think tank, defines cloud computing as "an emerging architecture by which data and applications reside in cyberspace, allowing users to access them through any web-connected device"[50] and according to Nicholas Bessmer, "cloud computing is the commoditized and centralized delivery of reliable, scalable, and easy to use computing."[51]

---

[43]Mell and Grance (2011, p. 2).

[44]Smith (2009).

[45]Vaquero et al. (2008, p. 2).

[46]See, in particular, Chap. 8, Part III.

[47]Reed (2010, pp. 2–3).

[48]Ambrust et al. (2009, p. 1).

[49]Marks and Lozano (2010, p. 28).

[50]Horrigan (2008).

[51]Bessmer (2013).

In this book, cloud computing is described in simple terms as a large network of data servers where end-users can submit their files remotely using only an Internet connection in order to process, store and transfer data and databases across multiple jurisdictions. Thus, they can benefit from different kinds of services and varying resources that are continually and rapidly evolving into different business models, which can save time and costs.

In reality, cloud computing had been around for several years before the concept came into existence. Most computer systems that we are familiar with are "single-device systems"; for example, your personal computer, smartphone, tablet, and "Kindle" electronic book are all single-device systems. As these devices are limited in processing and storage capabilities, cloud computing connects a bundle of single-device systems and enables them to all work together.[52]

The following are the best examples of cloud services: social networking sites such as Facebook or LinkedIn; webmail services such as Hotmail, Yahoo or Gmail; blogging or micro-blogging services such as Twitter; video sharing websites such as Youtube; business sites like e-Bay; picture sharing services such as Flickr[53] and Instagram[54]; and even ranking and rating sites such as Tripadvisor.[55] Other cloud computing services are IBM Cloud Computing, Cisco Cloud Computing, Microsoft Azure, Rackspace and Amazon Web Services (AWS).[56]

Another classical example is in the web server scope; for instance, let's imagine an SME that sells products online, like smartphone products or books. If a company hosts its website on a single server, the website could get crowded and overrun at some point in the year such as Christmas or Valentine's Day, which are periods of the year when customers buy more products. If this situation occurred, the company's website might not be able to sufficiently process and store its customer's information. However, if the company hosted its website "in the cloud," multiple servers are interconnected so that the processing, memory and storage capabilities are enhanced and shared. This cluster or network of computers, which are "in the cloud," can handle more data during peak load times than a single server.[57]

3.3.3 Advantages of Cloud Computing: Main Capabilities

Cloud computing has many benefits. From a service provider viewpoint, it reduces costs and "optimizes" the usage of different resources. From an end-user perspective,

---

[52]Griffith (2012).

[53]Pew Internet, *The Future of Cloud Computing*, p. 2, [online]. Available at: http://pewinternet.org/~/me-dia/Files/Reports/2010/PIP_Future_of_the_Internet_cloud_computing.pdf [Accessed 1 November 2013].

[54]Instagram, [online] Available at: http://instagram.com/# [Accessed 1 November 2013].

[55]Tripadvisor, [online] Available at: http://www.tripadvisor.de/ [Accessed 1 November 2013].

[56]Pistorious (2012).

[57]Griffith (2012).

cloud computing prevents the investment of substantial amounts of capital in terms of hardware, software, and other services.[58] If we consider the SME's website example given above, it may be noticed that resources can be scaled up or down depending on the processing or storage needs. This means that with cloud computing, online activities are much faster and easier to spread.[59] This also means cost savings for the company by only paying high costs during such peak load times, instead of having to pay for all the equipment and extra servers to cover such potential demand if this were to happen during such a busy time of the year.[60] Therefore, instead of buying extra powerful servers, they can be rented at a lower cost. As databases are moved to the cloud and distributed across different servers, cloud computing also enables a high degree of redundancy which offers user's backup capabilities. This means that if one server is down for any reason such as a shortage of power supply, there is usually enough data replicated on another server which avoids the problem of data loss.[61] Other typical capabilities also considered as beneficial characteristics are[62]:

3.3.3.1 Scalability

Dynamic Scalability—a synonym for "elasticity"[63]—refers to the constant fluctuation in the workload that is typical in the context of web-based applications which may occur at diverse frequencies such as daily, weekly, monthly, or even over longer periods of time.[64] Cloud computing is essentially scalable because users only use what they need. The best way to exemplify this in an everyday life situation is when we use electricity, as we only switch the lights on when it is necessary. Likewise, the user can utilize cloud computing resources from the cloud only when they are needed. This means that users no longer need to invest in buying expensive equipment but can simply rent the different cloud resources[65] (for example Central Processing Unit (CPU), Random Access Memory (RAM), hard drives, etc.)[66] available and pay for the amount of time used.

Amazon was one of the first companies to use dynamically scalable cloud resources; they started to sell cloud computing processing capabilities per hour via a service called "Elastic Compute Cloud" (EC2).[67] This is a web-based service which permits users to run applications in the Amazon Cloud Computing environment by

[58] Lindberg and Svensson (2010, p. 15).

[59] Schmidt and Cohen (2013, pp. 67–68).

[60] Schmidt and Rosenberg (2014, p. 25).

[61] Griffith (2012).

[62] Lindberg and Svensson (2010, p. 15).

[63] Rosenberg and Mateos (2011, p. 5).

[64] Agrawal et al. (2011, pp. 2–15).

[65] Barnatt (2010, p. 11).

[66] Ghosh (2012).

[67] Barnatt (2010, p. 11).

registering and creating an Amazon Machine Image (AMI) which contains the operating system, application programs and configuration settings. Once this is done, the AMI is uploaded to the Amazon Simple Storage Service called AmazonS3 and then the subscriber can use as much of the virtual machine (VM) as needed, from just a few to more than 1000 VM.[68] In this respect, scalability also refers to the database systems. Scaling a database uses a technique called "federating the database" which is also a synonym of scaling the database "out." It is important to understand that when someone increases the capacity of a server by adding more servers to the system, they are creating a database federation.[69]

3.3.3.2 Pay-As-You-Go

Cloud computing uses a different billing system in comparison to the traditional IT billing model which includes buying the hardware and software, installing the software system, testing and verifying the configuration and executing the application. In the classical computing model, the customers have to buy and own the entire system which needs to be renewed every 18 months, turning out to be very costly.[70] Typically, there is an annual contract and an initial startup fee. However, the cloud computing model breaks this economic limitation.[71] It offers a "pay-as-you-go" system where the hardware and software are leased from the cloud provider reducing the costs significantly to almost 95%.[72] In other words, the initial investment in a cloud offer is much lower than traditional IT services.[73]

The cloud computing billing practices are also referred to as "pay-per-use" and they include per gigabyte (GB) billing per user, or simply "per-use." This means that a company gets "on-demand" computational services[74] and is charged only on each usage of the cloud service.[75] The pay-per-use system is, in principle, the same for all cloud service models with some slight variations as follows: (i) Software as a Service (SaaS): the costs will depend on the number of users using the software application; (ii) Platform as a Service (PaaS): the cost will be calculated proportionally to the usage and size of the application being developed; and (iii) Infrastructure as a Service (IaaS): the cost will be charged based on the number of servers and storage usage.[76]

---

[68]Amazon Elastic Compute Cloud (Amazon EC2) [online]. Available at: http://searchcloudcomputing.techtar-get.com/definition/Amazon-Elastic-Compute-Cloud [Accessed 1 November 2013].

[69]Sukenari and Tamura (2012, pp. 33–37), Cherry (2008), Oracle White Paper (2011, p. 4).

[70]Hwang et al. (2012, pp. 196–197).

[71]Rosenberg and Mateos (2011, p. 6).

[72]Hwang et al. (2012, pp. 196–197).

[73]Metheny (2013, p. 23).

[74]Siddessh and Srinivasa (2014, p. 114).

[75]Wang (2010, pp. 1–2).

[76]Williams (2010, p. 26).

However, some cloud computing services are free of charge or take a lump-sum instead of recurring payments.[77]

In cloud computing, sometimes the billing system can turn out to be very complicated due to the different policies and types of payment methods available for different customers for the same kind of services. For this reason, the broker in the hybrid cloud scenarios depicted below in Sect. 3.5 may also provide billing services and offer more flexible and customized payment terms for each client.[78]

3.3.3.3 On Demand

"On demand" means that the cloud users can automatically and unilaterally "provision computing capabilities", such as network storage, anytime it is needed without any means of human interaction.[79] This means that end-users can log onto a website and have virtually unlimited access and supply to cloud services (i.e., computer power and storage) as needed,[80] at any time without the necessity to talk to a sales or technical staff member.[81]

3.3.3.4 Measured Service

This capability denotes the possibility of measuring the type of service, i.e., storage, processing, and bandwidth, to provide automatic means of control systems through a metering mechanism. This provides the possibility for a tailor-made business and payment model depending on the type of service.[82]

3.3.3.5 Ubiquity

This cloud computing capability is also usually referred to as "pervasive computing." These two words, "pervasive" and "ubiquitous" simply mean "existing everywhere." In other words, cloud computing devices are always available and they can not only be accessed remotely, but they can also be accessed by many users simultaneously.[83]

---

[77]Columbus (2013).

[78]Mukherjee and Loganathan (2014, p. 130).

[79]Srivastava and Kumar (2011, p. 150).

[80]Vivek (2015, p. 7).

[81]Williams (2010, p. 9), Metheny (2013).

[82]Lindberg and Svensson (2010, p. 16).

[83]De Filippi (2013, pp. 1–18), Tang (2010), Krcmar et al. (2014, pp. 18–19) (eds).

3.3.3.6 Maintenance and Security

On top of the capabilities mentioned above, "maintenance" and "security" services can also be added. As far as maintenance of the services is concerned, this is probably one of the most undisputed benefits of the cloud. Since the applications do not need to be installed on the customer's single device system (computer, laptop, mobile phones, etc.), this allows the cloud service provider to fix any software related problems (such as "bugs") and to provide any upgrades to all users instantly and simultaneously. The issue of security, however, is more controversial than maintenance. In theory, cloud service providers will have more computing resources and expertise to take the appropriate technical and security measures[84] to prevent the loss, destruction, alteration, access and disclosure of data.[85]

The drawback of this argument is related to the customer's fear to submit, for example, their valuable or even sensitive data to a place outside their control. This comes back to the issues of fear, risks and trust mentioned in the introduction of this work. According to Linderberg and Svensson, only time will tell whether cloud providers will be able to convince their clients that their data will not be in jeopardy due to the "off-site cloud storage." In their view, "new security standards and certification procedures" will most likely be able to attain an "objective" security standard.[86]

3.3.4 Disadvantages of Cloud Computing: Some Related Technical and Legal Issues

Paradoxically, some of the capabilities that are seen as beneficial in the technical sense might be seen as a disadvantage or even a "risk" in the legal sense. For instance, data replication for backup purposes might be seen as one of the main benefits of cloud computing as this prevents data loss in cases of accident. Even from a legal standpoint, this might be taken as beneficial if we were to consider data protection and data security issues. However, this also represents a hurdle if we have to consider data location and jurisdictional issues, assuming the customer is not fully aware of where the data has been replicated.

Another technical capability of the cloud, which might have a negative impact if some legal matters are not thoroughly considered, is called multi-tenancy. This feature refers to the ability to store and process data in a shared environment. This means that customers, consumers, and organizations (i.e., tenants) share the same infrastructure and *databases* in order to benefit from the multiple advantages of cloud computing, such as lower prices and better performance. The major concern in this "multi-tenant" environment is to ensure proper security mechanisms and make sure

---

[84] Lindberg and Svensson (2010, p. 16).

[85] Barnitzke et al. (2012).

[86] Lindberg and Svensson (2010, p. 16).

these tenants do not risk losing data while sharing different kinds of Internet resources including the "ownership" rights of their own data.[87] A more effective solution is the so-called "fine-grained multi-tenancy," where customers share the same resources but the data and access capabilities are "segregated," usually within the same application database. Examples include online word processing and spreadsheet tools, customer relationship management services such as Salesforce CRM, and other kinds of web services (i.e., Google Docs, etc.).[88]

From a technical point of view, in the case of SaaS, multi-tenancy is accomplished most of the time via a database configuration. In this case, the "isolation" is done at the application layer whereas in the case of IaaS this is provided via server virtualization and configuration.[89] This means that SaaS tenants share a database whereas IaaS tenants share resources. The best examples of SaaS multi-tenancy are Salesforce.com[90] or SmugMug[91] where customers use a pay per use application that enables them to upload unlimited numbers of photos and manage complex tasks. The data itself is stored in shared common databases as rows in tables. For security reasons, each customer or "tenant" has a unique ID which distinguishes one row from the other. Nevertheless, the risk is very high that an error in the configuration or the access control list may result in the loss or disclosure of data.[92] This book does not focus on data security issues; however, the risk of losing data due to sharing the same database is closely related to the problem of losing the "ownership" rights of data and databases if this is not fully and duly specified in the SLA, as we will discuss in future chapters.

As hinted above, the cloud is used in one way or another in most of life's daily activities. From my point of view, cloud computing offers more advantages than disadvantages. Cloud computing services are all over the Internet and it is not the issue of whether we should use cloud services or not anymore, but how to reduce the risks involved. This is especially when the major drawbacks and disadvantages of using the cloud are related to legal issues.

3.4 Cloud Deployment Models

There are different cloud computing models depending on the way they are deployed in the cloud and the way the service is delivered. The public cloud model is where a cloud service provider makes resources such as storage available to the general public and everyone with Internet access can sign up to these services.[93] The private

[87] Juniper Networks Inc. (2012, p. 3), White Paper.

[88] Pearson and Yee (2013, p. 6) (eds).

[89] Pearson and Yee (2013, pp. 3–5) (eds).

[90] Salesforce.com [online] Available at: www.salesforce.com [Accessed 1 December 2013].

[91] Smugmug.com [online] Available at: www.smugmug.com [Accessed 1 November 2013].

[92] Juniper Networks Inc. (2012, p. 4), White Paper.

[93] Kalpit (2013).

cloud (also known as internal cloud or corporate cloud) is a marketing term used by the media when an organization prefers to use a proprietary computing architecture that meets their particular needs. This model provides more control over the data in comparison to a third-party hosted service.[94]

In contrast to the public cloud, the private cloud is more expensive but also allows for better tailor-made customization services and more security mechanisms.[95] A community cloud is simply a cloud infrastructure that is shared by several institutions with common goals and activities within the same community.[96] Finally, the hybrid model is a combination of the first two previous clouds, public and private, and is specifically designed for organizations that need a more customized solution. Below are short descriptions and some examples of each model.

3.4.1 Public Cloud

By definition, a public cloud is one of the various types of deployment models characterized by the management and availability of computational resources that are external to the consumer's organization.[97] One of the main benefits of public clouds is the reduction of costs. This is because the applications and bandwidth are already covered by the cloud provider and are, therefore, very recommendable to SMEs that do not have the resources to invest in IT infrastructure.[98]

In this model, corporate boundaries are often delineated using firewalls. With the advent of cloud computing, these perimeters have become more and more borderless and now cloud computing resources are shared with other companies outside the firewall area in a public cloud.[99] In other words, a public cloud is a cloud infrastructure that is available to the general public over the Internet[100] (or to a select group of the public)[101] which is owned by a cloud service provider.[102] Some examples of the public model are Amazon Elastic Compute Cloud (EC2), IBM's Blue Cloud, Sound Cloud and Windows Azure.[103]

---

[94]Singh and Hemalatha (2012, p. 99).

[95]Weinschenk (2011).

[96]Black (2012, p. 211).

[97]Jansen and Grance (2011, p. 3).

[98]Kalpit (2013).

[99]Ballantine (2012).

[100]Black (2012, p. 213).

[101]Pistorious (2012).

[102]Black (2012, p. 213).

[103]Kalpit (2013). Windows Azure is a cloud system developed by Microsoft that allows applications to run from remote servers. It is hosted by Microsoft datacenter and its architecture includes storage services in the cloud. See Li (2009), introduction.

3.4.2 Private Cloud

Private clouds are the precursors of public clouds as they were first created by those organizations that are now offering public cloud services, such as Google and Amazon. Both companies developed a private cloud first that was intended for other lines of business such as Internet search engines and bookselling.[104] A private cloud is located within the company or institution environment, and its access is usually restricted to staff members. They are better suited for medium-sized and large companies.[105] For example, if the workload of the payroll department of a big company increases during certain times, i.e., at the end of the year due to the Christmas bonuses, it would need enough computing power to cope with the maximum workload. In this case, computing power is spread all over the company and the payroll department receives extra power when they need it. This model also allows the enterprise to save costs.[106] One example of this model is the Amazon Virtual Private Cloud (VPC).[107]

In general, cloud computing offers a favorable environment to deliver and provision database services. For instance, in a private cloud model, IT departments consolidate their servers, storage capabilities, and database workloads onto a common software and hardware infrastructure. Databases that are deployed on a private cloud model are less expensive and provide a more elastic, scalable, and metered quality of service.[108] From a technical point of view, public clouds and private clouds are essentially the same. The difference, however, lies in who is in control of the cloud and who the end-users are.[109]

3.4.3 Community Cloud

With regards to the target set of customers, a community cloud falls in between the public and private cloud categories[110] as it is shared by several institutions or by a "community of users."[111] It may be managed by one organization or all of them, or

---

[104]Rosenberg and Mateos (2011, p. 16).

[105]Santos (2012).

[106]Amrhein et al. (2009, p. 25).

[107]Amazon Virtual Private Cloud (VPC) allows you to create a virtual network topology with subnets and routing systems. If you are familiar and using Amazon Elastic Compute Cloud (EC2) resources you are aware that each instance you launch makes random selections of public IP addresses in the Amazon EC2 address space whereas Amazon VPC allows you to establish an "isolated portion of the Amazon Web Services (AWS) cloud—a VPC—and launch Amazon EC2 instances that have private (RFC 1918) addresses in the range of your choice".

[108]Oracle White Paper (2011, p. 5).

[109]Smoot and Tan (2012, p. 39).

[110]Jansen and Grance (2011, p. 3).

[111]Metheny (2013, p. 33).

by a third party on or off-premises.[112] For example, all government organizations within one country may share their cloud infrastructures in order to process data from their citizens and provide new services to them.[113] It is also usually provisioned by a group of people or organizations sharing the same concerns such as security, policy, or compliance considerations.[114]

3.4.4 *Hybrid Cloud*

The hybrid model is more complex as it involves a blend of private, community and/or public clouds.[115] For example, a company, hospital or university[116] can store their day to day data (and especially their sensitive data) in their private cloud, and use a public cloud for backup purposes.[117] A hybrid cloud can be made up of two or more clouds including private, community or public that "remain unique entities" but are connected through different technologies.[118]

According to Garg and Buyya, a hybrid cloud is "the deployment which emerged due to a diffusion of both public and private cloud advantages"[119] where companies can keep their critical data inside their private clouds. This enables them to have more control over their data and at certain peak load times they can simply use an external or public cloud.[120] It is expected that this model will grow considerably in the coming years and that the hybrid cloud storage architecture within this model will play an important role as new technology. Taking into account that data growth is such a "pervasive" problem, it is essential to find a way to overcome the problems of managing data and improve storage capabilities by fusing on-premises storage with cloud storage services.[121]

---

[112]Black (2012, p. 211).

[113]The Cloud Turorial.com, *Types of Clouds* [online]. Available at: http://thecloudtutorial.com/cloudtypes.html [Accessed 1 November 2018].

[114]Mell and Grance (2011, p. 3).

[115]Jansen and Grance (2011, p. 3).

[116]For a better understanding of the impact of cloud computing in higher education and on the IT organization of universities see Krcmar et al. (2014) (eds).

[117]Kalpit (2013).

[118]Black (2012, p. 212).

[119]Garg and Buyya.

[120]Garg and Buyya.

[121]Farley (2013), Williams (2010, p. 17).

3.5 Cloud Service Models

The concept of cloud computing is not "monolithic"[122] but emanates from the interaction of three concepts: Software as a Service (SaaS), Platform as a Service (PaaS), and Infrastructure as a Service (IaaS).[123] These three services together are often referred to as the "cloud computing stack."[124]

3.5.1 Software as a Service (SaaS)

Instead of installing and maintaining a software application in your own computer, SaaS provides the possibility of accessing the software via the Internet. It is also known as "web-based software," "on-demand software," or "hosted software" because the service provider is in charge of managing the application including access and security measures.[125] Instead of buying and downloading the computer software, users can rent it on a "pay-per-use" basis.[126] While the concept is not new, changes in technology have improved the way of delivering software services, making this model a less expensive and more practical solution for business entrepreneurs.[127]

In the same way one can rent a car or taxi in a day to day situation, SaaS can be used as "pay-as-you-go." Very good examples of this model are Google Apps, Salesforce.com, Microsoft Online Services[128] and WebEx.[129] In this respect, the myth between buying versus renting must be clarified. It is often mentioned to highlight the benefits of "buying" and downloading the software onto your device in comparison to renting a software on-demand and running it in the cloud. This is, however, a misleading comparison because there is no actual "purchase" of the software but a license to use (rent) the application.[130]

SaaS is a growing and extensive market, and services range from simple web-based email applications to more complex customer tailor-made management systems. A typical "SaaS-contract" would concentrate on the functional service descriptions, service level remedies, and interoperability issues.[131] SaaS spans a wide variety of services. For example, Framework as a Service (FaaS) is an extension of SaaS that

---

[122] McKendrick (2012).

[123] Stephenson (2012).

[124] The Chartered Institute for IT (2012).

[125] Salesfore.com, *What is SaaS?* [online]. Available at: http://www.salesforce.com/saas/ [Accessed 1 November 2018].

[126] Arockaim et al. (2012, p. 321).

[127] Waters (2005, pp. 32–36).

[128] Singh et al. (2012, p. 104).

[129] WebEx is a web-based service which enables users to attend, connect, schedule and share meetings in the cloud [online]. Available at: http://www.webex.com/ [Accessed 1 November 2013].

[130] Waters (2005, pp. 36–37).

[131] Lindberg and Svensson (2010, p. 14).

enhances the capabilities of the SaaS offering. It works as an adjunct for tailor-made applications that allow organizations to have specialized and customized features.[132]

3.5.2 *Platform as a Service (PaaS)*

Platform as a service is both hardware and software, and considered to be "a computing platform provided on a network that you can use."[133] PaaS allows any software developer to plan, build, design, create, test, and deploy their own application using an application programming interface (API) that is deployed to users and configured remotely online.[134] This service provides the possibility for developers from all over the world to work together on the same project while ensuring compatibility in any changes to the operating systems and reducing costs at the same time.[135]

PaaS also eases the deployment of cloud applications without the necessity of "buying" the different layers of hardware and software.[136] Examples of this model include Second Life, IS Tools, NING, Wolf Framework, 10Gen,[137] Google Application Engine (Google App),[138] Microsoft Windows Azure, Bunge Labs, Work Press, Force.com (which is part of Salesforce.com), Crunch Base and Orange Scape.[139]

3.5.3 *Infrastructure as a Service (IaaS)*

Infrastructure as a service provides the customer with the potential to provide different kinds of services such as processing, storage, networks and other primary resources including operating systems and different applications.[140] A good definition of IaaS may be given as follows: "a model in which an organization outsources the equipment used to support operations, including storage, hardware, servers, and networking components. The service provider owns the equipment and is responsible for housing, running, and maintaining it." This means that the whole service, including using the hardware as well as the platform for executing it, is carried out in the cloud, including items such as storage capabilities.[141] A very good example of this model

[132] Rosenberg and Mateos (2011, p. 16).

[133] Pistorious (2012).

[134] Menken (2010, pp. 13–14), Pearson and Yee (2013, p. 6) (eds).

[135] Kalpit (2013).

[136] Lindberg and Svensson (2010, p. 15).

[137] Menken (2010, pp. 63–77).

[138] Shroff (2010, p. 56), Rosenberg and Mateos (2011, p. 42).

[139] Creeger (2009), Pearson and Yee (2013, p. 6) (eds).

[140] Smoot and Tan (2012, p. 41), Lindberg and Svensson (2010, p. 15).

[141] Galorath (2012).

is Amazon EC2 and S3, which provides a computational and storage infrastructure in a "centralized and location transparent service."[142]

3.5.4 Software Infrastructure as a Service (SIaaS)

There is a new trend of cloud computing called Software Infrastructure as a Service (SIaaS) which is when a cloud provider offers both SaaS and IaaS simultaneously.[143] SIaaS denotes the software component of a cloud infrastructure, which is located in between the physical infrastructure and the cloud platform. More precisely, SIaaS provides "specific application support capabilities" and includes cloud management, application development, and integration services. The "cloud stack" is not a static model and is evolving into a rather more dynamic way of providing new services. Most cloud innovations are moving towards SlaaS as it offers the necessary capabilities which are essential for a cloud to work properly.[144]

3.6 Cloud Service Brokerage

The combination of the cloud computing stack and the different deployment services (private, public, hybrid and community clouds) give rise to several multi-cloud dynamic scenarios. The easiest of these scenarios was born out of the necessity of an end-user who owns a private cloud, either an individual, a private company, a university or a hospital, who needs to rent a public cloud during certain peak load times or for any other reason including security, costs and eco-efficiency. This typical scenario is called "cloud bursting", which is when you move computer workloads into an on-demand service to access additional capacity. Cloud bursting is an "application deployment model." This application is executed in a private cloud or server and "burst" into an infrastructure provider (public cloud) when needed. This scenario best depicts one of the main advantages of cloud computing where an organization only pays for extra computing capabilities when they are needed.[145]

If we add more infrastructure providers to the cloud bursting scenario, we have what is known as "federation scenario." In this scenario, several infrastructure providers (i.e., IPA, IPB, IPC and IPD) have an agreement in which any infrastructure provider (IP) can use each other's capacity, such as storage capabilities. The cooperation among all the IPs is carried out according to an internal agreement. However, only one of these cloud providers (either service provider or infrastructure provider) negotiates with the customer and seals the deal with the client. Therefore,

[142]Creeger (2009), Pearson and Yee (2013, p. 6) (eds).

[143]Zsigri et al. (2010, p. 1).

[144]Zsigri et al. (2010, p. 1).

[145]Rouse (2011).

this provider is the only one responsible even in the case of subcontracting with other IPs from the federation. The "principal" or "main" cloud provider can, however, set a series of legal restrictions, such as concerning trans-border transactions, with the other infrastructure providers to prevent virtual machines (VMs) migration across different jurisdictions. These restrictions should be placed within the SLA negotiations,[146] as will be explained in detail in the last part of this book.[147]

Now, if we add an intermediary to these two scenarios, we have the so-called cloud brokerage scenario depicted below in Fig. 3.1. This scenario, as well as the others, belongs to the category of hybrid clouds where the broker acts as an innovation intermediary between customers and infrastructure providers (IPA, IPB, IPC and IPD) that most suit the customer's needs. When a customer wants to use a cloud provider (either service provider or infrastructure provider), they usually compare the quality requirements with the SLAs of different cloud providers. For this purpose, the customer provides the broker with the necessary information so the latter can alleviate this task by helping the customer to select the cloud provider that best matches his expectations. The dictionary definition of a broker is "one that acts as an agent for others, as in negotiating contracts, purchases, or sales in return for a fee or commission; a person who acts as an intermediary in…negotiating agreements, etc."[148]

As cloud computing "as-a-service" offering proliferates[149] and more and more suppliers are added on to the service supply chain, the need for consumption support also increases.[150]

As in any business situation, the figure of a broker rises in order to mitigate the communication gap between the two and bring the different parties together. Gartner defines them broadly as "a type of cloud service provider that plays an intermediary role in cloud computing."[151] More specifically, a cloud brokerage scenario can be defined as "a business model in which a company or other entity adds value to one or more (generally public or hybrid, but also possibly private) cloud services on behalf of one or more consumers of those services."[152]

In other words, the broker fills the gap between the service consumer and cloud service provider[153] acting on the customer's behalf to carefully examine and analyze the provider's different offerings. Generally speaking, the broker helps to shop around and find which cloud provider better suits the customer company's needs.[154] The

---

146 Ferrer (2012, p. 71).

147 See, more specifically, Chaps. 8 and 9, Part III.

148 The Free Dictionary by Farlex, *Broker*, [online]. Available at: http://www.thefreedictionary.com/broker [Accessed 10 April 2016].

149 Lheureaux and Plummer (2011).

150 Mendham (2011).

151 Mendham (2011).

152 Plummer et al. (2010).

153 Plummer and Kenney (2009).

154 Mendham (2011).

brokers act as a support, communication and distribution channel, aided by finding the best criteria for their customers within the cloud computing market.[155]

Furthermore, Brian Prentice suggests that there are three kinds of cloud brokerage models, depending on the level of active involvement of the broker between the parties. In the first model, there is a "compositing" process, which means taking parts of different services and putting them together as a package. The second model also involves a compositing process but with an intellectual property added value. It could be considered a new and separate proprietary service as it provides its own way of delivering cloud services. The third model is the service as "property" or "platform provider" and is the one recommended by some consultancy companies, such as Gartner. This model operates in the same way a "retailer's floor space is rented out to other suppliers."[156] For example, the operator of a supermarket charges a fee for allocating the goods in a high traffic area in the supermarket with more visibility for the clients. The main question here is how independent the broker is and the legal relationship between with particular "floor space renters."[157]

One example of this is the proposal defined by the Global Inter-Cloud Technology Forum (GICTF). The Intercloud vision of the forum established a use-case scenario with the broker acting as a middle-man between the cloud customer and multiple cloud providers to support the former in choosing the appropriate provider that better fits with his requirements. Besides the "mediator" role of the broker, this entity, with the right tools, can add value services during the deployment and operation phases.[158] As Frank Kenney puts it, "the future of cloud computing will be permeated with the notion of brokers negotiating relationships between providers of cloud services and the service customers."[159]

3.7 Summary and Interim Remarks

This chapter focused on the fact that a considerable amount of life's activities involves the use of a cloud computing service in one way or another. At the outset, it examined the important role databases play in the various types of cloud service and deployment models. It surveyed different definitions and also analyzed the different cloud services and deployment models. Broadly speaking, it could be summarized that the two fundamental components of typical cloud architectures are the "back end" and the "front end" of services. The former is the "cloud itself" (servers, computers and data storage equipment). The latter is, for example, a web browser (the part which is

155 Korzeniowski (2014).

156 Korzeniowski (2014).

157 Korzeniowski (2014).

158 Global Inter-Cloud Technology Forum (2010, p. 17).

159 Gartner Inc. (2009).

perceived by the customer/end-user) , consisting of the network, applications, and interfaces which enable access to cloud computing services.[160]

Cloud computing is a fast-growing and evolving model that proffers dynamic and flexible solutions. There is a tendency to improve cloud services and it is associated with the inclusion of more stakeholders in the supply chain. In the midst of these various cloud services, the significant role of the intermediaries gives rise to a new hybrid way of providing services: cloud brokerage services. Besides the customers, the main parties in a typical cloud brokerage service are the brokers and the infrastructure providers. The brokers are directly accessed by the customers and interact with the customers and infrastructure providers as they offer economically efficient and added value services. Infrastructure providers offer computing, storage, and network resources required for hosting services. Their goal is to maximize their profits from tenants by making efficient use of their infrastructures, possibly by outsourcing partial workloads to partnering providers. The key element during service deployment, from a legal point of view, is the negotiation of the contractual terms in the SLA between the customers and infrastructure providers through the broker intervention.

References

Agrawal D et al (2011) Database scalability, elasticity and autonomy in the cloud. In: Yu J, Ho Kim M, Unland R (eds) Proceedings of the 16th international conference on database systems for advanced applications, DASFAA'11, vol. Part I. Springer, Berlin, pp 2–15

Amazon Elastic Compute Cloud (Amazon EC2). http://searchcloudcomputing.techtarget.com/definition/Amazon-Elastic-Compute-Cloud. Accessed 10 May 2019

Ambrust et al (2009) Above the clouds: a berkeley view of cloud computing, p 1. Technical Report No. UCB/EECS-2009-28 https://www2.eecs.berkeley.edu/Pubs/TechRpts/2009/EECS-2009-28.pdf. Accessed 10 May 2019

Amrhein D et al (2009) Cloud computing use cases: a white paper produced by the cloud computing use case discussion group. Version 2.0, p 25 http://opencloudmanifesto.org/Cloud_Computing_Use_Cases_Whitepaper-2_0.pdf. Accessed 10 May 2019

Arockaim L, Parthasarathi G, Monikandan S (2012) Privacy in cloud computing: a survey, p 321. http://airccj.org/CSCP/vol2/csit2331.pdf. Accessed 10 May 2019

Ballantine R (2012) Cloud computing: security compliance and governance, loc. 189, Kindle Edition

Barnatt C (2010) A brief guide to cloud computing: an essential guide to the next computing revolution, Kindle Edition, p 11

Barnitzke B, Corrales Compagnucci M, Forgó N (2012) Aspectos Legales de la Computación en la Nube: Seguridad de Datos y Derechos de Propiedad sobre los mismos, locs. 637 et seq., Kindle Edition. Editorial Albremática S.A., Buenos Aires

Bently L, Sherman B (2009) Intellectual property law, 3rd edn. Oxford University Press, Oxford, p 310

Bessmer N (2013) Cloud computing for small business, loc. 24, Kindle Edition

Black N (2012) Cloud computing for lawyers. American Bar Association, Chicago, p 211

Bort J (2011) 10 technologies that will change the world in the next 10 years. NetworkWorld. http://www.networkworld.com/article/2179278/lan-wan/10-technologies-that-will-change-the-world-in-the-next-10-years.html. Accessed 10 May 2019

[160] Lindberg and Svensson (2010, p. 16).

Butler B (2012) Cloud computing's most over-hyped terms. http://www.computerworlduk.com/indepth/cloud-computing/3376086/cloud-computings-most-over-hyped-terms/?intcmp=most_pop;cldcmptng;6. Accessed 10 May 2019

Buyya R et al (2009) Cloud computing and emerging IT platforms: vision, hype, and reality for delivering computing as the 5th utility. Futur Gener Comput Syst 25(6):599–616

Carey J (2007) Cloud terminology in a nutshell. http://www.lighterra.com/articles/cloudterms/. Accessed 10 May 2019

Carrol C (2014) What's a cloud services broker, and why do you need one? http://www.cio.com/article/2462417/cloud-computing/cloud-computing-whats-a-cloud-services-broker-and-why-do-you-need-one.html. Accessed 10 May 2019

Cherry D (2008) Scaling the database out, not up. IT Knowledge Exchange. http://itknowledgeexchange.techtarget.com/sql-server/scaling-the-database-out-not-up/. Accessed 10 May 2019

Columbus L (2013) Top 12 sites for free cloud computing & enterprise software research. Forbes. http://www.forbes.com/sites/louiscolumbus/2013/08/25/top-12-sites-for-free-cloud-computing-enterprise-software-research/. Accessed 10 May 2019

Columbus L (2014) Roundup of cloud computing forecasts and market estimates. Forbes. http://www.forbes.com/sites/louiscolumbus/2014/03/14/roundup-of-cloud-computing-forecasts-and-market-estimates-2014/. Accessed 10 May 2019

Creeger M (2009) Cloud computing: an overview. A summary of important cloud computing issues distilled from ACM CTO roundtables. ACM QUEUE. http://queue.acm.org/detail.cfm?id=1554608. Accessed 10 May 2019

De Filippi P (2013) Ubiquitous computing in the cloud: user empowerment -vs- user obsequity, pp 1 and 18. http://hal.archives-ouvertes.fr/docs/00/85/57/12/PDF/18_-_2013_Ubiquitous_Computing_-Cloud-ubiquity.pdf. Accessed 10 May 2019

Farley M (2013) Rethinking enterprise storage: a hybrid cloud model, Kindle Edition. Microsoft Press, locs 175, 228 and 1849

Ferrer A et al (2012) OPTIMIS: a holistic approach to cloud service provisioning. Futur Gener Comput Syst 28(1):71

Frost R (1984) Database management systems: practical aspects of their use. McGraw-Hill Book Company, New York, p 3

Galorath D (2012) Another look at the "As a Service" offerings. http://www.galorath.com/wp/another-look-at-the-as-a-service-offerings.php. Accessed 10 May 2019

Garcia-Molina H, Ullman J, Widom J (2002) Database systems: the complete book. Prentice Hall, New Jersey, p 1

Garg S, Buyya R Green cloud computing and environmental sustainability, p 8. http://www.cloudbus.org/papers/Cloud-EnvSustainability2011.pdf. Accessed 10 May 2019

Garthwaite E (2014) It's official: cloud is the most disruptive force for 20 years. ItProPortal. http://www.itproportal.com/2014/05/12/cloud-most-disruptive-force-for-20-years/. Accessed 10 May 2019

Gartner Inc. (2009) Gartner says cloud consumers need brokerages to unlock the potential of cloud services. Press Release. http://www.gartner.com/newsroom/id/1064712. Accessed 10 May 2019

Ghosh A (2012) Scalability in cloud computing. http://thecustomizewin-dows.com/2012/08/scalability-in-cloud-computing. Accessed 10 May 2019

Global Inter-Cloud Technology Forum (2010) Use cases and functional requirements for inter-cloud computing, p 17. http://www.gictf.jp/doc/GICTF_Whitepaper_20100809.pdf. Accessed 10 May 2019

Griffith R (2012) A short introduction to cloud computing: everything you need to know in around 1000 words, locs. 21 and 29, Kindle Edition

Hansen A (2004) Bioinformatik: Ein Leitfaden für Naturwissenschaftler, p 9. Birkhäuser, Berlin

Horrigan J (2008) Use of cloud computing applications and services. Pew Internet and American Life Project. http://www.pewinternet.org/~/media/Files/Reports/2008/PIP_Cloud.Memo.pdf.pdf. Accessed 10 May 2019

Hwang K, Fox G, Dongarra J (2012) Distributed and cloud computing: from parallel processing to the internet of things. Elsevier, Waltham, pp 196–197

Jansen J (2014) Top 10 predictions on the future of the cloud in 2014. http://www.businesstoday.org/articles/2014/01/top-10-predictions-on-the-future-of-the-cloud-in-2014/. Accessed 10 May 2019

Jansen W, Grance T (2011) Guidelines on security and privacy in public cloud computing, p 3. National Institute of Standards and Technology (NIST), Computer Security Division, Special Publication 800-144

Juniper Networks Inc. (2012) Securing multi-tenancy and cloud computing: security that ensures tenants do not pose a risk to one another in terms of data loss, misuse or privacy violation, White Paper, p 3. http://www.juniper.net/us/en/local/pdf/whitepapers/2000381-en.pdf. Accessed 10 May 2019

Kaku M (2013) A scientist predicts the future. International Herald Tribune. http://www.nytimes.com/2013/11/28/opinion/kaku-a-scientist-predicts-the-future.html?pagewanted=all. Accessed 10 May 2019

Kalpit J (2013) Learn cloud computing: simple'n easy. WAGmob, locs 246, 253, 258, 264 and 270, Kindle Edition

Kingfisher E (2011) Cloud computing explained: 92 practical tips for understanding the cloud's applications, software, strategies and services, loc 3, Kindle Edition

Knorr E, Gruman G (2008) What cloud computing really means? http://www.infoworld.com/d/cloud-computing/what-cloud-computing-really-means-031. Accessed 10 May 2019

Korzeniowski P (2014) Cloud brokerage market potential grows, but long-term future questionable. http://searchcloudcomputing.techtarget.com/tip/Cloud-brokerage-market-potential-grows-but-long-term-future-questionable. Accessed 10 May 2019

Krcmar H, Reussner R, Rumpe B (eds) (2014) Trusted cloud computing. Springer, Cham, pp 18–19

Lheureaux B, Plummer D (2011) Cloud service brokerage proliferates. http://www.gartner.com/DisplayDocument?doc_cd=226656&ref=g_noreg. Accessed 10 May 2019

Li H (2009) Introducing windows azure: learn windows azure to create next-generation, cloud-based applications. Springer, New York

Lindberg A, Svensson D (2010) IT law from a practitioner's perspective. In: Wahlgren P (ed) ICT legal issues: scandinavian studies in law, vol 56. Stockholm Institute for Scandinavian Law, Stockholm, p 13

Linthicum D (2015) Make sense of cloud service brokers. InfoWorld. http://www.infoworld.com/article/2903436/cloud-computing/make-sense-of-cloud-service-brokers.html. Accessed 10 May 2019

Lloyd I (2004) Information technology law, 4th edn. Oxford University Press, Oxford, p 509

Marks E, Lozano B (2010) Executive's guide to cloud computing. Wiley, Hoboken, p 28

McKendrick J (2012) SaaS, PaaS and IaaS: three cloud models; three very different risks. http://www.zdnet.com/blog/service-oriented/saas-paas-and-iaas-three-cloud-models-three-very-different-risks/8815. Accessed 10 May 2019

Mell P, Grance T (2011) The NIST definition of cloud computing. National Institute of Standards and Technology (NIST), US Department of Commerce, p 1. http://csrc.nist.gov/publications/nistpubs/800-145/SP800-145.pdf. Accessed 10 May 2019

Mendham T (2011) The role of a cloud broker: will cloud brokers find legitimacy in enterprise computing? http://www.cio.com.au/article/399699/role_cloud_broker/. Accessed 10 May 2019

Menken I (2010) Cloud computing certification kit specialist: platform management & storage management, 2nd edn. Emereo Pty Ltd., s.l, pp 13–14

Metheny M (2013) Federal cloud computing: the definitive guide for cloud service providers. Elsevier, Waltham, p 23

Mosco V (2014) To the cloud: big data in a turbulent world. Paradigm Publishers, Boulder, p 6

Mukherjee S, Loganathan S (2014) Role of broker in inter-cloud environment. In: Mahmood Z (ed) Continued rise of the cloud: advances in trends in cloud computing. Springer, London, pp 142–143

Oracle (2002) Database architecture: federated vs. clustered. An Oracle White Paper, p 4. http://www.oracle.com/technetwork/database/windows/clustercomp-134873.pdf. Accessed 10 May 2019
Oracle White Paper (2011) Database consolidation onto private clouds, p 5. http://www.oracle.com/us/products/database/database-private-cloud-wp-360048.pdf. Accessed 10 May 2019
Panettieri J (2013) Cloud services brokerage company list and FAQ. TalkinCloud. http://talkincloud.com/cloud-services-broker/cloud-services-brokerage-company-list-and-faq. Accessed 10 May 2019
Papazoglou M, Valder W (1989) Relational database management: a systems programming approach. Prentice Hall, Hertfordshire, p 2
Paragon Corporation (2003) Databases: past, present and future. http://www.paragoncorporation.com/ArticleDetail.aspx?ArticleID=20. Accessed 1 Dec 2013
Pearson S, Yee G (eds) (2013) Privacy and security for cloud computing. Springer, London, p 6
Pew Internet, The future of cloud computing, p 2. http://pewinternet.org/~/media/Files/Reports/2010/PIP_Future_of_the_Internet_cloud_computing.pdf. Accessed 10 May 2019
Pistorious M (2012) The quick guide to cloud computing and cyber security, loc. 109, Kindle Edition
Plummer D, Kenney F (2009) Three types of cloud brokerages will enhance cloud services. http://www.gartner.com/DisplayDocument?docCode=164265&ref=g_fromdoc. Accessed 10 May 2019
Plummer D, Lheureux B, Karamouzis F (2010) Defining cloud service brokerages: taking intermediation to the next level. Gartner. https://www.gartner.com/doc/1448121/defining-cloud-services-brokerage-taking. Accessed 10 May 2019
Popescu A (2009) The best cloud computing definition. http://jots.mypopescu.com/post/213246006/cloud-computing-definition. Accessed 10 May 2019
Reed C (2010) Information ownership in the cloud. CCLS Legal Aspects of Cloud Computing Research Project, pp 2–3. http://papers.ssrn.com/sol3/papers.cfm?abstract_id=1562461. Accessed 10 May 2019
Rosenberg J, Mateos A (2011) The cloud at your service: the when, how, and why of enterprise cloud computing. Manning Publications Co., Greenwich, p 1
Rouse M (2011) "Cloud Bursting" in essential guide: guiding the enterprise into a hybrid model. http://searchcloudcomputing.techtarget.com/definition/cloud-bursting. Accessed 10 May 2019
Santos S (2012) Advantages and options for private cloud computing. http://www.ibm.com/developerworks/rational/library/private-cloud-advantages-options/. Accessed 10 May 2019
Schmidt E, Cohen J (2013) The new digital age: reshaping the future of people, nations and business. Alfred A. Knopf, New York, pp 67–68
Schmidt E, Rosenberg J (2014) How google works. Grand Central Publishing, New York, p 25
Shroff G (2010) Enterprise cloud computing: technology, architecture, applications. Cambridge University Press, Cambridge, p 56
Siddessh G, Srinivasa K (2014) Realization of open cloud computing standards, forums and platforms. In: Mahmood Z (ed) Continued rise of the cloud. Advances and trends in cloud computing. Springer, London, p 114
Simovici D, Tenney R (1995) Relational database systems. Academic Press, Inc., San Diego, p 1
Singh A, Hemalatha M (2012) Cloud computing for academic environment. Int J Inf Commun Technol (ICT J) 2(2):99
Singh A, Vasanthi V, Hemalatha M (2012) A brief survey on architecture, challenges & security benefit in cloud computing. Int J Inf Commun Technol (ICT J) 2(2):104
Smith J (2009) Harnessing the power of cloud computing for M2M. http://www.numerex.com/files/wp/m2mCloudComputing.pdf. Accessed 10 May 2019
Smoot S, Tan N (2012) Private cloud computing: consolidation, virtualization, and service-oriented infrastructure. Elsevier, Waltham, p 39
Soumelidis D (2014) Cloud computing will disappear. http://www.nagarro.com/us/en/blog/post/27/Cloud-Computing-will-disappear. Accessed 10 May 2019

Srivastava K, Kumar A (2011) New approach of CLOUD: computing infrastructure on demand. TRIM 7:150. http://www.inflibnet.ac.in/ojs/index.php/TRIM/article/view-File/1249/1130. Accessed 10 May 2019

Stephenson D (2012) What is SaaS? Understanding the concepts of cloud computing. http://www.firmex.com/blog/what-is-saas-concepts-cloud-computing/. Accessed 10 May 2019

Sukenari T, Tamura M (2012) "InfoFrame Relational Store": a new scale-out database for big data, big data processing platforms. Nec Tech J 7(2):33–37

Tang B (2010) Definition: pervasive computing (ubiquitous computing). http://searchnetworking.techtarget.com/definition/pervasive-computing. Accessed 10 May 2019

Tenopir C, Soon Ro J (1990) Full text databases. Greenwood Press, Connecticut, p 1

The Chartered Institute for IT (2012) Cloud computing: moving it out of the office. loc. 46, Kindle Edition

Tutton R, Corrigan O (2004) Genetic databases: socio-ethical issues in the collection and use of DNA, Introduction. Routledge, Oxon, p 2

Ullman J (1988) Principles of database and knowledge base system, vol 1. Computer Science Press, Maryland, p 5

Valle G et al (2003) Introduzione alla Bioinformatica. Zanichelli, s.l, p 13

Vaquero L et al (2008) A break in the clouds: towards a cloud definition, p 2. http://dl.acm.org/citation.cfm?id=1496100. Accessed 10 May 2019

Vivek K (2015) Guide to cloud computing for business and technology managers: from distributed computing to cloudware applications. CRC Press (Taylor & Francis Group), Boca Ratón, p 7

Wang H (2010) Distributed systems meet economics: pricing in the cloud, pp 1–2. http://research.microsoft.com/pubs/158913/WangH.pdf. Accessed 10 May 2019

Waters B (2005) Software as a service: a look at the customer benefits. J Digit Asset Manag 1:32–36

Weinschenk C (2011) The public cloud, the private cloud and unified communications. http://www.itbusinessedge.com/cm/community/features/articles/blog/the-public-cloud-the-private-cloud-and-unified-communications/?cs=47587. Accessed 10 May 2019

Williams M (2010) A quick start guide to cloud computing: moving your business into the cloud. Kogan Page Limited, London, p 26

Williams A, Kersey P, Pruess M (2005) Biological databases: infrastructure, content and integration. In: Azuaje F, Dopazo J (eds) Data analysis and visualization in genomics and proteomics. Wiley, Chichester, p 17

Zsigri C et al (2010) Cloud ecosystem: taxonomy and value networks. OPTIMIS D7.1.1. http://www.optimisproject.eu/sites/default/files/OPTIMIS_D7.1.1%20Cloud%20ecosystem%20%20taxonomy%20and%20value%20networks_exec%20summary.pdf. Accessed 10 May 2019

Chapter 4
Law and Economics—Five Core Principles in the Cloud

"*We are all law and economics now*" [Lawrence Lessig (The work of Lawrence Lessig. See Oppenheimer and Mercuro 2004, p. 3)].

4.1 Introduction

By its very nature, the study of cloud computing transformations is an interdisciplinary endeavor, drawing on complex technical and legal issues that include a variety of other social disciplines. Consequently, structuring a coherent theoretical framework requires careful scrutiny that goes beyond the capacity of any single discipline. Therefore, in order to gain a holistic understanding of these complex issues and to resolve adequately some of these problems, this chapter focuses on the contributions and synergies across the disciplines of law and economics. To proceed, Sect. 4.2 opens with a narrative of the general foundations of law and economics. It discusses the different schools of thought featuring the main tenets of the economic analysis of law. The considerations against this backdrop and its contextualization in the cloud provide a good reference point to support the theoretical framework of this work. More specifically, this chapter discusses the hypothesis that individuals are rational agents, its assumption on market dependence and its focus on efficiency as the social goal of the law-making process. As a follow-up, this chapter introduces in Sect. 4.3, a quintet of straightforward arguments that should be taken into account in the elaboration of a contractual framework for cloud computing transactions. Finally, Sect. 4.4 concludes with the idea that we need to derive from these five core insights. Yet, this is not sufficient. Therefore, there is an increasing need to consider a revamp of the current legal system and facilitate a well-coordinated framework.

M. Corrales Compagnucci, *Big Data, Databases and "Ownership" Rights in the Cloud*, Perspectives in Law, Business and Innovation,
https://doi.org/10.1007/978-981-15-0349-8_4

4.2 Literature Review and Background Considerations: *The Three Schools of Thought*

The rudiments of what it is known today as the economic analysis of law, can be traced back to the "mercantilism" era during the 18th century, with Adam Smith's study *An Inquiry into the Nature and Causes of the Wealth of Nations*[1] (abbreviated as "The Wealth of Nations"). In this work, Adam Smith analyzed the mercantilist legislation and delineated its various economic implications. He argued in favor of free trade, exalting the individual's capabilities of regulating and bargaining their own prices and services. Notwithstanding his revolutionary thinking, his experience reflected the "pre-industrial" and "small-scale technology" of the era and did not anticipate the rise of "multi-national interests" and "large-scale" technological advances[2] that we encounter today on the Internet.

Law and economics is conceptually a form of utilitarianism.[3] The idea that individuals are, on average, fully rational and that they make choices that maximize their individual utility[4] found its clearer expression in the works of John Austin, John Stuart Mill and Jeremy Bentham. The latter was the progenitor of this movement and in his book, *Introduction to the Principles of Morals and Legislation* (1780), he criticizes the law for being too difficult to understand and argues for a utilitarian approach to morality and law. He reduces the law to its basic elements: pain and pleasure.[5] This principle of utility remained prevalent in the mainstream of economics for quite a long time and it was grounded in the belief that anything that produces or promotes pain and pleasure is the guide to answer the question of what is right or wrong.[6]

It must also be underscored from the outset that the basic ideas of economics are rooted in two main premises: scarcity and rationality. Scarcity means that there are limited resources available and that choices must be made while considering the desires of individuals.[7] Rationality means that when presented with a choice in the face of scarcity, individuals will act in a way so as to achieve the best combination and allocation of resources.[8] In other words, the assumption of rationality means no

[1]Smith (1776).

[2]Sutherland (1993) (ed).

[3]Some commentators believe that this categorization is partly misleading. According to Nicolas Georgakopoulos: "The deployment of the methods used by economic analysis of law does not depend on acceptance of a utilitarian moral philosophy…is not a methodological slave to any form of utilitarianism." Some jurists think that they can combine moral philosophical arguments with the economic analysis of law. From this perspective, law and economics is "agnostic." See Georgakopoulos (2005, p. 3).

[4]Burrows and Veljanovski (1981, p. 3) (eds).

[5]Bentham (1781).

[6]Sandel (2010, p. 23), Driver (2010).

[7]Malloy (1990, pp. 14–15), Duggan (1982, pp. 4–6).

[8]Malloy (1990, pp. 14–15).

more that individuals act with a conscious *intention* to accomplish their self-interests and goals.[9]

It was not until the beginning of the 1960s, however, when Ronald Coase and Guido Calabresi independently published two seminal and stylistically innovative works: *The Problem of Social Cost*[10] where Coase analyzed the best allocation of resources in relation to the rules of liability and *Some Thoughts on Risk Distribution and the Law of Torts*[11] where Calabresi observed the same phenomena.[12] Coase's theory holds that where the results of a bargaining process are reduced to zero, property rights will be rendered to those who value them the highest. On the other hand, the distinctive contribution of Calabresi was to rationalize a whole body of law by taking into account simple economic principles and to further develop a solid theory for its reform.[13] These two articles can be seen as the cornerstone for building the modern school of law and economics.[14]

Law and economics is a well-established area of research and is known today as a powerful legal tool, which is the dominant approach to law in the U.S. and has become unquestionably influential in governments and public bodies of other countries.[15] Like all schools of thought, law and economics does not represent a consistent movement. Unpacking all the different strands of the law and economics spectrum reveals the complexity and slightly different modes of variation. It will not be possible to discuss all these theories in depth and breadth. Therefore, I shall refer to a representative selection of them that will adjust for the unevenness of the cloud and Big Data market and enhance the framework I present in this book. As a starting point and in order to make this explanation less complicated, Parisi divides law and economics into three separate branches, which is the classification that I follow in this chapter. These three strands of thoughts are: (I) positive law and economics, (II) normative law and economics, and (III) functional school of law and economics.[16]

4.2.1 Positive Law and Economics (Chicago-Style)

The Chicago style explains the reasons why the law is the way it is.[17] Richard Posner is one the most notable forerunners of the Chicago school.[18] His treatise on the

[9]Veljanovski (1990, p. 34).

[10]Coase (1960, pp. 1–44).

[11]Calabresi (1961, pp. 499–553).

[12]Posner (1983, p. 4).

[13]Veljanovski (1990, pp. 21–22).

[14]Posner (1983, p. 4).

[15]Elkin-Koren and Salzberger (2013), Stray Ryssdal (1995), preface, Veljanovski (1982), Riis and Nielsen (1998) (eds), introduction.

[16]Parisi (2004, pp. 259–272).

[17]Medema (2015, pp. 70–74).

[18]Malloy (1990, p. 2).

economic analysis of law relies partly on Calabresi's insights on risk allocation and Coase's theory about the importance of transaction costs. Posner attempts to explain various aspects of the economic analysis to almost every field of law and his work stands as a keystone of modern economic scholarship.[19]

Some other harbinger exponents of the Chicago school of economics are Aaron Director, Frank Knight, Milton Friedman, George Stigler, Gary Becker, Armen Alchian and Harold Demsetz. Director transmitted the persuasive argument that "regulation was the proper function of markets, not government,"[20] which was, back then, a novel and important message. Knight's theoretical contribution did not lie in strict mathematical formulas and quantitative analysis but he imparted the idea of the development of economic thinking to pull apart from what he believed to be false premises that were becoming popular among economic theorists.[21] Friedman and Stigler's strength relied on evidence drawn from their empirical research arguing for less government intervention and market policies relying more on the voluntary exchange of private companies. In their conclusions, they affirmed that this would facilitate the progress of markets and assist in a more efficient allocation of resources.[22] The arguments adduced by Becker grasped the idea that "economics is the science of choice" across a wide breadth of human activities including race discrimination in labor markets,[23] crime and punishment,[24] marriage, and family law.[25]

Finally, it is worthy to note the contribution of Alchian and Demsetz on the economics of property rights. They seized the idea that legal-institutional provisions or *plans* that constrain the behavior of individuals and firms might have a significant impact on the scarce allocation of resources. Their main postulates are based on two parts. First, the more clarified property rights are, the more uncertainty is reduced, which leads to a better allocation of resources. Second, the appearance and development of new property rights can be understood as a "value-seeking behavior" caused by the application of techniques or technologies to the production of new goods and services as well as the development of new market opportunities.[26]

The general observation that I can make about the Chicago-style is that these developments can serve as a way to create economic stimulus. Cloud computing companies are viewed as profit maximizers. They take into account that all the activities surrounding the services they provide, such as the price they charge and their

[19]See, generally, Posner (1998).

[20]Mercuro and Medema (1997, pp. 51–54).

[21]Reder (1982, p. 6), Medema (2010, pp. 46–48).

[22]Mercuro and Medema (1997, p. 55).

[23]See, generally, Becker (1971).

[24]See, generally, Becker (1968, pp. 169–217), Benson and Zimmerman (2010).

[25]Becker (1978).

[26]The works of Alchian and Demsetz. See Mercuro and Medema (1997, pp. 51–57).

contracting practices, lead to the maximization of resources.[27] The same could be said about cloud computing end-users. They also need to make the most rational choice based on the price and the kind of services they need. A related inference can be drawn from the empirical discoveries that argued for less government intervention and market policies.

It is fair to say that regulations such as the Database Directive are not designed to be carved in stone; however, making further amendments to tackle these issues would be unwieldy because of the significant technological developments constantly taking place in the cloud market. It follows from the discussion that the best way to assist a more efficient cloud market should be brought in by the private sector. Clarifying "ownership" rights in data and databases can also be understood as "value-seeking behavior" through the development of new techniques and market opportunities.

4.2.2 Normative Law and Economics (Yale-Style)

The Yale-style uses economics to identify the best criteria for the most efficient and realistic policy, rule, measure, procedure, *schema or model.*[28] While the positive school of economics is more objective and based on real facts, the normative school of economics is subjective and based on values. The former ought to be approved or rejected, whereas the latter is based on opinions, and therefore does not need to be tested.[29] This is precisely the aim of this research through the use of the Extensible Markup Language (XML) Description Model for clarifying "ownership" rights of data and databases, which is essentially a schema where customers are under more control when using cloud services.

The information provided in this framework should be used in order to automate the negotiation process between the broker and the cloud infrastructure providers in cloud brokerage scenarios. The main purpose of providing such an XML-based definition is to bridge the gap between customers and cloud providers in order to grant customers the capacity to choose a cloud provider accordingly. With this approach, it is possible to "pre-filter" cloud providers that do not meet the legal requirements based on end-user input. I shall return to the details of this framework in Chap. 8 of this book.

[27] Here I take the shared properties of a firm as analogical inference and from this basis I infer that cloud service providers also share further property. See, generally, Mercuro and Medema (1997, p. 57).

[28] Schmalbeck (1983, p. 491), Miceli (1997), introduction. Some critics to the normative economic analysis claim that it lacks the moral and ethical values such as personal integrity that are overturned by the cost and benefits analysis. See, i.e., generally, Zerbe (2001, p. 8).

[29] Caplin and Schotter (2010).

4.2.3 *Functional School of Law and Economics (Virginia-Style)*

The Virginia-style offers a third alternative stressing individual choice and "market-like" mechanisms in the elaboration of laws.[30] Law and economics adopts a rather pragmatic approach and criticizes the traditional legal view that focuses on the concept of "fairness," as in corrective justice. While the traditional model focuses on the past and tries to correct and fix the situation retrospectively, the economics perspective suggests evaluating things prospectively because the past is over and proposes to address the problem in a way that makes things less likely to occur in the future.[31]

According to the economics view, individuals are "rational maximizers."[32] That is, they make *intentional* choices so as to pursue reliable and uniform ends using efficient means. Assuming that individuals are able to process and understand correctly all the information presented and available to them, including the alternative choices, they can classify all possible outcomes according to their desires and will choose the best option of goods or activities that maximize utility.[33]

The Virginia-style serves not only as a good reference to grasp the links between individual choices and the adoption of mechanisms to bolster the efficiency of the market. The idea I would like to propose is to search for a flexible and perhaps more realistic solution in light of the *behavioral* economic approach and choice architectures that take into account the cognitive traits of human agency. I shall also return to the topic of choice architectures in Chap. 5.

4.3 Combining the Three Schools of Thought: *Five Core Principles*

In sum, the economic analysis of law conveys a powerful view to the glitches and hitches than can arise in the law and in the process of decision-making to reach the best outcome. While these developments are built upon each other, and each theory is leading logically to the next, they are tinged with different nuances and overtones. An account of the main components of the law and economic theories are offered in

[30]Parisi (2004, pp. 259–272), Backhaus (2005) (ed), introduction.

[31]Miceli (2004, pp. 2–3).

[32]Parisi (2004, pp. 262–263). According to Posner and Parisi: "Law and economics rely on the standard economic assumption that individuals are rational maximizers, and study the role of law as a means for changing the relative prices attached to alternative individual actions. Under this approach, a change in the rule of law will affect human behavior by altering the relative price structure—and thus the constraint—of the optimization problem. Wealth maximization, serving as the paradigm for the analysis of law, can thus be promoted or constrained by legal rules." The work of Richard Posner and Francesco Parisi. See Sandeen (2010, p. 47). See, also, generally, Posner and Parisi (2003) (eds).

[33]Mercuro and Medema (1997, p. 57).

the forthcoming sections but it is important to note that it is very difficult to choose one specific school of thought and perhaps doing so would limit the scope of this analysis. Yet, the theoretical challenge is how to blend different school of thoughts and add some additional contributions to make the parallel developments that mirror and underpin the relations between all the stakeholders in cloud computing and Big Data transformations.

Below I introduce five core principles that should be taken into account while developing a more flexible and effective contractual framework in the cloud. These principles are specifically related to the clarification of database rights and "ownership" rights of data and suggest the following: (1) Reducing transaction costs and filling the gaps in SLAs; (2) Turning technological negative externalities into benefits; (3) Transforming the "tragedy of the commons" into "comedy"; (4) Swaying like a "Foucault pendulum" of "imperfect institutional choices"; and (5) Embracing the role of cloud brokers as a hub in supple cloud networks.

4.3.1 Reducing Transaction Costs in the Cloud: "Filling the Gaps" in SLAs

In a first step, I base my arguments in the abovementioned theory of Ronald Coase. He suggests that transaction costs introduce a certain degree of uncertainty between the parties and, therefore, are relevant at every stage of the negotiation.[34] To quote Williamson, transaction costs are part of the "New Institutional Economics" school[35] and are defined as "the cost of planning, [emphasis added] adopting and monitoring task completion under alternative forms of contracting."[36] For Barzel, the concept of transaction costs is closely related to that of "property rights." He defines transaction costs as "the costs associated with the transfer, capture, and protection of rights."[37]

The rationale behind law and economics is to try to reduce transaction costs while reaching private parties in negotiating and concluding agreements. The goal is to get as close as possible while minimizing the subsequent costs[38] of adjusting the "misalignments" of the agreement.[39] This is not to say, as many law and economics scholars have mistakenly conceived, that the initial allocation of legal entitlements does not matter from an efficiency point of view as long as the transaction costs of exchange are down to zero. The characterization of this trend has been spurred by

[34]Coase (1960, pp. 1–44).

[35]Williamson (1985, p. 16).

[36]Veljanovski (1982, p. 61).

[37]Barzel (1997, p. 4).

[38]Friedman (2000, pp. 8–18).

[39]Rutherford (2013, p. 603), see, also, Coase (1937, pp. 386–405), Commons (1934), Demsetz (1968, pp. 33–53), Williamson (1975). For an analysis of the effects of transaction costs between common law and other civil law based legal systems i.e., in Luisiana, see, generally, Brown (1997, pp. 2–3).

George Stigler in his conception of the so-called "Coase Theorem" (that, in reality, was never explicitly proposed by Coase).[40] On the contrary, Coase never assumed a world without transaction costs. Doing so would be to think of a utopia.

His argument is based on the way resources are used. According to him, legal decisions do not affect the way resources are allocated. As he asserts, "the delimitation of rights is an essential prelude to market transactions, but the ultimate result (which maximizes the value of production) is independent on the legal decision."[41] There are at least two interpretations to this proposition: (a) the *neutrality* version—the changes in the law do not affect the composition of the market, and; (b) the *efficiency* version—the efficient outcome arises despite the legal position.[42] We can conclude from this that delimitation of rights is an essential requirement to cloud computing transactions and the changes in the legal system might not affect directly the cloud market. This also tells us that the most efficient outcome might come from the negotiation inter partes.

It is said that cloud computing, and the Internet in general, reduces transaction costs. The impact of these effects is dramatic however not uniform. For instance, the hassles inherent to contracts remain still.[43] As cautioned earlier, SLAs are drafted on a "take it or leave it basis," which forces end-users to accept or reject the agreements outright. Instead, in order to achieve a favorable outcome, these agreements must set concrete, clear and well-defined "ownership rights" of data and databases to better satisfy not only current problems but also emerging trends such as Big Data. Yet, negotiating these clauses and writing down the terms with every single customer would be very costly and time-consuming. In hindsight, this is what Coase meant by the "high transaction costs" that need to be reduced and that have crystallized into a number of "economic-legal" truisms. Some of these formulas suggest that where transaction costs are high, one needs to structure the legal regime, or restructure the legal entitlements so as to reduce transaction costs or at least approximate the results that the parties would have arrived at in a "zero transaction cost world."[44]

According to Perkins, the Coase theory is particularly interesting and challenging for the clarification of "ownership rights" of information in cloud computing environments. One of the main reasons is that property rights are currently under heated debate swirling around several subjects including rights to share and access

---

40McCloskey (1998, pp. 367–371).

41Dittrich (2001, p. 35), Michie (2000, p. 117) (ed), Schmidtchen (2009, p. 32), Epstein (2011, p. 27).

42Veljanovski (1982, p. 49).

43Naughton (2013a, b).

44Gray (2012, p. 665) (ed), Posner (2003), Rittich (2002, p. 138). On the contrary, some commentators are very critical to the "market-based transaction cost" approach proposed by Posner and other proponents of the Chicago-style school of economics. According to i.a., Schlag, this approach does neither have the sort of "theoretical intelligibility nor the operational applicability to make the market-based transaction costs approach plausible." See Schlag (1989, pp. 1662–1700). See, also, generally, Williamson (1993, pp. 98–118).

to information. Thus, if these property rights can be asserted then the "best allocation of resources" can also be determined according to this theory.[45]

Kronman and Posner pleaded in favor of default rules (i.e., standard terms) as a mechanism to facilitate the negotiation process and reduce transaction costs.[46] Efficient default rules can help to fill the gaps in a contract and this may yield more profits or maximize the necessary surplus value.[47] Ayres and Gertner's article, *Filling Gaps in Incomplete Contracts: An Economic Theory of Default Rules*,[48] provides a theory of how to set efficient default rules through a variety of mechanisms. To achieve this end, they introduced the concept of a "penalty default rule" which is a rule designed to fill the gap in a contract with a term that would not have been otherwise chosen by the majority of the parties involved in the contract in question. This rule aims to incentivize at least one party of the contract to choose affirmatively the contractual clause they prefer. The purpose is to encourage or even force the involved parties to disclose information to the counterparty or third parties. This rule helps them to achieve more efficient results in cases where information is asymmetric.[49]

To avoid cumbersome bureaucratic procedures such as the manual checking of contractual clauses, this is in essence what the contractual model of this work will offer. The pervasive and dynamic nature of the cloud may result in confusion as to how to deal with these complex matters. My idea is to leverage the bargaining power of end-users and at the same time reduce the transaction costs. The contractual model that I will present in Chap. 8 will include a number of fields that are dictated by the relevant legal analysis and intellectual property compliance capabilities. More specifically, the schema will be broken down into three parts: database rights, "ownership" rights, and compliance. This will include a Boolean waiving system whereby the cloud provider can choose to keep or waive database rights. It will also contain a string field capability, which allows the inclusion of contractual clauses written in plain English as defined by the provider on a case by case basis. This can work as a kind of "penalty default rule" in order to "fill the gaps in incomplete contracts" as defined by Ayres and Gertner.

This legal framework will be implemented through a suitable XML schema model structure that an infrastructure cloud provider should fill in with its own information, and then make available to the public. Therefore, the brokers can read this information during the selection of infrastructure providers' procedures. This information must be included and displayed by an infrastructure provider and needs to be suitably adapted in a machine-readable way so it can be processed in an automated fashion. This kind of information is usually exposed for the infrastructure provider selection procedure in different group categories. Frequently, there is a legal information category that focuses on data protection and security issues. Therefore, this schema aims

[45]Perkins (2010), see, also, Cacciola and Gibbons (2012, pp. 1–32).

[46]DiMatteo and Janssen (2014, p. 99).

[47]Cooter and Ulen (2008, p. 220).

[48]Ayres and Gertner (1989, pp. 87–130).

[49]Ayres and Gertner (1989, pp. 91–92), Ayres (2006), De Geest (2011, pp. 228–229) (ed). But see Posner (2005, pp. 1–34), Maskin (2005, pp. 1–11).

at extending these capabilities including "ownership" rights issues. I will return to the technical specifications of this model in Chap. 8. For the moment, suffice it to say that this framework will nudge cloud providers to disclose the relevant information and incentivize end-users to choose the contractual clause (as default rule) they prefer when it comes to the clarification of "ownership rights" of data and databases.

4.3.2 Turning Technological Negative Externalities into External Benefits: The "Bee Metaphor"

Much of the economic approach to law attempts to solve the problem of the so-called "externalities." Externalities can be either negative or positive. Therefore, the second argument I submit in this section is how to turn negative externalities into positive ones. A negative externality is the effect of any activity of an individual or a firm that alter the production decision and thrusts a cost onto someone else.[50] According to Weigel, a negative (technological) externality "is when a person makes use of property rights in a way that increases her utility (or profit), and in doing so creates a side-effect that lowers the utility of another person without that person's help or prior consent."[51] Negative externalities are thus "ubiquitous and reciprocal."[52] They occur when the activity of one agent does not take other individuals' activity into account and affects their welfare negatively.[53]

Systems of property, torts and *contract law* may be used in such a way as to streamline the delimitation of rights into a particular direction.[54] Coase's solution to reduce negative externalities is by invoking the property rights theory as follows: "if trade in an externality is possible and there are no transaction costs, bargaining will lead to an efficiency outcome regardless of the initial allocation of property rights."[55] Environmental pollution, such as air pollution or chemical contamination poured into a river stream by a factory that causes harm and discomfort to the community, is the best example to describe a negative externality.[56] In this case, the legal question would be who is bearing the cost for the damages? There are many theories to solve this question. One of them is the Piguvian approach, which suggests imposing a tax on the pollutants.[57] What Coase and other economists however proclaim is for less government intervention: "regardless of who owns the right to control the

[50]Noll (2005, p. 21), Harrison (2003, p. 39).

[51]Weigel (2008, p. 44).

[52]Mercuro and Medema (1995, p. 101).

[53]Lewin (1995, p. 254).

[54]Mercuro and Medema (1995, p. 101).

[55]Coase (1960, pp. 1–3), see, also, Huang and Gao (2013, p. 124), Berderman (2010, p. 48).

[56]Coase (1960, pp. 1–3).

[57]See, generally, Pigou (1932).

environmental improvement...private negotiation can yield the efficient outcome without government regulatory intervention."[58]

This is precisely the problem I observe with database rights in the cloud. Consider the situation of a project about Big Data using any kind of medical or genetic scientific research. On the one hand, database rights may increase the utility or profit of database makers. On the other hand, the protective nature of database rights automatically raises the concern of whether information should be free, at least for the scientific community. Therefore, database rights may sometimes create a deterrent spill-over effect that could lower the utility of third parties and we can take the law of property and contract to delineate database rights and "ownership" of data into a particular direction.

The opposite is true for a "desirable"[59] or "positive" externality (also known as "external benefit" or "beneficial externality"),[60] which is when individuals receive some unexpected benefits or when the utility (or profit) of the third party is expanded. Honey production illustrates a good example of a positive externality.[61] Consider the scenario of an apiarist who possesses several beehives in a meadow for honey production, which is adjacent to a grove of apple trees owned by someone else.[62] In this scenario, the queen bee is nurtured on a special diet of royal jelly, which is collected by the worker bees, also known as "foragers." The foragers fly around the hive collecting the pollen from the flowers and through a fascinating dance called the "waggle dance," they communicate to the rest of the bees where the apple tree blossoms are located. The more they waggle the more flowers are supposed to be in the place they are facing, using the sun as an indicator for orientation.[63]

A positive collateral effect (as an external benefit) of this fascinating social behavior of honey bees suggests that bees (and "beekeepers") are not the only ones benefiting from the collection of pollen but many plants and trees depend on the pollination for their very survival. Bees and other insects have built up a symbiotic relationship with nature. Hence, the value created by the pollination may be more beneficial than the value generated by the harvested nectar itself.[64]

Under these circumstances, both the apiarist and the apple orchard owner can benefit from the bargaining of a contract where both parties are better off. Suppose they could design a mechanism to know how many trees are pollinated by the bee foragers, whereby they come to know that each beehive is capable of pollinating one acre of apple trees, duplicating the value of the apple trees production.[65] On this account, they could invest and share the expenses to allocate more beehives in strategic places. This is what Stephen Cheung describes as the "custom of the

[58] Hacket (2001, p. 130).

[59] Ver Eecke (2008, p. 65).

[60] Cavalcanti (2015, p. 73).

[61] Mankiv (2007, p. 2010), Beito et al. (2002, p. 406) (eds).

[62] See Nerlove et al. (1987, pp. 38–39); Cheung (1980).

[63] Frame (2013, pp. 173–175).

[64] Corrales (2010, pp. 5–13).

[65] Nicholson and Snyde (2010, pp. 598–599), Peterson (2009, p. 30).

orchards," which conveys the idea of a positive externality accruing to the apple orchard.

Therefore, a certain number of beehives are necessary to pollinate, on average, one specific area. If both parties negotiate a fee paid and purchase the correct amount of hives, then the bees will randomly collect the pollen around the apple orchard.[66] As long as this mechanism is cheap and transaction costs are low, these kinds of cooperation can bring some substantial revenues. This idea may not be perfect and needs a special mechanism to work effectively, yet it reinforces one of the recurring themes of this book, which is about the importance of choosing the right institutions and mechanisms when addressing the so-called "market failures."[67]

As an example, in the context of cloud computing and Big Data projects, an analogy can be drawn from this phenomenon and applied to genetic research that involves biological data taken from patients. The "bee metaphor" mirrors and resembles the relationship between patients and researchers where not only researchers receive scientific or economic benefits from the biological data taken from patients, but there is a mutual relationship where the group of patients, including their communities, should receive some benefits too. This relationship should be built up through a bilateral manifestation between patients and researchers in terms of a contractual agreement where the principle of "freedom of contract" fulfills the purpose of safeguarding the autonomies of the interested parties.[68]

In this book, I will argue and demonstrate how SLAs can develop some default rules that allow for the transformation of negative externalities into positive ones by following the example of honey production (the "bee metaphor"). The contractual model that I will present in Chaps. 8 and 9 will capture "ownership" rights of data and databases—sometimes seen as externalities—through the XML schema that will be used through the entire lifecycle of the SLA negotiation. This schema will be backed-up with a selection tool that takes Unified Modeling Language (UML) models and exports their options through a Graphical User Interface (GUI) for end-users to select which options they need. Insofar as "ownership" rights of data and databases can be ascertained and incurred through the SLA specification, the involved parties can recoup some of the negative collateral effects by generating similar beneficial externalities. According to Autor, the Coase theory implies that the market can *potentially* resolve or at least mitigate externalities if property rights are agreed upon and clearly asserted. A crucial interpretation of the Coase theory is that an externality may be settled not by "regulating the externality out of existence" but by giving the parties the possibility to negotiate so that the involved parties may come to terms with the best economical solution.[69]

From a law and economics point of view, a crucial role of contract law and property law is to reduce transaction costs in order to protect the rights holders of entitlements against negative externalities, by ensuring that these are negotiated among the parties

[66] Cheung (1973, pp. 11–33), Newmark (2009, pp. 195 et seq.) (ed), McCall (2010, pp. 166–167).

[67] Sandler (2001, pp. 65–67).

[68] Corrales (2010, pp. 5–13).

[69] Autor (2010, p. 4).

involved.[70] The Coase theory is a useful benchmark since it helps us to evaluate under which circumstances law is necessary, or when a contract between the parties may be adequate. On the other hand, reducing the transaction costs may be a critical point in reckoning the opportunities for self-regulation. If the transaction costs for negotiating the agreement between the parties are too high then the opportunities for self-regulation are restricted. However, there are many mechanisms to expand the design of cloud computing contracts by which transaction costs can be minimized.[71]

Under this theory, all externalities are internalized within the firm[72] because agents are able to consider them beforehand and negotiate them away and, as a consequence, the transaction costs are totally aligned. The Coasian method rests upon the assumption that the involved parties have sufficient and adequate knowledge about their preferences, have made a rational decision, and that transaction costs have been reduced to the very minimum.[73] This idea, when first introduced a few decades ago, seemed to be profound and important. Today this may sound somewhat intuitive. Nevertheless, it seems that Coase wanted to go one step further and he was implying a framework for the economic analysis of law in real case scenarios where transaction costs are too high.[74]

4.3.3 "Ownership" Rights of Data as a Commons: Transforming "Tragedy" into "Comedy"

The foregoing discussion leads us directly to the third core principle with the works of Oliver Williamson and Elinor Ostrom who shared the Nobel Prize award in the year 2009. Williamson received it for his analysis of "economic governance, especially the boundaries of the firm" and Ostrom received it for her analysis of economic governance with a main focus on "the commons."[75] By and large, they both studied ways of regulating transactions more broadly. Williamson's research focused on what kind of transaction should be carried out *intra* firms and what sort of transactions should be done within the market. According to him, one can either outsource the contract to an independent third party who can "mediate that transaction," which is in a sense one of the main proposals of this book, or one can take that transaction out of the market and organize it inside the firms. There are pros and cons in these alternatives and the challenge of this research is to look at the viable contractual alternatives to clarify "ownership rights" of data and databases in the most successful and effective way. As Williamson notes, what we need to do is to identify the most

---

[70]Hirsch (1988, pp. 18–19).

[71]Maata (2010, p. 133).

[72]Rutherford (2013, p. 208).

[73]Coleman (1983, p. 110).

[74]Richardson and Hadfield (1999, p. 34) (eds).

[75]www.Nobelprize.org, All Prizes in Economic Sciences [online]. Available at: http://www.nobelprize.org/no-belprizes/economic-sciences/laureates/ [Accessed 10 December 2018].

important attributes that define those transactions and examine whether they are deemed to be easy or complicated.[76]

The thesis of this rests upon the assumption that cloud computing contracts (or SLAs) may be too complicated for end-users to understand the terms of the contract. Successful negotiation between parties relies on reducing information asymmetry. In this case, the cloud provider will have more accurate information than end-users. This creates a disproportional balance in the negotiations, which can sometimes cause the transactions to go askew. A broker providing a flexible and standardized contract can curtail or even bypass the negotiation phase hence reducing transaction costs.[77]

In line with Williamson's logic, and referring to the works of Mair and Marti, "institutional voids" are "situations where institutional arrangements that support markets are absent, weak, or fail to accomplish the role expected of them."[78] They refer to the structural system where intermediaries are in place, but are not "properly functioning in the framework of institutional voids."[79] Nevertheless, in line with Schrammel, I argue that intermediaries can help end-users and SMEs overcome these obstacles as a "surrogate mechanism" filling the void left in the structure by traditional institutions.[80] Yahklef also suggests that with the advent of the Internet, the role of the intermediaries will change, but not disappear. Instead, they will acquire a more explicit and focused role involving favorable location and "infrastructural delivery systems and services."[81] My approach to transaction costs is to follow Common and Williamson by making different institutions places that foster the exchange of permanent relations.[82]

Ostrom, on the other hand, focused on the use of common-pool resources and the different routes to control such resources. Against the backdrop that advocates for state control and privatization, she modeled a theoretical framework and suggested that common-pools may offer a more productive and successful way instead of outside control.[83] The "commons" are those natural resources, such as lakes or rivers for fishing, irrigation systems, and community forests[84] which can be used for cattle grazing or for collecting fruits and medicinal plants. Researchers have realized that such resources may be exhausted in both laboratories and the field by individuals or community groups that want to maximize their resources. Ostrom carried out a lifetime empirical research and analyzed how the commons problem can be solved by communities who organize collectively and voluntarily to manage themselves rather than depending on the coercive governmental power. Neither the government

[76]See, generally, Williamson (1981a, b, pp. 548–577), (2002, pp. 171–195), (1996).

[77]Rose (1999, p. 64).

[78]Mair and Marti (2009, p. 422).

[79]Schrammel (2010, p. 508).

[80]See, generally, Schrammel (2014, p. 203).

[81]Yahklef (2000, pp. 39–55).

[82]Williamson (1981a, b, p. 41); see also Samuels and Schmid (1981) (eds).

[83]Ostrom (1990, 2000, pp. 29–52).

[84]Ostrom cites, for example, a forest reserve in Uganda. See Wall (2014, p. 89); see also Moran and Ostrom (2005) (eds).

nor the market has successfully dealt with the problem of common-pool resources. One of the main challenges identified by Ostrom is that the rules we use to govern our public and private institutions, or any kind of problem that we encounter, are designed to fit one area as a one size fits all solution.[85]

A typical problem that demonstrates negative externalities and illustrates the necessity for the clarification of property rights is the so-called "tragedy of the commons."[86] Ostrom studied different ways (both successful and unsuccessful) to solve this problem.[87] It happens when an individual who has a selfish interest disregards the well-being of the community in the pursuit of personal gain. The concept "tragedy of the commons" was coined by Garrett Hardin in his seminal article published in the Science journal a few decades ago.[88]

Hardin refers to cases in which resources owned by more than one individual are overused to the point that they might extinguish. The classical example dates back to medieval England where a "common" piece of land,[89] such as a pasturage, was set aside for public use. In this case, the grass may be overexploited to the point of diminishing returns and eventually damaged because each individual takes more than they should without taking the appropriate measures to keep the pasture in good and healthy conditions, i.e., by means of fertilization, etc. This produces a noticeably negative effect in the long term, oftentimes to the detriment of the whole community.[90] According to Ostrom, some of the most difficult challenges concerning the common dilemma is the management of large-scale resources that rely on international cooperation.[91] This refers to more intangible resources too, such as "knowledge" or "information,"[92] which is sometimes more difficult and costly to control.[93]

In contrast to Hardin, the other side of the coin is the so-called "comedy of the commons." This term is attributed to an article published by Carol Rose in 1986.[94] The "comedy of the commons" is also known as the "cornucopia of the commons"[95] or simply "inverse commons."[96] In the same line of thought, Susan Cox writes about the "triumph of the commons" as she believes "there is no tragedy on the commons."[97]

[85]Ostrom (2009, pp. 419–421).

[86]Harrison (2003, p. 40).

[87]Keohane and Ostrom (1995) (eds).

[88]Hardin (1968, pp. 1243–1248).

[89]Warren (2006, p. 1).

[90]Crowe (1969, p. 1103).

[91]Ostrom et al. (1999, pp. 278–282).

[92]Hess and Ostrom (2007, pp. 3–5).

[93]Felice and Vatiero (2012).

[94]Rose (1986).

[95]Bricklin (2006).

[96]See Warren (2006, p. 1).

[97]Cox Buck (1985, pp. 49–62), see, generally, Dahlman (1991, pp. 285–296). In this piece, Dhalman submits that in Hardin's syllogism there was actually no tragedy and that the problems were more complex.

In the "comedy of the commons," individuals share knowledge and information for the sake of the community rather than eliciting or removing resources for their own personal and selfish gain. It refers to "non-rivalrous" resources like data. Data may be seen as a "non-rivalrous good" and therefore has limitless potential to create social and economic value.[98] Most databases or research repositories like Big Data analyses may fall under this category.[99] One essential prerequisite for this is "data access." This movement is also known as "open data" in the public sector, "data commons" such as in science, or "data portability," which is a more restrictive concept to empower consumers.

Obstacles to data access can cause spillover effects in the upstream sector, such as universities and research institutions, but also in midstream and downstream collaboration. The term "open data" is often mentioned and promoted in the scientific community. It is also referred to in many international instruments such as the *OECD Declaration on Access to Research Data from Public Funding* (2004)[100] and the *OECD Council Recommendation Concerning Access to Research Data from Public Funding* (2006).[101] It is noteworthy to mention that the concept of open data is not only circumscribed to the public sector. UN Global Pulse (2012)[102] proposed the concept of "data philanthropy," by which the private sector shares data for the sake of the public interest. Two main corollaries are derived from this idea: (i) the "data commons," whereby some data are shared and made publicly available after adequate anonymization and aggregation; and (ii) the "digital smoke signals," where sensitive data are analyzed by private companies and the outcome of these studies shared with the government.

To avoid the "tragedy of the commons," I suggest a framework where private rights and common rights should not be treated as antagonistic options, but as an alternative tool to be implemented to solve those issues for which each may be best applicable.[103] Big Data shares many elements in common with natural resources. While data cannot be deteriorated, or expunged in the same way a forest would, placing obstacles to data access may have similar deterrent effects. For this reason, the contractual framework I propose allows for sufficient flexibility to create a commonly pooled resource for improving scientific research.[104]

These two claims, the "tragedy" and the "comedy" of the commons, help us to realize the crucial link that binds together "the boundaries of the firm" and the problem of "the commons" and some general inferences can be drawn about the lessons learned from Williamson and Ostrom. This analysis requires a dual focus. In Part III of this book, I will explore this subject in greater detail and I will provide flexible contractual constellations. To make the analysis easier to follow, and to

98 OECD (2015, pp. 187–188).
99 Borgman (2015, pp. 73–75).
100 OECD (2004).
101 OECD (2006).
102 Global Pulse White Paper (2012).
103 OECD (2015, pp. 187–188).
104 See, generally, Lane et al. (2014) (eds).

explore how such questions manifest themselves in practice, I will employ a use-case scenario[105] to illustrate how the "tragedy of the commons" can be avoided. I will also scale-up the propositions of this model from local communities to the international scope of cloud computing and Big Data environments.

4.3.4 Institutional Alternatives: The Foucault Pendulum of "Imperfect Choices in the Cloud"

Another argument takes into consideration recent extensions to traditional law and economics theories, as explained by Neil Komesar in his book, *Imperfect Alternatives: Choosing Institutions in Law, Economics, and Public Policy.*[106] Institutions such as the political process, the adjudicative process and *the market* are too large and complicated by nature. Komesar proposed a comparative institutional analysis and careful scrutiny of the main characteristics of such institutions. This analytical framework involves paying attention to how the role of each institution may predominate as a choice towards the social goal of the law-making process and how the role may swing from one institution to the other,[107] like a Foucault pendulum.

Komesar focuses on the potential routes that can lead to the strengthening of policy-making goals. This means that in his "deciding who decides" theory, he hashes out how choices are made through the selection of key institutions and how such choices should recast the Coasian approach with regards to the transaction costs and benefits. Komesar insists that this comparative approach must be "participation-centered," which means that the analysis of such transaction costs and benefits should be carried out *within* and *between* institutions. He implies that looking at one single institution such as the judiciary is a mistake and suggests a holistic interpretative approach among them.[108]

Kersch maintains that this analysis has advantages and disadvantages. On the one hand, a comparative approach can bring together different perceptions that a "single variable" cannot provide. On the other hand, narrowing down the analysis to one single institution can yield a more significant groundwork result and such comparative analytic reasoning is thanks to the literature that focuses on one particular key institution. According to Kersch, a weakness of Komesar's theory is that he limits this comparison to only three main institutions—markets, courts, and politics—and although he tries to argue that institutional choices must prevail, he seems to hint that judges should choose whether to focus on the judicial system or whether to leave it to the market or the political process. Everything seems to boil down to the rational

[105] See, more specifically, Chap. 8 with regards to the contractual framework and "Use Case Scenario 2" of Chap. 9. This scenario is about genetic research projects within clinical trials.

[106] Komesar (1994).

[107] Pierce (1995, p. 941), Komesar (1994, pp. 3–6), Hartmann and Kjaer (2015, pp. 157–158) (eds), Barani (2007, p. 118).

[108] Kersch (1996, pp. 13–15).

choice of one individual: the judge. The point he attempts to make is that judges should have an expanded vision that goes beyond the judicial system when it comes to interpreting the law and imparting justice.[109]

Another disadvantage of the Komesarian framework according to Kersch's view is that by focusing on the main characteristics of each institution, we are accepting a rather "static" and rigid model with all the flaws of typical institutional stagnation. This interpretation may also create some limitations and boundaries to what we understand as the concept of choice. In Kersch's opinion, Komesar seems to obviate the dynamic role of institutions that change over time.[110]

Komesar, however, expands the interpretation of institutions later on in his ensuing book *Law's Limits: Rule of Law and the Supply and Demand of Rights* [hereinafter "Law's Limit"]. He realized the importance of analyzing communities as an institutional alternative and observed how the informal norms of such communities are bound to the three key institutions he considered before. Likewise, he also recognized that the role of the "participation-centered" approach goes beyond the mere understanding of institutions and extends to the understanding of social goals and values.[111] In *Law's Limit*, Komesar focused again on the characteristics of the adjudicative process, however this narrow definition does not mean that the interpretation should be court centered. On the contrary, Komesar made a clear disclaimer that his approach should be construed more broadly as to embrace an understanding of its alternatives such as "legislatures, bureaucracies and informal communities."[112]

This last argument allows us to open the door wide and pay special attention to informal communities and relationships. As they come in a variety of forms, different tools must be employed to solve property rights quandaries. As explained by Robert Ellickson, individuals of a society may solve their discrepancies without making use of the law.[113] This idea is also supported by Ostrom in the world that she describes as being free of bureaucracies and informally governed. It is in this world which individual property rights are disassociated with the "tragedy of the commons."[114]

Upon first inspection, the advantages of "Komesar's Razor" points out a theory where greater weight is given to the institutions in a "world of networks."[115] Some general inferences can be drawn about "market transactions" and we can extend these ideas to cloud computing environments. The rationale for the integration of different institutional alternatives—although they might be imperfect by nature—suggests that we must choose the least imperfect choice available.[116] This approach may offer us

[109] Kersch (1996, pp. 13–15).

[110] Kersch (1996, pp. 13–15).

[111] Komesar (2001), preface.

[112] Komesar (2001, p. 9).

[113] See, generally, Ellickson (1994). In this book, Ellickson demonstrates that the law is not that important and that people can generally govern themselves by means of informal rules and social norms without the need for governmental control and coercive power.

[114] Ellickson (1994, p. 27).

[115] Ghosh (2014, p. 455).

[116] See Carolan (2009, p. 139).

the possibility to look at the cloud computing market in its multidimensional level that may contribute to the further extension and improvement of SLAs. This will offer end-users more choices[117] and will certainly influence their decision-making.[118]

This theoretical canvas is broad enough to encompass different aspects of the cloud market including the "communities" or smaller institutions, which may play an important role in asserting and clarifying "ownership rights" of data and databases in various ways. In this book, I will refer to such institutions and communities at different levels. In the following section, I will explain, for instance, the important role innovation intermediaries play in the cloud computing network, where I see the brokers playing a vital role as liaison between various institutions and communities. In addition, as I was persuaded and firmly convinced by Komesar's institutional choices and how its internal communities may streamline the roadblocks to the achievement of social goals, I will come back to this theoretical interpretation in future chapters such as in Chap. 6, where I will refer to the multi-layered levels of *trust* encountered in such intra-market communities and how they swing from one institution to the other.

4.3.5 Social Network Analysis (SNA): Cloud Brokers as a Hub

The final cut of these five core principles focuses on the role of the brokers as a hub in supple cloud networks. The analysis of social networks is not something new and goes beyond the study of social networks on the Internet.[119] This approach carefully examines the way the social network is structured. It studies the patterns and blueprint of the "relations" among the actors within a community as opposed to the "individual attributes" of its members.[120] In the words of Knoke and Yang, "the central objectives of network analysis are to measure and represent these structural relations accurately, and to explain both why they occur and what are their consequences."[121] An SNA is usually depicted in a figure called a "sociograph"[122] or a "sociomatrix."[123]

This paradigm includes theoretical and abstract thoughts as well as "methods and analytical techniques" to unveil the relationship between those individuals involved

[117]See generally, Purnhagen and Rott (2014, p. 833) (eds). In this book, the authors refer to the Komesarian approach as it can contribute "to the further development of European law on remedies that offers EU citizens access to basic services." As an analogy, I think that the Komesarian framework may serve to further develop contract law. With regard to the Komesarian approach in the context of the European Union, see, generally, Maduro (1998, p. 117).

[118]See, generally, Komarek (2012, p. 241).

[119]Cross and Thomas (2009).

[120]Giuffre (2013).

[121]The work of Knoke and Yang. See Giuffre (2013).

[122]Özyer et al. (2013) (eds).

[123]Marsden (2005).

Fig. 4.1 Triad relationship

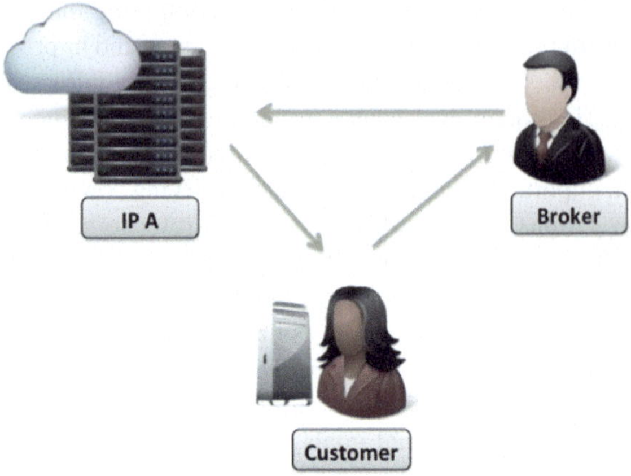

in social groups and how these relationships are influenced by different factors.[124] Cloud computing transactions frequently take part in complex relationships where several actors are involved. Hence, an SNA can be a powerful tool to elucidate and structure these crossroads.[125]

A crucial factor in understanding SNA is that the "unit" of analysis is not based on individual actors but rather groups of individuals and the way these individuals are interconnected. SNA breaks down into "dyads" and "triads" (groups of two or three individuals) and their "ties."[126] A triad occurs when three "nodes" (i.e., actors or social units such as individuals, companies or governmental agencies)[127] are linked to at least two "edges" and no more than three "edges," while a dyad is composed of only two "nodes" connected by one "edge."[128]

To understand this, focus on the correlation and linkage among a group of individuals beyond the role they play within the community.[129] These connectors are known today as service providers who play the important role of innovation intermediaries[130] or "brokers"[131] as depicted in Fig. 4.1, where in reality there is a triad relationship even though the actors do not know each other. For example, there is a triad relationship between the cloud customer, the broker and infrastructure provider A (IP A). On the other hand, the "length" (the number of arrows connecting each

[124]Prell (2012, pp. 1–10).

[125]Gunduz-Oguducu and Etaner-Uyar (2014, pp. 14–15) (eds).

[126]Actors are connected to each other by "social ties." This means that the relationship between two actors represents a tie. See Wasserman and Faust (2009). See also Berkowitz (1982, pp. 20–21, 119), Pryke (2012, pp. 87, 228).

[127]Tsvetovat and Kouznetsov (2011, pp. 4, 19), Prell (2012, pp. 140–141).

[128]Rees and Gallagher (2013), Freeman (2004, p. 24).

[129]Giuffre (2013).

[130]Pinheiro (2011).

[131]See Sodeur and Taube (2008, p. 100).

actor)[132] is crucial in the context of the sociograph as this represents the existence and numbers of intermediaries. This is also relevant in the framework of clarifying "ownership rights" in derived data, as this also means that the content of the information may change as the cloud provider adds and adapts the information submitted by the customer in order to provide the service.[133]

The neutrality of these intermediaries is, however, not per se guaranteed. Therefore, adding more providers to the supply chain may deter the deemed trust. The loss of this trust could generate the "implosion of the system" leading to a stunting effect and more users leaving the network. Cloud brokers may charge an additional fee thus adding more actors and intermediaries to the negotiation table that would increase the transaction costs. However, this would also contribute to the "social interface,"[134] which can save time and costs in the long-term. Since the cloud computing market is too complex, especially for individuals and SMEs, adding an intermediary with the technical expertise, legal knowledge and right tools (i.e., the contractual framework embedded in an open software toolkit that I present in Part III of this book) may improve and even lower deliberation and transaction costs.

The overriding assumption lies in the fact that if end-users could effortlessly assess the most convenient cloud provider and assert their "ownership" rights through an automated procedure implemented and orchestrated by the broker, then cloud computing transactions would increase. Legal uncertainties would be reduced and this would incentivize cloud customers to participate in the cloud market. In this vein, the broker will provide an added value service by clarifying "ownership" rights of data and databases rights between the involved parties, as will be explained in future chapters. The intermediary should act as a "trusted third party," assuring transparency and strengthening the trust to the functioning of the network.

4.4 Summary and Interim Remarks

Upon review of several theories and models introduced by leading scholars in the field of law and economics, and having contextualized them in the cloud computing and Big Data environments, the methods espoused here suggest that we need to supplement these ideas with some additional insights. Each of the positions herein examined offered plausible alternatives and have refined our general understanding of the law. Integrating some of these theories and recognizing how their constituent parts interact is a good point of reference. Yet, we need to go beyond that point of debate. My goal in the next part is to go one step further and to advance an approach that seamlessly connects the most important features of these earlier theory-driven considerations adding new elements and insights from other disciplines. Accordingly, by erecting a cross-disciplinary bridge, we may then be able to adjust a more

---

[132]Prell (2012, pp. 140–144).

[133]Teramoto (2013).

[134]Teramoto and Jurčys (2014, pp. 116–119).

generalized framework that can be applied to cloud computing and Big Data transformations. In the language of the previous theories employed here, the subsequent chapters will restate the implications of these findings and will add new elements found in more contemporary theories of law and economics, and behavioral law and economics, as well as other social sciences. Therefore, in Part II I present a new theoretical framework that I call "Plan-like Architectures."

References

Autor D (2010) Lecture note 13–externalities, the Coase Theorem and market remedies. Microeconomic Theory and Public Policy, Massachusetts Institute of Technology, p 4. http://ocw.mit.edu/courses/economics/14-03-microeconomic-theory-and-public-policy-fall-2010/lecture-notes/MIT14_03F10_lec13.pdf. Accessed 10 May 2019

Ayres I (2006) Ya-HUH: there are and should be penalty defaults. Faculty Scholarship Series. Paper 1172. http://digitalcommons.law.yale.edu/fss_papers/1172. Accessed 10 May 2019

Ayres I, Gertner R (1989) Filling gaps in incomplete contracts: an economic theory of default rules. Yale Law J 99(1):87–130

Backhaus J (ed) (2005) The Elgar companion to law and economics, 2nd edn. Edward Elgar Publishing, Cheltenham

Barani L (2007) The regulation of sport in the European union: courts and markets. In: Bogusz B, Cygan A, Szyszczak E (eds) The regulation of sport in the European union. Edward Elgar Publishing, Cheltenham, p 118

Barzel Y (1997) Economic analysis of property rights, 2nd edn. Cambridge University Press, Cambridge, p 4

Becker G (1968) Crime and punishment: an economic approach. J Polit Econ 76(2):169–217

Becker G (1971) The economics of discrimination, 2nd edn. University of Chicago Press, Chicago

Becker G (1978) The economic approach to human behavior. University of Chicago Press, Chicago

Beito D, Gordon P, Tabarrok A (eds) (2002) The voluntary city: choice community and civil society. The University of Michigan Press and the Independent Institute, Oakland, p 406

Benson B, Zimmerman P (2010) Handbook on the economics of crime. Edward Elgar Publishing, Cheltenham

Bentham J (1781) An introduction to the principles of morals and legislation. Dover Publications Inc., s.l

Berderman D (2010) Custom as a source of law. Cambridge University Press, Cambridge, p 48

Berkowitz S (1982) An introduction to structural analysis: the network approach to social research. Butterworth & Co., Toronto, pp 20–21, 119

Borgman C (2015) Big data, little data, no data. Scholarship in the networked world. The MIT Press, Cambridge, pp 73–75

Bricklin D (2006) The cornucopia of the commons: how to get volunteer labor. http://bricklin.com/cornucopia.htm. Accessed 10 May 2019

Brown J (1997) Transaction costs and vertical integrations. In: Zerbe R, Kovacic W (eds) Research in law and economics, vol 18. Jai Press Inc., Greenwich, pp 2–3

Burrow P, Veljanovski C (eds) (1981) The economic approach to law. Butterworths, London, p 3

Cacciola S, Gibbons R (2012) Coase meets the cloud: how and when can outsourcing IT improve organizational performance? pp 1–32. White Paper. http://www.analysisgroup.com/uploadedfiles/content/insights/publishing/coase_meets_the%20cloud.pdf. Accessed 10 May 2019

Calabresi G (1961) Some thoughts on risk distribution and the law of torts. Yale Law J 70(4):499–553

Caplin A, Schotter A (2010) The foundations of positive and normative economics: a handbook, handbooks of economics methodology. Oxford University Press, Oxford
Carolan E (2009) The new separation of powers: a theory for the modern state. Oxford University Press, Oxford, p 139
Cavalcanti J (2015) Effects of IT on enterprise architecture, governance and growth. IGI Global, Hershey, p 73
Cheung S (1973) The fable of the bees: an economic investigation. J Law Econ 16(1):11–33
Cheung S (1980) The myth of social cost. Cato Paper, No. 16. Cato Institute, s.l
Coase R (1937) The nature of the firm. Economica 4:386–405
Coase R (1960) The problem of social cost. J Law Econ 3:1–44
Coleman J (1983) The economic analysis of law. In: Kuperberg M, Beitz C (eds) Law, economics, and philosophy. Rowman & Allanheld Publishers, New Jersey, p 110
Commons J (1934) Institutional economic: its place in political economy. University of Wisconsin Press, Madison
Cooter R, Ulen T (2008) Law & economics, 5th edn, Pearson International Edition. Prentice Hall, Boston, p 220
Corrales M (2010) Protecting patients' rights in clinical trial scenarios: the "Bee Metaphor" and the simbiotic relationship. In: Bottis M (ed) An information law for the 21st century. Third international seminar on information law 2010. Nomiki Bibliothiki Group, Athens, pp 5–13
Cox Buck S (1985) No tragedy on the commons. Environ Ethics 7(1):49–62
Cross R, Thomas R (2009) Driving results through social networks: how top organizations leverage networks for performance and growth, loc. 117. Wiley (Kindle Edition), San Francisco
Crowe B (1969) The tragedy of the commons revisited. Science 166(3909):1103
Dahlman C (1991) The tragedy of the commons that wasn't: on technical solutions to the institutions game. Popul Environ 12(3):285–296
De Geest G (ed) (2011) Contract law and economics. Encyclopedia of law and economics, vol 6, 2nd edn. Edward Elgar Publishing, Cheltenham, pp 228–229
Demsetz H (1968) The cost of transacting. Quart J Econ 82:33–53
DiMatteo L, Janssen A (2014) Interpretive methodologies in the interpretation of the CISG. In: DiMatteo L (ed) International sales law: a global challenge. Cambridge University Press, New York, p 99
Dittrich M (2001) Internalisierung externer Effekte: Ein kritischer Vergleich der Ansaetze von Pigou und Coase, Diplomarbeit an der Technischen Universitaet Chemnitz Fachbereich Wirtschaftswissenschaften. Diplomica GmbH, Hamburg
Driver J (2010) The history of utilitarianism, stanford encyclopedia of philosophy. http://plato.stanford.edu/entries/utilitarianism-history/. Accessed 10 Oct 2018
Duggan A (1982) The economics of consumer protection: a critique of the Chicago School case against intervention. Adel Law Rev 2:4–6
Elkin-Koren N, Salzberger R (2013) The law and economics of intellectual property in the digital age: the limits of analysis. Routledge research in intellectual property. Routledge, Oxon
Ellickson R (1994) Order without law: how neighbors settle disputes, Revised Edition. Harvard University Press, Cambridge
Epstein R (2011) Liberty, property, and the law: private and common property. Routledge, New York, p 27
Felice F, Vatiero M (2012) Elinor Ostrom and the solution to the tragedy of the commons. American Enterprise Institute. http://www.aei.org/publication/elinor-ostrom-and-the-solution-to-the-tragedy-of-the-commons/. Accessed 10 May 2019
Frame D (2013) Framing decisions: decision making that accounts for irrationality, people, and constraints. Wiley, San Francisco, pp 173–175
Freeman L (2004) The development of social network analysis: a study in the sociology of science. Empirical Press, Vancouver, p 24
Friedman D (2000) Law's order: what economics has to do with law and why it matters. Princeton University Press, Princeton, pp 8–18 and 145–170

Georgakopoulos N (2005) Principles and methods of law and economics: basic tools for normative reasoning. Cambridge University Press, New York, p 3
Ghosh S (2014) Komesar's Razor: Comparative Institutional Analysis in a World of Networks. Wis Law Rev 455. Univ. of Wisconsin Legal Studies Research Paper 1244(2013)
Giuffre K (2013) Communities and networks: using social network analysis to rethink urban and community studies, locs. 143 and 149. Polity Press (Kindle Edition), Cambridge
Global Pulse White Paper (2012) Big data for development: opportunities & challenge. http://www.unglobalpulse.org/sites/default/files/BigDataforDevelopmentUNGlobalPulseJune2012.pdf. Accessed 10 May 2019
Gray C (ed) (2012) The philosophy of law: an encyclopedia, "Posner, Richard Allen," vol I–II. Routledge, London, p 665
Gunduz-Oguducu S, Etaner-Uyar A (eds) (2014) Social networks: analysis and case studies. Springer, Vienna, pp 14–15
Hacket S (2001) Environmental and natural resources economics: theory, policy, and the sustainable society, 2nd edn. M. E. Sharpe Inc., New York, p 130
Hardin G (1968) The tragedy of the commons. Science 162(3859):1243–1248
Harrison J (2003) Law and economics in a nutshell, 3rd edn. West Publishing Co., St. Paul, p 39
Hartmann E, Kjaer P (eds) (2015) The evolution of intermediary institutions in Europe: from corporatism to governance. Palgrave McMillan, New York, pp 157–158
Hess C, Ostrom E (2007) Introduction: an overview of the knowledge commons. In: Hess C, Ostrom E (eds) Understanding knowledge as a commons: from theory to practice. MIT Press, Cambridge, pp 3–5
Hirsch W (1988) Law and economics: an introductory analysis, 2nd edn. Academic Press, Inc., Boston, pp 18–19
Huang J, Gao L (2013) Wireless network pricing. Synthesis lectures on communication networks. Morgan & Claypool Publishers, San Rafael, p 124
Keohane R, Ostrom E (eds) (1995) Local commons and global interdependence: heterogeneity and cooperation in two domains. SAGE Publications, London
Kersch K (1996) Imperfect alternatives: choosing institutions in law, economics, and public policy (Book Review), vol 6(1), pp 13–15. www.Lawcourts.org
Komarek J (2012) Institutional dimension of constitutional pluralism. In: Avbelj M, Komarek J (eds) Constitutional pluralism in the European union and beyond. Hart Publishing, Oxford, p 241
Komesar N (1994) Imperfect alternatives: choosing institutions in law, economics, and public policy. The University of Chicago Press, Chicago
Komesar N (2001) Law's limits: the rule of law and the supply and demand of rights. Cambridge University Press, Cambridge
Lane J et al (eds) (2014) Privacy, big data, and the public good: frameworks for engagement. Cambridge University Press, New York
Lewin J (1995) Toward a new ecological law & economics. In: Malloy R, Braum C (eds) Law and economics: new and critical perspectives, vol 4. Peter Lang, New York, p 254
Maata K (2010) Law and economics from lawyers' point of view. In: Rosaeg E, Schaefer H, Stavang E (eds) Law and economics: essays in honor of erling eide. Cappelen Akademisk Forlag, Oslo, p 133
Maduro M (1998) We the court: the European court of justice and the European economic constitution: a critical reading of Article 30 of the EC treaty. Hart Publishing, Oxford, p 117
Mair J, Marti I (2009) Entrepreneurship in and around institutional voids: a case study from Bangladesh. J Bus Ventur 24(5):422
Malloy R (1990) Law and economics: a comparative approach to theory and practice. West Publishing Co., St. Paul, pp 14–15
Mankiv N (2007) Principles of microeconomics, 4th edn. Thomson South-Western, Mason, p 210
Marsden V (2005) Recent developments in network measurement, loc. 148. In: Carrington P, Scott J, Wasserman S (eds) Models and methods in social network analysis. Cambridge University Press (Kindle Edition), New York

Maskin E (2005) On the rationale for penalty default rules. In: Update version of the keynote presented at the "Symposium on Default Rules in Private and Public Law,". Florida State University College of Law, March 25, 2005, pp 1–11. https://www.sss.ias.edu/files/papers/econpaper58.pdf. Accessed 10 May 2019
McCall J (2010) The honeybee as teacher. In: Zambelli S (ed) Computable, constructive and behavioral economic dynamics, Essays in Honor of Kumaraswamy (Vela) Velupillai. Routledge, London, pp 166–167
McCloskey D (1998) Other things equal: the so-called Coase Theorem. East Econ J 24(3):367–371
Medema S (2010) Adam Smith and the Chicago School. In: Emmett R (ed) The elgar companion to the Chicago School of economics. Edward Elgar Publishing, Cheltenham, pp 46–48
Medema S (2015) From dismal to dominance? Law and economics and the values of imperial science, historically contemplated. In: Hatzis A, Mercuro N (eds) Law and economics: philosophical issues and fundamental questions. Routledge, Oxon, pp 70–74
Mercuro N, Medema S (1995) Schools of thought in law and economics: a *Kuhnian* competition. In: Malloy R, Braum C (eds) Law and economics: new and critical perspectives, vol 4. Peter Lang, New York, p 101
Mercuro N, Medema S (1997) Economics and the law: from posner to post-modernism. Princeton University Press, Princeton, pp 51–54
Miceli T (1997) Economics of the law: torts, contracts, property. Oxford University Press, Oxford, Litigation
Miceli T (2004) The economic approach to law. Stanford economics and finance. Stanford University Press, Stanford, pp 2–3
Michie J (ed) (2000) Reader's guide to the social science, vol 1. Routledge, London, p 117
Moran E, Ostrom E (eds) (2005) Seeing the forest and the trees: human-environment interactions in forest ecosystems. The MIT Press, Cambridge
Naughton J (2013a) Coase idea explains internet economics. The Japan Times. http://www.japantimes.co.jp/life/2013/09/10/digital/coase-idea-explains-interneteconomics/#.VEiNFtwxHFJ. Accessed 10 May 2019
Naughton J (2013b) How a 1930s theory explains the economics of the internet. The Guardian. http://www.theguardian.com/technology/2013/sep/08/1930s-theory-explains-economics-internet. Accessed 10 May 2019
Nerlove M, Razin A, Sadka E (1987) Household and economy: welfare economics of endogenous fertility. Economic theory, econometrics, and mathematical economics. Academic Press Inc., Orlando, pp 38–39
Newmark C (ed) (2009) Reading in applied microeconomics: the power of the market. Routledge, London, pp 195 *et seq*
Nicholson W, Snyde C (2010) Intermediate microeconomics and its application. Cengage Learning, Mason, pp 598–599
Noll J (2005) Rechtsökonomie: Eine anwendungsorientierte Einführung. Verlag Österreich, Vienna, p 21
OECD (2004) Declaration on access to research data from public funding. C (2004)31/REV1. http://acts.oecd.org/Instruments/ShowInstrumentView.aspx?InstrumentID=157. Accessed 10 May 2019
OECD (2006) Recommendation of the council concerning access to research data from public funding, 184. http://acts.oecd.org/Instruments/ShowInstrumentView.aspx?InstrumentID=159. Accessed 10 May 2019
OECD (2015) Data-driven innovation: big data for growth and well-being. OECD Publishing, Paris, pp 187–188
Oppenheimer M, Mercuro N (2004) Law and economics: alternatives economic approaches to legal and regulatory issues. Routledge, New York, p 3
Ostrom E (1990) Governing the commons: the evolution of institutions for collective action (Political Economy of Institutions and Decisions). Cambridge University Press, Cambridge
Ostrom E (2000) Reformulating the commons. Swiss Polit Sci Rev 6(1):29–52

Ostrom E (2009) A general framework for analyzing sustainability of social-ecological systems. Science 325:419–421
Ostrom E et al (1999) Revisiting the commons: local lessons, global challenges. Science 284(5412):278–282
Özyer T et al (eds) (2013) The influence of technology on social network analysis and mining, loc. 49. Springer, Vienna
Parisi F (2004) Positive, normative and functional schools in law and economics. Eur J Law Econ 18(3):259–272
Perkins A (2010) Property rights to information in the cloud–cloud based view on the Coase Theorem. http://cloud81.com/2010/11/21/property-rights-to-information-in-the-cloud-a-cloud-based-view-on-the-coase-theorem/. Accessed 10 May 2019
Peterson E (2009) A billion dollars a day: the economics and politics of agricultural subsidies. Wiley, Chichester, p 30
Pierce R (1995) A comment on "Imperfect Alternatives: Choosing Institutions in Law, Economics, and Public Policy". Calif Law Rev 83(3):941–951
Pigou C (1932) The economics of welfare, 4th edn. Mc Millan and Co., London
Pinheiro C (2011) Social network analysis in telecommunications, locs., 205, 221 and 220. Wiley (Kindle Edition), Hoboken
Posner R (1983) The economics of justice. Harvard University Press, Cambridge, p 4
Posner R (1998) Economic analysis of law, 5th edn. Aspen Publishers Inc., New York
Posner E (2003) Economic analysis of contract law after three decades: success or failure? Yale Law J 112(829). http://www.law.uchicago.edu/files/files/146.EAP_.Con-tractLaw.pdf. Accessed 10 May 2019
Posner E (2005) There are no penalty default rules in contract law, pp 1–34. http://www.law.uchicago.edu/files/files/237.eap_.default-rules.pdf. Accessed 10 May 2019
Posner R, Parisi F (eds) (2003) The economic foundations of private law. Elgar critical writings reader. Edward Elgar Publishing, Cheltenham
Prell C (2012) Social network analysis: history, theory and methodology. Sage Publications, London, pp 1–10
Pryke S (2012) Social network analysis in construction. Wiley, Oxford, pp 87, 228
Purnhagen K, Rott P (eds) (2014) Varieties in European economic law and regulation. Liber Amicorum for Hans Micklitz, Studies in European economic law and regulation 3. Springer, Cham, p 833
Reder M (1982) Chicago economics: permanence and change. J Econ Lit 20:6
Rees S, Gallagher K (2013) Detection via merged friendship-groups, loc. 737. In: Özyer T et al (eds) The influence of technology on social network analysis and mining. Springer, Vienna
Richardson M, Hadfield G (eds) (1999) The second wave of law and economics. The Federation Press, Leichhardt, p 34
Riis T, Nielsen R (eds) (1998) Law and economics: methodology and application. DJOF Publishing, Copenhagen
Rittich K (2002) *Recharacterizing restructuring: law, distribution and gender in market reform.* The Erik Castren Institute of international law and human rights. Kluwer Law International, The Hague, p. 138
Rose C (1986) The comedy of the commons: commerce, custom, and inherently public property. Faculty scholarship series, Paper 1828. http://digitalcommons.law.yale.edu/fss_papers/1828. Accessed 10 May 2019
Rose F (1999) Information age economy: the economics, concept, and design of information intermediaries. Physica-Verlag, Heidelberg, p 64
Rutherford D (2013) Routledge dictionary of economics, "externality", 3rd edn. Routledge, London, p 603
Samuels W, Schmid A (eds) (1981) Law and economics: an institutional perspective. Martinus Nijhoff Publishing, Boston

Sandeen S (2010) The value of irrationality in the IP equation. In: Flanagan A, Montagnani M (eds) Intellectual property law: economic and social justice perspectives. Edward Elgar Publishing, Cheltenham, p 47
Sandel M (2010) Justice–what's the right thing to do. Farrar, Straus and Giroux, New York, p 23
Sandler T (2001) Economic concepts for the social sciences. Cambridge University Press, Cambridge, pp 65–67
Schlag P (1989) The problem of transaction costs. South Calif Law Rev 62:1662–1700
Schmalbeck R (1983) The justice of economics: an analysis of wealth maximization as a normative goal. Columbia Law Rev 83:491
Schmidtchen D (2009) Transport, welfare and externalities: replacing the polluter pays principle with the cheapest cost avoider principle. New horizons in law and economics. Edward Elgar Publishing, Cheltenham, p 32
Schrammel T (2010) SME market entry in transition economies: the potential of cluster initiatives to fill institutional voids. In: Kakouris A (ed) Proceedings of the 5th European conference on innovation and entrepreneurship, ECIE 2010. University of Athens, Greece, p 508
Schrammel T (2014) Clusters as an instrument to bridge institutional voids in transition economies: lessons learned from southeast Europe. Springer Gabler, Wiesbaden, p 203
Smith A (1776) An inquiry into the nature and causes of the wealth of nations. Printed for W. Strahan and T. Cadell, London
Sodeur W, Taube V (2008) The flow of information in evolving social groups. In: Friemel T (ed) Why context matters: applications of social network analysis, 1st edn. VS Research, Wiesbaden, p 100
Stray Ryssdal A (1995) Legal realism and economics as behaviour: a scandinavian look at economic analysis of law. Juridisk Forlag AS, Oslo
Sutherland K (ed) (1993) Adam smith wealth of nations. Oxford University Press, Oxford
Teramoto S (2013) Sociomatrix, lecture notes taken during the Contemporary Issues of Intellectual Property Law course at the LL.M. Program in International Economic and Business Law (IEBL), Kyushu University, 23 Oct 2013
Teramoto S, Jurčys P (2014) Intermediaries, trust and efficiency of communication: a social network perspective. In: Fenwick M, van Uytsel S, Wrbka S (eds) Networked governance, Transnational business and the law. Springer, Berlin, pp 116–119
Tsvetovat M, Kouznetsov A (2011) Social network analysis for startups: finding connections on the social web O'Reilly, Sebastopol, pp 4, 19
Veljanovski C (1982) The new law-and-economics: a research review. Center for Socio-Legal Studies, Oxford
Veljanovski C (1990) The economics of law: an introductory text. The Institute of Economics Affair, London, p 34
Ver Eecke W (2008) Ethical dimensions of the economy: making use of hegel and the concepts of public and merit goods. Springer, Berlin, p 65
Wall D (2014) The sustainable economics of Elinor Ostrom: commons, contestation and craft, Routledge studies in ecological economics. Routledge, London, p 89
Warren A (2006) The inverse commons–a discontinuity in business models. The Farrell center for corporate innovation and entrepreneurship, Smeal College of Business, Penn State University, p 1. http://www.smeal.psu.edu/fcfe/more/white/in-vercom.pdf. Accessed 10 May 2019
Wasserman S, Faust K (2009) Social networks analysis: methods and applications, locs. 817, 1062. Cambridge University Press (Kindle Edition), New York
Weigel W (2008) Economics of the law: a primer. Routledge advanced texts in economics and finance. Routledge, London, p 44
Williamson O (1975) Markets and hierarchies: analysis and antitrust implications. Free Press, New York
Williamson O (1981a) The economics of organization: the transaction cost approach. Am J Sociol 87(3):548–577

Williamson O (1981b) Contract analysis: the transaction cost approach. In: Burrows P, Veljanovski C (eds) The economic approach to law. Butterworths, London, p 41
Williamson O (1985) The economic institutions of capitalism: firms, market, relational contracting. The Free Press, New York, p 16
Williamson O (1993) Transaction cost economics meets posnerian law and economics. J Inst Theor Econ (JITE) 149(1):99–118
Williamson O (1996) The mechanism of governance. Oxford University Press, New York
Williamson O (2002) The theory of the firm as governance structure: from choice to contract. J Econ Perspect 16(3):171–195
Yahklef A (2000) The internet as an opportunity to rethink the role of the intermediary. Consum Mark Cult 4(1):39–55
Zerbe R (2001) Economic efficiency in law and economics. Edward Elgar Publishing, Cheltenham, p 8

Part II
A New Theoretical Framework

Chapter 5
Plan-Like Architectures

"*We are all planning creatures*" (Bratman 2001, p. 203).

5.1 Introduction

After the previous considerations based on the economic analysis of law, the backbone of the theoretical framework of this work is substantiated in the theory submitted by Scott Shapiro in his book *Legality* (2011) where he adopts Michael Bratman's suggestion that we are all "planning agents."[1] By and large, this tenet refers to the collective intentions of people while carrying out a task together and is approached from both a psychological and normative perspective. The second main theory is grounded in the Lessig[2] approach that sees the code of computing architectures as a "constraint" and therefore as the main regulator. The way I conceive this model lies in between these two relevant theories and can be implemented and adjusted to the SLA frameworks of cloud and Big Data services.

This chapter is divided into five sections. Section 5.2 explains the rationale behind Plan Theory. This section is broken down into three parts. The first part introduces Plan Theory and discusses how can this be extended to larger groups of participants. The second part contextualizes and justifies the importance of Plan Theory for scaling up its implementation in the cloud. The third part examines how Shapiro sees norms as plans, or what he calls "plan-like norms," because they operate in the same way plans normally do. Section 5.3 combines the two approaches (Shapiro's "plan-like norms" and Lessig's approach). It is essentially at the juncture of these two theories

[1]Shapiro (2011, p. 120).

[2]Lessig (1998, pp. 661–691).

M. Corrales Compagnucci, *Big Data, Databases and "Ownership" Rights in the Cloud*, Perspectives in Law, Business and Innovation,
https://doi.org/10.1007/978-981-15-0349-8_5

where the main theoretical argument of this chapter lies. Finally, Sect. 5.4 concludes with the first part of the theoretical framework that I call *Plan-like Architectures*.

5.2 Plan Theory: We Are All Planning Agents

According to the approach of Bratman,[3] one of the unique characteristics of human conduct is the capacity to act together and share our intentions in cooperative ways. This is related to the necessity of guidance and coordination in order to achieve our goals and fulfill our desires. He introduced the notion of plans as a critical response to the "desire-belief" model that relates the intention of agents to certain desires and beliefs.[4]

Proponents who defend this theory[5] reduce the intention of human agency to a cluster of desires and beliefs. This is, however, a misleading approach. For Bratman, "we are planning creatures. We frequently settle in advance on plans for the future."[6] Oftentimes, we need to decide on different choices that are equally attractive and engaging to realize our desires and beliefs. We also direct our intentions to achieve larger plans.

Therefore, planning activity helps us to coordinate different kinds of tasks and achieve complex future goals over time vis-à-vis others.[7] Bratman developed a methodological planning theory that sees intention as a central notion to characterize peoples' actions and their states of mind.[8]

The relation between intention and intentional action, and the differentiation between intended and expected effects of one's intention, is fundamental for two main reasons. First, they are inextricably intertwined to various human emotions, moral attitudes and legal institutions. Second, such a portrayal can help us to understand, predict and coordinate human intra-personal and inter-personal activities.[9]

As we are rational agents (at least to some extent), we tend to do things purposively and deliberately. This indicates careful consideration and conscious intention that shapes the nature and future effects of our action plan. However, since deliberation takes time, effort and other limited resources, we need the appropriate mechanisms to allow deliberation to affect the present and influence the future. This leads us directly to the need for coordination mentioned before. This latter characterization

[3]Michael Bratman is a Professor in the Department of Philosophy at Stanford University. His work focuses on moral philosophy and the philosophy of action including many issues related to human agency and practical reason.

[4]Bratman (1984, pp. 375–405).

[5]See Audi (1973, pp. 387-403), Beardsley (1978), Churchland (1970, pp. 214–236).

[6]Bratman (1984, pp. 375–376).

[7]Bratman (1984, pp. 379–380).

[8]Velleman (1991, p. 277).

[9]Bratman (1999, pp. 1–2).

is what allows us to construct larger plans[10] from individual "micro" planning to a broader and collective "massive" macro planning.[11]

Consider the example of two friends who share the same intention of painting a house together. One of the main roles of the shared intention is to help the two individuals to coordinate their activities. There will be a bargaining of the means of how to successfully execute their plan. For instance, they will have to coordinate who is bringing the painting equipment (paints, brushes, paint strippers, ladder, etc.), then they will have to negotiate who is painting the bedroom, the living room, etc.[12]

This does not mean that plans are "once and for all."[13] They are not absolute, decisive and conclusive. This means that they are "revocable."[14] To quote Bratman, "such total plans are obviously beyond our limits. Rather, we typically settle on plans that are partial and then fill them in as need be and as time goes by."[15] Phrased differently, this means that plans are, in principle, incomplete. This incompleteness is of utmost importance for it takes the reasoning characteristics of the agents to start with a partial, or initial plan, as a first step. Then it requires a detailed plan to fill in as a more specific course of action.[16] Following the painting example given above, consider that the two friends realized that they did not achieve the expected color tone. To correct the problem, they can remove the paint, mix the paint with water to make it thinner or more transparent, and repaint the house with the new color blend.

Traditional views of law and economics tend to exhibit an archetype based on the forms of utilitarian "desire-belief"[17] models of human action. Nevertheless, this view is not always true. What is interesting about Bratman's thesis is that it goes beyond models that seem to overlook these complex realities[18] where intentions play a central role. Intentions are, for Bratman, "typically elements in the coordinating of plans: as such, intentions are distinctive states of mind, not to be reduced to clusters of desires and beliefs."[19] In order to understand intentions, we must understand the complex relationship between individual commitment and its cross-temporal functionality in cooperation with others.[20] These ideas are expounded below.

---

[10] Bratman (1999, pp. 2–3).

[11] Canale (2013, p. 19).

[12] Alonso (2008, p. 78).

[13] Bratman (1999, p. 3).

[14] O'Hagan (2001, p. 393).

[15] Bratman (1999, p. 3).

[16] Mohan (1990, p. 89).

[17] See Fischer (2005, p. 217) (ed).

[18] Mohan (1990, pp. 89–90).

[19] Bratman (1999, p. 3).

[20] O'Hagan (2001, p. 393).

5.2.1 Shared Agency Theory: From Individual Plans to Joint Plans

In his work titled, *Shared Agency: A Planning Theory of Acting Together* (2014), Bratman presented a full and updated version of his planning theory that started in 1987 with *Intentions, Plans, and Practical Reason.*[21] In this new book, he turns to a follow-up question: "What happens to our understanding of small-scale cases of acting together…when we take seriously the planning theory of our individual agency?"[22] This question is demonstrated in very simple examples that pervade our daily lives, such as walking with a friend, dancing together with a partner, conversing with a friend, singing in a duo with another person, painting a house together with someone and performing an experiment together with a colleague.[23]

Let us take the first example of walking down the streets in a crowded city. This takes a lot of coordination and responsiveness in order to avoid colliding with people. Walking around many people is, however, not the same as walking with someone, as you would a friend. That is, there is a big difference between walking alongside others and walking *together* with somebody. If these activities are performed alone, they involve intention and some sort of coordinated action is required as mentioned before. Nevertheless, if such activities are performed in tandem with another person, they involve something more likely referred to as a "shared intention" or "joint intention."[24]

Such activities can take place in large groups of people and can be performed at an institutional level in businesses, corporations or legal systems. However, to make things less complicated, I will refer in this section to what Bratman calls "Shared Cooperation Activity" (SCA) as having only two individual agents and no hierarchical relationship. For an SCA to take place, there is a need for a mutual response to each other's intention and action. There is also a need to form a common goal despite the different reasons for the achievement of such a goal.[25] A number of prominent philosophers have theorized about this subject and suggested that there is a new fundamental element introduced when you move from the individual case to a shared activity. The remaining of this section briefly describes the general features that are useful for our discussion.

According to John Searle[26] and Margaret Gilbert,[27] there is something that goes beyond a simple strategic equilibrium in cases of modest sociality. In Searle's opinion, there is a distinction between an "I-intention" and "we-intention" attitude that cannot

---

[21] Tuomela (2014).

[22] Bratman (2014a).

[23] Bratman (2014a), Westerlund (2015, pp. 822–836).

[24] Bratman (2013, 2014b).

[25] Bratman (1992, pp. 327–331).

[26] See, generally, Searle (1983, 1995).

[27] See, generally, Gilbert (2006).

be reduced to a sum of individual intentions.[28] This extra and foreign element suggests there is a kind of metaphysical and conceptual discontinuity as this represents a new concept and a specific mental state.[29]

In the same vein of reasoning, in Gilbert's point of view, there is also something fundamentally new. In her opinion, however, it is not a new state of mind but the establishment of a "joint commitment" primitive relationship that involves "distinctive mutual obligations" between the participants.[30] What is interesting about Gilbert's position is that she takes a normative approach (as in contract theory) in contrast to Bratman who takes a descriptive perspective. Gilbert uses the abovementioned walking example (shared action) to put her theory in simple terms to explain how people may enter, continue and leave acts of collective intentionality.[31]

In her account, those people walking alongside each other constitute the "plural subject" of a goal. Therefore, the fundamental conditions for collective conditions to exist are the following: (i) Consent in the formation of the agreement, i.e., people must be fully aware they are entering into an agreement. This agreement is sufficient to establish a group goal; (ii) Obligation: this agreement creates "obligations" among group members in order to achieve the final goal; (iii) "Right to rebuke": this obligation creates a necessary right to rebuke, which endows any member of the group with a tool to make sure the goal is achieved[32]; and (iv) Consent in the revocation of the agreement: there must be a joint consent among the group members in order to cancel the agreement.[33] Gilbert argues that the element missing in Searle's account is the previous agreement among the participants, and only if this requirement is met does it generate the obligations in the sort of "we-intention" model submitted by him. According to Gilbert, intentions cannot be made in terms of purely internal mind-states as Searle has suggested, but rather this has to take an external form for the parties to reach an agreement.[34]

Both philosophers (Searle and Gilbert) attempted to explain the planning theory within the scope of larger institutions taking into account these new elements. The central idea is that once we add this new structure of either "we intention" or "joint commitment," we pave the road for a whole new theory of thinking and acting together.[35] Contrary to this view, Bratman is resistant to introducing a distinctive new element of the human mind. He believes there is no need to introduce new features when moving from the individual to the shared case. The reason for that is

---

[28]Searle (2010, pp. 46–47), Searle (1990, pp. 401–416).

[29]Bratman (2013, 2014b).

[30]Bratman (2013, 2014a, b).

[31]Gilbert (1990, pp. 1–14).

[32]If you fail to give me what I have a right to through your promise, I have the standing, as your promise, to rebuke you on that account. Similarly, should you threaten to break your promise, I have the standing, as your promise, to command or insist that you act as promised, and thus pressure you to perform." The work of Margaret Gilbert, see Owens (2012, p. 50).

[33]Gilbert (2007, pp. 31–49), Gilbert (2000), But see Sheeney (2002, pp. 377–394).

[34]Gilbert (2007, pp. 31–49).

[35]Bratman (2013, 2014b).

what is known in Philosophy as "Ockham's Razor", also known as lex parsimoniae (the "law of parsimony"), which means that in the presence of several competing hypotheses—that lead to the same result—the one with the fewest assumptions should be chosen.[36]

He suggests following the "strategy of sufficiency" by taking into account the basic resources available in the planning theory and how these elements fit together to build up a model of shared intention. This construction provides sufficient conditions for a solid form of shared intentional activity. Once the individual planning agency theory has been pre-established, the same principles can be applied as an extension to larger groups of participants and institutions (i.e., to small-scale shared agency phenomena or so-called "modest sociality"). This is what Bratman calls the "continuity thesis." The eclectic position that Bratman seeks goes beyond the desire-belief model mentioned before and the associated models known in some other areas of social science.[37] This approach expands the individual planning agency by emphasizing special characteristics and interrelations between individual agents and their plans.[38]

In this approach, the intention of individuals is a fundamental element that goes beyond the bounds of such desires and beliefs typical of those traditional agency models. As Bratman has remarked, "such intentions are embedded in coordinating plans that play basic roles in the temporally extended structures that are characteristic of individual human agency."[39] The intentions of individuals are "plan states." For this plan to work, one needs to organize and coordinate such course of action in the present looking into the future.[40] Due to the resource-limited agency of individuals, these tend to be partial plans that need to be completed as time goes by.[41]

Human interaction needs very complex and delicate organizations that allow us to engage in these kinds of "cross-temporal" activities. Let us come back to the painting example. When the two friends make a plan to paint the house on the weekend, it would make no sense to try to fill in all the details at once. In this case, they would probably arrange to meet at a particular time. Additionally, they could agree and coordinate the color they want to paint the house. Depending on their skills and expertise they may also coordinate whether to use a specific paint material or a more complex refinishing system, which would largely depend on the amount and quality of the solvents per liter of paint used, but it would be very difficult to have the whole plan organized in advance. For example, they could also schedule to have lunch or take a coffee break when they feel hungry or tired. What happens in reality is that we conceive a general idea and then we set up a "partial" plan that will be filled in later.[42]

---

[36] Bratman (2013, 2014b).

[37] See, generally, Wend (1975) (ed).

[38] Bratman (2014a, pp. 10–11).

[39] Bratman (2014a, p. 11).

[40] Bratman (2014a, p. 15).

[41] Bratman (2013, 2014a).

[42] Bratman (2013, 2014b).

This is the reason why intentions are at the heart of this discussion. Intentions are plan-states that play a systematic role in supporting the "diaconic" organization of activities. We said that these plan-states are partial and that we can fill them in later. The inevitable question that arises here is how do we fill them in as time goes by? The answer is very simple. In planning (or intending), we have a range of different options. Sometimes these options are overlapping and we have to make a conclusive decision. Therefore, we settle on a particular option in a way that has stability over time and this is how the planning activity supports the organization over time. Furthermore, we can always draw on what Herbert Simons refers to as "resourcefulness." This partiality is thus grounded in the resourcefulness capacity of human agents that can refine or adjust their plans at a future stage.[43]

Finally, plans also *constrain* your thinking. They do what Bratman calls "filter multiple options." Let us come back again to the painting example. Consider now that the plan of painting the house together overlaps with another family commitment. That previous plan to do something with your family imposes a constraint on painting the house with a friend. Therefore, the only solution would be to postpone the painting activity to the following weekend. What plans do in these kinds of situations is that they not only pose problems but they filter possible solutions to the problems in order to ensure that plans *fit* together.[44]

Admittedly, this theory has some limitations. The first problem is that Bratman's continuity thesis does not cover larger and more complex organizational structures like corporations and institutions, as they are asymmetric and do not form part of the "modest sociality."[45] Nonetheless, Bratman has also hinted elsewhere that these kinds of planning structures can be applied and expanded to other fields of work and that there will be plenty of room in the shed to articulate a range of ideas associated with this theoretical investigation.[46] As far as this book is concerned, my pursuit in this chapter is to contribute to such debate and reflect that such basic philosophical conceptualization can be incorporated into more complex legal institutional frameworks, including cloud computing and Big Data transformations.

This is connected to the fact raised by James Coleman in his work on sociological theory entitled, *Foundations of Social Theory*,[47] where he elaborated on rational choice theories and extended them to more complex forms of social phenomena such as private and public organizations. Coleman demonstrated the links between individual rational choices with a much broader sociological conception of collective decision-making that extends towards the society as a whole.[48]

---

[43]Bratman (2013, 2014b).

[44]Bratman (2013, 2014b).

[45]According to Bratman: "The limitation is that my focus will be primarily on the shared intentional activities of small, adult groups in the absence of asymmetric authority relations within those groups, and in which the individuals who are participants remain constant over time." See Bratman (2014a, p. 7).

[46]Bratman (2014a, p. 8).

[47]See, generally, Coleman (1998).

[48]Coleman (1988, 1998, pp. 95–120).

5.2.2 *Laws Are Plans*

On the basis of this foregoing reconstruction, Scott Shapiro in his latest book *Legality* provides a good insight into the legal theory landscape and critically revisits the works of the most prominent contemporary legal theorists such as Herbert L. A. Hart,[49] Ronald Dworkin[50] and John Austin.[51] He starts by distinguishing between legal facts (dependent on other facts) and ultimate facts, and he uses this comparison as a heuristic device to answer the fundamental questions about the nature of the law by employing a method that he refers to as "conceptual analysis."[52] Shapiro borrows Bratman's thesis and seems to follow the Yale school of normative law and economics, which is also very critical to these kinds of "desire-belief" models. He puts forward a novel contribution to analytical legal positivism that categorizes "plans" as a kind of norm or "plan-like norms."[53]

Shapiro applies an analytical legal positivist methodology in the sense that he takes a neutral and independent stance with regards to the moral aims and principles that govern any given area of law.[54] The overarching idea that underlies this theory is that the law is tantamount to a plan. The legal activity is an enterprise of social planning.[55] The way to interpret the law, therefore, is equivalent to the way we interpret a plan. Thus, the legal system of a state is a very complicated and sophisticated structure that creates different types of plans that can be determined by the constitution as a "master plan."[56]

He focuses on the fact that a considerable amount of life's activities involve planning that guides us through the achievement of our goals and he explains the reasons why and how the law can assist and monitor human behavior by means of the concept of a plan. He sees the legal activity as a kind of "institutionalized social planning,"[57] whose aim is to compensate for the dearth of other forms of planning in order to clear up doubts and solve disagreements about the moral issues that we find in our communal life.[58]

---

[49] See, generally, Hart (1997).

[50] See, generally, Dworkin (1986).

[51] See, generally, Austin (1832, 1869).

[52] Shapiro (2011, pp. 12–13).

[53] Shapiro (2011, pp. 118 et seq).

[54] Stone (2011, p. 7). Stone actually believes that Plan Theory does not pertain only to the field of analytical legal positivism, but rather extends and even thrives in the context of natural law. For a full recount of positivism and the separation of law and morals, see Hart (1958, pp. 593–629).

[55] Shapiro (2011, p. 195).

[56] Shapiro (2011, pp. 205, 179 et seq).

[57] Shapiro (2011, p. 168).

[58] See, generally, Canale (2013, pp. 1–126).

The very nature of the law is to resolve these fundamental issues.[59] According to Shapiro, plans reduce and mitigate deliberation[60] and bargaining costs[61] under "circumstances of legality," such as in cases of uncertainty when society faces moral problems whose solutions are deemed to be complex, contentious and arbitrary.[62]

The value of planning stems also from its ability to coordinate the participants.[63] This view, in my opinion, dovetails with most law and economics paradigms discussed earlier in the previous chapter. The most fundamental premises of law and economics posit that forward thinking towards the identification of correct social welfare is key to the elaboration of law as well as the public policy mechanisms that incentivize all relevant actors. In this sense, Shapiro's Plan Theory is particularly relevant as he carefully examines the patterns of the relations among individuals in a society and establishes a similitude with the legal system consisting of planners, plan adopters and plan appliers.[64]

5.2.3 Simple Logic of Planning

Shapiro is perfectly aware that he needs to submit a solid theory of legal interpretation (meta-interpretive theory) that sustains his central thesis that the law is like a plan.[65] The term meta-interpretive stands for the different and most effective ways the interpreter seeks to understand the true intent (the true meaning) of the law. For example, legal texts should be read literally, purposively,[66] historically,[67] and comparatively.[68] This implies that the interpreter must choose among the different alternatives that can be combined with many other methods of interpretation.

Therefore, in Shapiro's enterprise, the way to interpret the law is very simple and straightforward, as it is exactly in the same way one interprets a plan.[69] How we interpret a plan is what Shapiro uses to explain his general theory of legal interpretation, which should contain the following factors: (i) the aim of the plan, (ii) the values it attempts to achieve, and (iii) the relation of *trust* between the planners and actors of the plan. This means that the legal system is not only an institution based on

[59]Shapiro (2011, p. 309).

[60]Shapiro (2011, pp. 124, 140).

[61]Shapiro (2011, pp. 139, 200, 275).

[62]Shapiro (2011, pp. 170–173, 213–214, 217, 309, 312, 337–339, 348).

[63]Shapiro (2011, p. 134).

[64]Shapiro (2011, pp. 118 et seq).

[65]Pino (2013, pp. 187–188).

[66]Ferrer Beltran and Ratti (2013, p. 182).

[67]See, generally, Easterbrook (1994, pp. 61–70).

[68]See, generally, Murray, Methods of Interpretation: Comparative Law Method, Report of Mr. Justice John Murray, President of the Supreme Court and Chief Justice of Ireland, Actes du colloque pour le cinquantiéme anniversaire des Traité de Rome, pp. 39–47.

[69]Pino (2013), Chap. 9 with further references.

power but also endowed with a level of trust between public officials and citizens.[70] The topic of trust certainly deserves further exposition. For this reason, I devote the whole next chapter to appropriately contextualizing the concept of trust.

Shapiro consistently argues with potential rivals, such as the proponents of the Dworkinian interpretive system, who reject the whole institutional framework of legal positivism. The Dworkin famous dictum, "lawyers are always philosophers,"[71] suggests that jurisprudence is always part of any lawyer's interpretation of the law. According to Dworkin, the only way to interpret and discover the content of the law is by invoking its moral and philosophical aims. Dworkin's conjecture is that the work of the legislator is comparable to the work of an artist who creates a great piece of art that reflects the best effort the artist can do. This determines the best outcome result and this is what he calls the "best-lights" analysis.[72]

Another pragmatic analysis of Dworkin operates from the assumption that the law should be interpreted like a "chain novel" or the script of a screenplay like in a soap opera. By drawing parallels between literary and judicial legal interpretation,[73] the point of comparison of Dworkin's "chain novel" metaphor[74] is that the interpretation of the law is always like a work in progress.[75] As an open narrative in a book in which each author takes the story where the other left it. The interpreters must take the story as it is and become acquainted with the main events of the plot, characters, themes, genre and previous arguments. Then they must follow-up the development of the storyline in order to find a solution from their own angle and perceptions. The overall purpose of legal theory is to provide a logical and well-organized explanation and justification.[76] There is no discontinuity or lacunas in the law even in what he refers to as the "hard cases," which are cases where the interpreter faces ambiguous linguistic expressions without legal precedents.[77]

Conversely, Shapiro contends that Dworkin's theory endorses a meta-interpretive practice which "defeats the very purpose of law."[78] Drawing from what he calls the "Simple Logic of Planning" (SLOP) , he makes sweeping assumptions that the "content of laws," inasmuch as they are equally comparable to plans, must be interpreted in a way that does not depend upon the resolution of problems that laws are meant to resolve.[79] In order to avoid getting lost in philosophical and moral abstractions,

[70] Pino (2013), Chap. 9 with further references, Shapiro (2011, pp. 335 et seq).

[71] Dworkin (1986, p. 380).

[72] Dworkin (1986, p. 308).

[73] Dworkin (1982, p. 182, 1996a, pp. 29–46), Levinson and Mailloux (1991, p. 271) (eds).

[74] Samuel (2013, p. 102).

[75] Bontekoe (2004, p. 24).

[76] Dworkin suggested that "judges are like authors jointly creating a chain novel in which each writes a chapter that makes sense as part of the story as a whole." For an in-depth rundown see Dworkin (1996b, p. 10). For a better treatment see also Wacks (2015, p. 147, 2014, p. 59), Culver (1999, p. 183) (ed), Samuel (2014, p. 183), Berns (1993, p. 149), Darian-Smith (2013, pp. 136–137).

[77] Dworkin (1975, pp. 1057–1109).

[78] Shapiro (2011, p. 307).

[79] Shapiro (2011, p. 307).

Shapiro's proposal according to the SLOP principle is the following, "the existence and content of a plan cannot be determined by facts whose existence the plan aims to settle…".[80]

According to Shapiro, the most apparent problem with Dworkin's famous analysis submitted in *Law's Empire* is that the meta-interpreter must engage in a dual, unnecessarily philosophical, and somewhat difficult, abstract methodology that involves the combination of a "fit" criterion; and a "moral justification." The threshold of this system conveys the elaboration of a list of the potential routes of interpretation, each with its own moral and philosophical justifications. This process includes an extrapolation of the competing principles on a ranking system where the selection of the option with the highest rank is applied to the legal system in question.[81]

Shapiro objects that this system of interpretation is only possible for a trained and skilled lawyer or judge and suitable for trustworthy legal systems.[82] Shapiro's severe criticism to the Dworkinian interpretive system—where lawyers or judges have to scrutinize retrospectively a series of moral and philosophical questions—points to another important limitation: "Having to answer a series of moral questions is precisely the disease that the law aims to cure. Dworkinian legal interpretation thus ends up reinfecting the patient after the contagion has been neutralized."[83] He claims that this may be like opening "Pandora's box," where there is a risk of creating insurmountable new moral problems that open up the interpretation from the start.[84]

This brings to the forefront new moral issues and re-opens a debate that the law was supposed to dissipate in the first place.[85] Shapiro copes with these matters under the caption of the "General Logic of Plans" (GLOP) argument as follows: "the interpretation of any member of a system of plans cannot be determined by facts whose existence any member of that system aims to settle."[86] The main difference between the SLOP principle and the GLOP argument is that SLOP refers strictly to the content and existence of plans, whereas GLOP concerns to their interpretation: "GLOP applies to the interpretation of a plan that is an element of some larger system."[87] If necessary for such interpretation, this can result in the creation of a new plan. It could be said that GLOP looks at the broader spectrum of the plan. The central idea is that the interpretation of a plan should not lead the interpreter to "answer a question that another plan is supposed to answer."[88]

---

[80] Shapiro (2011, p. 278).

[81] Shapiro (2011, pp. 282–307).

[82] Shapiro (2011, pp. 282–307).

[83] Shapiro (2011, p. 310).

[84] Shapiro (2011, p. 348).

[85] Shapiro (2011, p. 348).

[86] Shapiro (2011, p. 311).

[87] Shapiro (2011, p. 311).

[88] Shapiro (2011, p. 311).

5.2.4 Exclusionary Reasons

According to the traditional view of law and economics, an individual has to balance the various reasons in order to make a decision. According to Joseph Raz, however, some reasons are "exclusionary."[89] As soon as we take that factor into consideration, we exclude all other reasons and follow a particular direction to the exclusionary reason. Raz's opinion is that the law or legal rules are exclusionary reasons. For example, if the law says that you have to drive on the left side of the road, you do not measure the benefits of driving on the right side. Therefore, the idea of the "plan-like norms" submitted by Shapiro is very similar to what Raz referred to as "exclusionary reason."[90] What Shapiro seems to be essentially saying is that you have to follow and simply "stick" to the plan and exclude other reasons, i.e., "to follow the plan blindly, without making any further deliberation."[91]

Nevertheless, in his own words, he expressly states that plans "lower deliberation costs and compensate for cognitive incapacities."[92] In another passage he mentions a cooking example, which is about a group of friends who decide to jointly establish a "cooking club." In the beginning, the organization of the cooking activities take a lot of time and logistic organizational resources, such as deciding the time, place, and what to cook (i.e., deliberation costs). Then, the members of the cooking club decide to take further steps to make their plan run more smoothly. For example, instead of discussing the recipes for every meeting they just follow the recipes published in the New York Times Wednesday edition. This is what Shapiro calls the creation of "policies" that serve as a general plan. These policies "radically cut down on our deliberation and bargaining costs."[93]

With a little hindsight, when Shapiro comes to the SLOP argument and critiques Dworkin's interpretive thesis, he seems to imply that plans completely "remove" deliberation costs and that plans cannot be revisited. I have some issues with this. There are potential tensions between the SLOP argument and what he mentions to be a tool to "reduce" deliberation that he seems to exclude the possibility of re-visiting the plan.

I remain skeptical of the idea that plans may completely eliminate deliberation costs. To recall the picture presented in the previous section and coming back to the painting example, the two friends did not achieve their desired color tone and decided to repaint the house. Bratman seems to be more flexible with the idea of plans. For Bratman, plans are not perennial, they are only partial plans that can be adjusted in the future. The idea of revisiting the plan in order to fix any problem seems to be incompatible with the idea of Shapiro's SLOP narrative. Nonetheless, this should not be a reason to completely do away with Plan Theory. My suggestion is to go

---

[89] See, generally, Raz (1999).

[90] See, generally, Shiner (2005, p. 57).

[91] Pino (2013, p. 191).

[92] Pino (2013, p. 134).

[93] Pino (2013, p. 139).

instead to the roots of Plan Theory and take Bratman's more flexible approach, as I will explain in the subsequent sections.

5.3 Plan Theory in the Cloud: Plan-Like Architectures

After laying out this general theory, it is important to pause here for a moment as several characteristics of human shared agency merit attention. The overall purpose of referring to Bratman's and Shapiro's work is to begin to gradually sketch out a theoretical analysis. This idea is the starting point for making a proposition that squares well with the claims I made before about other theories of law and economics. As a practical matter, one such point of departure is Bratman's observation that humans are all "planning creatures" as they are constantly and *intentionally* making plans. This can range from the simplest to the most complex and sophisticated plan that involves "joint" or "shared" plans with others.

The second point of departure is that laws are plans according to Shapiro's narrative. If these logical assumptions are correct, I suggest turning to the basics of Plan Theory and fully contemplating the elements of the situation resulting in cloud computing and Big Data transformations. There is no doubt in my mind that all the stakeholders involved in any kind of Internet activities (end-users, cloud providers and brokers) are considered to be planning agents. Surely, they all engage in the cloud as planners, plan adopters or plan appliers, even though they are not fully aware of it. Therefore, the main focus of this section is to propose a more adequate and integrated framework within which Plan Theory could be brought to cloud and Big Data transformations. This approach—*Plan-like Architectures*—is designed to reduce deliberation costs and improve coordination among participants. The principles of this framework can be better explained under three main headings, as set out below.

5.3.1 Brokers as Main Planners

First of all, this section discusses the issue of intermediation and the role of intermediaries that affect the legal environment through the innovation process and economic growth. Innovation intermediary is a school of thought in innovation studies that can help to understand the role of governments, commercial firms, agencies and individuals.[94] Innovation intermediaries have been variously referred to as "brokers," "bridgers," or "change agents," as they form the linchpin that facilitates user innovation and creativity.[95] They may be generically defined as "an organization that bridges the gap between organizers that seek solutions to an innovation problem and

[94]Howells (2006, pp. 715–728).

[95]Stewart and Hyysalo (2008, pp. 295–325).

innovators that can provide a solution to an organizer's problem."[96] The number of innovation intermediaries has risen in recent years since they play a vital role in the distribution of and access to complex networks.[97] Besides providing direct links between the actors involved, they ensure fluidity and support for accessing all innovation factors.[98]

This book brings together different school of thoughts about innovation intermediaries. The first stream is the "diffusion and technology transfer" literature, where intermediaries promote and expedite the diffusion of information and uptake of new products and services. In this field of knowledge, the role of intermediaries is also fundamental for the formation of alliances, facilitating relationships and informal group collaborations, providing negotiation skills and formalizing agreements.[99]

The second stream belongs to the "innovation management" literature, which suggests that intermediaries take a more active role beyond mere brokering or networking.[100] They could be described as "architects" with a strong influence and valuable role in the creation of knowledge in collaborative innovation.[101]

Finally, the third stream belongs to the "systems and networks" literature, which takes a much broader view on innovation intermediaries and suggests their strong influence as the new drivers of the overall innovation system and policy framework. This stream holds the view that intermediaries (or brokers) link the key players in the market by orchestrating the system on a much deeper and strategic level. They also build up-close interactions and continuous communication with their clients, producing high added value products and services.[102] The fundamental insight of these three streams is that by improving the resources and capabilities of the firms, innovation intermediaries are also facilitating market development, albeit indirectly.[103] The primary focus is on their core roles of configuring, managing and brokering new technologies[104] and services in emerging Internet trends.

The second aim of this section is to highlight the cognitive biases[105] of cloud end-users and the centrality of brokerage, which shows how Plan Theory connects to the need of brokers as main planners and organizers. Following the same line of thought, I argue that the cloud computing market is very complex and that the planning theory submitted by Shapiro could be applied in order to reduce deliberation and bargaining costs in circumstances of legality, in particular in SLAs where the end-users also face intricate, contentious and arbitrary issues. Some issues are intricate because most

[96] Hallersted (2013, p. 35).

[97] Osorio et al. (2012, p. 201), Antikainen (2011, p. 189).

[98] Nauwelaers (2011, p. 474).

[99] Hallersted (2013, p. 35).

[100] Hallersted (2013, p. 36).

[101] Agogue et al. (2012, pp. 1–31).

[102] Hallersted (2013, pp. 36–37).

[103] Dalziel and Parjanen (2012, p. 120).

[104] See Stewart and Hyysalo (2008, pp. 295–325).

[105] I will expound these thoughts in Chap. 7, which focuses on Behavioral Law and Economics and Nudge Theory.

end-users lack the technical expertise to understand the different choices provided in the cloud service. Furthermore, they also lack the legal and technical knowledge to negotiate the terms and conditions of the SLA. They can be contentious because the uncertainties swirling around the failure of cloud providers to assert end-users' rights may give rise to future disputes and controversies. And finally, arbitrary issues exist since most SLAs belong to the so-called "click-wrap" or "click-through" category where users have no possibility of bargaining.

As conceptualized within Plan Theory, we are constantly making plans. It is part of our daily life activity. It is also not necessary that we have to be authors of all the plans that affect us in order to enjoy the benefits of planning.[106] Recall the members of the "cooking club." Instead of creating their own recipes, they reduce deliberation costs with the help of a wide range of recipes available in the New York Times. These are the "policies" that serve as a general plan in Shapiro's narrative. Another essential premise of Plan Theory is that plans are made by officials to solve information and coordination problems. Nevertheless, as I have tried to argue in the previous chapter, government intervention is not always necessary. In some cases, we should, therefore, resort to liaison and coordination arrangements by cloud brokers to solve problems and reduce transactions costs. The value of cloud brokers is to provide such "policies" that aid the achievement of the general plan. These "policies" are set out in Part III of this work with the improved SLA template that the broker can bring to the negotiation table. The SLA template within the proposed new contractual framework in this book can work as "recipe" to reduce deliberation and bargaining costs, as in the "cooking club" example.

According to Bratman, plans are not only important in the cognitive process of human agency but they also *constrain* your thinking and *filter multiple options* in the future. The value of cloud brokers is to *filter* multiple cloud providers that do not meet the legal requirements based on end-user's input and criteria. Additionally, cloud brokers aim to reap all the advantages of cloud computing and Big Data services while reducing risks. The management and engineers of cloud computing service providers are expected to understand the risks and the risk assessment methods. The main problem is that one cannot assume that end-users or companies will recognize and understand fully the potential risks or implications. The main question is how to make them informed about these complex legal and technical issues? This is where the strategic role of innovation intermediary services can effectively scope and *plan* cloud computing and Big Data projects.

Cloud brokers can help to bridge the gap and fill that information as they have the capacity, experience and technical skills to help end-users understand the actions they need to take. They can also help to manage and reduce various types of (legal) risks. The legal risk assessment framework, which is carried out by the broker (see infra Chap. 9), is based on a systematic analysis of threats and vulnerabilities. This assessment is designed to cope with the issue of sudden changes in the main plan. Plan Theory suggests that plans are not perpetual, but they are partial plans that are constantly changing. They can be adjusted in the future. Therefore, the broker is in

[106]Bridgeman (2009, p. 343).

the position to make a re-assessment of the legal risks involved and re-visit the plan as time goes by.

5.3.2 Code and Architecture Design

Shapiro uses the term "norm" as in "plan-like norms" so "one can cast one's net as widely as possible."[107] This is the reason why I think Plan Theory should not be limited and pigeon-holed exclusively under a sub-category of norms, as Shapiro explains, but rather a somewhat more elusive interpretation would grasp this concept as an extension to the four different modalities submitted by Lawrence Lessig, in particular the "architecture" modality that he sees as a constraint. I argue that plans could also be grouped as a sub-category of the architecture, especially when it comes to the Internet environment. The claim I make here is that the "architectural design" of the SLAs offered by cloud providers should facilitate the means to establish such trust with the end-users.

This idea is based on the "New Chicago School" approach submitted by Lessig in various books, such as *Code Version 2.0*[108] and *Free Culture: The Nature and Future of Creativity,*[109] where he proposes four different modalities that he sees as constraints. These modalities are "laws, social norms, market and *architecture*."[110] Laws are rules that attempt to regulate behavior. They impose penalties or punishment for behavior that is deemed unacceptable by society. They may also incentivize positive behaviors that are judged to be helpful to society. Norms are similar to laws in the sense that they also impose a conduct, however, the mechanism varies in a way that it is not the state but the society or the members of a community who enforce the norm on each other. Both laws and norms are similar since the constraint is imposed after the infringement took place. The third modality is the "market" which sets, however, a monetary constraint through a pricing mechanism. The market constraint in this case—contrary to laws and norms—is concurrent to the benefit that is sought. If you pay the price for a cloud computing service, for instance, you may benefit from that service simultaneously to the exchange of the fee (constraint). This does not mean that cloud market transactions exist separately from laws and norms as these are all entrenched in one way or another.[111]

Finally, the fourth modality is "architecture," which is the most relevant for the discussion in this book. Lessig's view of architecture as a constraint is taken from real-life examples from the physical world. For instance, a fallen bridge[112] and door locks are physical constraints which hinder one's ability to go beyond a certain

[107] Shapiro (2011, p. 41).

[108] Lessig (2006, pp. 120–137), Appendix, pp. 340–345.

[109] Lessig (2004, pp. 121–173).

[110] Lessig (2006, p. 123).

[111] Lessig (2006, pp. 314–340).

[112] Lessig (2004, p. 122).

point.[113] In the field of cloud computing and Big Data, this would be like installing a "firewall," which is a network security system that blocks and monitors the traffic system based on the security configuration rules.[114] In this case, the firewalls are also set out as a constraint. Similar to the market modality, the architecture has a concurrent consequence and not aposteriori as in the law and norm modalities.

These four modalities are, however, interrelated and sometimes one of them prevails over the others. For example, a law may influence the architectural design of a highway by increasing the number of bumps and signposts in order to encourage drivers to reduce speed and drive more carefully. A law may also manipulate market behavior by imposing higher taxes on petrol to persuade car drivers to drive slowly, assuming that most car drivers are aware of the fact that high speed consumes more gasoline.[115]

Lessig's approach of these four modalities as a constraint stresses the paramount importance of the role the architecture plays. This approach clearly holds great analytical insights for lawyers since the central issue is how the computer "code" becomes a prime regulator in online business transactions.[116] According to Lessig, "...the question here is not how the architecture of the Net will make it easier for traditional regulation to happen. The issue here is how the architecture of the Net—or its 'code'—itself becomes a regulator."[117] As he puts it, they are self-executed due to their "automatic nature" contrary to the other three modalities such as laws, norms and markets.[118] This approach also resembles the Komesarian framework, where the "code" can be expanded to address an even wider range of legal phenomena by adding the architecture modality as an adjunct to the institutional choices. Cyberspace "has no nature" but rather "a function of its design, its code."[119]

In the same vein, I concur with Lessig's approach about the importance of architectures and how the *code* stands out, but with a few reservations and observations. While cloud architectures can be seen most of the times as a constraint—such as in the "firewall" example—they may also offer more choices in order to improve the quality of the contracts and reinvigorate cloud computing transactions. The idea I would like to convey is to inject Plan Theory along with its trust elements into the "architectural design" of SLAs. This will help to display the relevant legal requirements, incorporating various legal issues currently not present such as database rights and "ownership" rights of data. This will also help in choosing an adequate cloud provider and outsourcing data and databases in a more reliable and automated way. This information should then be used to automate the negotiation process between the cloud broker (i.e., the entity in charge of finding the appropriate cloud resource and deploying the application service) , end-users and cloud service providers.

---

[113] Lessig (2006, p. 341).

[114] Boudriga (2009, pp. 21–23); see also, generally, Zwicky et al. (2000).

[115] Lessig (2004, pp. 112–123).

[116] Lessig (2006, p. 81).

[117] Lessig (2006, p. 81).

[118] Lessig (2006, pp. 342–343), see also, generally, Reidenberg (1998, pp. 553–593).

[119] Lessig (2002, p. 121), Lessig (1999, pp. 501–546).

This is in line with the foundational principles of the "Privacy by Design" approach[120] and purports to implement this concept as an analogy to IPR. In other words, cloud service providers should embrace IPR "ownership" rights of data and databases as a default mode of operation. With this new concept, this book posits that similar parallelisms should be drawn from the Privacy by Design approach, and allow the cloud market to adopt this principle globally. I suggest that the design of cloud computing architectures should include more capabilities, to include the clarification of database rights and "ownership" rights of data, and, therefore, they should be embedded into its entire lifecycle, as explained in greater detail in Part III of this book. A well-designed architecture is only useful if it helps the involved parties make better decisions, which is necessary for developing a consistent and consolidated SLA framework.

The purpose of this chapter is to outline in greater detail the relationship between the two scholarships. In the case of "architectures" and "code," the crucial question is how to extend Plan Theory to make SLAs more flexible. It seems that Lessig's approach to architectures as constraint mechanisms is very similar to Shapiro's theory in the sense that computer code aims to remove choices. The relationship between the two theories is that the same tensions found in Shapiro's SLOP narrative may also be found in Lessig's approach if we take the architecture modality only as a constraint. Therefore, the architecture modality must not be interpreted literally otherwise the structure of the architecture design would be somehow constraining (and removing) the choice possibility.

This book, however, seeks to see architectures not only as a "constraint," but as a "choice" as I will argue in Chap. 7. As hinted earlier, my suggestion is to go instead to the roots of Plan Theory and take Bratman's more flexible approach. This allows us to draft a more flexible plan. This will make the extensions of Plan Theory to the law of contract more malleable and feasible. More specifically in pulling Plan Theory down to the more practical level, SLAs in the cloud should be capable of being revisited, easily modified and subject to re-negotiation. The schema I will present in Part III of this book will enable SLA re-negotiation through the extension of the Web Services Agreement Specification (WS-Agreement). WS-Agreement is a language and specification protocol developed by IBM for the creation of SLAs based on initial offers that enable monitoring of those offers at runtime.[121]

The definition of WS-Agreement protocol is very general and is not built to incorporate the various elements that must be taken into consideration. It contains many relevant technical specifications but largely sidesteps questions of "ownership" rights of data and databases. Thus, from a legal perspective, it is not sufficiently far-reaching.[122] It is like an "empty canvas"[123] that does not contemplate the possibility of negotiation or changing an agreement at runtime. The extended version of the WS-Agreement will include the possibility of re-negotiation of the specific terms

[120] See Hustinx (2010, pp. 253–255), Cavoukian (2012).

[121] Bianco et al. (2008, p. 8).

[122] Sharaf and Djemame (2015, pp. 177–191).

[123] Schote (2012, p. 63).

with regards to database rights and "ownership" rights of data. As a rule of thumb, the result will show that offering more choices is a viable mechanism that provides more flexibility to the service provider and end-user.[124] These topics are outlined in greater detail in Part III (Chaps. 8 and 9) of this book.

5.3.3 *SLAs as Plans*

According to Gilbert, Plan Theory can take a normative approach—as a contract—and as we have seen in previous sections, these kinds of planning activities are equally useful when organizing the legal system. Sharing her outlook and shedding light on the current situation of the cloud market, the contractual framework I propose will allow for the circumvention of some of the deficiencies, particularly with standard SLAs that do not allow much room for negotiation let alone the re-negotiation of the contracts.

Curtis Bridgeman also draws from Bratman's approach and recent insights from Shapiro. According to Plan Theory, laws are like plans that are designed by the legal institutions in order to help individuals coordinate their communal life. Bridgeman extends Plan Theory to the law of contracts. He conceives contracts as plans, which are designed to clarify specific coordination problems even in circumstances where the involved parties are not able to trust each other. According to this view, a better understanding of Plan Theory will clarify the main issues of contract law.[125] As our needs become more complex, these "forward-looking intentions" have also become more difficult. Thus, plans help us to coordinate our behavior through time, both individually and with others.[126] In the same vein, the Internet became progressively more articulated and complex as globalization took hold. As cloud computing applications become more sophisticated and widespread, information becomes more difficult to handle and process. Therefore, plans are crucial in allowing us to coordinate and manage complex transactions with greater flexibility and therefore overcome challenges in the future.

If all norms and laws are plans, Bridgeman then argues that "contract law is a set of plans."[127] As a corollary, the thesis I propose in this book is built on Bridgeman's insights. Similarly, I argue that SLAs are plans; they belong to a specific category of plans that are embedded in the architecture design of the cloud and are meant to solve a particular kind of coordination and bargaining problem. According to Bridgeman, "we need to make shared plans non-optional and clear so that those with whom we would like to make bargains have a reason to trust us."[128] The law of contract

[124]Sharaf and Djemame (2015, pp. 177–191).

[125]Bridgeman (2009, pp. 341–342).

[126]Bridgeman (2009, p. 343).

[127]Bridgeman (2009, p. 344).

[128]Bridgeman (2009, p. 344).

provides the means and is the answer to this coordination problem. "It is a plan for creating private yet legally obligatory plans to make exchanges."[129]

The "Achilles heel" of such a process is how to choose and "filter multiple options" when there are no such options available in the current SLA frameworks. At the outset, the idea I have is to include the figure of the broker to assist end-users and cloud providers to "coordinate" their plan and use the abovementioned SLA specifications/XML Schema to provide them with a useful tool that is necessary to achieve their end goal. The complete process is as follows: First, the cloud broker issues the XML template with the new choices available. Then, the cloud provider uses the provided XML template to create a description. Thereafter, the end-user dictates which of the options she needs to be activated. To do so, end-user input may be obtained from web forms that are automatically created from schema/template files through tools like XSD Form.[130]

The XML is a markup language standard that aims to define a format that is both human and machine understandable. Thus, it may be edited by humans based on a template model, and the product can be processed by the appropriate software, following a relevant decision logic. For example, the template model dictates the available fields, the user selects the according values, and then relevant software may retrieve the XML based provider descriptions and *filter* them based on the user's requirements. Following the planning logic, since deliberation takes time, effort and other limited resources, this mechanism will assist coordination between the parties and reduce deliberation and transactions costs. Finally, if we take Plan Theory into account, "future-directed intentions" are treated as "elements of partial plans of action." If we take these premises for granted, then we also need a flexible contractual framework that allows for the *plan* to be re-formulated if needed.

5.4 Summary and Interim Remarks

How the major components of these two theories fit together has inspired and influenced this work to traced the central idea for the theoretical framework of this research. *Plan-like Architectures* attempts to work as a simplifying heuristic mechanism. Articulating this structural analysis will hopefully shed new light on the subject and strengthen the study of this work. It will allow the reader to critically evaluate the explicit assumptions I make with regards to the problems I observe within cloud computing contracts.

The purpose is to reveal the weaknesses in the current state of affairs of SLAs where end-users are vulnerable to being undermined, and where conflicts between the involved parties may occur. The overall purpose of this chapter was to explain the meaning, nature and challenges associated with cloud computing and Big Data transformations that are often experienced in the cloud market but unexplained

[129] Bridgeman (2009, p. 344).

[130] See Ilearian, XSD Form Features.

to cloud providers and end-users, so that we may act in a more efficient and effective way.[131]

Therefore, this chapter suggested that the use of innovation intermediary services that brings together interested parties such as end-users and cloud providers within a flexible SLA-based framework can promote broader participation, coordination and representation. In this sense, cloud brokers are a good option in extracting the full benefits of the cloud and Big Data market. The brokers in cloud scenarios could be seen as the central entities, or "main planners," with higher expertise and competences who can act as an interface to translate the technical and legal terms provided in the SLA. The remaining question is how to generate a climate of trust and strong business relations between the main planners, plan adopters or plan appliers. This will be addressed in the next chapter.

References

Agogue M, Ystrom A, Le Masson P (2012) Rethinking the role of intermediaries as an architect of collective exploration and creation of knowledge in open innovation. Int J Innov Manag 7(2):1–31

Alonso F (2008) Shared intention, Reliance, and interpersonal obligations: an inquiry into the metaphysics and interpersonal normativity of shared agency. A Dissertation submitted to the Department of Philosophy and the committee on graduate studies of Stanford University in Partial Fulfillment of the requirements for the degree of Doctor of Philosophy. ProQuest LLC, Ann Arbor, p 78

Antikainen M (2011) Towards collaborative open innovation communities. In: Chauvel D (ed) Leading issues in innovation research, vol 1. Academic Publishing International Ltd., Reading, p 189

Audi R (1973) Intending. J Philos 70:387–403

Austin J (1832) The province of jurisprudence determined. John Murray, London

Austin J (1869) Lectures on jurisprudence on the philosophy of positive law, 3rd edn. John Murray, London

Beardley M (1978) Intending. In: Goldman A, Jaegwon K (eds) Values and morals: essays in honor of William Frankena, Charles Stevenson and Richard Brandt. Springer, Dordrecht

Berns S (1993) Concise jurisprudence. The Federation Press, Annandale, p 149

Bianco P, Lewis G, Merson P (2008) Service level agreements in service-oriented architecture environments. Carnegie Mellon University, Pittsburgh, Software Engineering Institute, p 8

Bontekoe R (2004) Judicial discretion and right answers. In: Soeteman A (ed) Proceedings of the 20th IVR World Congress Pluralism and Law, Amsterdam, vol 4, Legal Reasoning. Franz Steiner Verlag, Stuttgart (2001), p 24

Boudriga N (2009) Security of mobile communications. Auerbach Publications (CRC Press), Boca Ratón, pp 21–23

Bratman M (1984) Two faces of intention. Philos Rev 93(3):375–405

Bratman M (1992) Shared cooperative activity. Philos Rev 101(2):327–331

Bratman M (1999) Intentions, plans, and practical reason, The Davis Hume Series, Philosophy and Cognitive Science Reissues. CSLI Publications, California, pp 1–2

Bratman M (2001) Taking plans seriously. In: Millgram E (ed) Varieties of practical reason. The MIT Press, Cambridge, p 203

[131] See, generally, Corvelle (2013) (ed), Asher (1984).

Bratman M (2013) Shared Agency, The Science Network (TSN), Stanford University. http://thesciencenetwork.org/programs/cogsci-2013/shared-agency. Accessed 10 May 2019

Bratman M (2014a) Shared agency: a planning theory of acting together. Oxford University Press, Oxford

Bratman (2014b) Acting and thinking together, Routledge Lecture in Philosophy, University of Cambridge http://upload.sms.csx.cam.ac.uk/media/1737335. Accessed 10 May 2019

Bridgeman C (2009) Contracts as plans. Univ Illinois Law Rev 2009(2):343

Canale D (2013) Looking for the nature of law: on Shapiro's challenge. In: Canale D, Tuzet G (eds) The planning theory of law: a critical reading, law and philosophy library, vol 100. Springer, Dordrecht, p 19

Cavoukian A (2012) Operationalizing privacy by design: a guide to implementing strong privacy practices, PhD. http://www.privacybydesign.ca/content/up-loads/2013/01/operationalizing-pbd-guide.pdf. Accessed 10 May 2019

Churchland P (1970) The logical character of action-explanations. Philos Rev 79:214–236

Coleman J (1998) Foundations of social theory. The Belknap Press of Harvard University Press, Cambridge

Coleman J (1988) Social capital in the creation of human capital. Supplement: organizations and institutions: sociological and economic approaches to the analysis of social structure. Am J Sociol 94:95–120 The University of Chicago Press

Craig J (2009) Raz and his critics: a defense of Razian authority, Master Thesis, Georgia State University. http://scholarworks.gsu.edu/philosophy_theses/49. Accessed 10 May 2019

Culver K (1999) (ed) Readings in the philosophy of law. Broadview Press Ltd., Ontario, p 183

Dalziel M, Parjanen S (2012) Measuring the impact of innovation intermediaries: a case study of Tekes. In: Melkas H, Harmaakorpi V (eds) Practice-based innovation: insights, applications and policy implications. Springer, Berlin, p 120

Darian-Smith E (2013) Laws and societies in global contexts: contemporary approaches. Cambridge University Press, Cambridge, pp 136–137

Dworkin R (1975) Hard cases. Harv Law Rev 88(6):1057–1109

Dworkin R (1986) Law's empire. Harvard University Press, Cambridge

Dworkin R (1982) Law as interpretation. Crit Inq Chic J 9(1):182

Dworkin R (1996a) How law is like literature. In: Ledwon L (ed) Law and literature: text and theory. Garland Publishing, New York, pp 29–46

Dworkin R (1996) Freedom's law: the moral reading of the American Constitution, Oxford University Press, Oxford, p 10

Easterbrook F (1994) Text, history, and structure in statutory interpretation. Harv J Law Public Policy 17:61–70

Ferrer Bertran J, Ratti G (2013) Theoretical disagreements: a restatement of legal positivism. In: Canale D, Tuzet G (eds) The planning theory of law: a critical reading, Law and Philosophy Library, vol 100. Springer, Dordrecht, p 182

Fisher J (ed) (2005) Free will: critical concepts in philosophy. Routledge, New York, p 217

Gilbert M (1990) Walking together: a paradigmatic social phenomenon. Midwest Stud Philos 15(1):1–14

Gilbert M (2000) Sociality and responsibility: new essays in plural subject theory. Rowman & Littlefield Publishers Inc., Lanham

Gilbert M (2006) A theory of political obligation. Oxford University Press, Oxford

Gilbert M (2007) Searle and collective intentions. In: Tsohatzidis S (ed) Intentional acts and institutional facts: essays on John Searle's social ontology. Springer, Dordrecht, pp 31–49

Hallersted S (2013) Managing the lifecycle of open innovation platforms. Springer, Wiesbaden, p 35

Hart H (1958) Positivism and the separation of law and morals. Harv Law Rev 71(4):593–629

Hart H (1997) The concept of law, 2nd edn. Oxford University Press, Oxford

Howels J (2006) Intermediation and the role of intermediaries in innovation. Res Policy 35(5):715–728

Hustinx P (2010) Privacy by design: delivering the promises. Identity Inf Soc 3(2):253–255. Springer. http://link.springer.com/article/10.1007/s12394-010-0061-z. Accessed 10 May 2019

Lessig L (1998) The new Chicago school. J Legal Stud 27(S2):661–691 The University of Chicago Press

Lessig L (1999) The law of the horse: what Cyberlaw might teach. Harvar Law Rev 113:501–546

Lessig L (2002) The future of ideas: the fate of the commons in a connected world. Vintage Books, New York, p 121

Lessig L (2006) Code. Version 2.0, Appendix. Basic Books, New York, pp 120–137, pp 340–345

Lessig L (2004) Free culture: the nature and future of creativity. Penguin Books, New York, pp 121–173

Levinson S, Mailloux S (1991) (eds) Interpreting law and literature: a hermeneutic reader. Northwestern University Press, Evanston, p 271

Mohan W (1990) Intention, plans, and practical reason. Int Stud Philos 22(3):89. Harvard University Press, Cambridge (Book Review)

Murray J Methods of interpretation: comparative law method, Report of Mr. Justice John L. Murray, President of the Supreme Court and Chief Justice of Ireland, Actes du colloque pour le cinquantième anniversaire des Traités de Rome. http://curia.europa.eu/common/dpi/col_murray.pdf. Accessed 10 May 2019, pp 39–47

Nauwelaers C (2011) intermediaries in regional innovation systems: role and challenges for policy. In: Cooke P et al (eds) Handbook of regional innovation and growth. Edward Elgar Publishing, Cheltenham, p 474

O'Hagan E (2001) Faces of intention: selected essays on intention and agency by Michael Bratman, Cambridge Studies in Philosophy. Cambridge University Press, New York (Book Review). Dialogue 40(2):393

Osorio D, Jimenez M, Arroyo L (2012) Open innovation through intermediaries in the web: a comparative case study. In: de Pablos Heredero C, López D (eds) Open innovation in firms and public administrations: technologies for value creation. Information Science Reference (IGI Global), Hershey, p 201

Owens D (2012) Shaping the normative landscape. Oxford University Press, Oxford, p 50

Raz J (1999) Practical reason and norm. Oxford University Press, Oxford

Reidenberg J (1998) Lex informatica: the formulation of information policy rules through technology. Texas Law Rev 76(3):553–593

Samuel G (2013) A short introduction to the common law. Edward Elgar Publishing, Cheltenham, p 102

Samuel G (2014) An introduction to comparative law: theory and method. Hart Publishing, Oxford, p 138

Searle J (1983) Intentionality. Cambridge University Press, Cambridge

Searle J (1990) Collective intentions and actions. In: Cohen P, Morgan J, Pollack M (eds) Intentions in communications. MIT Press, Cambridge. Reprinted in Searle J (2002) Consciousness and language. Cambridge University Press, Cambridge, pp 401–416

Searle J (1995) The construction of social reality. The Free Press, New York

Searle J (2010) Making the social world: the structure of human civilization. Oxford University Press, Oxford, pp 46–47

Shapiro S (2011) Legality. Harvard University Press, Cambridge

Sharaf S, Djemame K (2015) Enabling service level agreement renegotiation through extending WS-agreement specification. SOCA 9(2):177–191

Shiner R (2005) A treatise of legal philosophy and general jurisprudence: legal institutions and the sources of law, vol 3. Springer, Dordrecht, p 57

Schote N (2012) QoS-aware model-driven SOA using SoaML, Master Thesis, University of Twente, EEMCS–TRESE: Software Engineering Group, p 63

Stewart J, Hyysalo S (2008) Intermediaries, users and social learning in technological innovation. Int J Innov Manag 12(3):295–325

Stone M (2012) Planning positivism and planning natural law. Can J Law Jurisprudence, Forthcoming; Cardozo Legal Studies Research Paper No. 363:7. http://ssrn.com/abstract=1982143. Accessed 10 May 2019

Tuomela R (2014) Michael E. Bratman, shared agency: a planning theory of acting together. Oxford University Press, Oxford (Book Review) https://ndpr.nd.edu/news/49830-shared-agency-a-planning-theory-of-acting-together/. Accessed 10 May 2019

Velleman D (1991) Intention, plans, and practical reason by Michael E. Bratman. Philos Rev 100(2):277. Cambridge University Press, Cambridge (Book Review)

Wacks R (2014) Philosophy of law: a very short introduction. Oxford University Press, Oxford, p 59

Wacks R (2015) Understanding jurisprudence, 4th edn. Oxford University Press, Oxford, p 147

Wend D (1975) (ed) Utility, probability and human decision making. In: Selected Proceedings of an interdisciplinary research conference, vol II, Rome, 3–6 September 1973. D. Reidel Publishing Co., Dordrecht

Westerlund A (2015) Shared agency: a planning theory of acting together, by Michael E, Bratman. Aust J Philos 93(2):822–836. Oxford University Press, Oxford (Book Review)

Zwicky E, Cooper S, Chapman D (2000) Building internet firewalls, 2nd edn. O'Reilly & Associates Inc., Sebastopol

Chapter 6
Plans, Brokers and Trust

"In the cloud we trust" (Smith 2015).

6.1 Introduction

Having discussed the theoretical framework and how to construct Plan-like Architectures, this chapter follows on from the previous principles laid out in Plan Theory. What is more interesting about Shapiro's narrative is that he recommends resorting to the concept of *trust*. According to Shapiro, "plans…are sophisticated devices for managing trust and distrust: they allow people to capitalize on the faith they have in others or compensate for its absence."[1] This is, in my view, the key finding that should link cloud computing architectures with Plan Theory. This should be the linchpin for providing legal soundness in contractual relations. Trust has been identified as a new common currency[2] and has become one of the most important drivers in our global economy.[3]

The iceberg metaphor can help us understand in simple terms the different components and levels of trust. Like an iceberg, the greater part of trust determinants is under the surface and remains hidden to the observer.[4] Therefore, this chapter will attempt to make the hidden constructs and elements of trust more visible. Similarly, cloud end-users are frequently unaware of the complex technical and legal issues involved. They may lack the material information concerning the reliability of cloud

[1] Shapiro (2011, p. 334).

[2] Peterson (2016), foreword.

[3] Covey and Link (2012, p. 13); the work of Kenneth Arrow, see Hosseini (2015, p. 662).

[4] Glinz and Company (2016).

M. Corrales Compagnucci, *Big Data, Databases and "Ownership" Rights in the Cloud*, Perspectives in Law, Business and Innovation,
https://doi.org/10.1007/978-981-15-0349-8_6

and Big Data services. As a consequence, they do not notice the material risks and may hesitate to contract with a cloud provider.

Providing a framework of trust should, therefore, be based on input and parameter values extracted from innovation intermediary services. Coleman calls the third parties in this structure of social capital "intermediaries in trust."[5] The third party brings the two parties together and irons out the transaction because each one trusts the intermediary.[6] Higher levels of trust are achieved through a process of repeated interactions and information sharing.[7] Therefore, trust implies and represents a control and coordinating mechanism within uncertain environments.[8] This is where planning is required in a cloud collaborative network between third parties and is the key role of cloud brokers to perform market coordination.

The concept of trust has many facets and its nuances are beyond the scope of what can be usually captured in SLAs. Trust management originally entered the mainstream of computer science through the works of Blaze et al.[9] and involves the identification and analysis of trust relations at different levels.[10] These early works have spawned several versions of the most innovative trust management systems. The research community has, however, realized that trust management includes not only security controls,[11] but also privacy controls,[12] reputation,[13] and risk management.[14] Thus, this chapter seeks a revised and unified framework of trust by looking for links in previous research in various fields of social and computer sciences.

This chapter is divided into five sections. Section 6.2 provides an introductory background and a brief literature review focusing on the reasons why it is still not possible for the research community to agree on a formal definition of trust. For this reason, this section is broken down into a three-part structure: (i) part 1 explains the way Shapiro understands trust as an *attitude* within Plan Theory; (ii) part 2 contains key concepts and aspects of trust from the standpoint of social sciences and social capital; and (iii) part 3 delimits the notions of trust. The overall purpose of this section is to extract the essential elements of trust that can help us synthesize a better framework. After narrowing down the concept of trust and its main characteristics, Sect. 6.3 examines further technical aspects and approaches related to trust, with the main emphasis placed on contextualizing this within cloud computing and Big Data brokerage scenarios. The remainder of this section is dedicated to presenting alternative layered models and sets out the practical strategic requirements and actions

[5]Evidence of such structure abounds in our society. For example: real estate brokers, literary agency and political mediation. The work of James Coleman, see Baker and Obstfeld (1999, p. 92).

[6]Baker and Obstfeld (1999, p. 92).

[7]Dyer and Chu (2006, p. 224).

[8]Bijlsma-Frankema and Klein Woolthuis (2005), Chap. 1 with further references.

[9]Blaze et al. (1999, pp. 185–210), Noor et al. (2014, p. 13).

[10]Solhaug and Stolen (2012, pp. 1–5).

[11]Grandison (2007, p. 199).

[12]See Seigneur and Jensen (2004, pp. 93–107).

[13]See Carbo et al. (2003, pp. 135–155). See also Krukow et al. (2008, pp. 3781–3793).

[14]See Djemame et al. (2013). See also Josag et al. (2007, pp. 269–278).

to take into consideration. Section 6.4 explains how these different notions and the different layers of trust fit together within Plan-like Architectures. Finally, Sect. 6.5 concludes.

6.2 Literature Review and Background Considerations

Unraveling the complexities of the elusive notion of trust has been a recurrent subject throughout history. During the Enlightenment period, David Hume provided a clear description involving the notion of trust. In his *Treatise on Human Nature* (1737)[15] he illustrated the classical problem about trust with the "two farmers" often cited example,[16] which is also referred as the "collective action dilemma."[17]

> Your corn is ripe today; mine will be so tomorrow. Tis profitable for us both that I shou'd labour with you today, and that you shou'd aid me tomorrow. I have no kindness for you, and know that you have as little for me. I will not, therefore, take any pains on your account; and should I labour with you on my account, I know I shou'd be disappointed, and that I shou'd in vain depend upon your gratitude. Here then I leave you to labour alone: You treat me in the same manner. The seasons change; and both of us lose our harvests for want of mutual confidence and security.[18]

In this story, two farmers barely know each other and so have neither affection nor sympathy for one another. Despite this, they both agree to help each other and cooperate during the corn harvest season. The sociological consideration revealed in this short story is that people tend to reciprocate efforts or favors and implies that one places *confidence* on the other, which is important for our communal life.[19]

Over the past decades, there has been a rapid increase in literature using the notion of trust in various fields. According to Bachmann and Zaheer, trust has become one of the defining pillars for coordinating organizational relationships.[20] Similarly, in Reed's opinion, trust has proved vital in providing a framework for organizational analysis.[21] Many researchers have investigated a variety of approaches to building a framework based on the concept of trust.[22] Most recently, the topic of trust has been

---

[15]Hume (1737).

[16]Hollis (1998, p. 41).

[17]Tuomela (2000, p. 93).

[18]Branscomb and Keller (1999, p. 88) (eds).

[19]Cranston (2014, pp. 63–64).

[20]Bachmann and Zaheer (2006, p. 2) (eds).

[21]Reed (2001, pp. 201–228).

[22]McKnight and Chervany (1996), pp. 1-17.

addressed by scholars in many fields of social sciences, including psychology,[23] management,[24] marketing,[25] political science[26] and risk management.[27]

According to Grandison and Sloman, the existence of various definitions of trust in the current debate is due to two main reasons. First, trust is an abstract concept, is often related to other concepts such as reliability, safety, and certainty. Second, trust is a psychological state consisting of many facets including cognitive, emotional and behavioral dimensions.[28] Pettit, for instance, makes a distinction between the typical phenomena of reliance on people's behavioral dispositions as "active" or "interactive" reliance. Active reliance is when one person relies on a certain agent in conjunction with other people, whereas interactive reliance is when that person explicitly tells the agent that she is relying on him.[29] According to McCullagh et al., trust consists of three elements, i.e., commercial, technological, and behavioral,[30] while Kini and Choobineh make a useful distinction depending on three different perspectives of trust, i.e., individual, societal and relationship.[31] Baron, however, recognizes trust as a good, a belief and a behavior.[32]

Despite all these previous interpretations and classifications, little progress has been made in the appropriate conceptualization of this term. Susan Shapiro described these efforts very well, arguing that the concept of trust has been "applied to a host of units and level of analysis" which has brought a "confusing potpourri of definitions."[33] Sandro Castaldo endorsed this opinion and argued that this deficiency in the conceptualization has created a lot of miscommunication issues among scholars who often intended to contemplate the same construct but, in reality, they were applied to very different concepts or levels of trust.[34] Timothy Guinnane similarly argued that the attempt to conceptualize and delimit the notions of trust on the basis of the existing literature has created more confusion and more problems, rather than helping to resolve the difficulties.[35]

---

[23]See Kramer (1999, pp. 569–598).

[24]See Rousseau et al. (1998, pp. 394–404). In this study, the authors adopted a multidisciplinary and multilevel view of trust within and between organizations.

[25]Geyskens et al. (1998, pp. 223–248). In this study, the authors conducted a meta-analysis of empirical research and demonstrated the importance of trust in lowering the transaction costs and building a long-term successful relationship between businesses and consumers.

[26]See Ostrom (2005, pp. 97–98).

[27]See Slovic (1993, pp. 675–682).

[28]The work of Grandison and Sloman. See Joseph (2010, p. 243).

[29]Pettit (1995, p. 204).

[30]McCullagh et al. (1998, pp. 452–465).

[31]Dutton et al. (2005, p. 14).

[32]Barron (1998, pp. 185 et seq).

[33]Shapiro (1987, p. 625). Similarly, in the opinion of Barbara Misztal, trust is "a very imprecise and confusing notion and our intellectual understanding of trust is seriously underdeveloped." See Misztal (1996, p. 9).

[34]Castaldo (2002, p. 1).

[35]Guinnane (2005, pp. 1–2).

Regarding these controversies and gaps in the literature, Mutti writes, "the number of meanings attributed to the idea of trust in social analysis is disconcerting."[36] The author adds that "this deplorable state of things is the product of a general theoretical negligence. It is almost as if…social science has ended up losing its own trust in the possibility of considering trust in a significant way."[37] Similarly, Koza and Lewin convey the idea that research on trust "needs to advance beyond a catch-all residual in the unexplained random error."[38]

It is therefore particularly clear that there is still a high degree of uncertainty surrounding the terminology which shows the need to be more explicit about what exactly is meant by trust. This indicates that it remains a challenging theme as an "integral component"[39] that is present in our current society.[40] It could be said that the concept of trust has evolved enough over the years. It ranges from the most simplified definition to the more complex model representing different levels of trust. Nonetheless, research on trust has remained problematic for the following reasons: (i) Problem in conceptualizing trust itself; (ii) Lack of clarity and accuracy about the risk-trust relationship; (iii) Lack of a clear understanding of the various levels of trust; and (iv) The failure to consider the subjects of the trust relationship (trustor-trustee).[41]

It is also noteworthy to mention that trust could transcend the interpersonal level and take an institutional form whereby actors can build confidence without having physical contact and without knowing each other. This kind of "institution-based" trust rests in the assumption that institutions are everywhere and inevitable as a result of the "micro-level interactions of individual actors."[42] It also denotes that institutions are perceived to be trustworthy based on shared beliefs, norms and common values. These conditions, however, do not often exist within the cross-border and international level. Thus, building trust at the global perspective becomes a more difficult and challenging task.[43]

Before I delve into explaining the application of elements of trust within Plan-like Architectures, at the outset it is important to clarify that the concept of trust is always very subjective.[44] It can mean something completely different depending on the cultural background,[45] knowledge and experience of each individual.[46] Therefore, defining the concept of trust in a few words is a Herculean task that is fraught with

[36]The work of Antonio Mutti. See Mandelli (2004, p. 226). See, also, generally, Mutti (1987, pp. 223–247).

[37]See Mandelli (2004, p. 226), Mutti (1987, pp. 223–247).

[38]The works of Mitchell Koza and Arie Lewin. See Albers (2005, p. 203).

[39]Arzt and Gill (2007, p. 58).

[40]Silva et al. (2013, p. 42).

[41]Cohen (2015, p. 52).

[42]Cohen (2015, p. 52).

[43]Cohen (2015, p. 52). See, also, generally, Schwegler (2011, pp. 137–147).

[44]He et al. (2005, p. 541).

[45]Lee and Trim (2008, p. 91).

[46]See Jonker et al. (2004, p. 207).

difficulties and controversies as this has been tackled in the current literature from different angles.

This being said, one could start by explaining the double-edged nature of trust, which has branched out into two strands: trust as an *attitude* versus trust as an *act*. Some scholars tend to emphasize the emotional and psychological aspects of trust. They generally define this term as a kind of "attitude."[47] In other words, it refers to the psychological mental state or attitude of *X* towards *Y* concerning some potential desirable behavior.[48] There is also, however, the so-called "strategic view." According to this perspective, trust has very little, if anything, to do with psychological factors and human emotions.[49] Trust is rather a "decision" or "act" of "relying on, counting on, depending on Y."[50]

Proponents of this view argue that trust is necessary for cooperation and strategic *planning* based on the beliefs or expectations of the "trustor" vis-à-vis the potential "trustee." Such beliefs and expectations are based on a risk assessment that reduces and mitigates the uncertainties involved. The main partisans of this approach are inter alia Partha Dasgupta, John Dunn, Diego Gambetta, Russell Hardin and Niklas Luhmann.[51] In other words, this dyadic notion provides us with the conceptual link for the causal process of trust.[52] Both perspectives are closely intertwined and highly relevant for our discussion.

The following sections will present a thorough examination of some of the most widely recognized and debated notions of trust, taking into account different fields of social sciences, with the main emphasis on contextualizing this in the cloud computing and Big Data domains. In most cases these definitions are quite precise, indicating certain terms that should be included in the analysis. Some of these definitions are supplementary and sometimes overlapping. I do not intend to cover a complete outline of all fields and disciplines. These definitions are merely indicative for the purposes of building a legal construct with the necessary flexibility, but still limited in the scope of cloud computing and Big Data.

6.2.1 Attitudes of Trust (and Distrust) Within Plan Theory

According to Shapiro in his Plan Theory, different *attitudes* of trust can strongly influence the legal systems. The main issue is that Shapiro does not come up with a clear definition of trust himself. Nevertheless, this conceptualization has been left out intentionally and is vague in order to give the interpreter more room for interpretation. It seems that Shapiro implicitly admits that the notion of trust is a matter of context

[47] See Jones (1996, pp. 4–25).
[48] The works of Johannisson. See Castaldo (2002, p. 18).
[49] Miller (2000, pp. 38–45).
[50] The works of Johannisson. See Castaldo (2002, p. 18).
[51] Miller (2000, pp. 38–45).
[52] The works of Johannisson. See Castaldo (2002, p. 18).

because it could potentially apply to any situation. There might be some gaps in the accurate definition of trust, however, this is a good sign that the parties involved understand each other.

Therefore, he leaves in the hands of the interpreter the task of evaluating parameters and preconditions involved in construing the concept of trust. Instead of defining the term, Shapiro characterizes issues of trust and distrust as an *attitude* and he uses the history of the U.S. Republic to explain where the ideology of trust and distrust, or, as he puts in more dramatic terms the original distribution of "faith and suspicion," formed the basis of the U.S. Constitutional Order.[53]

This part of the U.S. legal history is precisely the same example I will refer to in this section to explain my argument regarding Plan-like Architectures. Before narrating this story in more detail, Shapiro clarifies that he is not a historian. The same disclaimer applies here. The story might be nuanced with imprecise facts; however, the analogy of the story serves as a good reference to explain further how attitudes of trust and distrust can and do influence the institutional design of legal systems.[54]

A full recount of the story is not necessary for present purposes. Therefore, suffice it to say that the radical political party called the "Whigs" played a decisive factor in the intellectual history of the revolutionary period. The Whigs influenced considerably the American political thinkers who subscribed to the classical doctrine of republicanism that believed that people could be trusted to exercise political power accordingly. To explain many years of history in a few lines, Shapiro divides it in three waves[55]:

The first wave was especially conspicuous in the period that followed the declaration of independence and is called "demoting the executive," as it was characterized by eliminating the "kingly office," termed by Thomas Jefferson.[56] In this wave, they dismantled the executive branch from its original functions and transferred many of its prerogatives to the legislative branch. This attitude of distrust towards the executive was echoed in the former regime where monarchs and aristocrats enjoyed and presumably abused their power.[57]

The second wave had several components, which takes it beyond the first wave. The same attitudes of distrust shifted away from the executive towards the legislative branch, described by Shapiro as "reining in the legislature period." In this wave, more trust was placed in the citizens who, according to the republican view, could exercise the power more responsibly. Additionally, three devices to monitor the state legislatures were given to the people; constitutions, conventions and instructions.[58]

Finally, the third wave, titled "losing faith in the people," included a greater amount of skepticism about the republican view. This wave explains how this new

[53] Shapiro (2011, pp. 312–313).

[54] Shapiro (2011, pp. 312–313).

[55] Shapiro (2011, pp. 313–316).

[56] Bailey (2010, p. 31).

[57] Shapiro (2011, pp. 316–318).

[58] Shapiro (2011, pp. 318–320).

attitude of trust granted to the citizens failed to achieve its goal and turned to the actual distribution and symmetric separation of powers, known as it is today. The current legal system might not be perfect but this historical event clearly shows how attitudes of trust and distrust may swing from one institution to another. This is what he calls the "economy of trust."[59] As Shapiro reminds us, "we can treat the trust attitudes underlying a system's institutional arrangements as a 'theory of trust.'"[60] This resembles the former simile of the Foucault Pendulum that I referred to when I described the Komesarian framework in relation to how the role of each institution may predominate as a choice towards the social goal of the law-making process and how such a role may oscillate from one institution to the other.[61]

Another meaningful example given by Shapiro is when a society is exposed to great challenges and faces difficulties in overcoming and solving complex legal issues by themselves. Given this setup, many of the citizens would feel frustrated and powerless to confront the situation while others would think they know what to do. This lack of trust could be the result of the "lack of character" of some individuals for decision-making[62] or the "lack of method for assuring trustworthy actors."[63] The former is an intrinsic lack of trust as this is coming from inside the individual. The latter has some extrinsic values as the individuals confronted with "issues of legality" feel confident to understand and solve these complex issues but lack the right tools or methods to confront these situations.[64]

As seen in the above examples, plans do not only allow planners to "compensate" and balance their lack of trust of others but they can also help them to "capitalize" on such trust. Plans can also play a multi-fold management role as they have a variety of sizes and shapes and can be blended to form complicated networks. According to Plan Theory, "the fundamental aim of the law is to rectify these deficiencies; moreover, the law pursues this aim by managing trust…through social planning."[65] In addition, Shapiro claims that "the only way to respect a plan's trust management function is to defer to its economy of trust, namely, the attitudes of trust and distrust that motivated its creation."[66]

On a more abstract level, Plan Theory posits a cogent positivistic theory of law. On a practical level, however, this might raise some debates as to how to interpret Plan Theory, taking into account that the author omits an explanation of the concept of trust in full details. As seen earlier, however, trust is a matter of context. Therefore, contextualizing trust is necessary to understand the contractual framework I submit in this book. My conjecture is to take Plan Theory and inject it into the overall

[59] Shapiro (2011, pp. 320–330).

[60] Shapiro (2011, p. 367).

[61] Komesar (1994, pp. 3–6). See also Pierce (1995, pp. 941–951). See, also, generally, Hartmann and Kjaer (2015, pp. 157–158) (eds).

[62] Shapiro (2011, pp. 331–352).

[63] Shapiro (2011, p. 337).

[64] Shapiro (2011, pp. 331–352).

[65] Shapiro (2011, pp. 213, 309 and 338).

[66] Shapiro (2011, p. 336).

framework of SLAs in the cloud. The characterization of trust and distrust typologies as an *attitude* seems to rely on rather broad ideas. On the positive side, it is too general and leaves, to some extent, substantial leeway for interpretation. However, perhaps this approach is too vague if we want to contextualize this in cloud computing and Big Data transformations. In the next section, I discuss some of these widely-accepted definitions that contain the main terms or expressions related to trust that would help to clarify the scope of this theoretical framework. I generally argue that we need to consider the different *levels* or *layers* of trust that are present today in the social and computer sciences.

6.2.2 *Different Notions of Trust: A Kaleidoscopic and Critical View*

In its most basic and generic form, trust is usually defined as "a relationship between a trustor (the principal that trusts someone) and a trustee (the principal being trusted)."[67] This definition is prima facie far too broad and is limited to the relationship between the involved parties rather than its form. It must be viewed in conjunction with other elements of trust. As hinted earlier, the notion of trust has different meanings[68] and has been characterized as an elusive and pervasive concept.[69] The debate in the literature extends further to different disciplines. The sections below recapitulate some of these definitions in an attempt to integrate considerations from different authors and to contextualize them in the field of computer science, and, more specifically, cloud computing and Big Data.

6.2.2.1 Trust From a Sociological Perspective

One of the most famous definitions of trust from a theoretical sociological point of view has been submitted by Niklas Luhmann. For Luhmann, trust is a mechanism that can reduce the complexities of society, which is generated by the interaction of individuals with different goals and perceptions. He also distinguishes the concepts of "trust," "confidence," and "familiarity,"[70] and the role they play in the so-called Luhmannian system theory.[71]

[67] Nielsen and Krukow (2003, p. 1).

[68] Williamson (1993, p. 453).

[69] Johns (1996, p. 76).

[70] See, generally, Luhmann (1973).

[71] See, generally, Luhmann (1987). See also Bechmann and Stehr (2002, pp. 67–75). For a simpler and clearer presentation of Luhmmans work, see Berghaus (2011), Kneer and Nassehi (2009), Baecker (2004) (ed).

He defines the notion of social trust not as a feeling, but a choice to place oneself at *risk*.[72] In other words, the agent believes that taking the risk is worthy and hopes the other will act accordingly in a benevolent way. This risk-based definition gives prominence to trust as a deliberate choice.[73] This definition is very useful for the purpose of this work for it takes into account its social nature, which is more suitable for "reputation-based systems"[74] in the cloud. I am also particularly interested in the way these concepts would function in the context of SLAs and the risk assessment framework that will follow in the last part of this book.[75] Contrary to the mainstream sociological studies, another reason why I think that Luhmann's concept of trust is relevant is that the central element of study in the Luhmannian system theory is not the individual or larger group formations but *communication*.[76]

This system allows us to connect with a much larger selectivity of the network and reduces process complexity.[77] Luhmann distinguishes different types of trust relations that reduce such complexity. The first relation is between trust and familiarity, which refers to past events. We tend to accept things that are more familiar to us and reject those things that are unfamiliar. For example, elderly people are often reluctant to use new technologies such as computers or the Internet because this is something completely new to them. One may argue that the reason for this is that it is just too complex for them to learn something technical. Yet, this is precisely another argument that invites you to think in terms of familiarity instead of trust.[78] Luhmann attempts to avoid confusion between familiarity and trust. Whilst familiarity is part of human life, trust offers a solution for a specific problem of risk. Familiarity refers to a past event. Trust, however, looks towards the future as it involves certain expectations.[79] For example, we use a cloud computing service because we expect this to be faster, cheaper, more convenient, etc.

Notwithstanding, Luhmann also observed a distinct difference between *trust* and *confidence*, which is perhaps one of the most important arguments in understanding the link between risk and trust. Both trust and confidence refer to "expectations which may lapse into disappointments"[80] about contingent events. But there is a major difference. Trust is always based on a risk assessment and a decision to take the risk or not, whereas confidence rejects the possibility of disappointment, not only because it is an event unlikely to happen but because there is no other choice.[81]

---

[72] Luhmann (1988, pp. 96–97).

[73] Pedersen (2015, p. 108).

[74] The Pace Project, *Practical Architectural Approach for Composing Egocentric Trust*, [online]. Available at: http://isr.uci.edu/projects/pace/trustdef.html. Accessed 10 May 2019.

[75] For further details see Chaps. 8 and 9 of this book (Part III).

[76] Jalava (2006, p. 2).

[77] Lane (1998, p. 16).

[78] Peters (2010, p. 160).

[79] Luhmann (1988, p. 95).

[80] Luhmann (1988, p. 97).

[81] Peters (2010, p. 289).

An example of this is when you are driving a car. You are usually confident that your car will not break down, or that another car will not leave the road and hit you while you are walking down the sidewalk. You need to feel confident and believe that these routine activities will not go wrong. Besides taking due diligence, such as checking the oil of your car or sending the car for its regular service, there is not much you can do about it. The other choice would be to live in a permanent state of fear and uncertainty without having any other alternative.[82]

Trust, on the contrary, presupposes a previous engagement on your side that puts you at risk and gives you the choice to do or not to do something. This is certainly true in the case of buying a second-hand car. There is a risk that the car may have a faulty item or defective engine system, which gives you the choice to buy it or not. It gives you the choice to avoid the risk if you are willing to waive the associated benefits. Both terms involve the possibility of disappointment, thus the distinction is a matter of perception and attribution. While confidence reacts on external attributions, trust refers to internal ones since the possibility of choosing poorly will give you a feeling of regret.[83] Finally, Luhmann also distinguishes two different kinds of trust: (i) *personal trust*, such as the kind of trust present in interpersonal relations, and (ii) *system trust*, such as the kind of trust present in technological systems (machines, computers, etc.).[84]

Many other sociologists followed the Luhmannian approach, such as Barber,[85] Sztompka, and Giddens,[86] who seem to be influenced by Luhmanns's account of trust as they also refer to trust as something that is risk-related.[87] Giddens, for instance, in his theory of structuration,[88] situates the concept of trust at the heart of sociological theories about contemporary society.[89] He examined the key role that trust plays in the everyday life of a society.[90] For Giddens, dynamic and modern societies with advanced welfare systems are based on an enormous sense of collective trust. They can succeed only by trusting the people of the society through accessing their wide-ranging skills, technical expertise and professional competences available on specific areas.[91] In describing this concept, Giddens well understands the great importance of "confidence" embedded in the very notion of trust. For Giddens, trust is an "abstract" concept and is defined as the "confidence in the reliability of a person or system regarding a given set of outcomes or events, where that confidence expresses a faith

[82]Luhmann (1988, p. 97).

[83]Luhmann (1988, pp. 97–98).

[84]Peters (2010, p. 288).

[85]Barber (1983).

[86]Giddens (1984).

[87]Jalava (2006, p. 8).

[88]This theory is based on both the structure and agents of a society. See, generally, Giddens (1986).

[89]Lewis and Weigert (1985, p. 967). For a more detailed overview, see Sztompka (1999).

[90]Appelrouth and Desfor (2008, p. 753).

[91]Bachmann and Zaheer (2006, p. 3) (eds).

in the probity or love of another, or in the correctness of abstract principles (technical knowledge)."[92]

To cite one of his several examples, if we were not able to trust in the air traffic control systems, which involve much more than technical matters, it would be too difficult for us to travel around the world and profit from doing business, networking, learning different cultures, languages, etc. In other words, we are much better off if we trust and rely on human expertise.[93] Another important aspect of Gidden's account is what he calls "active trust," which requires actors to "continuously and intensively communicate" with each other.[94]

This means that trust is not only an initial act, but a permanent process.[95] Giddens conceptualization of trust also involves the implicit intersections of trust versus risk,[96] in the sense that they rely on future individual or collective human actions to reduce potential danger.[97] In the same vein, according to Amerland, every definition of trust can be boiled down to one single element, "confidence." The way we establish, measure and keep trust is nothing more than an intuitively inherent risk assessment exercise we undertake in order to know exactly what we are getting involved in. Ultimately, the general question that end-users will ask themselves is: is it safe to enter this agreement?[98]

This is also in line with the studies and experiments carried out by Toshio Yamagishi. There is a general misconception that Japanese society, especially Japanese business practices, is more trusting than others.[99] This common characterization is based on the belief system that Japanese people feel safer and have a high degree of confidence and trust. According to his empirical research, however, Yamagishi explored a number of comparisons between the U.S. and Japanese society, and he found out that this idea is not reasonable or realistic.[100]

He supported his argument with clear evidence that what has been characterized in Japan as "trust" might be better labeled as an assurance of mutual cooperation in commitment relations, which does not necessarily mean that the Japanese do generally trust more than other societies. Building on the idea of the link between social uncertainty and cooperation,[101] Yamagishi argued that the Japanese tend to place more reliance on social structures and sanctions to reinforce agreements. This means that Japanese society is actually less likely to trust strangers when those sanctions are not in place.[102]

---

[92]Blegvad (1995, p. 153).

[93]Bachmann and Zaheer (2006, p. 3) (eds).

[94]The work of Giddens. See Bijlsma-Frankema and Klein Woolthuis (2005, p. 28).

[95]The work of Giddens. See Bijlsma-Frankema and Klein Woolthuis (2005, p. 28).

[96]See, generally, Giddens (1991).

[97]Craib (1992, p. 67).

[98]Amerland (2015, pp. 116–117).

[99]Yamagishi (2011, pp. 12 et seq).

[100]Yamagishi and Yamagishi (1994, p. 131).

[101]Yamagishi (2005, pp. 15, 352–370).

[102]The work of Toshio Yamagishi. See Hawley (2012, p. 38).

Yamagishi and colleagues also studied the relationship between trust-building and risk-taking behaviors. They arrived at the conclusion that a series of risk-taking behaviors is fundamental to building mutual trust. Assessing the degree of risks and the probability of the realization of such risks is thus a critical element in trust-building for the American society, but less so for the Japanese.[103]

Following the same logic of order, I will examine in Chap. 9 the technical functions of trust, confidence, and risk in Luhmannian's framework. Although my analysis will not be limited to Luhmann's own account of trust, I find this theoretical discussion particularly useful as this can be successfully implemented within the risk assessment framework of the overall broker architecture. The risk assessment framework in the broker architecture contains a software component, a *confidence* service, which is the interface that allows an end-user or the broker service to request a reliability measure for a provider's probability of failure (PoF).[104] The confidence service works in tandem with the risk assessor component, which provides the functionality to compute the reliability of the service.[105] What the confidence service does is provide a statistical estimate of the confidence that can be placed in the providers PoF.

This approach will be used and extended to clarify database rights and "ownership" rights of data along with other policies and technical assurances to increase the degree of confidence of end-users in using cloud[106] and Big Data services. The impartiality of this assessment provides end-users with additional risk information to improve their decision-making process.[107] Therefore, this framework is crucial for raising the confidence level in cloud computing transactions and Big Data services.[108]

6.2.2.2 Trust from a Psychological Perspective

Paul Slovic was one of the first researchers to study the nature of trust and its relationship with risk perception. In his study of the nature of trust, he arrived at the conclusion that trust is "fragile"; "It is typically created rather slowly but it can be destroyed in an instant—by a single mishap or mistake."[109] The premise that trust can take years to earn and only seconds to brake later became widespread in literature and even media. Whether this axiom is true or false is not very relevant here. What it matters now is to point out that Slovic distinguishes two types of information: (i) "negative (trust-destroying) events" and (ii) "positive (trust-building) events,"[110]

---

[103]Cook et al. (2005, pp. 121–142).

[104]Gourlay et al. (2009, p. 37).

[105]Gourlay et al. (2008, p. 438).

[106]See Kahn et al. (2012, p. 121).

[107]Details are beyond the scope of this chapter; however more details can be found in Chap. 9. See Townend et al. (2013, pp. 287, 289 and 398).

[108]Padgett et al. (2009, p. 284).

[109]Slovic (1993, p. 677).

[110]Earle et al. (2007, pp. 1–2).

which is in my view related to what Shapiro earlier referred to as "attitudes of trust and distrust."

A clear example of a "negative (trust-destroying) event" is what happened in the Volkswagen (VW) diesel-emissions scandal. Being one of the largest car manufacturer companies in the world, VW knowingly and willfully installed "device defeat" software in 11 million cars.[111] This device served to manipulate and understate their NOx emissions data in laboratory tests[112] to deceive millions of customers as well as environmental and tax authorities. This was an evident blow to the brand's reputation and trust that took VW years to build.[113]

However, another aspect of trust is that it could be repaired through "positive (trust-building) events" even after it has been broken. The levels of trust can increase and decrease over time. In the case of VW, it may take several years to regain the confidence and trust of its customers not only because it breached different types of trust but also because it acted illegally. The reasons why restoring trust can take a long time is because trust is a belief system that allows confidence to enter the mechanism of predicted outcomes in situations where making a rational analysis is difficult. Therefore, restoring trust "is more than a case of making up for what has been damaged or is missing."[114] According to Robinson and Rousseau, when trust is lost, what happens is a "breach of a psychological contract."[115] The repair of trust is the result of complex cognitive and interpersonal processes that even affects the people who are not directly involved.[116]

The psychological understanding of trust is commonly based on "attributes" between trustors and trustees and focuses on a number of personal cognitive behavior skills.[117] In this sense, trust may also be conceptualized as a psychological state of society based on positive expectations. According to Rousseau et al., trust is "a psychological state comprising the intention to accept vulnerability based upon positive expectations of the intentions or behavior of another."[118] In line with Rousseau and colleagues, my understanding of trust in this book is part of a "meso" concept, integrating a mix of micro-level psychological processes and macro-level institutional arrangements.[119] Along similar lines, Earle et al. define trust as "the willingness, in expectation of beneficial outcomes, to make oneself vulnerable to another based on a judgment of similarity of intentions or values."[120]

A more descriptive and perhaps most popular definition outlining some of these elements is the one given by Morton Deutsch in 1962, who is considered by many

---

[111] Amerland (2015, p. 238).

[112] Lee and Vachonp (2016, p. 102).

[113] Davis (2016, p. 137).

[114] Amerland (2015, pp. 321–322).

[115] See Robinson and Rousseau (1994, pp. 245–259), Robinson (1996, pp. 574–599).

[116] Amerland (2015, pp. 325–327).

[117] Rousseau et al. (1998, p. 393).

[118] Rousseau et al. (1998, p. 395). See also Walczuch et al. (2001).

[119] Dietz et al. (2010, pp. 9–10).

[120] Earle et al. (2007, p. 30).

one of the founders of modern theory and research on trust.[121] Deutsch states the following:

> (a) an individual is confronted with an ambiguous path, a path that can lead to an event perceived to be beneficial or to an event perceived to be harmful; (b) he perceives that the occurrence of these events is contingent on the behavior of another person; and (c) he perceives the strength of a harmful event to be greater than the strength of a beneficial event. If he chooses to take an ambiguous path with such properties, he makes a trusting choice; else he makes a distrustful choice.[122]

An interesting feature of this definition[123] points out the subjective dependency level of the way the individual perceives his reality. The word *perceives* in the definition denotes a high degree of personal subjectivity, which is implicit in the views and choices that the individual makes.[124] Deutsch distinguished two types of trust: interpersonal and mutual. Interpersonal trust is *unilateral*, i.e., the trust that one individual places on another. Whereas mutual trust is *reciprocal*, or the kind of trust that individuals share with each other with regards to their behaviors.[125] This definition has been widely adopted as a trust framework by many social networks and online models.[126]

Similarly, Deutsch also defined trust as being an expectation of events. By way of illustration, Deutsch considers an example of a young couple willing to hire a baby sitter to look after their child. The couple has a choice to trust or not. They consider the advantages and disadvantages depending on their perceptions or expectations of the occurrence of the events. One of the typical characteristics of trust is the presence of negative and positive outcomes. In this case, they expect the baby sitter to perform her duty of care well so they can enjoy their evening out. Yet, they also consider the potential negative event of harm resulting from intent or negligence. In this scenario, the expected loss from the negative event is greater than the positive outcome. Therefore, the choice to trust it is not based on a rational decision. If the situation were reversed, the choice to trust would be grounded on economic rationality.[127] Nevertheless, trust goes beyond the mere expectations, as some social psychologists have pointed out. For instance, Lewis and Weigert argued that trust is more than predictability, but also confidence in the presence of risk.[128]

What is especially relevant in Deutsch's conceptualization of trust is the implicit notion of *vulnerability*. The fact that the trustor feels exposed to a hazardous event and the idea that, in light of trust, there are necessarily inherent risks and uncertainty. For Castelfranchi, however, Deutsch's definition is too narrow because it ignores the "evaluation component," which makes the expectation to be a "reason-based"

[121] Simpson (2007, p. 587).

[122] The work of Morton Deutsch. See Chakrabarti (2007, p. 216).

[123] Marsh (1994, p. 26).

[124] Chakrabarti (2007, p. 216).

[125] Corritore et al. (2013, p. 1170).

[126] Cugelman et al. (2008, p. 51).

[127] Kini and Choobineh (1998, pp. 51–61).

[128] Lewicki and Bunker (1996, p. 116).

choice.[129] Deutsch's analysis was further refined to cover the element of "confidence," where he defined trust as "confidence that [one] will find what is desired [from another] rather than what is feared."[130] This definition was drawn up almost four decades ago and the confidence element was accepted as an appropriate base for many standard dictionary definitions.[131] The Oxford English Dictionary defines trust as the "confidence or faith in a person or thing, or in an attribute of a person or thing."[132] Similarly to the sociological approach, trust is delineated and hinged by the concept of "confidence,"[133] which involves the mental effort and belief that things will be fine, and "reliance," which denotes a more common and mechanical habit to accept that things will not go wrong.[134]

6.2.2.3 Trust in Social Capital

For many years, economists perceived three types of capital: financial capital, physical capital (which comprises both fixed and moveable assets), and human capital (which refers to knowledge and skills of individuals). To these, the notion of social capital has been added as another form of resource.[135] Social capital refers to the value given by social networks and pays special attention to the social connections of individuals and the benefits derived from the cooperation and the associated norms of reciprocity of the network.[136] The main representatives of these ideas are Robert Putnam, Pierre Bourdieu and James Coleman. Putnam's widely-known definition of social capital as "features of social life—networks, norms and trust—that facilitate co-operation and co-ordination for mutual benefit,"[137] refers here to social organizations as a "community level" resource[138] that can improve the efficiency of society.[139]

---

[129] Castelfranchi (2003, p. 189).

[130] Deutsch (1973, p. 148).

[131] Chakrabarti (2007, p. 216).

[132] See Oxford English Dictionary. Another example is the Collins dictionary, which defines trust as the "reliance on and confidence in the truth, worth, reliability, etc., of a person or thing," [online]. Available at: http://www.collinsdictionary.com/dictionary/english/trust. Accessed 10 May 2019.

[133] Venters et al. (2011, p. 262).

[134] Kidder (2010, p. 1).

[135] Sunderland (2007, p. 1).

[136] Putnam (2000, pp. 16–18).

[137] Putnam (1995, pp. 65–78).

[138] Baum and Ziersch (2003, pp. 320–323).

[139] Putnam et al. (1993, p. 167).

This entails “individual attitudes” and “behavioral networks”[140] (institutions, relationships, and customs) that can effectively improve the economic development of society.[141]

Bourdieu and Wacquant conceive social capital as “the sum of the resources, actual or virtual, that accrue to an individual or a group by virtue of possessing a durable network of more or less institutionalized relationships of mutual acquaintance and recognition.”[142] In this definition, the authors see social capital primarily as the “resources” available, and secondly, this is linked to the “relationships” of individuals[143]; i.e., “resources embedded in social networks.”[144] Phrased differently, this means that an individual gains and improves social capital as a result of interactions with other individuals who have and share resources.[145] Coleman, like Bourdieu, conceptualizes social capital as a network attribute.[146] According to Coleman, the forms this social capital can take on are primarily obligations, expectations and trustworthiness.[147] In Coleman’s view, it is rather the links within the social network that constitute social capital. The main difference is that in Bourdieu’s inquiry, the individual’s external network provides access to capital, whereas Coleman’s viewpoints out the links within and between networks.[148]

Francis Fukuyama also believes that the concepts of trust and social capital are closely related. According to Fukuyama, trust can be embodied in the smallest and most basic forms of society, such as immediate family members, and can be extended towards larger groups of people, such as the nation. He believes that trust is the expectation that emanates within a community of people who wish to cooperate regularly and is transmitted through cultural mechanisms.[149]

Fukuyama provides the example of northern and southern Italy to explain the influential role of trust in building social capital. It is well known that the northern part of Italy is more industrialized and developed than the southern part, despite being under the same national regime. The industrial and economic success that has grown in the northern region of Italy is attributed to the trust and social capital factors that are not present in the south. As his main point, he argues forcefully against economists who typically claim that group formations are the result of voluntary

[140] Rose and Weller (2003, p. 201). See, also, generally, Rose (2000, p. 155), Ouderkirk (2007, p. 5).

[141] The World Bank, Overview: Social Capital, [online]. Available at: http://web.world-bank.org/WBSITE/EXTERNAL/TOPICS/EXTSOCIALDEVELOPMENT/EXTTSOCIALCAPITAL/0,,content-MDK:20642703~menuPK:401023~pagePK:148956~piPK:216618~theSitePK:401015,00.html. Accessed 8 March 2019. See, also, generally, Nannestad (2009, p. 311), Bartee and Brown (2007, p. 33). According to Toshiyuki Ojima, this is also important for the promotion of health. See Ojima (2011, p. 133).

[142] Bourdieu and Wacquant (1992, p. 119).

[143] Stirling et al. (2012, p. 355). See also Bofota (2012, p. 10).

[144] Beckert and Zafirovski (2006, p. 605) (eds).

[145] Stirling et al. (2012, p. 355). See also Allbritton (2007, p. 36).

[146] Westlund (2006, pp. 1–2).

[147] Ishiyama and Breuning (2011, p. 195) (eds).

[148] Westlund (2006, pp. 1–2). See, also, generally, Haubarer (2011, p. 147).

[149] Fukuyama (1996).

agreements between individuals who made a rational choice that cooperation is in their best interest in the long-term. Basing his conclusions in cultural comparisons, he argues that contracts, legal regulation, and self-interest are important factors of association but not as effective as the bonds created based on the moral consensus that gives the members of a community the basis for mutual trust.[150]

In the past three decades, many other authors have also argued that the concept of trust and social capital are "mutually reinforcing"[151] and it became an economic axiom that a market economy cannot function without trust.[152] Diego Gambetta (1988),[153] James Coleman (1990), Robert Putnam (1993), Francis Fukuyama (1995), and La Porta et al. (1996) have all claimed that trust or social capital plays a central role in the cooperative performance of people and the institutions of a society that leads to socially efficient and beneficial outcomes. La Porta et al. have argued, for example, that this is particularly relevant for the performance of large organizations.[154] Gambetta, for instance, defines trust as follows:

> trust (or, symmetrically, distrust) is a particular level of the subjective probability with which an agent assesses that another agent or group of agents will perform a particular action, both before he can monitor such action (or independently of his capacity ever to be able to monitor it) and in a context in which it affects his own action.[155]

The above definition of trust is important for it helps us to understand the difference between the individual and the social dimensions of trust. While the individual dimension of trust occurs between the interactions of two agents, the social dimension is often built on existing *intermediaries*[156] who can provide procedural and technical assistance. This definition also shows that trust is subjective and that it is not directly or immediately affected by actions that the trustor can monitor.[157] Whilst Gambetta uses the term *subjective probability,* this can also refer to an expectation.[158] Therefore, trust in this context can also be seen as a prediction of the agent's future action.[159] For Castelfranchi and Falcone, however, trust goes beyond *subjective probability*. They argue in favor of a cognitive perspective with a complicated structure of goals

---

[150] Fukuyama (1996, pp. 26, 101).

[151] Fu (2004).

[152] Bruni and Sugden (2000, pp. 21–45). See also Weigl (2008, p. 77).

[153] Gambetta (1988) (ed).

[154] La Porta et al. (1997, pp. 333–338).

[155] Gambetta adds two additional explanations to this definition: (i) "when human beings say they trust someone or that someone is trustworthy, they implicitly mean that the probability that he will perform an action that is beneficial or at least not detrimental to them is high enough for them to consider engaging in some form of cooperation"; and (ii) "correspondingly when humans say that someone is untrustworthy, they imply that that probability is low enough for us to refrain from doing so." The work of Diego Gambetta. See Weitzenboek (2012, p. 77). See also Gambetta (2000, pp. 213–237).

[156] Stockheim (2006, p. 142).

[157] Scarlat and Maries (2009, p. 142).

[158] Wierzbicki (2010, p. 36).

[159] Liu and Issarny (2004, p. 50).

and beliefs, where the trustor recognizes a "degree of trust" and makes an estimation of the potential risks involved in making a decision on whether or not to rely on the trustee. This is what they call a "threshold of risk acceptance/avoidance."[160]

Dasgupta defines trust "in the sense of correct expectations about the actions of other people that have a bearing on one's own choice of action when that action must be chosen before one can monitor the actions of those others."[161] The resulting definition captures the essential idea of both the purpose and nature of trust[162] as it emphasizes the hidden predicting action before the individual can monitor such action.[163] It also shows the relationship of trust in the context of social dilemma where there is a strong bond to trust someone based on reciprocity. In this context, boundedly rational individuals will be willing to trust based on prior knowledge, training and experience.[164]

Coleman also considers trust to be an important element of social capital.[165] He explains that trust is like making a "conscious bet," in which a risk-reward tradeoff must be reached under certain circumstances. A calculation between what you can win and lose to proceed to trust someone.[166] Elinor Ostrom and James Walker in their book *Trust and Reciprocity*, consider that trust is very important for the design of institutions to facilitate continuous individual improvement in social dilemma situations. They both share a broad view about trust, which is defined as "the willingness to take some risk in relation to other individuals on the expectation that the others will reciprocate,"[167] According to Williamson, individuals who are in charge of adapting the interfaces of contractual relationships have a personal and organizational stake. If the agents can trust each other, contract negotiation will be less complex and less expensive under a regime of greater trust.[168] These definitions are deep-rooted in the notion of reciprocity, which is ideal in most circumstances but may be too restrictive in a sense that it is limited to a reciprocal relationship.[169]

For Russel Hardin, trust as such is essentially difficult to define, but is fundamental for the creation and conservation of society. For him, much of what can be identified as trust in a wide range of situations can be best articulated as "encapsulated interest."[170] That is, one actor trusts another when the latter is believed to have strong reasons

---

[160] Castelfranchi and Falcone (2000, pp. 1–10).

[161] Dasgupta (2000, p. 52).

[162] Bhuiyan (2013, p. 11).

[163] Chami and Fullenkamp (2002, p. 6).

[164] Ostrom and Ostrom (2014, p. 143).

[165] Houlihan and Groeneveld (2011, p. 4).

[166] Swedberg (2003, p. 45).

[167] Walker and Ostrom (2005, p. 382) (eds), Walker and Ostrom (2009, p. 91).

[168] Williamson (1985, pp. 62–63, 66, 293).

[169] Bratianu (2015, p. 268).

[170] "On this account, I trust you because I think it is in your interest to take my interest in the relevant matter seriously in the following sense: You value the continuation of our relationship, and you therefore have your own interests in taking my interests into account. That is, you encapsulate my interests in your own interests." See Hardin (2004, p. 6).

to act in his best interest.[171] In other words, trust is a cognitive process based on inter-personal reciprocity.[172] This judgment based on the other interest in fulfilling my trust is what encapsulates our own in a specific issue.[173] Hardin even goes further to suggest this is a rational model, which is the base for long terms relations.[174] He claims, however, that much of the great doubts and confusion in the current debate fail to address the distinction between the usual or "vernacular" meaning of *trust* in contrast to *trustworthiness.* Hardin also roundly criticizes the schemes proposed by Coleman, Putnam and Fukuyama, in which trust is seen as a strong element of social capital.[175]

Such studies alone are not enough for creating a trustworthy framework. Mutual trust manifests in multiple variable configurations and complex interrelated layers that must be addressed. By and large, we could start referring to the framework proposed by Ostrom in which there are different layers and structural elements in the community and government that impinge trust, reciprocity and reputation. At the bottom of the structure lies the trust among individuals. The middle layer belongs to the community at large and at the top of the pyramid lies the legal community, including regulators and the government.[176]

One of the limitations of focusing only on the ideas of trust and social capital is that they do not propose a specific risk assessment methodology that looks to calculate and minimize potential risks at these various layers. Another limitation when social capital is established in a social network is that we automatically assume that we trust the network and there is a certain degree of camaraderie among the participants. While this is good for economic growth, the question is: how can we reassess the risks and reduce the uncertainties over time if trust levels are so high? A good example of this problem can be found in general audits. At first, the accountants of a company may invest a lot of money and resources in a risk assessment method. However, they usually repeat the same risk analysis over the years and the gap between reality and the annual report gradually increases. Similar analogies may be found in auditing companies, which employ the same risk assessment procedure within the social capital network over several years. The risk assessment criteria must be updated through time on a regular basis otherwise the probability that a new risk may appear remains still.

Yet, with these conceptual revisions in mind, it is possible to move towards a more specific understanding of the concept of trust in cloud computing and Big Data environments. In the preamble of the foregoing discussion, I like the overall idea that the concepts of mutual trust and social capital are inexorably linked. However, I think we can clearly reject the notion that cultural values can help us to build mutual trust in cloud computing contracts. As I will further discuss in this chapter, I see SLAs

[171] Farrel (2009, p. 11).

[172] McMyler (2011, p. 113).

[173] Shapiro (2012, p. 100).

[174] Baert and Carreira da Silva (2010, p. 119).

[175] Zsolnai (2005, pp. 268–269). See also Ruokonen (2013, pp. 1–3).

[176] The work of Elinor Ostrom. See Sajise et al. (2003, p. 223).

in cloud computing transactions as things that could be seen as new legal forms of collaborations. They could provide more choices and create new opportunities for collaborations that are not under the current contractual regime. This should be addressed when individuals in cloud computing and Big Data settings attempt to fashion rules to improve their personal and joint outcomes. This new contractual framework can help to create better legal relations based on mutual trust. This means that the SLAs must be more flexible if we want to pursue innovation and economic growth. This flexibility comes through enabling the actors to engage in new forms of collaborations in the sense that they have more choices to start a new project.

6.2.3 Delimiting the Concept of Trust

In an empirical meta-analysis, Castaldo examined 72 definitions of trust to tease out the exact data about different fields of social sciences, such as management, marketing, psychology, and sociology.[177] This cluster analysis provides great value to follow our discussion and allows us to move forward to study the details of the necessary components and recurring links between these terms. A description of the main elements of trust is set out below. It follows the same sequence and logical order as they appear in the definitions.[178] These elements are:

(i) The "*construct*", where trust is perceived as an "expectation, a belief, willingness, and an attitude". This is an essential point to further analyze the concept of trust.[179]
(ii) The "*subjects*" of the trust relationship, placing more emphasis in "whom trust is placed"[180] (i.e., the "trustee"),[181] such as individuals, groups, organizations, institutions, etc. In this case, depending on the nature, characteristics and values of the trustee, the type of trust will take a more simple or elaborate form such as "personal," "inter-organizational" and "institutional" trust.[182]
(iii) "*Actions*" and "*behaviors*" which highlight the behavioral nature of trust. According to Castaldo, this is essential for "recognizing the concept of trust itself."[183] This behavioral facet of trust has been generally referred and operationalized as "a trustor's intended risk taking behavior."[184] This means that the trustor and trustee behavior will be based on actions that are consistent in

[177]Castaldo (2002, p. 2).
[178]Castelfranchi and Falcone (2010, p. 9).
[179]Castaldo (2002, p. 7).
[180]Castaldo (2002, p. 7).
[181]Castelfranchi and Falcone (2010, p. 9).
[182]Castaldo (2002, p. 7).
[183]Castaldo (2002, p. 7).
[184]The works of Clark and Payne, Curral and Judge. See Barling and Cooper (2008, p. 100) (eds).

a decision to trust. Cunning and Bromiley recognized and stepped up the complex multi-dimensional and structural nature of trust based on its behavioral aspect. Such recognition is an important step forward in realizing the full scope of trust.[185]

(iv) "*Results*" and "*outputs*" of behavior are two essential components of trust. This means that the actions of the trustee are assumably expected to be both beneficial and predictable for the trustor. This way, basic levels of predictability and optimal expectation can guarantee to plan ahead.[186]

(v) *The "risk"* of the "*decisional situation.*" This means that the decision to trust will be inherently replete with risks and uncertainty. Johannisson, among others, argued that the trustor has to willingly put herself in a situation of vulnerability with regard to the trustee. Risk, uncertainty and ambiguity are the fundamental pillars or key elements that espouse any such belief or expectation to trust.[187]

In broad strokes, this sequence motif reveals the continuation of a pattern that often regards trust as an *attitude*, *belief*, *expectation* or *willingness* to put oneself in a vulnerable position in order to avoid or diminish the likelihood or source of risk and uncertainty arising from any transaction. It also suggests a cross-cutting and multi-dimensional nature, covering the behavioral aspects based on reciprocal actions consistent in a decision to trust. These elements are the key takeaway that calls for the implementation of sophisticated ways to factor risk and uncertainty within a framework of trust. For this reason, this book features a chapter on behavioral law and economics (see infra Chap. 7) and risk assessment based on a specific analysis of *threats* and *vulnerabilities* (see infra Chap. 9). This way, basic levels of predictability and optimal expectation can guarantee to plan in advance,[188] as pointed out within Plan Theory.

Oomsels and Bouckaert also provide a comprehensive table with an overview of 33 different definitions of trust, many of which have already been discussed here, which allows us to visualize a pattern. The pattern stems from both "cognition and affection" and could be characterized by the willingness to put oneself in a vulnerable state that is required in risky or contingent situations. This leads to "risk-taking" behavior, which is hinged on the "positive expectations of a trustee." Both authors consolidate these patterns into the following definition of trust: "the intentional and behavioral suspension of vulnerability by a trustor on the basis of positive expectations of a trustee."[189]

Mayer and Davis, in their integrative model of organizational trust, presented a cross-disciplinary analysis of trust[190] that applies to a wide range of relationships

[185] The works of Cummings and Bromiley. See Castaldo (2002, p. 7).

[186] Castelfranchi and Falcone (2010, p. 9), Castaldo (2002, p. 7).

[187] Castelfranchi and Falcone (2010, p. 9). The works of Johannisson. See Castaldo (2002, p. 7).

[188] Castelfranchi and Falcone (2010, p. 9). The works of Johannisson. See Castaldo (2002, p. 7).

[189] Oomsels and Bouckaert (2014, pp. 5–7).

[190] Mayer et al. (1995, pp. 709–734).

in an organizational setting. This model considered other important factors that pattern the relationship between the trustor and trustee.[191] Other studies neglected this important relationship and considered trust as an umbrella concept that encompasses a broad spectrum as a social phenomenon. The proposed model defines trust as "the willingness to a party to be vulnerable to the actions of another party based on the expectation that the other will perform a particular action important to the trustor, irrespective of the ability to monitor or control that other party."[192] This definition has inspired the works of Johnson-George and Swap who stated that the "willingness to take risks may be one of the few characteristics common to all trust situations"[193]; and Kee and Know who concluded that in order to study trust there must be something meaningful at stake and the trustor must be fully aware of the risks involved.[194]

Feeling vulnerable means that there is something valuable to lose. Thus, Mayer et al. concluded that "making oneself vulnerable is taking risk. Trust is not taking risk per se, but rather it is a willingness to take risk."[195] The breaking down of these concepts tally with what has been argued in the previous sections. Risk is an essential component of trust because the decision to trust is primarily based on an individual's assessment of the negative outcomes.[196] Therefore, in order to create mutual trust, a risk assessment framework must be implemented and should include a systemic approach by which *threats* and *vulnerabilities* can be specifically identified.[197]

6.3 The Role of Cloud Brokers for Strengthening Mutual Trust

The concept of trust takes on a particular meaning in the context of ICT systems and varies significantly from the notions of personal and inter-personal trust discussed in some social sciences.[198] Notwithstanding that the concept of trust in the social sciences is frequently conceptualized in an informal framework, the extant literature discussed briefly above serves as a good reference point and source of inspiration when attempting to construct a model of trust in cloud and Big Data scenarios. While informal trust-based relationships are very important here, it is integral to achieve some degree of formality to ensure that the level of trust is not solely dependent upon individuals. In computer sciences, this notion has to be formalized in a sense that it needs a systematic structure to ensure its implementation.[199]

[191] Mayer et al. (1995, p. 711).
[192] Mayer et al. (1995, p. 712).
[193] Mayer et al. (1995, p. 712).
[194] Mayer et al. (1995, p. 712).
[195] Mayer et al. (1995, p. 712).
[196] Kini and Choobineh (1998, pp. 51–61).
[197] Kahn et al. (2012, p. 123), Djemame (2012, p. 12).
[198] Fuchs et al. (2010, p. 200).
[199] Nielsen and Krukow (2003, p. 1).

Kini and Choobineh define trust as "a belief in the system characteristics, specifically belief in the competence, dependability, and security of the system, under conditions of risk."[200] In the same line of thought, a non-profit organization established by several major software developers and hardware vendors—known collectively as the Trusted Computing Group (TCG)—has introduced the concept of "trusted computing."[201] This holds a special meaning depending on the particular properties and aspects of a technical system,[202] such as trust in security[203] and reputation-based management systems.[204]

Regrettably, the problem I observe is that the concept of trust in the cloud seems to be blurred by the shade of meanings emanating from the media and the commercial nature of the Internet. The concept of trust in this context is frequently used as a tool for marketing purposes without any solid foundations. It became completely detached from the traditional social sciences such as psychology, sociology and the overall ideas of social capital. Moreover, due to the increasingly complex privacy[205] and security[206] challenges, the concept of trust in the cloud seems to be limited to only two aspects: transparency and reputation. These aspects are certainly important when the main focus of attention is given to increasing the protection of customer's personal data from third parties. In this sense, cloud providers often characterize trust within the scope of privacy and security in the attempt to avoid data leaks and assure that customer's data is safe and in compliance with data protection legislation.[207] However, this approach to transparency and reputation in the context of security and privacy is, in my view, too limited and we need to go beyond that point.

As seen above on several occasions, the advent of cloud computing and Big Data has also brought the emergence of innovation intermediaries (or brokers) . They act as "gatekeepers" between end-users and cloud providers that provide platforms and services to support transactions on the Internet. They also act as a representative of or as a proxy for end-users since they may lack the material information concerning the reliability of the services. Therefore, the experience and expertise provided by cloud brokers could bring innovative services to the negotiation table. They can use the resources and technical skills they have to extend the trust parameter values beyond the current state of the art.

---

[200] Kini and Choobineh (1998, pp. 51–61).

[201] See, generally, Trusted Computing Platform Alliance (2001).

[202] Fuchs et al. (2010, p. 200).

[203] According to Yan Zheng, we cannot have security without resorting to a certain degree of trust. For example, in a Global System for Mobile Communications (GSM) technology, established more than two decades ago, there is an authentication system, which allows users to make secured phone calls. See, generally, Zheng (2010), foreword.

[204] Fuchs et al. (2010, p. 274). For example, the notions of trust and reputation of the XenoTrust Architecture System. See Dragovic et al. (2003, p. 60).

[205] See, generally, Robinson et al. (2011).

[206] For example, Edward Humphreys (Convenor of the International Standardization Organization (ISO) working group and manager of the ISO/IEC 27001, ISO/IEC 27002 and the cloud security standard ISO/IEC 27017, thinks that creating a climate of trust is one of the most important requirements when outsourcing IT. See, generally, Humphreys (2007), Gasiorowski-Denis (2015).

[207] See, generally, Burger et al. (2013).

Cloud brokers are also gaining momentum and recognition not only for providing intermediation and identifying dependable cloudservice providers, but also for providing cloud service aggregation and arbitrage.[208] In this context, trust may also play a key role in the coordination of cloud computing contracts, devoting special attention to measures which will make it possible to collaborate in scientific research at the global scale. This is the reason why one of the central themes of this book sees the role of intermediaries as a means of achieving mutual trust in cloud computing and Big Data transformations.

Chircu et al. carried out empirical research to assess the amount of trust a consumer has in electronic commerce intermediary and the level of expertise that end-users need in order to use such intermediary services. The results in this study confirmed what other academics and practitioners in the field alike have hypothesized with regard to the importance of trust and expertise as decisive factors when it comes to the adoption intention in complex transactions.[209] Similarly, I also argue in favor of finding solutions through proactive intermediary mechanisms to fine-tune the procedures built on a flexible contractual framework.

Cloud brokers could, for example, provide negotiation services that allow for the clarification of "ownership" rights of data and databases as I will further explain in the forthcoming chapters. The extension of these negotiation capabilities should be embedded in a well-structured contractual framework that takes into account all the main elements and attributes of trust. Within this trend, two options should be brought to the forefront: (i) the broker may only bring the parties together to conclude agreements; or (ii) the broker may also take part of the negotiations on behalf of end-users, bringing its infrastructure and expertise as a virtual cloud provider. The main distinction between these two options is that in the latter the broker no longer appears solely as a mediator but is instead offering added value services in the best interest of end-users.[210] This two-tier structure allows the parties to choose for a more flexible framework and to trust each other even though they never met in the past.[211]

End-users, on the other hand, can also be depicted as having two faces: one is the individual or "personal user" of the Internet in general and the other is the employee of a company or large organization using a cloud service. Personal users are less concerned about risks because there is not much at stake. They use any kind of cloud computing services such as Google, Amazon or storage cloud services such as Dropbox. They upload personal data or documents and keep them in the cloud for storage and back-up purposes. As this is their own personal information, they usually do not face any material problems or any kind of liability issues. Eventually, they may face some risks if they lose their mobile phones or their laptops are stolen together with their passcodes.[212]

---

[208] See Pawar et al. (2014, pp. 237–244).

[209] Chircu et al. (2000b, pp. 1–7).

[210] Djemame et al. (2006, p. 7).

[211] See Herzberg et al. (2000, pp. 2–15).

[212] See, generally, Hoog and Strzempka (2011, p. 94).

Additionally, the same individual or personal user may be simultaneously the employee of a company, university, or governmental agency. In this case, the managers of information system divisions of such organizations may demand employees use in house system services, private or hybrid clouds. They are generally vulnerable to two different kinds of risks. These are the general risks attached to the failure of the cloud services[213] and the risks associated with governance and accountability.[214]

In light of this, the first and most important question before us is of a technical nature—how can end-users protect themselves and their customers from running such risks? It is important thereby to raise risk awareness of potential failures among the parties concerned and how to identify appropriate responses. The other question is how can the intermediaries or brokers help with the different faces of users in order to strengthen their confidence, and, make more effective and smart choices? This question is also technical but more of a practical matter as it requires greater coordination. It implies the idea that end-users must rely on a trusted third party involved in the negotiations. Both questions merit a well thought out and reasoned answer as there are several attributes and elements of trust that should be taken into account. Some of the most important factors are explained below.

6.3.1 The Double Nature of Trust

First, we should depart from the psychological and emotional aspects of trust, which characterizes trust as an "attitude." In this framework, there are, from my point of view, two important issues to bear in mind. The first one is what Shapiro calls the "economy of trust" within Plan Theory. Similarly, to the story of the birth of the U.S. Republic where attitudes of trust (and distrust) moved between different branches within three waves,[215] I suggest allocating more trust in the services provided by innovation intermediaries. In this respect, brokers can act as trusted third parties who can negotiate and bargain the contractual terms on behalf of the end-users and help them to choose a cloud provider that can better satisfy their needs and demands. The role of these innovation intermediaries could compensate for the lack of trust by deferring its trust management functions to their brokerage services.

Secondly, this is also in line with the ISO standards[216] where trusted third parties, also known as certification authorities (CA), are identified as important nodes to secure the authenticity and legal admissibility based on web service protocols.[217] The idea of implementing a model of trust as a hierarchical tree is very important.

[213] See, generally, Zabolotnyi et al. (2014, p. 566).

[214] Niezen and Steijn (2015, pp. 203 et seq).

[215] Shapiro (2011, pp. 316–330).

[216] See ISO/DIS 17068—Information and Documentation—Trusted Third Party Repository for Digital Records.

[217] Crucially, a certificate is issued and digitally signed by the CA using a public key infrastructure (PKI) cryptographic system. See Butterfield and Ngondi (2016, p. 77).

By definition, the CA are considered the root of all trust relationships. Engaging with trusted third parties may also guarantee an expected threshold of reliability and increase the confidence between parties who have never met before.[218] By way of an analogy, we could refer here to other types of professional services such as those found in the legal field. Here the trust framework is designed to reassure the public and relies on several factors, such as through the use of licenses and memberships issued by the bar association, their adherence to a professional code of ethics and the faculty of a professional body that monitors and disciplines its members.[219]

The same analogy can be drawn upon other types of professional services, such as in the medical field. Even though the trusted third party may not be entirely reliable, the first aspect of trust is guaranteed by the license of the doctor. Patients may choose to contact doctors based on the good reputation of the institution in which they work, such as a well-known and prestigious hospital. Fugelli described, in simple terms, the essence of patient's trust in relation to a doctor as being "the belief that the doctor is acting in the patient's best interest."[220] This is also related to the double nature of trust as the two fundamental trust levels.[221] In other words, there is trust in a known individual, in this case trust in one's doctor (*personal trust*), and trust in the profession of medicine or health care system (*impersonal trust*).[222]

Personal trust is more emotional and depends on different factors like the affective ties of individuals.[223] Impersonal trust is more rational and allows people, even strangers, to interact with each other. It applies to the "macro-and meso-levels" and is broken down in two: systemic trust (confidence) and societal trust.[224] Recall that for Luhmann and Giddens, impersonal or generalized trust (i.e., in formal institutions, such as technical and professional knowledge systems)[225] is what makes you interact confidently and trust in professional services around the world.[226]

Unfortunately, the very nature of trust is more complex and, in real life, there are many other aspects to consider. Through interactions with professional services, communication may improve or deteriorate as time goes by. This means that neither a trusted third party's credentials (i.e., the license of a lawyer or doctor) nor authentication protocols can guarantee 100% reliability of the service and there is only one aspect on which to establish trust.

---

[218] Purser (2004, p. 15).

[219] See Lauziere (2002, p. 48).

[220] The work of Fugelli. See McDonald (2004), introduction.

[221] Huemer et al. (2000, p. 129).

[222] Healy (2016, p. 311).

[223] Huemer et al. (2000, p. 129).

[224] Chavdarova (2007, p. 279).

[225] Mehta (2007, p. 156).

[226] Johnstone (2011, p. 3).

6.3.2 Deferring Accountability to Cloud Brokers

In order to promote lasting commercial relationships, cloud brokers should recognize that they need to show not only high levels of skills and expertise but also replicate the same climate of trust-based relationships that we find in traditional intermediary services like travel agencies or financial institutions.[227] In this sense, Zanini and Migueles approach trust as a fundamental element in the planning and execution of diverse organizational tasks and its "mediating relationship with organizational performance."[228] They conclude that trust is the very cornerstone on which to build relational contracts.[229] Rubinstein and Wolinsky suggested that intermediaries lower the probability of running risks associated with trading and, as a consequence, lower the proportion of unsuccessful trades. This leads to an increase in mutual trust measures in the cloud market and its institutions.[230]

Nevertheless, coming back to the topic of CA that issue certificates on the Internet, they often exclude or overly limit their scope of liability. These clauses are usually included in a certificate policy document.[231] On the one hand, it is true that CA shall not be held liable for damages arising from the use of the certificate in excess of that value limit or for any other purpose.[232] On the other hand, this structure of liability seems comparatively favorable to the CA in an effort to create a less risky environment for them, but it seems unfairly detrimental to end-users.[233]

In this sense, cloud brokers play a significant role in evaluating suitable service and infrastructure providers taking the necessary steps of due diligence to conclude a contract on the best terms for their principals.[234] However, a certain degree of liability should be delegated to the brokers in order to guarantee neutrality and transparency. For this reason, an important approach is that the broker becomes accountable for ensuring that such identified user requirements are fully met when the cloud service is running. According to Guinnane, trust is implicitly derived from older notions of information and the ability to invoke sanctions. Trust exists because of the information available about the parties involved in a transaction and the ability to impose sanctions upon each other.[235]

---

[227] Chircu et al. (2000a, p. 1).

[228] Zanini and Migueles (2013, pp. 77–87).

[229] Zanini and Migueles (2013, pp. 77–87).

[230] The works of Rubinstein and Wolinsky. See Tarnacha (2008, p. 43). See, also, generally, Rubinstein and Wolinsky (1987, pp. 581–593).

[231] Skevington and Hart (1998, p. 60).

[232] See Articles 11 and 12 of the working paper submitted to the Working Group on Electronic Commerce at its thirty-second session: incorporation by reference: proposal by the United Kingdom of Great Britain and Northern Ireland: note by the Secretariat (A/CN.9/WG.IV/WP.74). United Nations Commission on International Trade Law (UNCITRAL), p. 175, Yearbook, Vol. XXIX, New York: United Nations Publication.

[233] Gladstone (2004, p. 227).

[234] As a way of analogy, this could be compared to the duty of diligence of real estate brokers. See Pivar and Harlan (1995, pp. 19 et seq).

[235] Guinnane (2005, pp. 1–2).

Once the broker has run a risk assessment, they then proceed to sing the SLA as a main representative of the end-user. If the requirements of the expected QoS are not achieved, the broker intermediary must pay a penalty fee to the end-user. For example, if the risk of a sub-job is high (i.e., likely to fail), the broker must find another cloud provider and re-negotiate the SLA in the best interest of the end-user. This means finding an optimal trade-off between the costs of the new cloud service and the penalty fee that the broker would need to pay in the event that the SLA fails.[236] This is in line with the theories of law and economics discussed above in previous chapters where transaction costs and a cost-benefit analysis should be taken into account. In addition, this system provides an assurance that transactions will be carried out in conformity to the end-users' requirements, and therefore, offers an extra layer for the strengthening of the trust framework.

6.3.3 Risk, Vulnerability and Threat

Three elements are of vital importance to furthering the development of trust. These elements are *risks, vulnerabilities and threats*. Trust cannot be fully achieved unless all these elements are at the same time effectively addressed in the cloud computing architecture. This means that we should resort to the so-called *strategic view*, which goes beyond human emotions. The way Luhmann characterized trust here is very important. Recall that trust for Luhmann has nothing to do with feelings, but is rather a *choice* to put oneself at *risk*.[237] Trust and risk are often two sides of the same coin.[238] Although they seem different and even opposite to some extent, they share the same ground. Trusting a third party implies taking risks. In fact, trust is born out of risky situations.[239]

Therefore, creating more trust has a lot to do with how individuals handle risk and uncertainty. In addition to what has been said in previous sections, it is opportune to cite here Chiles and McMakin, who define trust as "increasing one's vulnerability to the risk of opportunistic behavior of one's transaction partner, whose behavior is not under one's control in a situation in which the costs of violating the trust are greater than the benefits of upholding the trust."[240] This means that without the risk dimension and the notion of vulnerability to opportunistic behavior, there is no need to trust.[241]

In other words, while risk is usually seen as producing negative effects, modern theories of risk management recognize it as also having a positive impact. According to Mayer et al., trust as an action is "the result of a specific calculation weighing the

[236]Djemame et al. (2006, p. 7).

[237]Luhmann (1988, pp. 96–97).

[238]Swartz and Iacobucci (2000, p. 358) (eds).

[239]Pennanen (2006, p. 39).

[240]Chiles and McMackin (1996, p. 85).

[241]Smigielska and Wierbinski (2015, pp. 275–276).

likelihoods of both positive and negative outcomes."[242] A typical example can be seen in the foreign exchange market where traders have to evaluate the pros and cons of short buying or selling stocks. There is, of course, the risk of losing money but they also have high expectations to make long-term profits based on hard data.[243]

Short selling stock corresponds to *unlimited* risk and buying stocks to *limited* risk. The difference between limited and unlimited risk is related to the amount of gain or loss. To use a more dramatic example, if you jump from a train, you run the risk of dying; this is unlimited risk. However, if you run, there is only a risk of breaking a leg, i.e., limited risk. The question in this example would be: which one would you prefer the most? The answer is very simple. You would prefer to choose the option where the least risks are likely to occur and the best possible reward is presented to you.[244]

This approach is relevant to the contractual framework proposed in this book, which incorporates a risk assessment methodology. This framework sets out to identify the most vulnerable parts of the SLA, which is run and managed by a cloud brokerage service. Consider the scenario where end-users are searching for a cloud service to execute an application. This could consist of a single job or multiple sub-jobs. They might have strict deadlines and other obligations to take into account thus reducing transaction and deliberation costs is a key aspect of this process.

The current state of the art of cloud computing transactions does not include risk management within their infrastructures, or they only cover basic security and privacy issues. Usually, they follow a "best-effort" approach only. Within this scenario, if end-users are part of a big company, they may have to negotiate the SLA and define all the business and legal aspects with the cloud provider. Negotiating these requirements is often particularly complex and sensitive. On other occasions, if end-users are individuals or "personal users", they might face the constraints of click-wrap agreements where no negotiations are possible. Therefore, the role of the broker may offer the resources they need to negotiate contracts and define the criteria for reducing the legal risks involved. This approach is unique as it provides risk assessment information at the level of individual components in comparison to previous efforts, which are based on node or machine level risk assessments. The advantage of this probabilistic approach is the provision of more detailed options for the risk assessment leading to more efficient utilization of resources.[245]

Cloud computing and Big Data bring new threats. Therefore, the threat component in addition to the element of vulnerability is an essential feature linking the two sides of the trust-risk equation. It is no doubt that some of these threats are related to virtualization and multi-tenancy, which serve as the basis for cloud computing architectures. Some of these "tenants"—who might have opposite goals—share the

---

[242]The work of Mayer et al. See Wintterlin and Blobaum (2016, p. 77).

[243]Fontanills et al. (2001, p. 72).

[244]Fontanills et al. (2001, p. 72).

[245]See Sangrasi and Djemame (2011); Sangrasi and Djemame (2012, pp. 321–330), Sangrasi et al. (2012, pp. 445–452).

same physical infrastructure and pool of resources.[246] This also stems from the traditional security triad requirements of confidentiality, integrity and availability (CIA taxonomy).[247]

The Cloud Security Alliance has identified a list of the top threats for critical areas in cloud computing.[248] This taxonomy is, however, incomplete. Many authors have suggested modifications to the CIA requirements in order to take account of the different developments of Big Data and extend its range of choices.[249] Due to the massive data mining tools available in the cloud, Internet users can now run data mining algorithms by distributing data on different computers.[250] Therefore, the aim that sits at the core of this research is to extend the range of this taxonomy list and focus not only in the typical CIA requirements but also to consider other threats related to "ownership" rights of data and databases.

6.3.4 Trust and Reputation: Beyond Track Records

A reasonable development of trust may be based on due diligence or track records, i.e., the assessment or estimates by trustworthy third parties. For example, a closer look at the behavior of the employees of big companies, universities, or governmental agencies, suggest that trust can usually be placed on a trustworthy provider. This is often the situation when an organization contracts with a provider of software services that enjoys a very good reputation in the market. Contracting with them can alleviate the degree of responsibility of those individuals in charge when there is a risk that arises.[251]

The assessment of third parties may bring, however, some problems in a long-term perspective. For example, the risk assessment of new companies such as new mergers and acquisitions (M&A) or initial public offerings (IPOs) are usually more rigorous. Nevertheless, if the same risk assessment is done repeatedly during the following years, it is very difficult to maintain the granularity of the assessment and due diligence every year. The same holds true with auditing companies. If the audit is carried out by the same personnel, the quality of the auditing may gradually deteriorate. In other words, the assessments or estimates by trustworthy third companies tend to overlook some risks as time passes by.

There are a number of criteria used to assess risk when it comes to a service/cloud provider such as, (i) past SLA performance; (ii) geographical information (useful for the threat/vulnerability levels) ; (iii) certifications and standard compliance; (iv)

[246] Marinescu (2013, p. 278).

[247] See McCarthy (2006, p. 60).

[248] See Cloud Security Alliance (2013).

[249] Thomborson (2010, p. 17).

[250] Tsai et al. (2015, pp. 1–32).

[251] For a reputation trust model example. See Sinn (2008, pp. 130 et seq).

business stability; (v) general infrastructure practice; and (vi) general privacy practice. Each of these has sub-criteria. Indeed, when risk is assessed for a new company, it is usually more rigorous. Not to mention the fact that some information is missing or the data available is not useful (i.e., past SLAs). From my understanding, even if the risk assessment is done repeatedly over the following years, it is required to go through the finer-grain detail/criteria again, even if this is a tedious exercise because the environment and conditions may have changed. This is what actually happens in real life. If we consider Health & Safety risks (i.e., fire safety in a building), the "last year" assessment recommendations are reviewed but the current assessment itself needs to re-consider all aspects in relation to the building, people, etc. However, this may be left to interpretation.

Here again, we can find some other examples and learn important lessons from the experience of other disciplines in suggesting ways where repeated communication and past information could be a good resource for the development of mutual trust. In the field of financial services, for instance, we often find that disclosure of track records (such as repeated communication, repeated resolution of conflicts and information based on previous transactions) may establish or develop mutual trust.[252] A similar type of transaction occurs when a private equity fund/firm attempts to improve the target company through major structural management changes. This type of situation usually happens at the beginning of a take-over when the buyer firm can be very hostile to the management of the target company and some of the shareholders may be reluctant to join the new buyer firm. However, after they have gone through repeated negotiations and communicated frequently, they develop social capital and therefore mutual trust.

In the same vein, Mui et al. define trust as "a subjective expectation an agent has about another's future behavior based on the history of their encounters."[253] This definition is particularly important in the context of cloud computing and Big Data as it suggests that there is an implicit notion of reputation or track record based on previous interactions.[254] Trust and reputation have become the focus of active research in several cloud computing open systems. Alhamad et al. have proposed, for example, a trust model that comprises a high-level abstract architecture for cloud computing. Such a model takes into account information about previous experiences with regard to SLA service levels.[255] In line with this research stream, this book conveys the idea that trust and reputation—along with risk—are key components used by the broker to evaluate the service of the cloud provider.[256]

Attracting interested new customers to the cloud network presupposes a high level of trust in the reliability of the cloud services. The risk assessment framework developed in Chap. 9 offers innovative concepts that will help cloud providers win the merited user's trust by making the PoF of SLAs publicly available. This, in turn,

[252]See Eriksson (2015, p. 186).

[253]The work of Mui et al. See Munesh and Sareen (2012, p. 26) (eds).

[254]Alzaid et al. (2013, pp. 67–68).

[255]Alhamad et al. (2010).

[256]Pawar et al. (2014, p. 243).

enables greater transparency and increases end-user's confidence in proportion to the amount of additional information available to them. Similar to other daily life services, end-users usually choose cloud providers based on their previous experiences or their reputation by referrals from other customers.[257] Unfortunately, word of mouth is not enough to predict the future performance of cloud providers. Since data and databases are one of the most important assets that a customer or an organization might have, they prefer to use self-hosted resources instead of handing over management of their data to third parties. As a result, this lack of trust slows down the broader adoption of cloud services.[258]

On the one hand, cloud providers carefully scrutinize the SLAs since they are fully aware of the potential threats that might lead to paying high penalties to end-users. Therefore, they do not entirely trust their own capability to provide the requested quality of service (QoS). On the other hand, end-users do not completely trust cloud providers since they are also aware of possible resource outages.[259] Data breach scandals of some cloud providers, such as the Dropbox hack attack, have also led to the erosion of trust in cloud services on the global scale. In 2012, Dropbox cloud services, which are frequently used for file-sharing or backup purposes, announced that a software glitch at Dropbox allowed any visitor to log in the account of millions of customers using any password.[260]

In the end, the company admitted that more than 68 million usernames and passwords had been leaked. The full scale of the hack, however, only came to light in the middle of 2016.[261] Therefore, the question is: how can end-users trust cloud providers when incidents of this kind occur on a regular basis? By using the risk assessment framework provided in Chap. 9, end-users no longer need to rely on the "word of mouth" reputation of cloud providers or base their decisions solely on their past experience and track-records. Instead, they are able to correctly estimate the risk for their business based on the published PoF. This approach integrates different layers of trust and focuses on risk awareness and management services orchestrated by a cloud broker.

A similar type of reasoning can be found in the insurance industry. Most insurance is sold through insurance agents or brokers who can offer different policies directly to individuals or companies.[262] Many of these intermediaries are offering even more automated e-services to customers. By using new information and communication technologies, brokers can significantly expand their capacity to acquire and compare prices as well as different modalities of insurance policies.[263]

The cloud broker can also act as a mediator in the negotiation of SLAs. This will enable end-users to deal with several cloud providers at the same time. Moreover, the

---

[257] Battre et al. (2007, p. 193).

[258] Battre et al. (2007, p. 193).

[259] See Srinivasan (2014, p. 150).

[260] Simpson (2014, p. 114).

[261] Mendelsohn (2016).

[262] Graham and Xie (2007, p. 78).

[263] See Janovs and Fomin (2011, p. 231).

broker can take the position of a provider and act as a kind of "higher level provider" for workflow job executions by allocating sub-tasks over different cloud providers. This approach will allow the cloud broker to execute a service if the QoS is very high. This includes legal criteria requested by end-users. In such cases, the broker can engage with different cloud providers that can fulfill the SLA, thus lowering the PoF and general risks involved.

6.3.5 *Gaining User's Trust Through Websites and Social Networks*

As seen above, a reputation-based trust management system takes into account a specific approach to assess and manage trust. This approach to trust and reputation has been proposed in various fields of distributed systems such as peer-to-peer networks, e-commerce, pervasive computing, and grid and cloud computing.[264] The trust framework based on reputation-based systems should, however, also allow alternative approaches that include other individual parameters to calculate trust.

For example, an innovative approach carried out within the OPTIMIS project included two trust assessor components within the architectural design of its toolkit. Each component evaluates specific parameters (including legal ones) that are calculated for service and infrastructure providers. This framework calculates the level of trust an end-user may have with a service provider, taking into account two aspects: (i) the past experience between the end-user and the cloud providers (i.e., "direct interaction"); and (ii) the behavior of the cloud service provider with other end-users and the feedback provided by them with regards to such service (i.e., "recommended feedback"). This model takes into consideration different levels of trust and the level of preference a user may have for the cloud provider when relying exclusively on the reputations provided by the network.[265]

The framework includes a selection procedure and a social networking tool as a component within the same package. It contains a query system in which the end-user requests a service to be fulfilled. The system generates a list of candidates who can perform the task and calculates a set of trust values associated with the services. End-users may select the service provider from the provided list and are free to decide whether they want to use the cloud service or not. If they proceed to choose a cloud provider, they can submit their own rating after using the cloud service. Then, a list of "good" and "bad" services is stored in a database system, which is going to be used by the trust manager component for future calculations of trust values for the service.[266]

---

[264] See Zheng (2010), preface.

[265] Corrales Compagnucci (2016, p. 219).

[266] Corrales Compagnucci (2016, p. 219).

This approach enables cloud users to have better judgment about the reliability of cloud computing services based on the opinion of other end-users.[267] The social network within this framework may help to compensate for the lack of trust end-users might have towards cloud service providers thus adding an extra layer of trust to the reputation-based framework.[268] Similar analogies may be found in the hotel and accommodation industry. Intermediary services such as Tripadvisor[269] and platforms services such as Airbnb[270] allow previous guests of a hotel or private housing to write a review through their own web platform. This provides additional information for other customers. If the review reveals poor quality services, it is likely to negatively influence the decision of other potential customers who are considering visiting that establishment.[271]

In addition, some companies have decided to spend less time negotiating the complexities of SLAs and instead have moved their SLA to a so-called "Trust Site." For example, Salesforce.com has created a trust site[272] where they can make their SLA and policy framework publicly available (i.e., security policy and privacy policy). A Trust Site contains current and historical information with regards to uptime performance or any other metrics the customers need to know in order to gain trust.[273] This is, in my view, a simple and straightforward concept in which many legal issues could be brought to create more transparency and trust between cloud providers and end-users. For example, a "data portability" policy framework could be added to the Trust Site so issues of "ownership" rights of data and databases could be more clearly spelled out.[274] This view takes into account the classical interpretation of the concept of trust in the online environment that is rooted in elements of *transparency*.

Another good example of this trend is the CloudTrust Protocol (CTP) where cloud users can elicit information about the elements of transparency endowed in the SLA and policy frameworks. What the CTP does is to provide further evidence of relevant information concerning the compliance, security, privacy, integrity and other elements currently being performed in the cloud. Therefore, cloud users will be more aware and empowered to make the right decisions and choose the cloud provider that complies and fits their needs. These "elements of transparency" are inextricably entwined and rooted in the concept of digital trust[275] and could, therefore, provide a good venue for managing the economy of trust suggested by Shapiro.[276]

[267] Da Silva and Zisman (2012, pp. 328–343).

[268] Corrales Compagnucci (2016, pp. 219–220).

[269] Tripadvisor. Available at: https://www.tripadvisor.com. Accessed 10 May 2019.

[270] Airbnb. Available at: https://www.airbnb.com. Accessed 10 May 2019.

[271] Dinnen and Hassanien (2013, p. 71).

[272] See Salesforce.com.

[273] See Aber Law Firm.

[274] Corrales Compagnucci (2016, p. 219).

[275] See Cloud Security Alliance.

[276] Corrales Compagnucci (2016, p. 219).

6.3.6 *Blockchain 2.0: The "Trust Machine"*[277]

Another radical and novel idea would be to follow the principles underlying the decentralized cryptographic technology that enables Bitcoin called the "blockchain." Blockchain is the verification system behind Bitcoin that allows people who do not know or trust each other to build a large digital record of "who owns what" that will enforce the consent of everyone concerned.[278] The blockchain "acts as a consistent transaction history on which all 'nodes' eventually agree."[279] It is essentially a public ledger with the potential to store and transfer tangible assets (physical properties such as cars, real estate property, etc.) and intangible assets (such as votes, genomic data, reputation, intention, information, software and even ideas).[280]

In other words, the blockchain allows parties to send, receive and store value or information through a distributed peer-to-peer network of several computers. Each transaction is distributed across the entire network and is recorded on a block only when the rest of the network ratifies the validity of the transaction based on past transactions and taking into account the previous blocks.[281] Each block follows the other one successively and this is what creates the blockchain. Each block contains a unique fingerprint using cryptographic hash codes techniques to secure authentication similar to those used in electronic signatures.[282]

To put it in simple terms, the technology behind it could be compared to that of a database, although the way of interaction is different in the sense that it is maintained and updated by a network of participating computers rather than a single company or organization.[283] For this very reason, a blockchain can be regarded as an authoritative database with a very high level of trust.[284]

If we take the Bitcoin as an example, the "coins" themselves are not physical assets, nor even digital files, but entries in a public ledger using its own unit of account. Therefore, owning a Bitcoin is more like a declaration of owning something, which is recorded on the blockchain.[285] The distributed nature of this technological model has profound implications on the de-centralization of the financial system where

---

[277] on October 31, 2015, the Economist Featured the Blockchain on its Front Cover Page: "the Trust Machine: How the Technology Behind Bitcoin Could Change the World" [online]. Available at: http://www.economist.com/printedition/covers/2015-10-29/ap-e-eu-la-me-na-uk. Accessed 10 May 2019.

[278] The Economist, The Great Chain of Being Sure About Things, October 31, 2015 [online]. Available at: http://www.economist.com/news/briefing/21677228-technology-behind-bitcoin-lets-people-who-do-not-know-or-trustTrust-each-other-build-dependable. Accessed May 10, 2019.

[279] Wattenhofer (2016, p. 85).

[280] Swan (2015, p. 16).

[281] Kost de Sevres (2016).

[282] Mougayar (2015).

[283] Mougayar (2015).

[284] Stark (2016).

[285] The Economist, Bitcoin: The Next Big Thing, May 9 2015 [online]. Available at: http://www.economist.com/news/special-report/21650295-or-it-next-big-thing. Accessed May 15, 2019.

intermediary authorities (such as banks or governmental institutions) are no longer needed.[286]

These crypto-currency systems based on decentralized blockchains have allowed the emergence of the so-called "smart contracts."[287] According to Kost De Sevres, smart contracts are "self-executing, autonomous computer protocols that facilitate, execute and enforce commercial agreements between two or more parties."[288] Another definition of smart contracts that focuses on the blockchain technologies is given by Wattenhofer *as* "an agreement between two or more parties, encoded in such a way that the correct execution is guaranteed by the blockchain."[289] The blockchain creates more transparency and allows the otherwise mutually distrustful parties to contract safely without intermediaries.[290] This is because the pervasive nature of cloud computing allows the node of a blockchain to be supported outside of the organization by a neutral third party.[291] Therefore, it is fair to say that the blockchain itself becomes the trusted (distributed) third party. In addition, this enables the blockchain to also act as a mediator in conflict situations.[292]

The idea of smart contracts was generalized by computer scientist Szabo in (1997a). He argued that many kinds of contracts—including those attempting to delineate property rights—can be embedded in computer software and hardware architecture. A typical example of a smart contract in its earliest and simplest form is the vending machine, which is designed to transfer the ownership of a good (i.e., a can of soda) for the exchange of money. The vending machine is in control of the property—by being physically sealed—and thus can enforce the "contract" that he called "contract with bearer,"[293] since anyone with money can engage in a transaction with the vendor.[294]

By extending the logic underlying mechanic devices, such as the vending machine, Szabo suggested that the computer code could be used in place of vending machines. This idea could be implemented to negotiate more complex transactions, forge strategic relationships, and coordinate transactions arising under diverse jurisdictions. Instead of transferring the ownership of a can of soda, a smart contract could transfer ownership of shares, real estate, intellectual property rights[295] and, in the case of this research, "ownership" rights of data and databases.

As way of an example, we could borrow here again the initiatives of some financial services institutions, which are investing in blockchain distributed ledger technology. This could guarantee the secure exchange of any type of customer's personal data as

[286] Huang (2015, p. 3).

[287] Weber et al. (2016, p. 330), Kosba et al. (2015, p. 1).

[288] Kost de Sevres (2016).

[289] Wattenhofer (2016, p. 88).

[290] Kosba et al. (2015, p. 1).

[291] Linthicum (2016).

[292] Wattenhofer (2016, p. 88).

[293] Szabo (1997a).

[294] Szabo (1997b).

[295] Stark (2016).

a fundamental "Privacy-by-Design" approach for a trusted digital identity service. It is a well-known fact that some of the largest Internet companies profit from the collection and analysis of consumers' personal data. Most consumers do not realize how their data is being used.

Therefore, in this way, some have argued that financial institutions such as banks could be in a better position to orchestrate the blockchain as intermediaries to control and safeguard the digital identities of consumers. At the time of writing this book, Canadian and Dutch banks are, for example, working on a national digital identification service project. This will let online customers use their bank account login information to access other commercial and government services, and, at the same time, capitalize on the trust based on the majority of the nodes who are part of the blockchain.[296]

6.4 Trust and Plan-Like Architectures: How It All Fits Together

Through the sections of this chapter, we emphasized how attitudes of trust (and distrust) can shift from one institution to another and how this oscillation can influence and substantially change the whole legal system of a country. We also mentioned that such attitudes have an intrinsic and extrinsic value depending on the confidence of each individual and whether the right tools are in place to solve complex issues. Finally, we stressed that the main idea of a plan is to compensate and balance the lack of trust. This is precisely the situation one may observe on the Internet. My general claim is that issues of trust are highly influential when it comes to entering cloud computing transactions. The lack of trust of end-users often corresponds to those intrinsic or extrinsic values and not having the right tools to tackle the complex legal and technical issues found in cloud and Big Data transformations.

In this respect, there are two main ideas to take away: (i) the role of innovation intermediaries (cloud brokers)—provided with the right contractual framework as part of a software toolkit—may help to balance and compensate the lack of trust; and (ii) search for cues in the cloud market that leads to a better understanding of the different levels of trust and construct in a framework that can be adjusted to SLAs. This will provide more flexibility to interpret Plan Theory and will potentially influence the cloud computing and Big Data market to constantly grow and evolve.[297]

In the words of Shapiro, "the task of institutional design, therefore is to capitalize on trust while simultaneously compensating for distrust: to allocate enough power so that problems may be solved, but not so much that this power can be abused and

---

[296] Schenker (2016).

[297] Corrales Compagnucci (2016, p. 221).

exploited."[298] Therefore, this chapter calls for the implementation of a more flexible contractual framework where different levels of trust complement each other.[299]

For a deeper understanding, we may now recapitulate and turn back to the roots of Plan Theory that have inspired and motivated Shapiro to elaborate further on his "plan positivism."[300] According to Bratman, our necessity for plans are essentially entrenched in two very general needs. On the one hand, we are (on average) rational agents.[301] This means that deliberation and rational reflection helps to embody our intentions into a more physical manifestation at the time of action. Deliberation demands time and other limited resources. In my view, end-users are limited in their ability to make a rational and informed decision if the click-wrap types of outsourcing agreements available on the Internet do not provide the chance for negotiation.[302]

On the other hand, end-users have urgent needs for *coordination*. In order to accomplish complex goals, they need to coordinate their activities with others. Therefore, they set their goals as "partial plans" in the present with an eye towards the future. This means that their plans are partially incomplete and subject to further modifications and clarifications until they take better shape in the future. According to Bratman, plans work as a "framework reason" for screening and selecting the best options, and removing those options that are not relevant.[303]

Plans are everywhere; the same holds true for cyberspace. End-users who want to use a cloud or Big Data service must sign an SLA, though this agreement may end up being too complex for them and is set up on a "take it or leave it" basis. Either they subscribe to the predefined terms and conditions, or they cannot use the cloud. Therefore, this book elaborates on a more flexible contractual framework, which embraces the concept of trust in its multi-faceted and inter-institutional dimensions. This contractual framework will include a new template, which allows for more tailored options and a screening procedure—through the centrality of the cloud broker—to select the relevant cloud providers. Insofar as this approach has considerable sway at trust layers, this will likely work as a kind of "framework reason," as Bratman puts it, and yield significant optimal results for cloud computing and Big Data services.[304]

6.5 Summary and Interim Remarks

Cloud computing and Big Data services carry the promise of flexibility and unlimited choices. From a legal point of view, however, a closer look reveals a different reality. The bone of contention is that the choicesprovided in SLAs are too limited or perhaps even guided towards outcomes more favorable to cloud providers. While Plan Theory

---

[298] Shapiro (2011, p. 338).

[299] Corrales Compagnucci (2016, p. 221).

[300] Shapiro (2011, p. 178).

[301] Bratman (1999, pp. 2–3).

[302] Corrales Compagnucci (2016, p. 221).

[303] Celano (2013, p. 153), Corrales Compagnucci (2016, p. 221).

[304] Corrales Compagnucci (2016, p. 221).

lends itself as a powerful analytical metaphor, the linchpin and value of connecting plans and cloud architectures are to bring to the forefront the prospect of choice and the multi-layered elements of trust.

As the pace of cloud computing steadily spreads all over the world, increasingly vexing questions concerning cloud architectures and their institutional frameworks must be addressed and answered. The aim of this chapter was therefore to systematize a framework that increases the mutual trust within the involved parties of cloud computing and Big Data services.

While some notions of trust are closely interlinked, the coverage of the trust taxonomy and ontology is not uniform. The frequently fragmented definitions over various disciplines have, on occasion, given rise to controversy.[305] However, most of the trust definitions analyzed in this chapter bear some connections to risk. This calls for a risk-based approach, whereby all of the involved parties are made aware of relevant risks and, in particular, a more tailor-based mechanism that can assess the risks related to "ownership" rights of data and databases.

Yet, such a framework requires efficient and strategic planning that reflects a sophisticated multi-layered approach in the design of SLAs. The implementation of such a framework should be geared towards gaining a better understanding of our perception of the varying degrees of trust that must be present. It will allow us to facilitate and strengthen its application in the cloud. The value of this framework does not lie in the segregation of these terms but rather in the integration and incorporation of its elements in different proportions, in order to bring out their significance in cloud and Big Data transformations. When combined with a strong risk management framework, adopting a multi-layered and multi-dimensional construct to trust provides a choice that can be more flexible and create competitive cost advantages for cloud businesses.[306]

After outlining the virtues of some of these well-accepted theories in the field of conventional law and economics, and discussing some of the benefits of conceptualizing this within the scope of Plan-like Architectures, the last part of this theoretical framework will draw on a deeper understanding of how the complexities of the human mind may influence our decision to trust. By borrowing some elements from the new insights of behavioral law and economics, the following chapter will focus on how to develop interfaces between cloud providers and end-users, taking into account the centrality of the broker and Nudge Theory, so we can develop better cloud choice architectures.

References

Albers S (2005) The design of alliance governance systems. Koelner Wissenschaftsverlag, Koeln, p 203

Alhamad M, Dillon T, Chang E (2010) SLA-based trust model for cloud computing. In: 13th International Conference on Network-Based Information Systems. IEEE, Takayama

Allbritton M (2007) A model of contractual project-based work: personal social network connectivity. ICT use, and self-monitoring, p 36. PhD thesis, Syracuse University, The School of Information Studies, Paper 6, Syracuse

[305] Castelfranchi and Falcone (2010, p. 2).

[306] Castelfranchi and Falcone (2010, p. 3).

Alzaid H et al (2013) Reputation-based trust systems for wireless sensor networks: a comprehensive review, pp 67–68. In: Fernandez-Gago C et al (eds) Proceedings of 7th IFIP WG 11.11 International Conference on Trust Management VII, IFIPTM 2013. Springer, Heidelberg
Amerland D (2015) The tribe that discovered trust: How trust is created, lost and regained in commercial interactions. New Line Publishing, s. l, pp 116–117
Appelrouth S, Desfor L (2008) Classical and contemporary sociological theory: text and readings. Sage Publications, Inc., Los Angeles, p 753
Artz D, Gill Y (2007) A survey on trust in computer science and the semantic web. Web Semant Sci Serv Agents World Wide Web 5(2):58
Bachmann R, Zaheer A (2006) (eds) Handbook of trust research. Edward Elgar Publishing, Cheltenham, p 2
Baecker D (2004) (ed) Einführung in die Systemtheorie. Carl-Auer Verlag, Heidelberg
Baert P, Carreira da Silva F (2010) Social theory in the twentieth century and beyond, 2nd edn. Polity Press, Cambridge, p 119
Bailey J (2010) Thomas Jefferson and executive power, 1st edn. Cambridge University Press, Cambridge, p 31
Baker W, Obstfeld D (1999) Social capital by design: structure, strategies, and institutional context, p 92. In: Leenders R, Gabbay S (eds) Corporate social capital and liability. Kluwer Academic Publishers, Norwell
Barber B (1983) The logic and limits of trust. Rutgers University Press, New Brunswick
Barling J, Cooper C (2008) (eds) The SAGE handbook of organizational behavior, vol. 1, Micro Perspectives. Sage Publications, Los Angeles, p 100
Barron J (1998) Judgment misguided: intuition and error in public decision making. Oxford University Press, Oxford, pp 185 et seq
Bartee R, Brown II (2007) School matters: Why African American students need multiple forms of capital. Peter Lang, New York, p 33
Battre D et al (2007) Gaining users' trust by publishing failure probabilities, p 193. In: Third International Conference on Security and Privacy in Communications Networks and the Workshops (SecureComm 2007). IEEE, Nice
Baum F, Ziersch A (2003) Glossary—social capital. J Epidemiol Community Health 57(5):320–323
Bechmann G, Stehr N (2002) The Legacy of Niklas Luhmann. Society 39(2):67–75
Beckert J, Zafirovski M (2006) (eds) International encyclopedia of economic sociology. Routledge, London, p 605
Berghaus M (2011) Luhmann leicht gemacht: Eine Einführung in die Systemtheorie. Boehlau Verlag, Koeln
Bhuiyan T (2013) Trust for intelligent recommendation. Springer, New York, p 11
Bijlsma-Frankema K, Klein Woolthuis R (2005) Trust under pressure: trust and trust building in uncertain circumstances, Chapter 1 with further references. In: Bijlsma-Frankema H, Klein Woolthuis R (eds) Trust under Pressure: empirical investigations of trust and trust building in uncertain circumstances. Edward Elgar Publishing, Cheltenham
Blaze M et al (1999) The role of trust management in distributed systems security. In: Vitek J, Jensen C (eds) Secure internet programming: security issues for mobile and distributed objects. Springer, Berlin, pp 185–210
Blegvad B (1995) How to cope with uncertainty: trust and law, p 153. In: Karlsson M, Jonsson O (eds) Law, justice and the state: nordic perspectives, Proceedings of the 16th World Congress of the International Association for Philosophy of Law and Social Philosophy (IVR), Reykjavik, May 26–June 2. 1993, vol IV. Franz Steiner Verlag, Stuttgart
Bofota Y (2012) Social capital, human capital and economic development: theoretical model and empirical analyses. Presses Universitaires de Louvain, Louvain, p 10
Bourdieu P, Wacquant L (1992) An invitation to reflexive sociology. Polity Press, Cambridge, p 119
Branscomb L, Keller J (1999) (eds) Investing in innovation: creating a research and innovation policy that works. The MIT Press, Cambridge, p 88

Bratianu C (2015) Organizational knowledge dynamics: managing knowledge creation, acquisition, sharing, and transformation. IGI Global, Hershey, p 268
Bratman M (1999) Intention, plans, and practical reason. The David humer series, philosophy and Cognitive Science Reissues. CSLI Publications, Cambridge
Bruni L, Sugden R (2000) Moral canals: trust and social capital in the work of Hume Smith and Genovesi. Econ Philos 16(1):21–45
Burger R, Cachin C, Husmann E (2013) Cloud, trust, privacy: trustworthy cloud computing whitepaper http://www.tclouds-project.eu/downloads/TClouds_12_final_150dpi.pdf. Accessed 10 May 2019
Butterfield A, Ngondi G (2016) A dictionary of computer science, 7th edn. Oxford University Press, Oxford, p 77
Carbo J et al (2003) Trust management through fuzzy reputation. Int J Coop Inf Syst 12(1):135–155
Castaldo S (2002) Meanings of trust: a meta-analysis of trust definitions. EURAM, Stockholm, p 1
Castelfranchi C, Falcone R (2010) Trust theory: A Socio-Cognitive and Computational Model. Chichester: John Wiley & Sons.
Castelfranchi C, Falcone R (2000) Trust is much more than subjective probability: mental components and sources of trust, pp 1–10. In: Proceedings of the 33rd Hawaii International Conference on System Sciences, https://www.eecis.udel.edu/~decker/courses/886f04/pubs/castelfranchi00.pdf. Accessed 10 May 2019
Castelfranchi C (2003) For a "Cognitive Program": explicit mental representations for Homo Oeconomicus (The case of trust), p 189. In: Dimitri N, Basili M, Gilboa I (eds) Cognitive processes and economic behavior. Routledge, London
Celano B (2013) What Plans can do for legal theory? In: Canale D, Tuzet G (eds) The planning theory of law: a critical reading. vol 100. Springer, Dordrecht
Chami R, Fullenkamp C (2002) Trust as a means of improving corporate governance and efficiency, p 6. IMF Working Paper, International Monetary Fund (IMF)
Chakrabarti A (2007) Grid computing security. Springer, Berlin, p 216
Chavdarova T (2007) Business relations as trusting relations: the case of bulgarian small business, p 279. In: Roth K (ed) Social networks and social trust in the transformation countries. Lit Verlag GmbH & Co. KG Wien, Zurich
Chiles T, McMackin J (1996) Integrating variable risk preferences, trust, and transaction cost economics. Acad Manag Rev 21(1):85
Chircu A, Davis A, Kauffman R (2000a) The role of trust and expertise in the adoption of electronic commerce intermediaries, p 1. MISRC Working Paper http://citeseerx.ist.psu.edu/viewdoc/download?doi=10.1.1.194.9152&rep=rep1&type=pdf. Accessed 10 May 2019
Chircu A, Davis G, Kauffman R (2000b) The role of trust and expertise in the adoption of electronic commerce intermediaries, pp 1–7. MISRC Working Paper http://citeseerx.ist.psu.edu/viewdoc/download?doi=10.1.1.194.9152&rep=rep1&type=pdf. Accessed 10 May 2019
Cloud Security Alliance (2013) The notorious nine, cloud computing top threats in 2013. Top Threats Working Group https://downloads.cloudsecurityalliance.org/initiatives/top_threats/The_Notori-ous_Nine_Cloud_Computing_Top_Threats_in_2013.pdf. Accessed 10 May 2019
Cohen A (2015) Fairness in the workplace: a global perspective. Palgrave Macmillan, London, p 52
Cook K et al (2005) Trust building via risk taking: a cross-societal experiment. Soc Psychol Q 68(2):121–142
Corrales Compagnucci M (2016) "Plan-like Architectures" for mutual trust in the cloud, p 219. In: Fenwick M, Wrbka S (eds) Flexibility in modern business law: a comparative assessment. Springer, Tokyo
Corritore C et al (2013) Foundations of trust for e-health, p 1170. In: Information Resources Management Association, User-driven healthcare: concepts, methodologies, Tools and Applications, 1st edn. Medical Information Science Reference (IGI Global), Hershey
Covey M, Link G (2012) Smart trust: creating prosperity, energy, and joy in a low-trust world. Free Press, New York, p 13
Craib I (1992) Anthony Giddens. Routledge, London, Routledge Revivals, p 67

Cranston J (2014) Questionable dismissal, pp 63–64. lulu.com, s. l
Cugelman B, Thelwall M, Dawes P (2008) Website credibility, active trust and behavioral intent, p 51. In: Oinas-Kukkonen H et al (eds) Proceedings of 3rd. International Conference on Persuasive Technology, Oulu, Finland, June 2008. Springer, Berlin
Da Silva I, Zisman A (2012) A framework for trusted services, pp 328–343. In: Liu C et al (eds) Proceedings of 10th International Conference on Service-Oriented Computing, ICSOC 2012, Shanghai, China, November 12–15, 2012. Springer, Berlin
Dasgupta P (2000) Trust as a commodity. In: Gambetta D (ed) Trust: Making and breaking cooperative relations, electronic edn. Department of sociology, University of Oxford http://www.sociology.ox.ac.uk/papers/gambetta213-237.pdf. Accessed 10 April 2019
Davis D (2016) Creative strategy and the business of design. HOW Books, Blue Ash, p 137
Deutsch (1973) The resolution of conflict. Yale University Press, New Haven, p 148
Dietz G, Gillespie N, Chao G (2010) Unraveling the complexities of trust and culture. In: Saunders M et al (eds) Organizational trust: a cultural perspective. Cambridge University Press, Cambridge, pp 9–10
Dinnen R, Hassanien A (2013) Handling customer complaints in the hospitality industry, p 71. In: Eid E (ed) Managing customer trust, satisfaction, and loyalty through information. Business Science Reference (IGI Global), Hershey
Djemame K, Gourlay I, Padgett J (2006) Introducing risk management into the grid, p 7. In: Proceedings of the Second IEEE International Conference on e-Science and Grid Computing, e-Science'06. https://pc2.uni-paderborn.de/uploads/tx_sibibtex/RiskDje06.pdf. Accessed 10 May 2019
Djemame K et al (2013) Legal issues in clouds: towards a risk inventory. Phil Trans R Soc A 371(1983) https://royalsocietypublishing.org/doi/full/10.1098/rsta.2012.0075. Accessed 10 May 2019
Dragovic B et al (2003) Managing trust and reputation in the xenoserver open platform, p 60. In: Nixon P, Terzis S (eds) Proceedings of First International Conference on Trust Management, iTrust 2003, Heraklion, Crete, Greece, May 28–30 2003. Springer, Berlin
Dutton W et al (2005) The cyber trust tension in e-government: balancing identity, privacy, security, p 14. In: Lips M, Taylor J, Bannister F (eds) Public administration in the information society: essays on risk and trust. IOS Press, Amsterdam
Dyer J, Chu W (2006) The role of trustworthiness in reducing transaction costs and improving performance: empirical evidence from the United States, Japan and, Korea, p 224. In: Kramer R (ed) Organizational trust: a reader. Oxford University Press, Oxford
Earle T, Siegriest M, Gutscher H (2007) Trust, risk perception and the TCC model of cooperation. In: Siegrist M, Earle T, Gutscher H (eds) Trust in risk management: uncertainty and scepticism in the public mind. Earthscan, London, pp 1–2
Eriksson K (2015) Financial services quality: people, processes and performance, p 186. In: Harrison T, Estelami H (eds) The routledge companion to financial services marketing. Routledge, New York
Farrel H (2009) The political economy of trust: institutions, interests, and inter-firm cooperation in Italy and Germany. Cambridge University Press, Cambridge, p 11
Fontanills G, Gentile T, Cawood R (2001) The stock market course. Wiley, New York, p 72
Fuchs A, Guergens S, Rudolph C (2010) A formal notion of trust—enabling reasoning about security properties, p 200. In: Nishigaki M et al (eds) Proceedings of 4th IFIP WG 11.11 International Conference on Trust Management IV, IFIP Advances in Information and Communication Technology, vol. 321, IFIPTM 2010, Morioka, Japan, June 16–18, 2010. Springer, Berlin
Fukuyama F (1996) Trust: the social virtues and the creation of prosperity. Simon & Schuster, New York
Fu Q (2004) Trust, social capital, and organizational effectiveness. Master Thesis submitted for the Master in Public and International Affairs, Faculty of the Virginia Polytechnic Institute and State University http://www.ipg.vt.edu/papers/qhfumajorpaper.pdf. Accessed 10 May 2019

Gambetta D (1988) (ed) Trust: making and breaking cooperative relations. Basil Blackwell Ltd, Cambridge MA

Gambetta D (2000) Can We Trust Trust? pp 213–237. In: Gambetta D (ed) Trust: making and breaking cooperative relations, electronic edition. Department of Sociology, University of Oxford http://www.sociology.ox.ac.uk/papers/gambetta213-237.pdf. Accessed 10 May 2019

Gasiorowski-Denis E (2015) Trust and confidence in cloud privacy, ISO News http://www.iso.org/iso/es/news.htm?refid=Ref1921. Accessed 10 May 2019

Geyskens I et al (1998) Generalizations about trust in marketing channel relationships using meta-analysis. Int J Res Mark 15(3):223–248

Giddens A (1984) The constitution of society: outline of the theory of structuration. Polity Press, Cambridge

Giddens A (1986) The constitution of society: outline of the theory of structuration. Polity Press, Cambridge

Giddens A (1991) The consequences of modernity. Stanford University Press, Stanford

Gladstone J (2004) International Cyberlaw, p 227. In: Bidgoli H (ed) The internet encyclopedia, Vol. 2 (G–O). Wiley, Hoboken

Glinz & Company (2016) Digital trust: towards a more sustainable approach to personal data, p 3, White Paper. http://iceberg.digital/iceberg_whitepaper_2016.pdf. Accessed 10 May 2019

Gourlay I, Djemame K, Padgett J (2009) Evaluating provider reliability in grid resource brokering, p 37. In: 1th IEEE International Conference on High Performance Computing and Communications. IEEE Computer Society

Gourlay I, Djemame K, Padgett J (2008) Reliability and Risk in Grid Resource Brokering, p 438. In: 2nd IEEE International Conference on Digital Ecosystems and Technologies (IEEE DEST 2008). IEEE Computer Society

Graham L, Xie X (2007) The United States insurance market: characteristics and trends, p 78. In: Cummins D, Venard B (eds) Handbook of international insurance: between global dynamics and local contingencies. Springer, New York

Grandison T (2007) Trust management tools, p 199. In: Ronggong S, Korba L, Yee G (eds) Trust in e-services: technologies, practices and challenges. Idea Group Publishing, Hershey

Guinnane T (2005) Trust: a concept too many, pp 1–2. Discussion Paper No. 907, Economic Growth Center, Yale University http://aida.wss.yale.edu/growth_pdf/cdp907.pdf. Accessed 10 May 2019

Hartmann E, Kjaer P (2015) (eds) The Evolution of intermediary institutions in Europe: From Corporatism to Governance. Palgrave McMillan, New York

Hardin R (2004) Distrust: manifestations and management, p 6. In: Hardin R (ed). Distrust. Russell Sage Foundations, New York

Haubarer J (2011) *Social* Capital Theory: Towards a Methodological Foundation, p 147, 1st edn. Springer Fachmedien Wiesbaden GmbH, Wiesbaden

Hawley K (2012) Trust: a very short introduction. Oxford University Press, Oxford, p 38

He R, Niu J, Zhang G (2005) CBTM: A trust model with uncertainty quantifications and reasoning for pervasive computing, p 541. In: Pan Y et al (eds) Proceedings of Third International Symposium on Parallel and Distributed Processing and Applications, ISPA 2005, Nanjing, China, November 2005. Springer, Berlin

Healy J (2016) Improving health care safety and quality: reluctant regulators. Routledge, New York, p 311

Herzberg A et al (2000) Access control meets public key infrastructure, or assigning roles to strangers, pp 2–15. In: Proceedings of IEEE Symposium on Security and Privacy S&P 2000. IEEE Computer Society, Los Alamitos

Hollis M (1998) Trust within reason. Cambridge University Press, Cambridge, p 41

Hoog A, Strzempka K (2011) iPhone and iOS forensics: investigation, analysis and mobile security for Apple iPhone, iPad and iOS Devices. Elsevier, Waltham, p 94

Hosseini H (2015) Insufficient social capital and economic underdevelopment, p 662. In: Altman M (ed) Handbook of contemporary behavioral economics: foundations and developments. Routledge, New York

Houlihan B, Groeneveld M (2011) Social capital, governance and sport, p 4. In: Groeneveld M, Houlihan B, Ohl F (eds) Social capital and sport governance in Europe. Routledge, New York
Huang P (2015) A dissection of bitcoin. Lulu.com, p 3, s l
Huemer L, Von Krogh G, Roos J (2000) Knowledge and the Concept of Trust, p 129. In: von Krogh G, Roos J, Kleine D (eds) Knowing in firms: understanding, managing and measuring knowledge. SAGE Publications, London
Hume D (1737) A treatise of human nature. In: Selby-Bigge LA, Nidditch PH (eds) 1975. Clarendon Press, Oxford
Humphreys E (2007) Implementing the ISO/IEC 27001 information security management system standard, information security and privacy series, 1st edn. Artech House, Boston
Ishiyama J, Breuning M (2011) (eds) 21st century political science: a reference handbook, p 195, vol 1. Sage Publications, Los Angeles
Jalava J (2006) Trust as a decision: the problems and functions of trust in Luhmannian systems theory, p 2. PhD thesis, Published by the Department of Social Policy, University of Helsinki, Helsinki
Janovs V, Fomin V (2011) Development of e-services in latvian insurance industry: the critical role of quality benchmarking, p 231. In: Skersys T et al (eds) 11th IFIP WG 6.11 Conference on e-Business, Building the e-world ecosystem. Springer, Heidelberg
Johns J (1996) A concept analysis of trust. J Adv Nurs 24(1):76
Johnstone S (2011) A history of trust in ancient Greece, p 3. The University of Chicago Press, Chicago
Jones K (1996) Trust as an affective attitude. Ethics 107(1):4–25
Jonker C et al (2004) Human experiments in trust dynamics, p 207. In: Jensen C, Poslad D, Dimitrakos T (eds) Proceedings of Second International Conference on Trust Management, iTrust 2004, Oxford, UK, March/April 2004. Springer, Berlin
Josag A et al (2007) Security usability principles for vulnerability analysis and risk assessment, pp 269–278. In: Proceedings of Twenty-Third Annual Computer Security Applications Conference, 2007. ACSAC 2007. IEEE Computer Society, Los Alamos
Joseph B (2010) E-government adoption landscape zambia: context, issues, and challenges, p 243. In: Reddick C (ed) Comparative e-government. Springer, New York
Kahn A et al (2012) Security risks and their management in cloud computing, p 121. In: IEEE 4th International Conference on Cloud Computing Technology and Science, IEEE Computer Society
Kidder R (2010) Trust: a primer on current thinking, p 1. Institute for Global Ethics. http://www.touroinstitute.com/trust.pdf. Accessed 10 May 2019
Kini A, Choobineh J (1998) Trust in electronic commerce: definition and theoretical considerations. https://pdfs.semanticscholar.org/9db5/5d845b43a09ac26868f23df851c19bea95e0.pdf. Accessed 10 May 2019
Kneer G, Nassehi A (2009) Niklas Luhmanns Theorie sozialer Systeme. Wilhelm Fink GmbH & Co., Verlags-KG, Paderborn
Komesar N (1994) Imperfect alternatives: choosing institutions in law, economics and public policy. The University of Chicago Press, Chicago
Kosba A et al (2015) Hawk: the blockchain model of cryptography and privacy-preserving smart contracts, p 1 https://www.weusecoins.com/as-sets/pdf/library/Hawk%20-%20The%20Blockchain%20Model%20of%20Cryptography%20and%20Privacy-Preserving%20Smart%20Contracts.pdf. Accessed 10 May 2019
Kost de Sevres N (2016) The blockchain revolution, smart contracts and financial transactions. https://www.dlapiper.com/en/uk/insights/publications/2016/04/the-blockchainrevolution/. Accessed 10 May 2019
Kramer R (1999) Trust and distrust in organizations: emerging perspectives, enduring questions. Annu Rev Psychol 50:569–598
Krukow K, Nielsen M, Sassone V (2008) Trust models in ubiquitous computing. Phil Trans R Soc A 366:3781–3793
La Porta R et al (1996) Trust in large organizations. American Economic Review Papers and Proceedings 87(2):333–338

Lane C (1998) Introduction: theories and issues in the study of trust, p 16. In: Lane C, Bachmann R (eds) Trust within and between organizations: conceptual issues and empirical applications. Oxford University Press, Oxford
Lauziere L (2002) Dependence and interdependence in the lawyer-client relationship, p 48. In: Law Commission of Canada (ed) Personal relationships of dependence and interdependence in law. UBC Press, Vancouver
Lee K, Vachonp S (2016) Business value and sustainability: an integrated supply network perspective, p 102. Palgrave MacMillan, London
Lee Y, Trim P (2008) Strategic marketing decision-making within Japanese and South Korean Companies, p. 91. Chandos Publishing, Oxford
Lewicki R, Bunker B (1996) Developing and maintaining trust in work relationships, p. 116. In: Kramer R, Tyler T (eds) Trust in organizations: frontiers of theory and research. SAGE Publications, Thousand Oaks
Lewis D, Weigert A (1985) Trust as a social reality. The University of North Carolina Press, Soc Forces 63(4):967
Linthicum D (2016) Linking up blockchain and cloud. https://www.cloudtp.com/doppler/linking-blockchain-cloud/. Accessed 10 May 2019
Liu J, Issarny V (2004) Enhanced reputation mechanism for mobile ad hoc networks, p 50. In: Jensen C, Poslad S, Dimitrakos T (eds) Trust management. iTrust 2004. Lecture notes in computer science, vol 2995. Springer, Berlin
Luhmann N (1973) Vertrauen: Ein Mechanismus der Reduktion sozialer Komplexität. Ferdinand Enke Verlag, Sttutgart
Luhmann N (1987) Soziale Systeme: Grundriß einer allgemeinen Theorie. Suhrkamp Verlag, Frankfurt am Main
Luhmann N (1988) Familiarity, confidence, trust: problems and alternatives. In: Gambetta D (ed) Trust: making and breaking cooperative relations. Basil Blackwell Ltd., Oxford, pp 96–97
Mandelli A (2004) Exploring the origins of new transaction costs in connected societies, p 226. In: Huotari M, Iivonen M (eds) Trust in knowledge management and systems in organizations. Idea Group Publishing, Cambridge
Marinescu D (2013) Cloud computing: theory and practice. Morgan Kaufmann, Waltham
Marsh S (1994) Formalizing trust as a computational concept, p 26. Submitted in partial fulfillment of the degree of Doctor of Philosophy. http://www.cs.stir.ac.uk/research/publications/techreps/pdf/TR133.pdf/. Accessed 10 May 2019
Mayer R, Davis J, Schoorman F (1995) An integrative model of organizational trust. Acad Manag Rev 20(3):709–734
McCarthy C (2006) Digital libraries: security and preservation considerations, p 60. In: Bidgoli H (ed) Handbook of information security, information warfare, social, legal, and international issues; and security foundations, vol 2. Wiley, Hoboken
McCullagh A, Little P, Caelli W (1998) Electronic signatures: understand the past to develop the future. Univ N S W Law J 21(2):452–465
McDonald E (2004) Difficult conversations in medicine. Oxford University Press, Oxford
McKnight H, Chervany N (1996) The meanings of trust, pp 1–17 http://misrc.umn.edu/workingpapers/fullpapers/1996/9604_040100.pdf. Accessed 10 May 2019
McMyler B (2011) Testimony, trust, & authority, p 113. Oxford University Press, Oxford
Mehta A (2007) Trust in a Time of Crisis: The Mass Media as a Guardian of Trust, p. 156. In: Bakir V, Barlow D (eds) Communication in the age of suspicion: trust and the media. Palgrave Macmillan, Hampshire
Mendelsohn T (2016) Dropbox hackers stole e-mail addresses, Hashed passwords from 68 M accounts. http://arstechnica.co.uk/security/2016/08/dropbox-hackers-stole-email-addresses-hashed-passwords-68m-accounts. Accessed 10 May 2019
Miller J (2000) Trust: the moral importance of an emotional attitude. Practical Philosophy 3(3):38–45

Misztal B (1996) Trust in modern societies: the search for the bases of social order, p 9. Polity Press, Cambridge
Mougayar W (2015) Understanding the blockchain: we must be prepared for the blockchain's promise to become a new development environment. https://www.oreilly.com/ideas/understanding-the-blockchain. Accessed 10 May 2019
Munesh K, Sareen M (2012) (ed) Trust and technology in B2B e-commerce: practices and strategies for assurance, 1st edn. IGI Global, Hershey, p 26
Mutti A (1987) Trust: a fragile concept, a solid reality (in Italian: "La Fiducia. Un Concetto Fragile Una Solida Realtà"). Rassenga Italian di Sociologia 2:23–247
Nannestad P (2009) Making Integration Work, p. 311. In: Svendsen G, Svendsen G (eds) Handbook of social capital: the troika of sociology, political science and economics. Edward Elgar Publishing, Cheltenham
Nielsen M, Krukow K (2003) Towards a formal notion of trust, p 1 https://userscs.au.dk/krukow/research/publications/online_papers/TaFNoT03.ps. Accessed 10 May 2019
Niezen M, Steijn W (2015) Understanding the cloud: the social implications of cloud computing and the need for accountability, pp 203 et seq. In: Felici M, Fernández-Gago C (eds) Proceedings of First Summer School on Accountability and Security in the Cloud, Cloud Accountability Project, A4Cloud, Malaga, Spain, June 2–6, 2014. Springer, Cham
Noor T, Sheng Q, Bouguettaya A (2014) Trust management in cloud services, p 13. Springer, Cham
Ojima T (2011) Social capital and population approach, p 133. In: Muto T, Nakahara T, Nam E (eds) Asian perspectives and evidence on health promotion and education. Springer, Tokyo
Oomsels P, Bouchaert G (2014) Studying interorganizational trust in public administration: a conceptual and analytical framework for "administrational trust". Public Perform Manag Rev 37(4):5–7
Ostrom E (2005) Understanding institutional diversity. Princeton University Press, Princeton, pp 97–98
Ostrom E, Ostrom V (2014) Choice, rules and collective action: the Ostroms on the study of institutions and governance. ECPR Press, Colcherster, p 143
Ouderkirk S (2007) Social capital and the third choice, p 5. Master thesis, Graduate School of Binghamton University, New York
Padgett J et al (2009) Risk-aware SLA brokering using WS-agreement, p 284. In: 2009 International Conference on Advanced Information Networking and Applications Workshops, IEEE Computer Society
Pawar P et al (2014) Trust assessment using cloud brokers, pp 237–244. In: Zhou J et al (eds) Proceedings of 8th IFIP WG 11.11 International Conference on Trust Management VIII. IFIPTM 2014, Singapore, July 7–10, 2014. Springer, Heidelberg
Pedersen E (2015) An outline of interpersonal trust and distrust, p 108. In: Liisberg S, Pedersen E, Dalsgard A (eds) Anthropology & philosophy: dialogues on trust and hope. Berghahn, New York
Pennanen K (2006) How Consumers build trust in e-commerce: towards a trust formation model, p 39. In: Gonzalez S, Luna D (eds) Latin American advances in consumer research, vol 1. Association for Consumer Research, Duluth
Peters W (2010) Verifiability of electronic voting: between confidence and trust, p. 160. In: Gutwirth S, Poullet Y, De Hert P (eds) Data protection in a profiled world. Springer, Dordrecht
Peterson (2016) The 10 laws of trust: building the bonds that make a business great, Foreword. Amacom, New York
Pettit P (1995) The cunninng of trust. Philos Public Aff 24(3):204
Pivar W, Harlan D (1995) Real estate ethics: good ethics = good business, 3rd edn. Dearborn Financial Publishing, Chicago, pp. 19 et seq
Porta RL et al (1997) Trust in large organizations. Am Econ Rev Pap Proc 87(2):333–338
Purser S (2004) A practical guide to managing information security. Artech House, Inc., Norwood, p 15
Putnam R, Leonardi R, Nonetti R (1993) Making democracy work: civic traditions in modern Italy. Princeton University Press, Princeton, p 167

Putnam R (1995) Bowling alone: America's declining social capital. J Democracy 6(1):65–78
Putnam R (2000) Bowling alone: the collapse and revival of American community. Simon & Schuster, New York, pp 16–18
Reed M (2001) Organization, trust and control. Organ Stud 22(2):201–228
Robinson N et al (2011) The cloud understanding the security, privacy and trust challenges. RAND Corporation, Santa Monica
Robinson S (1996) Trust and breach of the psychological contract. Adm Sci Q 41:574–599
Robinson S, Rousseau D (1994) Violating the psychological contract: not the exception but the norm. J Organ Behav 15:245–259
Rose R (2000) Getting things done in an anti-modern society: social capital networks in Russia, p 155. In: Dasgupta D, Serageldin I (eds) Social capital: a multifaceted perspective. The World Bank, Washington
Rose R, Weller (2003) What does social capital add to democratic values? p 201. In: Badescu G, Uslaner E (eds) Social capital and the transition to democracy. Routledge, London
Rousseau D et al (1998) Not so different after all: a cross-discipline view of trust. Acad Manag Rev 23(3):393–404
Rubinstein A, Wolinsky A (1987) Middlemen. Quart J Econ 102:581–593
Ruokonen F (2013) Trust, trustworthiness, and responsibility. In: Mäkelä P, Townley C (eds) Trust: analytic and applied perspective. Rodopi B.V, Amsterdam, pp 1–3
Sajise P, Fellizar F, Saguiguit G (2003) The road to community-based resource management in the Philippines: entries, bends, tolls and dead ends, p 223. In: Persoon G, van Est D, Sajise P (eds) Co-management of natural resources in Asia: a comparative perspective. Nias Press, Copenhagen
Sangrasi A, Djemame K (2011) Component level risk assessment in grids: a probabilistic risk model and experimentation. In: Proceedings of the 5th 2011 IEEE International Conference on Digital Ecosystems and Technologies (IEEE DEST 2011), Daejeon
Sangrasi A, Djemame K (2012) Risk assessment modeling in grids at component level: considering grid resources as repairable. In: Omatu S et al (eds) Distributed computing and artificial intelligence. Springer, Berlin, pp 321–330
Sangrasi A, Djemame K, Jokhio I (2012) Aggregating node level risk assessment in grids using an R-out-of-N model. Commun Comput Inf Sci 281:445–452
Scarlat E, Maries I (2009) Towards an increase of collective intelligence within organizations using trust and reputation models, p 142. In: Nguyen N, Kowalczyk R, Chen S (eds) Proceedings of 1st International Conference on Computational Collective Intelligence: Semantic Web, Social Networks and Multiagent Systems, ICCCI 2009. Springer, Berlin
Schenker J (2016) How blockchain will allow banks to become brokers of personal data. https://medium.com/@jennifer.schenker/how-blockchain-will-allow-banks-to-become-brokers-of-personal-data-7d2971ed222e#.ol7rm22ps. Accessed 10 May 2019
Schwegler U (2011) Vertrauen in interkulturellen Kooperationsbezihungen. In: Dreyer E, Hößler U (eds) Perspektiven interkultureller Kompetenz. Vandenhoeck & Ruprecht GmbH & Co., Goettingen, pp 137–147
Seigneur J, Jensen C (2004) Trading privacy for trust, pp 93–107. In: Jensen C, Posland S, Dimitrakos T (eds) Proceedings of Second International Conference on Trust Management, iTrust 2004, Oxford, UK, March/April 2004. Springer, Berlin
Shapiro S (1987) The social control of impersonal trust. Am J Sociol 93(3):625
Shapiro S (2011) Legality. Belknap Press, Cambridge MA
Shapiro S (2012) The grammar of trust, p 100. In: Pixley J (ed) New perspectives on emotions in finance: the sociology of confidence, fear and betrayal. Routledge international studies in money and banking. Routledge, London
Silva E et al (2013) Inferring hidden trust relationships in social networks for encouraging collaboration and cooperation among individuals, p 42, In: Antunes P et al (eds) Proceedings of 19th International Conference on Collaboration and Technology, CRIWG 2013, Wellington, New Zealand, October/November. Springer, Berlin

Simpson J (2007) Foundations of interpersonal trust, p 587. In: Kruglanski A, Higgins T (eds) Social psychology: handbook of basic principles, 2nd edn. The Guilford Press, New York
Simpson T (2014) Computing and the search for trust, p 114. In: Harper R (ed) Trust, computing, and society. Cambridge University Press, Cambridge
Sinn R (2008) Software security technologies: a programmatic approach. Cengage Learning, Stamford, pp 130 et seq
Skevington P, Hart T (1998) Trusted third parties in electronic commerce, p 60. In: Sim S, Davies J (eds) The internet and beyond. Springer, Dordrecht
Slovic P (1993) Perceived risk, trust, and democracy. Risk Anal 13(6):675–682
Smigielska G, Wierzbinski B (2015) The role of trust and culture in building mutual relations in business competitive market, pp 275–276. http://www.asecu.gr/files/11th_conf_files/21.pdf. Accessed 10 May 2019
Smith B (2015) In the cloud we trust. http://news.microsoft.com/stories/inthecloudwetrust/. Accessed 10 May 2019
Solhaug B, Stolen K (2012) Uncertainty, subjectivity, trust and risk: How it all fits together, pp 1–5. In: Meadows C, Fernández-Gago C (eds) 7th International Workshop on Security and Trust Management, STM 2011, Copenhagen, Denmark, June 27–28, 2011. Springer, Berlin
Srinivasan S (2014) Risk management in the cloud and cloud outages, p 150. In: Srinivasan S (ed) Security, trust, and regulatory aspects of cloud computing in business. Information Science Reference (IGI Global), Hershey
Stark J (2016) How close are smart contracts to impacting real-world law? http://www.coindesk.com/blockchain-smarts-contracts-real-world-law/. Accessed May 10 2019
Stirling W, Giraud-Carrier C, Felin T (2012) A framework for the design and synthesis of coordinated social systems, p 355. In: Aberer K et al (eds) Proceedings of 4th International Conference on Social Informatics, SocInfo 2012 Lausanne, Switzerland, December 2012. Springer, Berlin
Stockheim T (2006) Supply network optimization: coordination based on scheduling, negotiation, and trust, p 142. Books on Demand GmbH, Frankfurt
Sunderland D (2007) Social Capital, Trust and the industrial revolution, 1780–1880. Routledge Explorations in Economic History. Routledge, London, p 1
Swan M (2015) Blockchain: blueprint for a new economy, 1st edn. O'Reilly, Sebastopol, p 16
Swartz T, Iacobucci D (eds) (2000) Handbook of services marketing and management. SAGE Publications, Thousand Oaks, p 358
Swedberg R (2003) Principles of economic sociology. Princeton University Press, Princeton, p 45
Szabo N (1997a) Contracts with bearer. http://szabo.best.vwh.net/bearer_contracts.html. Accessed 10 May 2019
Szabo N (1997b) The idea of smart contracts. http://szabo.best.vwh.net/smart_con-tracts_idea.html. Accessed 10 May 2019
Sztompka P (1999) Trust: a sociological theory. Cambridge University Press, Cambridge
Tarnacha A (2008) The impact of platform certification on a platform-based product market: the case of mobile applications. ProQuest LLC., Ann Arbor, p 43
The PACE Project (2019) Practical architectural approach for composing egocentric trust. http://isr.uci.edu/projects/pace/trustdef.html. Accessed 10 May 2019
The World Bank (2019) Overview: Social Capital http://web.worldbank.org/WBSITE/EXTERNAL/TOPICS/EXTSOCIALDEVELOPMENT/EXTTSOCIALCAPITAL/0,,contentMDK:20642703~menuPK:401023~pagePK:148956~piPK:216618~theSitePK:401015,00.html. Accessed 10 May 2019
Thomborson C (2010) A framework for system security, p 17. In: Stavroulakis P, Stamp M (eds) Handbook of information and communication security. Springer, Heidelberg
Townend P et al (2013) Risk assessment and trust in services computing: applications and experience, pp 287, 289 and 395. In: 2013 IEEE 10th International Conference on Services Computing, IEEE Computer Society

Trusted Computing Platform Alliance (2001) Trusted form alliance announces v.1.0 specifications for trusted computing. https://web.archive.org/web/20030719234815/, http://www.trustedcomputing.org/docs/tcpa_final.pdf
Tsai C et al (2015) Big data analytics: a survey. J Big Data 2(21):1–32
Tuomela R (2000) Cooperation: a philosophical study. Kluwer Academic Publisher, Dordrecht, p 93
Venters C et al (2011) Provenance: current directions and future challenges for service oriented computing, p. 262. In: Proceedings of the 6th IEEE International Symposium on Service Oriented System Engineering (SOSE 2011), s.l
Walczuch R, Seelen J, Lundgren H (2001) Psychological determinants for consumer trust in e-retailing. In: Proceeding of the Eight Research Symposium on Emerging Electronic Markets (RSEEM 01) http://citeseerx.ist.psu.edu/viewdoc/down-load?doi=10.1.1.64.9004&rep=rep1&type=pdf. Accessed 10 May 2019
Walker J, Ostrom E (2005) (eds) Trust & reciprocity: interdisciplinary lessons from experimental research, p 382. A volume in the Russel Sage Foundation on Trust. Russell Sage Foundation, New York
Walker J, Ostrom E (2009) Trust and reciprocity as foundations for cooperation, p 91. In: Cook K, Levi M, Hardin R (eds) Whom can we trust? How groups, networks, and institutions make trust possible. Russel Sage Foundation, New York
Wattenhofer R (2016) The science of the blockchain, p 85. Inverted Forest Publishing, s. l
Weber I et al (2016) Untrusted business process monitoring and execution using blockchain, p 330. In: La Rosa M, Loos P, Pastor O (eds) Proceedings of 14th International Conference on Business Process Management, BPM 2016, Rio de Janeiro, Brazil, September 18–22, 2016. Springer, Cham
Weigl T (2008) Strategy, structure and performance in a transition economy: an institutional perspective on configurations in Russia, p 77, 1st edn. Gabler Verlag, (Springer), Wiesbaden
Weitzenboeck E (2012) A legal framework for emerging business models: dynamic networks as collaborative contracts (corporations, globalization and the law). Edward Elgar Publishing, Cheltenham, p 77
Westlund H (2006) Social capital in the knowledge economy: theory and empirics, pp 1–2. Springer, Berlin
Wierzbicki A (2010) Trust and fairness in open, distributed systems, p 36, Studies in computational intelligence. Springer, Berlin
Williamson O (1985) The economic institutions of capitalism: firms, markets, relational contracting. The Free Press, New York, pp 62–63, 66, 293
Williamson O (1993) Calculativeness, trust, and economic organization. In: John M (ed) Olin Centennial Conference in Law and Economics at the University of Chicago. J Law Econ 36(1):453
Wintterlin F, Blobaum B (2016) Examining journalist's trust in sources: an analytical model capturing a key problem in journalism, p 77. In: Blobaum B (ed) Trust and communication in a digitized world: models and concepts of trust research. Springer, Cham
Yamagishi T (2005) Cross-societal experimentation on trust: a comparison of the United States and Japan, pp 15, 352–370. In: Ostrom E, Walker J (eds) Trust and reciprocity: interdisciplinary lessons for experimental research. Russell Sage Foundation, New York
Yamagishi T (2011) Trust: the evolutionary game of mind and society. Springer, Tokyo, pp 12 et seq
Yamagishi T, Yamagishi M (1994) Trust and commitment in the United States and Japan. Motiv Emot 18(2):31
Zabolotnyi R, Leitner P, Dustdar S (2014) Building elastic java application services seamlessly in the cloud: a middleware framework, p 566. In: Ramanathan R (ed) Handbook of research on architectural trends in service-driven computing. Information Science Reference (IGI Global), Hershey
Zanini M, Migueles C (2013) Trust as an element of informal coordination and its relationship with organizational performance. Economia 14(2):77–87
Zheng Y (2010) Trust modeling and management in digital environments: from social concept to system development. Information Science Reference, Hershey
Zsolnai L (2005) The rationality of trust (Russell Hardin: trust and trustworthiness. New York: 2002, Russell Sage Foundation), (Book Review). Int J Soc Econ 3:268-269

Chapter 7
Framing Choice Architectures

"*We are all choice architects now!*" (Stewart 2015, p. 78) (The Institute of Practitioners in Advertising).

7.1 Introduction

This chapter is about cloud architectures, freedom of choice, and the legitimate scope of cloud brokers in softly nudging end-users and cloud providers—as a new form of soft paternalism—that can help them make better decisions without coercing or neglecting their choices. I attempt to examine these issues by taking into account the recent theories within behavioral law and economics, which are steadily on the rise and increasingly relevant as a point of reference in policy-making and regulation over the past decade. In this regard, behavioral economics offers a normative framework, which helps us better understand the pitfalls of the decision-making process.

My goal in this chapter is to advance a fresh approach to the economic analysis of contract law in cloud computing transactions that is based on a more reliable and accurate understanding of choice and human behavior. I attempt to build on early driven theories of behavioral economics and outline a framework addressing the potential applications of behavioral insights.

The unifying idea of this interdisciplinary analysis is to integrate the tools of traditional law and economics, but taking human behavior for granted.[1] Thus, it aims

[1] See, generally, Jolls et al. (1998, pp. 1471–1550).

M. Corrales Compagnucci, *Big Data, Databases and "Ownership" Rights in the Cloud*, Perspectives in Law, Business and Innovation,
https://doi.org/10.1007/978-981-15-0349-8_7

to assist in bridging the gap between "Plan Theory" with "heuristics"[2] and systematic errors responsible for the "fallacies" of interpretation[3] known as "biases."[4]

In this chapter, I use the works of Daniel Kahneman and Amos Tversky with regards to risk-management and uncertainty. The central discussion of behavioral law and economics, especially in Kahneman and Teversky's contribution, is about heuristics and biases. I also apply the idea of "nudges." In this context, to nudge means "to alert, remind, or mildly warn another."[5] The intrinsic idea of nudges lies in helping people to make good decisions without coercing them to make any particular choice. Many of the policies that behavioralists recommend can and have been adequately implemented by the public and private sector in various countries.[6]

This chapter is divided into five sections. Section 7.2 reviews the literature and provides some general background considerations. This section is broken down into three parts. The first part revisits Daniel Kahneman's own account of human psychology: that human agents are run by two different ways of thinking and being aware of this dual-system can help to reduce the legal risks in cloud SLAs. Only by combining these two ways of thinking can the two aims converge. The second part explains the main ideas of nudges and choice architectures. It uses both illustrative and metaphorical examples to discuss the pervasive nature of architectures. They are always around us and often inadvertently influence the decisions we make. The last part of this section discusses what Sunstein calls "behavioral market failures" and the "libertarian paternalism" movement along with different types of nudging categories and techniques.

Section 7.3 outlines how we can turn certain nudging techniques into simpler and more effective SLAs. This section explains how default rules, warnings, and information disclosures can help end-users improve their decision-making when choosing a cloud provider. Section 7.4 highlights the relationship between the various theories discussed in this chapter. This section recapitulates the main findings of both Kahneman's cognitive biases approach and Sunstein's justification to gently nudge individuals in cases of market failures.

Therefore, this chapter discusses, in general, the advantages and disadvantages of such theories with a critical view on the most salient points. The most important thing to remember here is that these biases and heuristics are going to have a certain effect on a choice to *trust*. As a corollary, it also examines the impact of these heuristics in designing cloud architectures as a *plan* and takes into consideration these biases in order to compensate for the lack of trust. Finally, Sect. 7.5 concludes with the theoretical framework of this work that has been encapsulated in a new paradigm with a more purposive and cloud-market-oriented approach.

---

[2]Tversky and Kahneman (2004, pp. 203–220).

[3]Viale (2012, p. 25).

[4]About "heuristics" and "biases" see Heukelom (2014, pp. 71–96), Gilovich et al. (2002) (eds), Kahneman et al. (1982) (eds).

[5]Safire (2004, p. 242).

[6]Safire (2004, p. 242).

7.2 Literature Review and Background Considerations

As a body of learning, the field of behavioral economics is as old as the discipline of law and economics itself. The marrying of psychology and economics can be traced back to 1958 and emerged as an independent "bona fide" sub-discipline of economics.[7] This field analyzes a variety of psychological, emotional,[8] social and cognitive factors that induce economic decision-making.[9] It became apparent very early that this discipline needed to be united with the law in order to manage firms effectively or to influence public policy and economic decision-making. Behavioral law and economics blends insights from cognitive psychology and economy as the overarching framework to discuss legal issues. Behavioral law and economic's fundamental premise stems from an innate human propensity to err in making decisions.[10]

The idea to incorporate the findings of behavioral and social sciences when shaping law and government policies has now entered the mainstream of modern law and economics. It became increasingly popular by the works of Richard Thaler and Cass Sunstein. They argued that improved choices, default rules and information disclosure could softly nudge citizens to make better decisions, improve welfare and enhance the efficiency of government.[11] According to the 2015 World Development Report, "the promise of this approach to decision making and behavior is enormous, and its scope of application is extremely wide… Research shows that small differences in context, convenience, and salience have large effects on crucial choices…"[12]

---

[7]Angner and Loewenstein (2016).

[8]See, generally, Zeiler and Teitelbaum (2015) (eds).

[9]Minton and Kahle (2013).

[10]See, i.e., Jolls et al. (1998, pp. 1471–1550).

[11]In the United Kingdom for instance, the Prime Minister David Cameron established a "Behavioral Insights Team" (Cabinet Office*),* with the specific objective of including the psychological analysis of human behavior into policy-making initiatives in various areas such as anti-smoking, energy efficiency, consumer protection, organ donation, etc. See Behavioral Insights Team, [online]. Available at: http://www.behaviouralinsights.co.uk. Accessed 10 May 2019. See also Wright (2014). In the United States, the Obama administration has created a team in 2013 in order to do empirical research of behavioral sciences. On September 2015, President Obama signed an executive order, which encouraged federal government agencies to use behavioral science insights to better understand and serve the American people. Executive agencies are invited to "nudge" people to make better decision by means of reminders, notifications, warnings and reframing citizens' choices. See Executive Order—Using Behavioral Science Insights to Better Serve the American People, The White House, Office of the Press Secretary, (September 15 2015), [online]. Available at: https://obamawhitehouse.archives.gov/the-press-office/2015/09/15/executive-order-using-behavioral-science-insights-better-serve-american. Accessed 10 May 2019. In the European Union, the Directorate-General for Health and Consumers has also shown some interest to focus on behavioral economics. See Consumer Policy Toolkit, Org. For Econ. Cooperation & Dev., [online]. Available at: https://www.oecd.org/sti/consumer/consumer-policy-toolkit-9789264079663-en.htm. Accessed May 10 2019. See, i.e., the "Green Behavior" report from the European Commission. See Sunstein (2014, pp. 33–36).

[12]World Development Report (2015).

According to an article published by The Economist, "this body of work is best understood as a set of exceptions that modifies but leaves intact the canonical model of rational choice, not least since it is irrational to suppose that, in general, people behave irrationally."[13] On this account, behavioralists are not saying that individuals behave irrationally. On the contrary, they concur with the idea that individuals are fully rational, but sometimes they make mistakes due to certain limitations to that rationality. The stimulus, and central idea, is to take this "bounded rationality" into account.[14]

The term "bounded rationality" was coined by Herbert Simon and it means simply that there are some "boundaries" to that rationality.[15] He used the scissor's metaphor[16] to concisely explain the interaction between cognitive strategies and the structure of environmental context.[17] He suggested that there is a dual limitation process that individuals face while making a decision. One blade of the scissor is the cognitive bias and the other the environmental constraints, such as a finite amount of time, lack of information,[18] and lack of resources available.[19] Contrary to the prevailing approach in traditional economics, it has been more widely acknowledged recently that individuals do not behave as perfectly rational actors. There are obvious boundaries to one's own willpower and self-control.[20]

More recently, behavioral scientists have also shown that individuals often tend to act unselfishly and may be too optimistic. This is because they rely on the limited resources available to perceive and process information more accurately through the abovementioned mental shortcuts known as "heuristics and biases." The technical definition of a heuristic is "a simple procedure that helps find adequate, though often imperfect, answers to difficult questions."[21] In this case, the heuristic question is "the simpler question that you answer instead."[22] This being said, behavioral law and economics may offer us some new insights or certain cues for legal reform.[23]

---

[13]The Economist (2006).

[14]See generally, Munro (2009).

[15]Simon (1972, p. 162), Pomerol (2012, pp. 70 and 71), Lahti (2010, p. 35), Simon (1998, pp. 270–274).

[16]As Herbert Simon pointed out: "Human rational behavior (and the rational behavior of all physical symbol systems) is shaped by a scissors whose two blades are the structure of task environments and the computational capabilities of the actor." See Simon (1990, p. 7).

[17]Clark et al. (2012), preface, Reb et al. (2014, p. 14), Gigerenzer (2000, p. 125).

[18]Gigerenzer and Selten (2002, p. 4). See, also, generally, Simon (1955, pp. 99–118), Simon (1984).

[19]Viale (2012, p. 25).

[20]Jolls (2004, pp. 1–3).

[21]Kahneman (2011, p. 98).

[22]Kahneman (2011, pp. 97 and 98). The etymology of the word "heuristics" comes from Greek "heureka," which literally means, "I have found (it)" from the verb "heuriskein" (to find). This expression became famous as it was supposed to be shouted by Archimedes (c. 287–212 B.C.E.) when he found the solution to a scientific problem. See: Online Etymology Dictionary [online]. Available at: http://www.etymonline.com/index.php?term=eureka. Accessed May 10 2019, Utts (2014, p. 348).

[23]See, generally, Sunstein (2000) (ed).

This approach provides more structured choices without restricting or neglecting an individual's right to choose and can lead to more positive outcomes.[24] Richard Thaler, Cass Sunstein and other forerunners focused on these psychological traits of human behavior, which may offer a more realistic foundation to law and economics.[25]

This movement is also known as "libertarian paternalism." This concept is the union of two ideas that seem to contradict each other. The libertarian aspect lies in the general principle that people know what is good for them and therefore should be free to do whatever they want to do. Whereas the idea of paternalism "attempts to influence the choices of affected parties in a way that will make choosers better off."[26] According to Thaler and Sunstein, this idea is not an "oxymoron,"[27] but both possible and totally legitimate for private and public institutions to influence decision-making without coercion. This is also called "soft paternalism" because it respects freedom of choice, while at the same time attempts to guide people's choices towards the promotion of welfare. Thaler and Sunstein themselves are one of the stalwarts of this movement.[28]

The backbone of this approach is substantiated in the empirical research carried out by Daniel Kahneman in his book, *Thinking, Fast and Slow*. In this book, he adopts his own account of human psychology by stating that we all have two ways of thinking, which he calls "thinking fast" (System 1) and "thinking slow" (System 2).[29] Thaler and Sunstein adopt this paradigm and streamline it to various matters of public policy (i.e., education, healthcare, finance, etc.).[30] This dual-system way of thinking is further explained below.

---

[24] As Sigal Ben-Porath pointed out, "choice does seem like an appropriate, straightforward solution to the shortcomings of the alternative, choice-less vision of the predestined life." See Ben-Porath (2010).

[25] Heukelom (2014, pp. 1–10 and 168).

[26] See Thaler and Sunstein (2003).

[27] Oxymoron is "a figure of speech by which a locution produces an incongruous, seemingly self-contradictory effect." For example: "cruel kindness", [online]. Available at: http://dictionary.reference.com/browse/oxymoron. Accessed 10 May 2019. According to the Merriam-Webster dictionary, oxymoron is: "a combination of words that have opposite or very different meanings," [online]. Available at: http://www.merriam-webster.com/dictionary/oxymoron. Accessed May 10 2019.

[28] Thaler and Sunstein (2003, pp. 1–3). But see White (2013). White argues generally against the idea of paternalistic nudges by the government and makes a positive claim in favor of individual choice and autonomy.

[29] The terms System 1 and System 2 were first coined by Stanovich and West and will be used along this work. See Stanovich and West (2000, pp. 645–665).

[30] Corrales and Jurčys (2016, pp. 533–536).

7.2.1 Two Ways of Thinking: "Fast" and "Slow"

By virtue of his early works on "cognitive biases"[31] and his seminal paper on "prospect theory"[32] co-authored by Amos Tversky, Daniel Kahnemman devoted much of his career to challenging the *Homo Economicus,*[33] or economic man, human agency theory.[34] This theory sees individual actors as maximizers of their own well-being. This approach became prevalent among John Stuart Mill's critics and gave birth to various ramifications in mainstream economics throughout behavioral economics and other social sciences through the abovementioned "rational choice theory."[35]

Kahneman focuses on what he calls "imperfect rationality" and criticizes the rational agent model, which plays a key role in the economic analysis of many social sciences including inter alia economy, psychology, sociology and law. As seen earlier, the rational agency theory is constructed based on the assumption that economic agents are rational enough to assume the choice that is more beneficial for their own self-interest.[36] Kahneman's dual-system theory, however, indicates how individuals can divert from that rational way of thinking.

According to Kahneman, there are two ways of thinking: "thinking fast" (System 1) and "thinking slow" (System 2). The previous is emotional, impulsive and difficult to control. The latter is reflexive, measured and more flexible. Individuals tend to use System 1 and use easier questions instead of more difficult ones (i.e., legal and technical). This works as a kind of mental shortcut that every so often may lead to error-making.[37]

For Kahneman, the human brain operates as having two different fictitious characters, with each possessing different skills, personalities and attributes, because this is the easiest and most efficient way for the human brain to process and endow itself with information. One of these agents (System 1) operates automatically and effortlessly and is the one that we use most of the time without being fully aware of the processes in such decision-making. It is very fast and perceptive.[38] For example, when somebody asks you to name the capital of France or what 2 + 2 is, the answers come to your mind in an instant without deliberate thought.[39]

---

[31] See Tversky and Kahneman (1974, pp. 1124–1131).

[32] Kahneman and Tversky (1979, pp. 263–292).

[33] See generally, Kirchgaessner (2000).

[34] Holt (2011).

[35] The term "homo economicus" as we understand it conceptually today, was first coined by John Stuart Mill in his *Essays of Some Unsettled Questions of Political Economy* (1844) and in his *Principles of Political Economy*. Noteworthy, this concept permeated the academic literature and became notorious as a pejorative term by Mill's adversaries. See Rodriguez-Sickert (2009, p. 223).

[36] Catino (2013, p. 100). See, also, generally, Reason (1990), Jackman and Miller (2007, p. 20).

[37] Kahneman (2003, p. 698).

[38] Kahneman (2003, p. 698).

[39] Kahneman (2003, p. 698), Kahneman (2011, pp. 20–26).

The other agent (System 2) is slower, more flexible and consciously monitored. It has two functions: one of them is to compute more difficult tasks like finding the results of 567×18. In this case, the answer to that question (which is 10,206) does not come as easily as in the previous $2 + 2$ example. Here, one needs to spend some time and effort in order to find the result. Another function of System 2 is to supervise the behavior of the mind. The main characteristic of this model is that individuals need to work laboriously in order to find a solution.[40]

Being aware of these two types of mental operations goes hand in hand with the systematic framework of this research. System 1 focuses on how the information is presented (i.e., it relies on shortcuts and illusions) whereas System 2 overturns present biases and heuristics, detects errors and recognizes omissions. Constant developments and changes taking place in the field of ICT, especially in the area of cloud computing and Big Data, has posed serious challenges and threats to employees and management teams. Advances in technology are happening so fast that it is difficult for them to assess how to collect, store, and process data for competitive advantages.[41]

It is therefore even more overwhelming to choose the right cloud provider. As seen in previous chapters, an additional way businesses and organizations can leverage cloud computing and prevent these heuristics and biases is through the experience and technical expertise of cloud brokers. End-users and companies can make faster and better decisions by using intermediary services involved in these processes. This chapter covers a variety of techniques that will enable end-users to overcome these heuristics and biases and make better decisions about companies and organizations.

7.2.2 Nudge Theory and Cloud Brokerage Architectures

Nudge theory mainly operates by "designing" or "re-shaping" choices that influence and encourage individuals and society to improve and enforce decision-making provided by the government, companies and other authorities.[42] Choice architectures

---

[40]Kahneman (2003, p. 698), Kahneman (2011, pp. 20–26). See also Stanovich (2010). In this book, Stanovich established the difference between rationality and intelligence and suggests that some individuals are closer to System 1 and some others are closer to System 2. He also established a distinction of two parts of System 2, what he calls "two separate minds." According to him, System 2 has a dual-process and must be divided into the "reflective mind" and the "algorithmic mind." According to Stanovich's concept, superficial or "lazy" thinking is a flaw in the reflective mind, and explains how individuals can behave sometimes irrationally. See also Kahneman (2011, pp. 48–49). In evolutionary terms, System 1 is older than System 2. It relates to our animal instincts and is broken down in a subset of systems that include both our innate abilities and "domain-specific knowledge" learnt from a "domain-general learning" system. System 2 is more recent and belongs only to humans. It allows abstract and hypothetical ways of reasoning and thinking. It is linked to language and intelligence but is limited in memory capacity. See Evans (2003, pp. 454–459).

[41]Raisinghani et al. (2015, p. 188).

[42]Businessballs.com, *Nudge Theory* [online]. Available at: http://www.businessballs.com/nudge-theory.htm. Accessed May 10 2019.

are present from the very moment that we use the law to try to influence society. This includes the very idea of nudges. The Collins dictionary definition of a nudge is "to push or poke (someone) gently…to give (someone) a gentle reminder or encouragement."[43] Similarly, the Oxford dictionary defines nudge as to "prod (someone) gently, typically with one's elbow, in order to draw their attention to something," or simply "to touch or push (something) gently or gradually."[44]

For Thaler and Sunstein, a nudge refers to "any aspect of the choice architecture that alters people's behavior in a predictable way without forbidding any options or significantly changing their economic incentives."[45] To put this in simpler terms, a nudge is "every small feature in the environment that attracts our attention and influences the decision that we make."[46] Nudges can be very helpful for individuals and society. Some of these nudges may be regarded as more controversial than others. For example, road signs are undeniably helpful for the community, thus they can be hardly regarded as controversial (unless they have been misplaced). They give instructions and warn road users to drive more carefully.[47]

Thaler and Sunstein mention a good example of a visual 3D illusion painted on the road close to a curve in Chicago's Lake Shore Drive. The painting resembles a speed bump that nudges drivers to tap their brakes and slow down. This illusion creates the same effect of a real bump that uses vertical deflection. The advantages of using this road illusion are manifold: (i) it cost roughly only 500 US$ instead of 2000 US$; (ii) there is no danger for ambulances and similar emergency vehicles; and (iii) it avoids a water flood. The drawback is that regular drivers can get used to the illusion, thus reducing its effectiveness.[48] The 3D illusion and road sign examples are created by someone called a "choice architect," which is just a fancy term for someone who has "the responsibility for organizing the context in which people make decisions."[49]

This is also evident in the case of a cafeteria or restaurant, where someone has to decide where to put the salad bar, hamburgers, muffins and coffee. That person is a "choice architect" because how they arrange the food and drinks will influence the decisions of customers. If the salad bar is placed at the entrance and within visible range, it is most likely that the customers will take the salad first as a healthier

---

[43]English Collins Dictionary, *Nudge* [online]. Available at: http://www.collinsdictionary.com/dictionary/english/nudge. Accessed May 10 2019.

[44]Oxford Dictionary, *Nudge*, [online]. Available at: http://www.oxforddictionaries.com/es/definicion/ingles_americano/nudge. Accessed May 10 2019.

[45]Thaler and Sunstein (2009, p. 6).

[46]Willis (2015).

[47]See generally, Jamson (2013, p. 298), Avineri (2014); Nudge.org, What if a Speed Limit Sign Told You the Most Efficient Speed to Drive? [online]. Available at: http://nudges.org/2009/06/25/what-if-a-speed-limit-sign-told-you-the-most-efficient-speed-to-drive/. Accessed 10 May 2019; Nudge.org, *Choice Architecture for the Road* [online]. Available at: https://nudges.wordpress.com/2008/06/05/choice-architecture-for-the-road/. Accessed May 10 2019.

[48]Nudges.org, 2008, *Another Visual Trick to Nudge Drivers to Slow Down* [online]. Available at: http://nudges.org/?s=lake+shore+drive. Accessed May 10 2019.

[49]Thaler and Sunstein (2009, p. 3).

choice.[50] Thus they need a nudge to make better decisions.[51] In this context, the definition of architecture seems to be very broad and goes beyond the physical space of the restaurant. As in the Daily Grill restaurant example, Sunstein explains how the healthier Simply 600 (calories) menu is also a form of architecture. This means that every restaurant, including their menus, contain choice architectures.[52]

Why Nudge? The Politics of Libertarian Paternalism[53] ["Why Nudge"] is one of the most recent attempts by Sunstein to offer a new approach to the role of government and his libertarian paternalism approach. In this book, he shares his personal experience from the time he worked as an Administrator of the White House Office of Information and Regulatory Affairs (OIRA) and discusses numerous empirical studies conducted by cognitive psychologists and economists. Why Nudge is a follow-up of the book, *Nudge: Improving Decisions About Health, Wealth, and Happiness*, co-authored with Richard Thaler, which lays out the principles of how people often and persistently engage in making poor decisions that run counter to their best interests in a long-term perspective. This book was about choice architecture and opened up with probably one of the most humorous and real-world illustrations of a nudge in bathroom urinals at the Amsterdam Schiphol airport. It turns out that men are often a bit careless and not fully attending to the task they have when it comes to using the urinal in the men's room. As an experiment in human behavior, they etched the image of a black fly (that looks very real) into the porcelain of each urinal just above the drain in order to prompt them with a target to aim at. After this experiment, "spillage" on the men's bathroom floor was considerably reduced by 50 to 80%. This is an interesting, simple and inexpensive example of a nudge that gives people a gentle push in the right direction, reducing cleaning costs and showing how small changes can make a big difference.[54]

In Why Nudge, Sunstein explains what he means by choice architectures and nudges. He uses both illustrative and metaphorical examples to discuss the pervasive nature of architectures. They are always around us and, often inadvertently, influence the decisions that we make. The story by the late novelist David Wallace that Sunstein refers to reflects, in metaphorical terms, the central idea of choice architectures, which often exists without individuals even recognizing them.

> There are these two young fish swimming along, and they happen to meet an older fish swimming the other way, who nods at them and says, 'Morning, boys, how's the water?' And the two young fish swim on for a bit, and then eventually one of them looks over at the other and goes, 'What the hell is water'?[55]

The sentiment expressed in this quotation embodies the view that there is always background architecture in place by which all individuals are affected even though

---

[50] Thaler and Sunstein (2009, p. 3), Sunstein (2014, pp. 12, 25, 91, and 164).

[51] Behavioral Economics is expanding to different fields in addition to law. See Heshmat (2011), introduction.

[52] Sunstein (2014, pp. 11, 12, 15, 25, and 28).

[53] Sunstein (2014, pp. 1–221).

[54] Thaler and Sunstein (2009, p. 20), Clark (2010, p. 176), Evans-Pritchard (2013), Sommer (2009).

[55] Wallace (2008).

they do not recognize it. The immediate point of this illustrative story, translated into our daily life activities, suggests the ubiquitous nature of the Internet and cloud architectures that affect the choices we make. The same holds true for cyberspace. This story resembles the cloud computing metaphor introduced by Eric Schmidt that I quoted at the beginning of Chap. 3 as follows: "You never visit them, you never see them. But they are out there. They are in a cloud somewhere. They are in the sky, and they are always around. That's roughly the metaphor."[56] The story of the two young fish and the cloud computing metaphor suggest that if you are a user of cloud computing services and engaging with contractual agreements, there is always the equivalent of water in the background, which is affecting the decisions you make whether you are fully aware or not, just as fish are swimming in water whether they recognize it or not.[57]

A choice architecture serves as a material counterpart of the "interface" (i.e., menu, ordering and structure) of different choices that are available for individuals. How these options are listed or represented, or even created in the first place, will influence the quality of the decisions we make. By way of illustration, besides the canonical cafeteria and restaurant examples, there are many other kinds of architectures and nudges around us, such as the default settings of a printer machine (double-sided or single-sided), that can have a large-scale environmental and economic impact. This is another example that shows how small nudges are not trivial and can make a substantial difference in the long term.[58]

The notion of "architecture" obviously varies in different disciplines and there are many concepts provided in the literature. Even in the computer science field, there are many definitions available. Therefore, the concept of architecture that I appeal to for this book is that of the standard and widely accepted definition given by the Institute of Electrical and Electronics Engineers (IEEE). According to the IEEE ISO Standard 42010, architecture is defined as follows: "the fundamental organization of a system embodied by its components, their relationships to each other and the environment, and the principles guiding its design and evolution."[59] Bloomberg provides a very broad definition and in his view, not only is the technology framework part of such architecture, but so too are the people using the system.[60]

In computer jargon, software architecture is a metaphor that resembles the architecture of a building. It has to do with the high-level structure of the software components, where they are located and who uses them according to the defined roles/actors in the system. Each layer of the software structure comprises different component elements and how they are designed to work with other software components.[61] In

[56]Lindberg and Svensson (2010, p. 13).

[57]Sunstein (2014, p. 25).

[58]Felin (2014, p. 3).

[59]Ramanathan et al. (2009, p. 171), Eppinger and Browning (2012, p. 7), Abraham et al. (2012, p. 116).

[60]See Bloomberg (2013, p. 12).

[61]Clements et al. (2010, p. 19), Perry and Wolf (1992, p. 44).

the context of this research, I take a very broad interpretation of the concept of software architecture so that the risk assessor component and SLA specifications can be included within the definition. Software architecture is about making vital choices and decisions to the design of the software.[62]

Choice architectures embrace the idea of nudges. They usually consist of disclosures, warnings and default rules. They are inevitable and everywhere.[63] "Nudging" provides useful resources that are supposed to enhance an individual's welfare. A meaningful example for embedding default rules in the construction of architectures is related to the choice of postmortem organ donation process.[64] There are generally two main default systems worldwide: (i) opt-in rule, which requires explicit consent from the deceased; and (ii) opt-out rule, whereby consent is automatically assumed. This means that in the latter system, the default is that you are a donor.[65]

The procedure varies greatly from country to country. In some jurisdictions, such as in some areas of the United States, this requires the deceased to have previously signed up in a state registry.[66] In some other jurisdictions, such as Japan and most European countries, you are given this option when you obtain or renew your driver's license. Usually, there is a box to check either as an opt-in or opt-out rule. Opt-out default systems make the percentage of organ donation much higher than opt-in systems.[67] For example, in countries such as Spain, Austria, France, Hungary, Poland and Portugal, which all have opt-out policies, there has been a substantial increase in levels to over 99% of donors registered[68] In comparison to countries with an opt-in system like Denmark (4.35%) and the Netherlands (27.5%).[69] This is because people tend to prefer the option which does not require further deliberation costs.[70]

In the next chapter, I will discuss how to embed default rules within the end-user's interface. For the moment, suffice it to say that opt-in or opt-out rules are greatly attributed to the culture of a society, and may change based on the users' experience. Empirical studies conducted in countries such as Germany, United States and Austria showed that signing up for organ donation in an opt-in system was generally considered to be a virtuous act of benevolence, whereas abstaining to donate under an opt-out system was commonly viewed as egotistic and antisocial.[71]

Another iconic example of a nudge in a rather more technical context is a global position system (GPS). They are designed to show people the best and/or shortest route possible. However, individuals still have the freedom to choose another route,

[62]See generally, Jansen and Bosch (2005, pp. 109–120).

[63]Sunstein (2014, pp. 1–30 and 179).

[64]Ben-Porath (2010, p. 11).

[65]Heshmat (2015, p. 243).

[66]Detels et al. (2015, p. 782).

[67]See John et al. (2013, p. 104), Quigley and Stokes (2015, p. 64), Thaler (2009), Hamilton and Zufiaurre (2014, p. 18).

[68]Leitzel (2015, p. 137).

[69]Shafir (2013, p. 496).

[70]Cahn (2013, p. 148).

[71]Zamir (2015, p. 103). See, also, generally, Davidai et al. (2012, pp. 15201–15205).

and if they do so, there is a risk they will end up getting lost.[72] In the context of this work, cloud brokers are important choice architects in many of the areas that I will discuss here. The notion of a nudge in this context implies the principle to help end-users and cloud providers to make better choices and warn them about potential risks and mistakes. Nudging occurs when behaviors are stimulated through "indirect suggestions."[73] The dominant mood in the current debate seems to emphasize, or even amplify, either the "business-to-consumer" relationship or the "government-to-citizen" approach. The first refers to how private companies use different nudging techniques to influence consumer buying behavior such as in an advertisement.[74]

In the second relationship, there is no direct intervention from the government by means of policies, regulations or enforcement.[75] It focuses on the extent at which government paternalism may be justified.[76] Either way, these two modalities always target consumers or citizens directly. It is, however, a slightly new approach that I seek to highlight in this book. I propose a new argumentation framework of "indirect nudging," by which cloud brokers will play a key role in setting the generally applicable nudging techniques, based on an automated contractual framework. The main argument here is *not* to nudge consumers or citizens directly but to approach *cloud providers* instead. This new approach could be interpreted as a modified extension of the industry's "choice editing" role[77] that is also strongly related to the Sunstein narrative. The central idea would be to think of cloud brokers as main *planners* of choice architectures.

7.2.3 Behavioral Market Failures, Different Types of Nudges and Soft Paternalism

The nudging idea is nothing new, but justifying it based on dormant and veiled rationality is. As hinted in the previous section, it has existed for many decades, especially in the private sector. Marketing agencies have always relied on nudging strategies to capture the attention of consumers in order to influence their behavior and sell their products.[78] The crucial question in Sunstein's narrative seems to boil down as to whether the government is allowed to use these kinds of nudging techniques as in the organ donation example. Could be this seen as a kind of paternalism? This idea is very controversial as it conflicts with autonomy and freedom.

A key strand of Sunstein's argument is to challenge John Stuart Mill's so-called "Harm Principle," by showing that in some instances people are prone to error and

---

[72] Sunstein (2014, pp. 28, 73, 74, 77, and 149).

[73] Biddle et al. (2015, p. 377).

[74] See Dold (2016, p. 50), Blythe (2013, p. 426).

[75] Biddle et al. (2015, p. 377).

[76] See Le Grand and New (2015, pp. 1–3), Van Aaken (2015, p. 88).

[77] Abbots and Lavis (2016, p. 155).

[78] Gigerenzer (2015, pp. 361 and 362).

some paternalistic interventions are needed.[79] The "Harm Principle" suggests that an individual's actions should only be constrained to prevent harm to others. According to Mill's oft-quoted principle, "the only purpose for which power can be rightfully exercised over any member of a civilized community, against his will, is to prevent harm to others."[80] The justifications for the "Harm Principle" are grounded in the principle that individuals know best what is good for them and that governments do not have access to all the necessary information.[81]

This is what Sunstein calls the "Epistemic Argument," which is sometimes wrong. Sunstein questions and challenges this argument by outlining a non-exhaustive list of cognitive circumstances where humans make various mistakes. This is what he labels as "Behavioral Market Failures" and provides a justification for the government to step in.[82] Sunstein also discusses what he calls the "paternalistic toolbox," where he distinguishes different types and sizes of paternalism. The gist of the matter is whether public officials are poised to offer a legitimate intervention for citizens to increase welfare. To some extent, they should promote the best rational choice by providing the means for improved decision-making. This might not always be possible but it provides a strong argument for the government to intervene, especially in cases of market failure.[83]

The first category refers to the soft versus hard paternalism dichotomy.[84] In traditional hard paternalism, the "nanny state" uses its coercive power to order its citizens to do what is in their best interests.[85] Soft paternalism holds the view that government intervention is legitimate and justified only when the person is consciously aware and acts voluntarily.[86] Mill's famous example of the person who is about to cross a damaged bridge (so-called "Bridge Exception") illustrates this point clearly.[87] Consider the case where the government could not communicate the risks of a bridge that is about to collapse because of language limitations (i.e., the intervened person does not speak the local language and thus she can neither read the signs nor understand any warning signals given). In this scenario, the government's use of force to stop her from crossing the bridge would be justified as her liberty consists of doing what she wants, and falling and dying is most probably not her desire in this case.[88]

Nonetheless, if such a person is fully aware of the danger and wants to commit suicide, then the soft paternalistic view would allow this person to carry on with her will. The hard paternalistic view would justify, however, the use of force to

---

[79] Sunstein (2014, p. 28).

[80] Mill (1859, pp. 21 and 22).

[81] See, generally, Brown (1972, pp. 133–158), Perry (1988, p. 92), Riley (2015, p. 11).

[82] For more details on "behavioral market failures" and default rules as good nudging techniques, see Sunstein (2015, pp. 206 and 218).

[83] Sunstein (2014, pp. 63–72).

[84] White (2016, p. 26), Prinz (2013, p. 182).

[85] Bishop (2009, p. 296).

[86] Tanner (2007, p. 200), Hartley (2012, p. 70), Angner (2016, p. 264).

[87] See, generally, Jackson (2006, pp. 68 and 69).

[88] Sunstein (2014, pp. 63–99).

stop the person from crossing the bridge even if she knows the danger and wants to voluntarily take her own life. This could be interpreted broadly or narrowly. The main difference according to Sunstein would be the ability to influence without imposing material costs. Nudges would be regarded as soft if they imposed zero or very small costs to the choosers. The second main category is the distinction between means paternalism and ends paternalism. Here again, GPS is a good example of a nudge based on means paternalism. As pointed out earlier, individuals using GPS have the freedom to choose another route.[89] This is the ideal kind of paternalism that Sunstein tries to promote and these is the kind of nudges that I aim to propose in this book.

7.3 Turning Nudges into Simpler and More Effective SLAs

Borrowing the ideas of Kahneman, Thaler, Sunstein, and others as an analogy, the effects of default rules, warnings and information disclosure are germane to SLAs where the involved parties are still free to make a choice. When designing a contract, it is important to follow the nudge theory and apply it correctly to the case. The point is to help both end-users and cloud providers to make better decisions and to facilitate continuous mutual communication and feedback. This is also related to the need to keep informed decisions at every stage. Informed consent is a process and is an event. Therefore, even after a decision has been made, making repeated decisions is the key. Fostering rationality within cloud computing transactions and preventing mistakes when it comes to clarifying "ownership" rights of data and database rights takes a good *architecture*. This is precisely the kind of framework I propose in order to balance intuition and rationality. In other words, the ideas underlying the contractual model of this book is to make the laborious work of System 2 easily accessible for end-users and cloud providers so they can make better and faster decisions. The overall idea is to have a systematic SLA framework in order to improve decision-making. This will, in my view, reduce deliberation and transaction costs and will optimize cloud computing transactions.

In this section, I will explain how the very simple idea of nudges in cloud brokerage architectures can align with SLAs, making them less complicated. SLAs are not drafted in a vacuum. They are made in an environment where many components and features converge. This being said, the correlation between nudges, choice architectures and SLAs are of equal importance when drafting an SLA, if not the most important thing for targeting various stakeholders at the global scale. Why should cloud providers care? Many cloud providers do not understand or simply resist the idea that clarifying legal issues is a key contributor to the end-user's quality of service, which then contributes to building more trust and potentially bringing more customers on board. In order to provide a more well-rounded view, this section offers a brief and non-exhaustive list of the key points to be remembered from our earlier discussions about nudges and choice architectures. All of the below should

[89] Sunstein (2014, pp. 66–99 and 119–158).

be generally taken into account as nudges[90] that can help at every level of cloud computing transactions.

(i) An effort to raise awareness about the main legal issues that should be taken into account. In this case, the focus is on the addition of more capabilities and/or parameters required to achieve dynamic management of database rights and "ownership" rights of data;
(ii) An effort to provide concise, clear and simple information about these rights;
(iii) An effort to inform the involved parties about the importance of clarifying database rights and "ownership" rights of data;
(iv) A disclosure mechanism imposed on cloud providers that collate the information with end-user specification requirements so that end-users can clearly see whether the target infrastructure provider meets the eligibility criteria for a specific service requested;
(v) A default rule designed to clarify database rights and "ownership" rights of data;
(vi) Graphic warnings and reminders that alert the involved parties about the potential legal risks so they have the freedom to choose a different "route";
(vii) An initiative by which cloud brokers can nudge cloud providers, in a machine-readable format, to disclose information, to enable end-users to track and find the providers that best fit their needs.

This list is just a sampling of the nudges that must be implemented in the contractual framework. I will have more to say about this in the following sections and future chapters when I examine the risk assessment and the specifications of SLAs in more detail. The overall idea is that with soft nudging techniques already implemented in the architecture design, SLAs can radically improve. As hinted earlier, it turns out that the solution is not in clarifying the contractual clauses per se. That is only one part of the equation. What we need to do is to change the architecture design of the SLAs by creating more choices and implementing effective nudging techniques not only between end-users and cloud providers but essentially between cloud brokers and cloud providers. Cloud brokers can create an interface that enables improved choices between end-users and cloud providers. Below I will explain two main types of nudging techniques that will be specifically embedded in the architecture design of the computer code of the OPTIMIS toolkit.

[90]In this section, the basis for nudges in SLAs are inferred to be similar in certain aspects to other kind of nudges explained by Cass Sunstein. See Sunstein (2013a, pp. 38 and 39). See, also, generally, Minton and Kahle (2013), Thaler et al. (2010).

7.3.1 *Warning Signs for Risk Management in Cloud Brokerage*

An important nudging technique refers to warning signs with regards to risk management and contracts. Learning how to spot potential risks can help end-users and cloud providers intervene and take early action. This is strongly related to a behavioral heuristic that Tversky and Kahneman call the "availability heuristic."[91] This heuristic is set to judge frequency and probability in that it influences the options a person considers.[92] Individuals tend to substitute difficult technical or legal questions and relate them to simpler ones that they can understand better. The heuristic question here is the easier question that is answered instead.[93]

Yet, how many people are able to make judgments of probability without comprehending precisely what probability is? Kahneman and Tversky concluded that people must somehow simplify the impossible or difficult task. The answer they found is the following: "when called upon to judge probability, people actually judge something else and believe they have judged probability."[94] System 1 makes this substitution if the answer to a related question comes readily available to the individual's mind. Now and again, substitution will take place and a heuristic answer will be validated by System 2. Recall that one of the main attributes (or rather weaknesses) of System 2 is being lazy. Therefore, the heuristic question may be easily endorsed without much scrutiny by a sluggish System 2.[95] To explain this in simple terms and by paraphrasing the words of Kahneman, individuals are not very good at assessing risks since this involves technical and complex processes.

Moreover, for a host of reasons, it is self-evident that System 2 should always prevail while drafting SLAs. Taking some time to plan the contractual terms and conditions objectively and deliberately is crucial in order to rationally assess all the relevant risks involved, rather than skimming through the pages of a contract, which is something typically done in System 1.[96] What seems to be less obvious is that drafting a clear and automated contractual model using System 2, which includes a risk assessment tool, is a good means for reducing deliberation costs.[97] For this reason, the SLA framework of this book includes customized and automated techniques to manage and reduce the risks involved while selecting and using a cloud computing infrastructure.

One of the central ideas of this book is to make SLAs more useful and universally accessible. Therefore, the information presented in the SLA is very important. This

---

[91]Gilovich et al. (2002, p. 3). See also Hardman (2009, p. 24), Kahneman et al. (1982, p. 201).

[92]Tversky and Kahneman (1973, pp. 207 and 208).

[93]Kahneman (2011, p. 98).

[94]Kahneman (2011, p. 98).

[95]Kahneman (2011, pp. 97–104).

[96]Contract Clarity, *Thinking Fast and Slow for Contracts*—part 1, [online]. Available at: http://contractclarity.co.uk/articles/thinking-fast-and-slow-for-contracts-part-1/. Accessed May 10 2019.

[97]Contract Clarity, *Thinking Fast and Slow for Contracts*—part 1, [online]. Available at: http://contractclarity.co.uk/articles/thinking-fast-and-slow-for-contracts-part-1/. Accessed May 10 2019.

is exactly the situation I examine in Chaps. 8 and 9 within the contractual and risk assessment framework, respectively. The risk assessment framework includes methodologies, evaluation, mitigation, and monitoring strategies. On the one hand, it provides the architecture and technology design to assure higher confidence to cloud end-users. On the other hand, it increases reliable and cost-effective productivity by optimizing resources available for cloud infrastructure and service providers.[98]

While making hasty decisions using System 1, end-users may be influenced by their own biases, ignoring the probabilities and underestimating the risks involved. "We are often confident even when we are wrong, and an objective observer is more likely to detect our errors than we are," as Kahneman ably put it.[99] This is the reason why I suggest that brokerage services can play the role of that subtle "objective observer" very well. The risk assessment tool, which is embedded within the cloud brokerage SLA framework, can help end-users (and cloud providers), to reduce such heuristics and biases in real-time.[100] In tandem with the correlated mitigation strategies, this will increase confidence and create more trust within cloud computing transactions.[101]

Therefore, the broker who is responsible for creating/planning the programming code of the risk assessor component and the descriptions based on the XML schema is also a "choice architect", and thus a "main planner." I argue that cloud brokers can give end-users and cloud providers some helpful warning nudges through the risk assessment mechanism and other tools available such as the XML Description Schema that I will present in the next chapters. Therefore, clarifying database rights and "ownership" rights of data can only be successfully achieved if incorporated at early stages of the design architecture and taken into account throughout the whole lifecycle of the cloud service provision. This includes the technical implementation of warning signals to improve decision-making without coercion.

To explain this in as simple words as possible, the risk assessment component essentially operates as in the GPS system example. It signals the best "route" to take by sending some warning signs about specific legal issues. This will allow the involved parties more freedom to continue or change their course of action. This is the kind of paternalism that does not override people's freedom or judgments about their own ends. The same question about the legitimacy of the government to softly nudge its citizens as a kind of "libertarian paternalism" or "soft paternalism" in Sunstein's narrative could be posed to cloud brokers. The main question would be whether cloud brokers could act paternalistically? Or, to put in other words, to what extent can cloud brokers step in when there are cases of market failures? This

---

[98]See Djemame et al. (2011, p. 119).

[99]Kahneman (2011, p. 4).

[100]Berman (2012). But see Devlin (2012). Berman actually refers to how the Big Data phenomenon can help us to reduce our biases taking into account the advanced technologies present in the new database systems. Contrary to this view, Devlin points out that Big Data certainly can detect more patterns and analyze statistics more accurately, however, humans still need the recognize these patterns and make a choice. As an analogy, I take the Big Data example and I refer to the risk assessment model that I will further explain in Chap. 9.

[101]Djemame et al. (2011, p. 119).

is pertinent especially where people are likely to err and it is necessary to provide the means for improved decision-making. In my view, the "paternalistic" intervention of cloud brokers could be legitimized in some instances if we take the *soft* paternalistic approach in Sunstein's narrative as demonstrated in the GPS iconic example.

7.3.2 Default Rules and Information Disclosure as Prime Nudges

Another nudging strategy refers to default rules and information disclosures. According to Sunstein, freedom of choice is emphatically a good thing and it is always present in our daily life and business as well as in our social and political participation. Some may argue that in a democratic society this is a blessing.[102] Yet, it may also become a staggering burden when too many choices are available and we do not know what to choose.[103] Choosing takes time and effort. It requires a great deal of study and deliberation. Thus, choice may also become a burden. Sometimes, "choosing not to choose" is a better option that can yield lower transaction and deliberation costs, making it more cost-effective for end-users. This can also improve their social welfare and respect their freedom.[104] That choice is of particular relevance in cloud computing contracts since it leaves considerable room for end-users to focus on what matters for their own businesses.

On this account, default rules are probably one of the most efficient nudges. Disclosure requirements most definitely fall into the same category too. They can have a significant and lasting impact since they tend to stick.[105] They are "ubiquitous" and very powerful.[106] The GPS system can serve here again as a well-worn example of a prime nudge. GPS is an electronic device set out as a default mechanism. It enables individuals to choose not to choose the best route available to their destinations. It selects a "default route" allowing them to exercise their freedom by following or ignoring the route. In this era of technology,[107] with the coming of cloud-based computing and fully automated contracts, it is now possible to identify tailor-made default rules to the end-user's needs. Contracts can consist, in large measure, of default rules. Thus, applying a series of default rules as prime nudges with an opt-out mechanism can aid to personalize and enhance the efficiency of SLAs. The

[102]Sunstein (2015, preface, pp. 95, 105, and 192).

[103]See Iyengar and Lepper (2000, pp. 995–1006). In this empirical research, the authors challenged the assumption that the more choice, the better. In three different experiments, they arrived to the conclusion that people are more likely to choose or buy something when limited choices are available. For example, it is easier to choose and buy jam or chocolate from a limited array of 6 options rather than a more extensive selection of 24 or 30 choices.

[104]Sunstein (2015, preface, pp. 27, 36, and 145).

[105]Sunstein (2013b, p. 11).

[106]Thaler et al. (2013, p. 430).

[107]Sunstein (2015, preface, pp. 6 and 104).

contractual framework that I will present in the next chapter will include an XML schema with a set of pre-defined parameters necessary for choosing a cloud provider accordingly.

More specifically, the XML-based definition schema contains customized default rules that can help to clarify "ownership" rights of data and databases in an automated fashion. In addition, it will also include a "pseudo-code" as an extension to the SLA framework. A pseudo-code is the best way to *plan* a computer program before the actual code is written. The central idea of this pseudo-code is to allow the disclosure of information imposed on cloud providers. This will allow cloud brokers to collate the information with end-user specification requirements. The pseudo-code has been designed with a set of specific legal questions that follows a programming logic, whereby cloud brokers can automatically check the legal compliance. This list of legal questions aims at nudging cloud providers. This is where framing questions based on the "indirect nudging" approach could be implemented more effectively. I will address this in more detail in the next chapter.

Many reasons can justify this approach. Consider the following, legal people can exercise their rights by default but they can also forsake specific rights. In most civil cases and even some criminal actions, individuals can waive their rights to sue before court. They can also exchange their ownership titles in return for something. The same rules can apply to database rights and "ownership" rights of data. The SLA will essentially embrace the choice to "trade" or "waive" such rights, which are typically not covered in cloud transactions. These capabilities are now included by default in the OPTIMIS toolkit.[108]

Another parallel can be drawn from financial agents and general power of attorney for administrative or legal acts. People hire trustworthy agents based on their skills and expertise. They authorize them to act on their behalf for a wide range of financial, economic and legal aid. Under these circumstances, people act as "principals," hiring agents to replace them when needed. In other words, they are choosing not to choose.[109] In the same vein, the main themes of this book puts forward a number of tools and practical solutions through the agency of a broker as a representative of end-users. For present purposes, therefore, the crucial point is to recognize, by analogy, that end-users are relying on the broker's ability to elicit and convey information from cloud providers based on the automatic default settings incorporated into the SLAs. In doing so, they are also choosing not to choose.

[108]OPTIMIS is an open source toolkit designed to help cloud service providers to build and run applications in the cloud. New features that include the clarification of database rights and "ownership" rights of data have been implemented. The toolkit has been integrated into the OpenNebula Ecosystem and the Infrastructure-as-a-Service cloud computing project OpenStack, [online]. Available at: https://opennebula.org/the-optimis-toolkit-is-now-available-in-the-opennebula-catalog/. Accessed May 10 2019.

[109]See, generally, Sunstein (2015, pp. 9 and 139).

7.4 The Relation Between Plans, Nudges and Choice Architectures

In this chapter, we have analyzed the so-called "bounded rationality" principle, by which all human beings have flaws and limitations. They tend to take impulsive decisions. They are also unrealistically optimistic and are strongly affected by default rules. Because they are prone to procrastination and often thinking in a short-term perspective, default rules can create a lot of damage (but alternatively, can also cause a lot of good). The advantages of this cognitive-based approach are evident. System 1 is a doer, not a *planner*, whereas System 2 thinks more about the probabilities. Understanding how people think and how they fail to plan can help us design better choice architecture environments.[110] By extension, such insights can also be used in making default mechanisms that better shape SLAs in the cloud.

The question that remains is how to put all these topics together. Is there a common theme among these theories? In what way can we put these, sometimes contradicting, terms together? The theoretical framework of this book is a cross-disciplinary enterprise truly shaped by economists, sociologists, psychologists and philosophers. The path I took to develop this theoretical construct led me from normative concepts in legal philosophy and methodology to more empirical studies about behavioral law and economics as a critique of the status quo in the way SLAs are drafted on a take it or leave it basis.

As for the question of choice architectures, I am quite sympathetic to the reasoning behind some of the nudging ideas. The default settings in the printer machine and GPS examples remind us of what Lawrence Lessig said in his book *Code Version 2.0*. He extended the notion of regulation to include not only legal structures but technological architectures written in software and hardware codes. This was also a reaction to libertarianism due to the outpouring of liberal ideas with the advent of the Internet.[111] Similar to the typical and old software engineering truisms, choice architectures capture broadly-applicable principles of software and hardware construction, where designing more customized applications and options as default rules can lead users to make better decisions.

This is where Plan Theory along with the notions of trust come to the forefront as a venue to justify the role of choice architects in nudging people. The motivation for this is that sufficient thoughts do not exist about the relationship between behavioral law and economics and the more "orthodox" or conventional views of law and economics. Therefore, this is an effort to engage in such a debate. To fit the legal questions of this research, cloud architectures and SLAs, in particular, have to be thoroughly redefined in relation to these rights. The plea I make is to suggest a reform of cloud architectures founded on the belief and abilities of nudges. I developed this argument for the small scale and the specific problem of clarifying database rights and "ownership" rights of data that can make a big difference as a whole.

---

[110] Sunstein (2015, pp. 12 and 13).

[111] See, generally, Lessig (2006).

7.5 Summary and Interim Remarks

The advantages of thinking about *Plan-like Architectures* are manifold. This notion encompasses various dimensions of "frame choices" on the normative level. It is contingent on cloud architectures where brokers are allowed to use various active nudging techniques to influence cloud providers and as a corollary improve the decision-making of end-users. This new flow of "indirect nudging" techniques breeds a new paradigm. Improved choices, warning signals, information disclosures and default rules should be embedded in the architecture design of the computer code. This will reduce deliberation costs, improve welfare and enhance the efficiency of cloud computing transactions. It will also increase the likelihood that the involved parties will be better off.

More deliberation in designing cloud choice architectures would be a desirable improvement. Here is the reason why crafting SLAs as customized *plans*, which are grounded in the notion of *trust*, may help to solve the shortcomings of the much-criticized one-size-fits-all approach. The biases and heuristics in the behavioral economics approach are going to have far-reaching effects in a choice to trust. Thus, shifting the focus on trust fits very well with the idea of nudging. The bottom line is, since architectures are inevitable and since choice architects will bias decisions in one way or another, ignoring them is not a solution. On the contrary, this will make choice architectures more likely to be poor or in favor of choice architects. The operative broader question is not to nudge end-users but to approach cloud providers so they can improve choice architectures and influence better decision-making.

References

Abbots E, Lavis A (eds) (2016) Why we eat, how we eat: contemporary encounters between foods and bodies. Routledge, London, p 155

Abraham R, Aier S, Winter R (2012) Two speeds of EAM-A dynamic capabilities perspective. In: Aier S et al (eds) Trends in enterprise architecture research and practice-driven research on enterprise transformation, 7th workshop, TEAR 2012, and 5th working conference, PRET 2012, held at the open group conference 2012 Barcelona, Spain, October 2012, Proceedings. Springer, Berlin, p 116

Angner E (2016) A course in behavioral economics, 2nd edn. MacMillan Education Palgrave, London, p 264

Anger E, Loewenstein G (2016) Behavioral economics, Elsevier's handbook of the philosophy of science, vol 5. http://www.cmu.edu/dietrich/sds/docs/loewenstein/BehavioralEconomics.pdf. Accessed 10 May 2019

Avineri E (2014) Nudging safer road behaviors. http://www.rannaorf.org.il/webfiles/files/Nudge_in_Road_Safety_final.pdf. Accessed 10 May 2019

Ben-Porath S (2010) Tough choices: structured paternalism and the landscape of choice. Princeton University Press, Princeton, p 11

Berman D (2012) So, what's your algorithm? Wall Str J, Business Technology. http://www.wsj.com/articles/SB10001424052970203462304577138961342097348. Accessed May 10 2019

Biddle S, Mutrie N, Gorely T (2015) Psychology of physical activity: determinants, well-being and interventions, 3rd edn. Routledge, London, p 377

Bishop M (2009) Essential economics: an A to Z guide, The Economist, 2nd edn. Bloomberg Press, New York, p 296
Bloomberg J (2013) The agile architecture revolution: how cloud computing, rest-based SOA, and mobile computing are changing enterprise IT. Wiley, Hoboken, p 12
Blythe J (2013) Consumer behavior, 2nd edn. Sage Publications, Los Angeles, p 426
Brown D (1972) Mill on liberty and morality. Philos Rev 87:133–158. In: Smith G (ed) (1998) John Stuart Mill's social and political thought: critical assessments, vol II. Routledge, London, p 103
Cahn N (2013) The new kinship: constructing donor-conceived families. New York University Press, New York, p 148
Catino M (2013) Organizational myopia: problems of rationality and foresight in organizations. Cambridge University Press, Cambridge, p 100
Clark G, Strauss K, Knox-Hayes J (2012) Saving for retirement: intention, context, and behavior. Oxford University Press, Oxford
Clark R (2010) I'm just saying. Dog Ear Publishing, Indianapolis, p 176
Clements P et al (2010) Documenting software architectures: views and beyond, Carnegie Mellon software engineering institute (SEI) series in software engineering, 2nd edn. Addison Wesley, Upper Saddle River, p 19
Corrales M, Jurčys P (2016) Cass Sunstein, why nudge: the politics of libertarian paternalism, New Haven/London: Yale University Press, 2014 (Book review). Mod Law Rev 79:533–536
Davidai S, Gilovich T, Ross L (2012) The meaning of default options for potential organ donors. Proc Natl Acad Sci 109(38):15201–15205
Detels R et al (2015) Oxford textbook of global public health, vol 1, 6th edn. Oxford University Press, Oxford, p 782
Devlin B (2012) Big data, big mistakes? Smart data collective https://www.smartdatacollective.com/big-data-big-mistakes/. Accessed 10 May 2019
Djemame K et al (2011) A risk assessment framework and software toolkit for cloud service ecosystems. In: Cloud computing 2011, The second international conference on cloud computing, GRIDs, and virtualization, p 119
Dold M (2016) Condorcet's jury theorem as a rational justification of soft paternalistic consumer policies. In: Mathis K, Tor A (eds) Nudging—possibilities, limitations and applications in european law and economics. Springer, Cham, p 50
Eppinger S, Browning T (2012) Design structure matrix methods and applications. The MIT Press, Cambridge, p 7
Evans J (2003) In two minds: dual-process accounts of reasoning. Trends Cognit Sci 7(10):454–459
Evans-Pritchard B (2013) Aiming to reduce cleaning costs, works that work. https://worksthatwork.com/1/urinal-fly. Accessed 10 May 2019
Felin T (2014) Nudge: managers as a choice architect. The saïd business school's working paper series, University of Oxford, p 3. http://papers.ssrn.com/sol3/papers.cfm?abstract_id=2523922. Accessed 10 May 2019
Gigerenzer G (2000) Adaptive thinking: rationality in the real world. Oxford University Press, Oxford, p 125
Gigerenzer G (2015) On the supposed evidence for libertarian paternalism. Rev Phil Psych 6:361–362
Gigerenzer G, Selten R (eds) (2002) Bounded rationality: the adaptive toolbox. The MIT Press, Cambridge, p 4
Gilovich T, Griffin D, Kahneman D (eds) (2002) Heuristics and biases: the psychology of intuitive judgement. Cambridge University Press, Cambridge
Hamilton D, Zufiaurre B (2014) Blackboards and bootstraps: revisioning education and schooling. Sense Publishers, Rotterdam, p 18
Hardman D (2009) Judgment and decision making: psychological perspectives. Wiley, Chichester, p 24
Hartley D (2012) Education and the culture of consumption: personalization and the social order. Routledge, London, p 70

Heshmat S (2011) Eating behavior and obesity: behavioral economics strategies for health professionals. Springer, New York

Heshmat S (2015) Addiction: a behavioral economic perspective. Routledge, New York, p 243

Heukelom F (2014) Behavioral economics: a history. Cambridge University Press, New York, pp 71–96

Holt J (2011) Two brains running, The New York Times, Sunday book review, Nov 25, 2011. http://www.nytimes.com/2011/11/27/books/review/thinking-fast-and-slow-by-daniel-kahneman-book-review.html?_r=0. Accessed 10 May 2019

Iyengar S, Lepper M (2000) When choice is demotivating: can one desire too much of a good thing? J Pers Soc Psychol 79(6):995–1006

Jackman R, Miller R (2007) Before norms: institutions and civic culture. The University of Michigan Press, Ann Arbor, p 20

Jackson J (2006) Ethics in medicine: virtue, vice and medicine. Polity Press, Cambridge, pp 68–69

Jamson S (2013) The role of acceptance in behavioral adaptation. In: Rudin-Brown C, Jamson S (eds) behavioral adaptation and road safety: theory, evidence and action. CRC Press, Boca Ratón, p 298

Jansen A, Bosch J (2005) Software architecture as a set of architectural design decisions. In: Nord R et al (eds) 5th working IEEE/IFIP conference on software architecture WICSA 2005, papers and working session results, proceedings, Pittsburgh, Pennsylvania, November 6–10, 2005. IEEE Computer Society, Los Alamitos, pp 109–120

John P et al (2013) Nudge, nudge, think, think: experimenting with ways to change civic behavior. Bloomsbury, London, p 104

Jolls C, Sunstein C, Thaler R (1998) A behavioral approach to law and economics. Stanford Law Rev 50:1471–1550

Jolls C (2004) Behavioral law and economics, Public law and legal theory, research paper no 130, John M. Olin center for studies in law, economics, and policy, research paper no 342. Paper prepared for the economic institutions and behavioral economics conference held in Helsinki in June of 2004, pp 1–3

Kahneman D (2003) A perspective on judgment and choice: mapping bounded rationality. Am Psychol 58(9):697–720

Kahneman D (2011) Thinking, fast and slow. Penguin Books, London, p 98

Kahneman D, Slovic P, Tversky A (eds) (1982) Judgment under uncertainty: heuristics and biases. Cambridge University Press, Cambridge

Kahneman D, Tversky A (1979) Prospect theory: an analysis of decision under risk. Econometrica 47(2):263–292

Kirchgaessner G (2000) Homo oeconomicus: Das ökonomische Modell individuellen Verhaltens und seine Anwendung in den Wirtschafts- und Sozialwissenschaften. Mohr Siebeck, Tübingen

Lahti A (2010) Globalization & the nordic success model—part I. Ventus Publishing ApS (e-book), s l, p 35

Le Grand J, New B (2015) Government paternalism: nanny state or helpful friend? Princeton University Press, Princeton, pp 1–3

Leitzel J (2015) Concepts in law and economics: a guide for the curious. Oxford University Press, Oxford, p 137

Lessig L (2006) Code. Version 2.0. Basic Books, New York

Lindberg A, Svensson D (2010) IT law from a practitioner's perspective. In: Wahlgren P (ed) ICT legal issues: Scandinavian studies in law, vol 56. Stockholm Institute for Scandinavian Law, Stockholm, p 13

Mill J (1859) On liberty. Oxford University Press, Oxford, pp 21–22

Minton E, Kahle L (2013) Belief systems, religion, and behavioral economics: marketing in multicultural behavioral insights team. http://www.behaviouralinsights.co.uk. Accessed 10 May 2019

Munro A (2009) Bounded rationality and public policy: a perspective from behavioral economics, the economics of non-market goods and resources, vol 12. Springer, Dordrecht

Perry D, Wolf A (1992) Foundations for the study of software architecture. Softw Eng Notes 17(4):40–52
Perry M (1988) Morality, politics & law. Oxford University Press, New York, p 92
Prinz A (2013) Should the state care for the happiness of its citizens? In: Brockmann H, Delhey J (eds) Human happiness and the pursuit of maximization: is more always better? Springer, Dordrecht, p 182
Pomerol J (2012) Decision-making and action. Wiley, London, pp 70–71
Quigley M, Stokes E (2015) Nudging and evidence-based policy in Europe: problems of normative legitimacy and effectiveness. In: Alemanno A, Sibony A (eds) Nudge and the law: a European perspective, modern studies in European law. Hart Publishing, Oxford, p 64
Raisinghani M et al (2015) Cloud computing in the 21st century: a managerial perspective for policies and practices. In: Aljawarneh S (ed) Advanced research on cloud computing design and applications. Idea Group, Hershey, p 188
Ramanathan J, Rammath R, Desai A (2009) Adaptive IT architectures as a catalyst for network capability in government. In: Saha P (ed) Advances in government enterprise architecture. Information science reference (IGI Global), Hershey, p 171
Reason J (1990) Human error. Cambridge University Press, Cambridge
Reb J et al (2014) Performance appraisals as heuristics judgments under uncertainty. In: Highhouse S, Dalal R, Salas E (eds) Judgment and decision making at work, The organizational frontiers series. Routledge, New York, p 14
Riley J (2015) The right to liberty. In: Schefczyk M, Schramme T (eds) John Stuart Mill: Über die Freiheit. Walter de Gruyter GmbH., Berlin, p 11
Rodriguez-Sickert C (2009) Homo economicus. In: Peil J, van Staveren I (eds) Handbook of economics and ethics. Edward Elgar Publishing, Cheltenham, p 223
Safire W (2004) The right word in the right place at the right time: wit and wisdom from the popular "on language," first printed edition. Simon & Schuster, New York, p 242
Shafir E (ed) (2013) The behavioral foundations of public policy. Princeton University Press, Princeton, p 496
Simon H (1955) A behavioral model of choice. Quart J Econ 69(1):99–118
Simon H (1972) Theories of bounded rationality. In: McGuire C, Radner R, Arrow H (eds) Decision and organization: a volume in honor of Jacob Marschak, study in mathematics & managerial economics, 1st edn. North-Holland Pub. Co., Amsterdam, p 162
Simon H (1984) Models of bounded rationality: economic analysis and public policy, vol 1. The MIT Press, Cambridge
Simon H (1990) Invariants of human behavior. Annu Rev Psychol 41:1–20
Simon H (1998) Rationality in psychology and economics. In: Wiener Katz A (ed) Foundations of the economic approach to law, interdisciplinary readers in law. Oxford University Press, Oxford, pp 270–274
Sommer J (2009) When humans need a nudge toward rationality, The New York Times. http://www.nytimes.com/2009/02/08/business/08nudge.html?_r=0. Accessed 10 May 2019
Stanovich K (2010) Rationality and the reflective mind, 1st edn. Oxford University Press, Oxford
Stanovich K, West R (2000) Individual difference in reasoning: implications for debate? Behav Brain Sci 23(5):645–665
Stewart D (ed) (2015) The handbook of persuasion and social marketing: historical and social foundations, vol 1. Praeger, Santa Barbara, p 78
Sunstein C (ed) (2000) Behavioral law & economics. Cambridge University Press, Cambridge
Sunstein C (2013a) Simpler: The Future of Government. Simon & Schuster, New York, pp 38–39
Sunstein C (2013b) Deciding by default. Univ Pa Law Rev 162(1):11
Sunstein C (2014) Why nudge? The politics of libertarian paternalism, Storrs lectures on jurisprudence. Yale University Press, New Haven & London, pp 33–36
Sunstein (2015) Choose not to choose: understanding the value of choice. Oxford University Press, Oxford, pp 206 and 218

Tanner M (2007) Leviathan on the right: how big-government conservatism brought down the republican revolution. Cato Institute, Washington, D.C., p 200
Thaler R (2009) Opting in versus opting out, The New York Times. http://www.nytimes.com/2009/09/27/business/economy/27view.html?_r=0. Accessed 10 May 2019
Thaler R, Sunstein C (2003) Libertarian paternalism is not an oxymoron, University of Chicago public law & legal theory working paper no 43, pp 1–3. http://chicagounbound.uchicago.edu/cgi/viewcontent.cgi?article=1184&context=public_law_and_legal_theory. Accessed 10 May 2019
Thaler R, Sunstein C (2009) Nudge: improving decisions about health, wealth, and happiness. Penguin Group, New York, p 6
Thaler R, Sunstein C, Balz J (2010) Choice architectures. http://papers.ssrn.com/sol3/papers.cfm?abstract_id=1583509. Accessed 10 May 2019
Thaler R, Sunstein C, Balz J (2013) Choice architecture. In: Shafir E (ed) The behavioral foundations of public policy. Princeton University Press, Princeton, p 430
The Economist (2006) The perils of prosperity: can you be too rich? http://www.economist.com/node/6849948. Accessed 10 May 2019
Tversky A, Kahneman D (1973) Availability: a heuristics for judging frequency and probability. Cognit Psychol 4:207–208. http://people.umass.edu/biep540w/pdf/Tversky%20availability.pdf. Accessed 10 May 2019
Tversky A, Kahneman D (1974) Judgment under uncertainty: heuristics and biases. Science 185(4157):1124–1131
Tversky A, Kahneman D (2004) Judgment under uncertainty: heuristics and biases. In: Shafir E (ed) Preference, belief, and similarity: selected writings. The MIT Press, Cambridge, pp 203–220
Utts J (2014) Seeing through statistics, 4th edn. Cengage Learning, Stamford, p 348
Van Aaken A (2015) Judge the nudge: in search of the legal limits of paternalistic nudging in the EU. In: Alemanno A, Sibony A (eds) Nudge and the law: a european perspective. Hart Publishing, Oxford, p 88
Viale R (2012) Methodological cognitivism, vol 1: mind, rationality, and society. Springer, Berlin, p 25
Wallace D (2008) Plain old untrendy troubles and emotions, The Guardian. http://www.theguardian.com/books/2008/sep/20/fiction. Accessed 10 May 2019
White M (2013) The manipulation of choice: ethics and libertarian paternalism. Palgrave Macmillan, New York
White M (2016) The crucial importance of interests in libertarian paternalism. In: Mathis K, Tor A (eds) Nudging—possibilities, limitations and applications in European law and economics. Springer, Cham, p 26
Wright O (2014) The nudge team started out as a sort of mission impossible: how the government's successful behaviour insights team has had a profound effect on whitehall, The Independent. https://www.independent.co.uk/news/people/profiles/the-nudge-team-started-out-as-a-sort-of-mission-impossible-how-the-government-s-successful-behaviour-9117793.html. Accessed 10 May 2019
Willis O (2015) Behavioral economics for better decisions, ABC.net. http://www.abc.net.au/radionational/programs/allinthemind/better-life-decisions-with-behaviouraleconomics/6798918. Accessed 10 May 2019
World Development Report (2015) Mind, science and behavior. A world bank group flagship report. http://www.worldbank.org/content/dam/Worldbank/Publications/WDR/WDR%202015/WDR-2015-Full-Report.pdf. Accessed 10 May 2019
Zamir E (2015) Law, psychology, and morality: the role of loss aversion. Oxford University Press, Oxford, p 103
Zeiler K, Teitelbaum J (eds) (2015) Research handbook on behavioral law and economics. Edward Elgar Publishing, Northampton

Part III
A New Contractual Model

Chapter 8
New Template for SLAs

"*Consensus facit legem*" (Consent makes the law—Latin maxim).

8.1 Introduction

The notion that theory and practice are somewhat disconnected is often criticized. Most theories and models fail to address the links that put together theory and research into effective practice.[1] To fill this gap, this chapter attempts to demonstrate how Plan-like Architectures can be particularly applied as a methodological tool in the real world of cloud computing and Big Data. The overarching aim, and challenge, is to explain how the legal problems identified in this book have been technically implemented and solved.

More specifically, this chapter explains in detail how these legal issues should be communicated in the SLA. It explores the necessary avenues for choosing the right cloud provider and what actions are required to effectively incorporate the information related to "ownership" rights of data and databases into SLAs. It proposes an innovative framework keeping in mind the overall goal to execute the management of these legal requirements.

Certain methodologies will be examined in order to advance the specifications of a new template for an improved choice architecture within the SLA framework. This can be used by infrastructure providers in order to implement the necessary legal requirements. With this in mind, we can return to the iceberg metaphor introduced at the beginning of this book. The same metaphor could be applied to identify the

[1] Boniface and Seymour (2012) (eds), foreword.

M. Corrales Compagnucci, *Big Data, Databases and "Ownership" Rights in the Cloud*, Perspectives in Law, Business and Innovation,
https://doi.org/10.1007/978-981-15-0349-8_8

legal void found in SLAs. The terms and conditions that the layperson or end-user can read in SLAs are just the tip of the iceberg.

In other words, whether or not these agreements address particular terms and conditions does not matter if they are disconnected from what the computer software can actually do. What is of utmost importance, from a pragmatic point of view, is that the computer code takes on additional form[2] and end-users can unequivocally express their true *intentions*. Plan-like Architectures can be realized by embedding not only the legal issues, but the explicit consent of end-users within the architecture design as well.

This chapter is divided into three main sections; each of which provides a concise review of the core theories and models relevant to the area of the topics covered. This will help to combine the systematic theoretical base of Plan-like Architectures and allow the practical techniques to be built step by step, hence making the ensuing theory-practice gap come full circle back into the discussion of well-designed architectures again.

Most lawyers and legal scholars prefer to focus their attention on the topic of legal regulation. They hardly discuss the implementation of embedding legal concepts into man-machine interfaces and operational systems. Therefore, since this is not an area that the majority of legal scholars tend to address explicitly, this chapter contains a mixture of case law material, hypothetical scenarios, anecdotal examples and incidents that will help every lawyer grapple with issues of architecture and design.

After this introduction, Sect. 8.2 explains the essential background information concerning SLAs and XML. They are both integral parts of the contractual framework. Most SLA offerings, however, are based on a "take it or leave it" basis and empirical studies suggest that the average consumer rarely reads the terms of service. Section 8.3 is based on a special survey that was responded to by a group of experts in the field of computer science and IT law. This section also contains some anecdotal incidents and jurisprudence as examples of the challenges and contrasting images when it comes to delineating the central question with regards to "ownership" rights of data and databases.

Section 8.4 presents a sui generis contractual model and explains in detail how to fine-tune and effectively embed these legal issues at the earlier stages of the architectural design. It also includes selection tools that use XML and Unified Modeling Language (UML) models and can later export their options through a Graphical User Interface (GUI) for end-users to select which options they need. Finally, the contractual model includes a pseudo-code that follows a conditional programming logic. This pseudo-code contains a set of legal questions that have been specifically designed to *nudge* cloud providers to disclose information and effect the necessary changes into their own SLA specifications and underlying resources.

[2]See, generally, Donaldson and Siegel (2001, p. 144).

8.2 Background Considerations: SLAs and XML

SLAs are nothing more than contracts between a cloud service provider and a customer. They are comparable with outsourcing agreements in a way that they provide the specific terms and services that the provider needs to fulfill. An SLA may be defined as: "an explicit statement of expectations and obligations that exist in a business relationship between two administrations, i.e., service provider and end-user (customer)."[3] In other words, SLAs are formal, legally binding contracts used to specify and guarantee, usually in measurable terms, the delivery and expectations of services, including its sanctions and penalties if such services are not delivered according to the defined terms.[4]

In traditional outsourcing agreements, the customer deals directly with the service provider, knowing exactly where the physical infrastructure lies. Nonetheless, SLAs in the cloud differ in a way that the numbers of IT resources, which are made available to the customer, vary depending on the customer's demand and therefore they are unaware of the exact location of the IT infrastructure.[5]

SLAs resemble contracts related to web hosting services,[6] outsourcing, SaaS and Application Service Provider Agreements (ASP).[7] Their structure is similar to software license agreements. Nevertheless, taking into consideration the subject matter, they are comparable to hosting and outsourcing contracts.[8] SLAs can vary in shape and wording depending on the cloud provider and the type of service being provided.[9] The main legal issues that are usually considered are those related to inter alia data protection, data security, jurisdictional issues, and intellectual property.[10]

This chapter focuses only on answering the research questions of this book with regard to those issues related to the clarification of "ownership" rights of data and databases. The contract terms and conditions between the customers and cloud providers defined at the outset also describe the separation of responsibilities between the parties at both organizational and operational levels. The current state of the art in terms of contractual issues shows that there is little or no room for negotiation between the parties involved. Instead, there are different kinds of contracts the customer can choose.[11]

As mentioned earlier, this book deals with the entire lifecycle of the SLA. This being said, it is important to point out some of the main characteristics of the "pre-contractual" negotiation phase. The quality of information provided at this stage

---

[3]Sheshasaayee and Swetha (2016, p. 574).

[4]Wu (2014, p. 20), Jin and Machi-Raju (2002), Ron and Aliko (2001).

[5]Carstensen et al. (2012, p. 244).

[6]See, generally, King and Squillante (2005, pp. 195) et seq.

[7]Harney (2002, p. 126).

[8]See, generally, Bragg (2006, p. 49), Svirskas (2004, pp. 96) et seq.

[9]Matthews and Gillespie (2002, pp. 143) et seq.

[10]Other related issues are with regard to negligence and law enforcement access. See Balboni (2011, p. 165).

[11]Waschke (2015, p. 122).

must be accurate and complete to enable end-users to come to an informed decision. This part should deal with basic questions with regards to the quality of the service (QoS). It should also include questions related to database capabilities including, but not limited to, power of virtual machines, storage capacity, location of data[12] and issues related to the clarification of "ownership" rights of data and databases.

It is not possible to discuss all the pre-contractual issues here or even a representative number of them. What I would like to stress in this chapter, however, is the way to present the information to end-users, which should be seen as an *ongoing process* and not a single event. This process goes beyond the pre-contractual phase and extends further to the service deployment and operation stages.

There are several reasons why information does not come across to cloud users in the most efficient way. This information must come in the right format. That is, in a *standardized and machine-readable* fashion. The current meaning of informed consent in online click-through agreements can, however, beeasily over-stated. The significance of this has been examined by the House of Commons Science and Technology Committee in the UK. They found out that end-users usually just sign up without really reading and knowing what they are actually signing up to. They were particularly critical of the complexities surrounding terms and conditions, describing them as "more complex than Shakespeare."[13]

This was evidenced in 2014, when the Article 29 Data Protection Working Party recommended Google change its privacy policy to avoid "indistinct language".[14] Furthermore, a study of Facebook's Data Policy in 2015 concluded that it was unclear "to what extent user data is shared with other entities such as 'Facebook Companies,' 'Third Party Partners' and 'Customers,' nor what the exact identity is of these entities."[15] Thus, end-users should be able to make simple *choices*. It must be easy to understand, without technical or legal jargon.[16] In this sense, the word "choice" involves two different meanings: (a) the possibility of *what* to choose; and (b) the *way* of choosing.[17] In the context of this book, this refers to being able to choose how to allocate "ownership" rights of data and databases, and the most appropriate form to convey such a choice.

In other types of services like broadband or telephone provision, the legal terms of the SLA are given in written form. These sorts of agreements are signed by the parties like a normal contract. In cloud computing and Big Data environments, the idea is very similar. However, since the agreements are managed automatically by the provider, they are expressed in an XML format called Web Service Agreement

---

[12]See, Verite and Helberger (2013) EU Cloud Computing Expert Group: Discussion Paper Pre-Contractual Information Requirements and Cloud Services [online]. Available at: https://ec.europa.eu/info/law/law-topic/consumers/consumer-contract-law_en. Accessed May 10 2019.

[13]Anderson (2015, p. 159).

[14]Anderson (2015, p. 159). See also Letter from the Article 29 Data Protection Working Party to Google on Google Privacy Policy (Appendix: List of Possible Compliance Measures. Ref. Ares (2014)3113072).

[15]Anderson (2015, p. 159), Van Alsenoy et al. (2015).

[16]Power et al. (2006, p. 84).

[17]Sunstein (2015), introduction.

(WS-Agreement).[18] For this reason, the idea I propose in this chapter is to provide a *template model for improving templates* in SLAs. This can be done by selecting the infrastructure provider that can provide such a framework by using a specially designed XML schema during SLA negotiations. The XML is a markup language standard,[19] which aims to define a format that is both human and machine understandable. Thus, it may be edited by humans based on a template model, and the product can be processed by the corresponding software, following a relevant decision logic.

For example, the template model dictates the available fields, the user selects the appropriate values through a user-friendly interface, and then the relevant software retrieves the XML-based provider descriptions and filters them, taking into account the end-user's requirements. As explained in the triad (SNA) relationship,[20] the information provided in the schema should be used to automate the negotiation process between the broker and the infrastructure provider. The main purpose of providing such an XML-based definition is to bridge the gap between end-users and cloud providers in order to grant customers the capacity to keep more control over their data and choosing cloud providers, which comply with their requirements.

This chapter takes into account previous work related to the OPTIMIS European funded-project concerning the XML definition for data protection and security issues and extends the work to include the possibility of clarifying "ownership" rights of data and databases. In the following sections, I will explain the details of this new contractual framework, which are aligned with the main findings gleaned from a unique survey.

8.3 Empirical Study and Optimized Solutions

The analysis in this section departs from the survey conducted by Queen Mary University of London that looked at standard terms and conditions. It showed that cloud providers do not usually express "ownership" of IPRs, particularly the content and data uploaded to the cloud by the end-users.[21] Nevertheless, as discussed earlier, the nature of cloud computing implies the constant generation of new data, which is derived from the data submitted to the cloud. Hence, it is important to design a framework that establishes a clear understanding of "ownership" rights with regards to this new data.

---

[18] Kirkham et al. (2012, pp. 156–160). See also Open Grid Forum, *Guide to WS-Agreement Model & Protocol*, [online]. Available at: http://wsag4j.sourceforge.net/site/wsag/overview.html. Accessed May 10 2019; see also Web Service Agreement Specification, [online]. Available at: https://www.ogf.org/documents/GFD.107.pdf. Accessed May 10 2019.

[19] See Extensible Markup Language (XML) 1.0 (5th edn), [online]. Available at: http://www.w3.org/TR/REC-xml/. Accessed May 10 2019.

[20] See Chap. 4.

[21] Bradshaw et al. (2010, pp. 31–32).

For this reason, I conducted a special survey[22] that looked at the main legal problems aassociated with "ownership" rights of data and databases. The survey was submitted to academics and law practitioners working in the field of IT and IP law, and to various sectors of the IT industry such as service and infrastructure providers, software developers and datacenter provisioning services. The data collected revealed elevated concern in this subject matter and suggested the need for better criteria to solve these issues. It also showed a lack of awareness of database rights as less than 40% of respondents were acquainted with the provisions of the Database Directive, especially in the IT sector. On the other hand, more than 90% of the respondents conveyed that a contract for cloud services should include language clearly affirming and specifying "ownership" rights of data and databases.

As outlined in the methodology section of this book, the survey was sent to 100 experts in the field of ICT and IT law, from which approximately 40% worked in the academic, research and education sectors. The remainder worked in law firms and other fields of the IT industry including cloud service providers, software developers, data center provisioning services, IT management, wholesale and retail companies. This also included insurance companies as well as other financial, communication and technology services. The survey was sent via email to selected expert groups and followed up by phone or email as necessary. Most of the surveyed experts were located in the EU (more than 62%) including all the cloud service providers due to the relevance of the provisions of the Database Directive in the EU and the potential implications in other jurisdictions.

Nevertheless, to ensure geographic representation, the questionnaire was also sent to a random sample of leading experts in North America (about 7%), Central and South America (about 13%), and Africa and the Middle East (about 5%). Not surprisingly, only 38% of the respondents were aware of the provisions of the Database Directive, in particular those located within the EU jurisdiction, whereas 62% were not aware of the database right, particularly those experts without a legal background or those located outside of the EU.

These statistics may reflect the necessity of raising awareness with regards to the provisions enshrined in the Database Directive and the potential implications on a global scale. The survey provides information about current practices and how the industry views potential problems if database rights are not fully addressed, which is critical to designing effective contracts. The intent of the survey was to accomplish four main tasks: (i) improve estimates with regard to the implementation of database rights in cloud computing and Big Data environments from a global perspective; (ii) identify the perceptions and practices of the cloud computing industry with regard to the Database Directive and "ownership" rights of data; (iii) recommend strategies to clarify "ownership" rights of data and databases in order to mitigate potential risks among the involved stakeholders; and (iv) provide an effective and pragmatic contractual framework to prevent the monopoly of information and future controversies between the involved parties.

---

[22]This empirical study was based on a survey carried out among 100 different stakeholders throughout different world regions.

The survey contained a set of 10 questions that covered the most important provisions of the Database Directive while using a cloud service provider. In particular, the questions were grouped into 3 categories as follows: (i) location of databases and jurisdictional issues: defined as the "glocalizational" conundrum further examined in Sect. 8.3.1; (ii) contractual issues: click-through vs. negotiated agreements which are further discussed in Sect. 8.3.2; and (iii) "ownership rights" of new data: this question has been divided into two sections. While Sect. 8.3.3 deals with the question of "ownership" rights in consumer data, Sect. 8.3.4 focuses on "ownership" rights in biological/genetic data.

Finally, the results of the survey were considered when a mechanism was designed that allowed customers to have more control when using cloud services. The database right is only applicable within the jurisdiction of European Member States, and therefore, the right extends only to makers or right holders who are nationals or habitual residents of a European Member State. Because cloud computing is a global issue and databases can be easily reproduced on VMs running in the cloud in a matter of seconds, cloud providers should offer their customers the ability to keep their database rights or waive them. This does not only depend on their specific locations but also, and more importantly, on their specific needs. For example, if the cloud service is needed for scientific research using Big Data, then end-users could choose to waive database rights and share that data in a common pool, so everyone can tap into this new information.

8.3.1 Database Rights and the "Legal Glocalization" Conundrum

The first thing to consider while planning an SLA framework is the so-called "legal glocalization" problem. According to Annupan Chander, legal glocalization "would require the creation or distribution of products or services intended for a global market but customized to conform to local laws—within the bounds of international law."[23] Given the global capabilities of cloud service provisioning, there are potentially different jurisdictions involved.

Therefore, the survey contained a set of questions about jurisdictional issues. Approximately, 85% of surveyed participants considered that clarifying which legal jurisdiction would be applied was an important point of negotiation. Database rights are particularly problematic in the field of cloud computing as they could be potentially "ex-ported" overseas to a jurisdiction without database right protection. Therefore, database rights should only be implemented in jurisdictions where this right exists and limited to a "geographic location" due to its territorial nature. In addition,

[23]Chander (2013, pp. 11, 16, 137, 143, 144, 145 and 169).

as hinted in the preceding chapters, an "unconditional waiver" should be incorporated as an alternative for scientific databases and/or for databases transferred across different jurisdictions outside of the EU/EEA countries.[24]

The survey also contained one specific question about the elaboration of International Standard Contractual Clauses (ISCC), which can address database rights. The question was whether the ISCC could be a good venue to address these potential uncertainties. This main idea was inspired from the Standard Contractual Clauses (SCC) framework in the field of data protection, whereby European Member States may transfer data safely to a "white list" of countries using the SCC provided by the European Commission. Almost 75% of the surveyed participants agreed with this idea while about 5% disagreed and approximately 20% did not know whether this could be a good venue to approach this problem. Some of the comments provided by the respondents showed a certain degree of skepticism as to whether the drafting of these clauses could be possible at an international level due to the territorial nature and regional approach of database rights. Not to mention the difficulties of enforcing this internationally. Many of the responses gathered from this survey led me to shift the original purpose of elaborating the ISCC and encouraged me to find a more pragmatic solution.

Therefore, I arrived at the conclusion that instead of clarifying the contractual clauses per se, both database rights and, more generally, "ownership" rights of data should be embedded in the architecture design. As mentioned in the introduction of this chapter, the terms and conditions are just the tip of the iceberg, but what is more important is the hidden architecture; the software code that can work more effectively as a normative framework. In my opinion, this is a very good approach because it grants end-users the possibility to negotiate their rights while keeping the transaction costs very low. All in all, this solution offers a good blend that keeps the benefits of negotiated terms and, at the same time, the practical aspects of click-through agreements. In the next sections, I will explain this approach in more detail.

8.3.2 Click-Through or Negotiated Terms? A Blended Approach

As hinted above, SLAs belong to the "adhesion contracts" category. These are standard contracts offered by one party (in this case the cloud provider) to another (end-user) on an essentially "take it or leave it basis," whilst ruling out any possibility of negotiation.[25] In these types of contracts, one party establishes all the conditions arbitrarily, in so far as the other party can only accept or reject the offer.[26] Depending

[24]See, generally, The work and principles of the Creative Commons (CC) licenses. Keller and Maracke (2007). See also OpenAIRE, *Creative Commons 4.0: It's here!* [online]. Available at: https://www.openaire.eu/launch-of-creative-commons-40-license. Accessed May 10 2019.

[25]Soliz and Gasteazoro (1992, p. 79).

[26]Borda (1974, p. 14).

on the cloud service, this might be agreed upon by the parties. Most of the publicly available contracts on the Internet are, however, limited to an "on-line click-through" agreement.[27]

The current state of the art in terms of contractual issues shows that there is little or no room for negotiation between the involved parties. Instead, there are different kinds of SLAs that the user can select. For this reason, it is important to differentiate at the outset from "negotiated contracts," also known as "arm's length contracts," and the "adhesion" or "standard form" contracts known as "click-wrap" or "click-through" for on-line agreements and "shrink wrap" for products offered off-line.[28] The main problem related to the SLA in cloud computing transactions is that they do not offer their cloud customers the possibility to assert "ownership" rights of data and databases. As pointed out by Davison, the problem is that "contracts for access databases may not in fact have the customized features,"[29] which are necessary, in my view, for the optimization of cloud computing and Big Data.

Currently, end-users may only accept the terms and conditions displayed on a computer screen by ticking a box or clicking on an icon. According to Davison, this situation is likely to happen in electronic databases because of the contractual automating procedures, where there is no negotiation over the terms and conditions. These types of contracts have been described in the academic environment "as one in which a contract may be formed but in fact there is no agreement in the sense that there is no meeting of the minds of the individual parties and the terms are completely non-negotiable."[30]

For this reason, there was a specific question addressed by the survey regarding the most efficient way to clarify "ownership" rights of data and databases. The specific question was whether a negotiation of the terms and conditions should occur before entering into a contractual relationship between cloud providers and customers, or, whether a click-through agreement would be more practical. According to the survey conducted, the answers were disputed as nearly 49% of the respondents believed that a click-through agreement would be more practical than a negotiation of the terms and conditions. Almost 45% thought that the negotiation of the terms and conditions was a better choice. The rest of the respondents were undecided.[31]

Besides the multiple-choice question between "negotiated terms" and "click-through" agreements, the survey allowed the respondents to expound on the answers as open-ended questions. The answers given by the respondents revealed that negotiations should be agile and that it would be extremely impractical to negotiate on all kinds of cloud services and use as this would depend mainly on three factors: (i) *the type of user*: individual or private users may not be in a position to negotiate, and, the level of technical and legal knowledge of the average consumer may not be high enough to warrant the negotiation of terms and conditions, whereas corporate users

[27] Wrinkler (2011), Kunz et al. (2001), Ezor (1999).

[28] Derclaye (2008, pp. 174–175).

[29] Davison (2003, p. 40).

[30] Davison (2003, pp. 40–41).

[31] Survey results.

or professional contract partners might be in a better position to negotiate; (ii) *the type of service*: it depends on the complexity of the applications and infrastructure as well as the value of the cloud services; and (iii) *the type of data*: it depends on the relevance of the data involved.[32]

The current state of affairs is that only large companies signing contracts of high economic value are in a position to negotiate the terms and conditions as they have the technical and legal expertise as well as the financial resources to bargain for a better deal. Nevertheless, as previously discussed in the law and economics theoretical framework, within the five core principles,[33] transaction costs would be too high to negotiate agreements with all entities and users operating in the cloud. With professional contract partners, this may be another issue but with individual consumers or smaller enterprises, the negotiation of the terms is not realistically feasible.[34] For this reason, this book highlights the importance of the broker intermediarie's role in facilitating transactions between cloud providers and cloud customers. The cloud broker could provide added value services such as clarifying specific terms using the expanded SLA framework that I will explain further below. This would also bring more transparency and create more trust for both parties. The broker could act as a middleman and offer SLA negotiating services, which could contain a blend of the efficacy of click-through agreements and more negotiation capabilities.

The ideal contractual framework should allow the involved parties to reach a mutually beneficial agreement on an equal basis. End-users should be able to rely on the fact that the agreement is reasonable otherwise it will feel like a "deadlock" and they would refrain from using such cloud services. Clarifying database rights and, more generally, "ownership" rights of data will enhance the mutual trust between the parties and maximize cloud transactions. The basic requirement would be that these options are expressed in simple terms so end-users could be more aware and easily identify the benefits of clarifying these rights.

This idea is consistent with the results of the survey. More than 73% of the respondents thought that the contractual terms should use terminology addressed to the layperson and general public, whereas less than 21% believed this should be drafted in strictly legal terms. This approach could be achieved with the inclusion of default rules as discussed in the previous chapter. By clicking some boxes with reference to these specific rights within the SLA, an intermediate position between the two types of contracts could offer end-users, such as private customers and SMEs, the opportunity to engage in a more balanced transaction.

[32]Survey results.

[33]See Chap. 4 above.

[34]Survey results.

8.3.3 "Ownership" Rights in Consumer Data

Given the potentiality of cloud computing and Big Data to generate new data out of the data submitted to the cloud, the questionnaire submitted to the group of experts contained a specific question related to "ownership" rights of data. The question referred to the necessity of including language specifying the "ownership" rights of data, i.e., language specifying what happens to the results of any processing of this data that occurs while on the cloud provider's system. Survey results indicated that 97% thought this was an important aspect of negotiation and highly relevant to clarify at a contractual level, while only 3% estimated this as not being relevant at all.[35]

Since end-users use the cloud and Big Data services not only to store data but also to analyze and create new information, the key question was who is the "owner" of this new data? To some extent, the answer to this question lies on where and when the new information is generated. In many cases this is a collaborative process between customers and provider, and, as both parties have a legal interest, this is certainly a critical point of negotiation. For this reason, this should be clearly asserted before the processing of new data. The current state of legal affairs seems to fail in addressing these issues appropriately.[36]

The Japan Railway Suica card incident is probably one of the most notorious examples in Japan with regards to the question of who is the "owner" of the processed data collected (i.e., Big Data). The East Japan Railway (JR East) is a train company that decided to sell information from the processed travel records of its prepaid Suica cards to a third-party company (Hitachi) without the consent of its 43 million customers. The Suica card is a rechargeable smart train pass that can also be used to purchase goods in a number of stores.[37]

When the incident became public, the railway company claimed that this was "anonymized" data related to only "statistical information," which in principle would not violate data protection laws. JR East apologized for the incident and offered its customers the chance to opt-out of the data collection by sending an email.[38] Nevertheless, some customers claimed that the advanced analytic tools of private marketing companies could make it possible to identify the patterns of such "anonymous" data and establish links to customers' commuting and buying behaviors.[39]

Although it is arguable whether JR East actually violated Japan's Personal Information Protection Act (Act No. 57 of 2003, the "PIPA" Act), this incident created uproar and concerns among Japanese society. Consumers felt offended by the behavior of JR East who simply claimed the "ownership" rights of such data as a unilateral

---

[35] Survey results.

[36] See Reed (2010, pp. 1–22).

[37] Corrales Compagnucci and Jurčys (2016).

[38] Corrales Compagnucci and Jurčys (2016); See also Metcalfe (2013).

[39] Corrales Compagnucci and Jurčys (2016); See also Editorial (2013) *JR Sells Commuters' data*, The Japan Times, [online]. Available at: https://www.japantimes.co.jp/opinion/2013/08/03/editorials/jr-sells-commuters-data/#.XRw0uS2B0_U. Accessed May 10 2019.

decision. They thought that this behavior was not the most desirable, or appropriate, for the company while exercising their fiduciary duty as a faithful trustee. As a consequence, JR East received several complaints from customers and decided to terminate its contract with Hitachi.[40]

Further, this case raised public awareness of the need for having a more clear-cut, explicit set of rules regarding data disclosures.[41] Against this backdrop and after years of debates, substantial amendments have been made to the PIPA Act. Among the most notable changes is one that merits special attention in the context of Big Data and the Internet: the disclosure of such Big Data must be reported to the competent authority and must also be communicated to the public.[42]

Nevertheless, despite modifications in the legal framework of the substantive law and several institutional changes in order to strengthen the data protection regime, the government lawmakers were not discussing issues of respect to general consumers. The discussion concerning "ownership" rights of data is inherently related to the concept of respect with regards to the origin and source of data. The legal discussion of data protection, non-disclosure of information and the confidentiality of data is not enough. The implementation of the concept of respect in regulation or even at a contractual level seems to be very difficult. However, the practical implementation of this concept embedded into the user interface or user experience seems to be more feasible. The nature of this concept can be gleaned from the experience of how to establish informed consent in the medical field. Informed consent and decision-making are an ongoing process. It is a continuous effort to ensure meaningful communication and respect for patient autonomy.[43] Thus embracing this concept could also help to build a trustful relationship.

Most legal scholars tend to cluster somewhere towards very conventional concepts and normative approaches related to database rights, privacy, data protection and security. However, we must strike a balance between integrity, availability and confidentiality. Within the scope of Big Data, when a service company is collecting data, Big Data does not solely belong to the connecting company. The company is a fiduciary and as such, it has fiduciary obligations to the beneficiaries whose data is held in their databases.[44] Consumer consent is not only related to gathering information but also how it is managed and disseminated. It also depends on the type of data.[45] If service companies see their overall role as being fiduciary trustees, and if

---

[40] Corrales Compagnucci and Jurčys (2016); See also Editorial (2013) *JR sells commuters' data*, The Japan Times, [online]. Available at: https://www.japantimes.co.jp/opinion/2013/08/03/editorials/jr-sells-commuters-data/#.XRw0uS2B0_U. Accessed May 10 2019.

[41] Crawford (2015).

[42] Amended Act on the Protection of Personal Information (Tentative Translation), 2016, [online]. Available at: http://www.ppc.go.jp/files/pdf/280222_amendedlaw.pdf. Accessed May 10 2019; Durham (2016); Corrales Compagnucci and Jurčys (2016).

[43] For a comprehensive view with respect to patient's autonomy and informed consent in the medical field, see Maclean (2009, p. 42), see, also, generally, Veatch (1997, p. 195) et seq.

[44] About fiduciary responsibilities of Big Data, see, i.e., Berman (2013, pp. 201–211).

[45] Stimmel (2015, p. 209).

they explain that the use of Big Data will benefit the individuals, then the attitudes of the customers towards sharing data will be more positive.

Most cloud service providers or online companies are not very good at letting their customers know the purpose of garnering and sharing their data. They are not very transparent and constantly run foul of customer opinion.[46] Therefore, contextualizing this is very important for developing mutual trust. Commercial retail banks, airline companies and security houses, for example, are much better at interacting with their customers. They explain to them that the purpose of analyzing Big Data will improve the value of personalized services, expand business transactions and enhance customer cooperation and experience. According to a global consumer survey from Infosys, 88% of the surveyed people were willing to share their online data with retailers if they receive some sort of benefit as an exchange, such as "special offers or royalty points." Additionally, according to the Data and Privacy Study 2014 from LSE: SDL, 79% would be willing to participate if this was a company they trusted.[47]

There are two main approaches to deal with "ownership" rights of data in the literature. One such solution is to treat data as an extension to the notion of property rights. This is derived from John Lock's ideas and principles that follow the "natural rights theory of the social contract."[48] In the context of this doctrine, he introduced the concept of "monautopoly," which means the "monopoly of oneself." That is, the individual owns his body and the labor he or she produces.[49] This notion extends beyond lands and tangible goods to the data that the person also generates. If we take this model into account, data could be considered as an asset and thus could be liquidized.[50] This data could also be traded on a number of market places. If so, a more ambitious goal would be to determine virtual values and set up data exchanges as much as we have trade stocks or securities in the stock exchange market today.[51] Furthermore, this is what traditional law and economics theories say: that markets are very good at self-organizing.[52]

The other solution would be to "waive" individual property (or "ownership") rights and think of data as a "common" where end-users cannot be easily excluded. According to Yochai Benkler, the commons would be a form of "non-property," presumably because in his understanding the notion of property refers to a kind of "exclusive ownership."[53] This approach is derived from the empirical work of Elinor

[46]Davenport (2014, p. 167).

[47]Bakey (2014).

[48]For some authors such as Henry Mitchell, there is actually a clear distinction between "natural rights theory" and "social contract theory." In the first case the state *recognizes* IP rights and argues they should be permanent as any other property rights, whereas in the second case, the state *creates* them for a limited period of time. See Mitchell (2005, p. 10).

[49]Andersen (2006, pp. 112–113).

[50]See Morabito (2015, p. 75), Fisher (2009).

[51]There are already many companies trading data, including consumer's data. See Mayer-Schoenberger and Cukier (2013, pp. 118) et seq.

[52]See Lipsey and Chrystal (2011, p. 7).

[53]Wall (2014, p. 80).

Ostrom as discussed above in the five core principles of law and economics.[54] As seen earlier, this theory evolved from the study of natural pooled resources (forests, lakes, fisheries, etc.) to non-rivalrous information and other assets,[55] such as the case of Big Data. By and large, this model considers placing data in the public domain as a shared pool of resources where everyone can get access and tap into it. Viewed from this perspective, one may think of this common data as a public good, just like roads, public libraries and parks. Most data repositories would fall into this category.[56] Therefore, this model is particularly interesting in the context of scientific research with regards to genetic and biological databases coming from groups of patients or participants.[57]

Admittedly, these two approaches rest on opposite ideas. They are opposed to the definition of "ownership" rights itself. Nonetheless, I follow these two approaches, but I go beyond them in the sense that I combine these two criteria and make them fit into the same template. This will allow end-users to choose either approach and customize it to fit their best interests. To the best of my knowledge, this hasn't been done yet. There is currently no template embedded into the architectural design of computer software that allows end-users to choose a more specific framework that defines "ownership" rights of data. At the same time, one must not take these two approaches as the only two models. The impression is often that these two paradigms are mutually exclusive and exhaust any other options available. The weakness of this is that each of them lacks the precision in explaining how this could be adopted in the integral components of the man-machine interface and operational system. Therefore, the perspective I take in this chapter aims at discovering different parameters and considers additional sources of variation when planning and designing the template.

This alternative approach offers a number of advantages. First, combining different "ownership" rights models into one single template makes it possible to take a more flexible and universal framework, which can then be tailored based on end-user criteria. Second, since the template uses the structure of the source code, it allows the implementation of automatic embedded commands, but keeps the possibility of including any kind of contractual clause written in plain language. Third, it gauges the true intentions of end-users and offers them a deeper understanding of the scope and options they have. Following the same line of thought examined in the previous section, I suggest creating a new contractual model which includes a subset of specific questions during SLA negotiations. Within this framework, the customer may choose to keep, waive or even share the "ownership" rights of this new data. This will allow cloud customers, particularly those with less negotiation power, skills and resources like end-users and SMEs, the possibility to negotiate or further clarify their rights.

Moreover, the rationale behind this framework is consistent with the idea of the broker linking the involved parties (customers and cloud providers) and assisting the

---

[54] See above Chap. 4.

[55] Reichman et al. (2016, p. 3).

[56] Borgman (2015, p. 73).

[57] See, i.e., generally, Gochfeld et al. (2001), Chap. 12 with further references.

cloud customers in making better-informed decisions. A practical solution would be to let cloud customers fill in a set of questions about "ownership" rights in the same way an online survey is filled in. Similarly, in the clarification of database rights, by clicking some boxes regarding the "ownership" rights of new data, the broker could use this information to find the cloud provider that best suits customer needs. For example, one set of questions could contain a reference to data mining tools (i.e., whether the customer would be willing to allow the utilization of data mining tools to process the information submitted to the cloud). If the customer clicks "no" then the broker should find a cloud provider who is not analyzing and generating information by means of data mining tools. If the customer clicks on "yes" then another set of questions could pop up in order to clarify the distribution and allocation of "ownership" rights in the best way (i.e., whether customers would prefer to keep the "ownership" of data or simply waive their rights). The "ownership" rights of this new Big Data that was generated could also be shared by both parties and perhaps a bargaining strategy could be employed (i.e., a discount offered by the provider). The possibilities of clarifying "ownership" rights of data are manifold. This process could also be used to improve communication and increase the "mutual trust" within cloud computing transactions. As soon as cloud providers start realizing the importance of clarifying this during SLA negotiations prior to the generation of new data, the potential of cloud transformations and Big Data could be fully utilized.

8.3.4 "Ownership" Rights in Biological Data

The ethical and legal issues surrounding informed consent and "ownership" rights of biological data are far more delicate and they deserve to be discussed in a whole book on their own. Therefore, it is not the purpose of this section to answer these questions from a theoretical point of view but to bring forward a pragmatic solution that can help the involved parties (patients-doctors/participants-researchers) to improve their communication and to clarify this in a more efficient and automated fashion.

This being said, I will start by only painting the overall picture of the legal landscape. Then, I will illustrate this problem by referring to a gloomy court decision in the US where issues of "ownership" rights in biological data were raised and disputed among a group of participants and researchers of a hospital. I will then move forward to contextualize this into the technological framework that we find today in cloud-based applications and Big Data services to finally explain the concepts underlying the proposed contractual framework.

When it comes to the question of "ownership" rights of biological data, it should not come as a surprise that the opinion is divided among legal scholars and other groups of experts. To start within the framework of this section, it is important to understand the distinction between "biological material" and "biological data." The first one stands for the corporeal body tissue such as blood, urine, serum, etc. The second one refers only to data collected from the excised tissue.[58] It is only the information that has been extracted from the tissue that matters in the context of cloud computing and Big Data.

Broadly speaking, the current debate of "ownership" rights in biological data also stands at the juncture between the property paradigm and the common approach. One of the legal theorists who defends the property model is Graeme Laurie. He concurs with the property paradigm as an extension of personality rights to certain parts of the human body. This concept is easier to depict when it comes to biological material but is more difficult to grasp when it comes to (intangible) biological data derived from genetic samples.[59] According to Laurie, "ownership of information is a difficult concept to fit into the property paradigm, but it is by no means impossible to do so."[60] In his view, property rights in biological data fall under the scope of intellectual property. Nevertheless, the rights are granted in this domain because new information has been added to the total sum of human knowledge. And, as with any IPR, it attempts to work as a reward and incentive to others to contribute in the same way.[61]

Rule and Hunter are also proponents of the property rights and market model. In their views, property rights in personal data create a new equilibrium of power. For these two authors, there is a thriving market for data. This concept of ownership lays in a market model which provides a substantial value to biological data; therefore, participants may ask for monetary or non-monetary compensation in exchange to their biological data.[62]

Yet, the prospect of establishing more property rights over biological material and data has led various international soft law treaties, such as the Council of Europe Convention on Human Rights and Biomedicine, to endorse the view that "the human body and its parts shall not, as such, give rise to financial gains."[63] In the same vein, the UNESCO International Declaration on Genetic Data (the "UNESCO Declaration") approves the position of conferring "ownership" rights to biological data but rejects the so-called market model. Article 8 (a) of the UNESCO Declaration clearly states that "prior, free, informed and express consent, without inducement by financial or other personal gain, should be obtained for the collection of human genetic data, human proteomic data or biological samples…".[64] In this sense, Article 4 of the

[58]For example, "genotype" information. A genotype is "the genetic makeup of an organism, described as a combination of alleles for a gene." See McHugh and Bannerman (2010, p. 280).

[59]Tutton (2004, p. 30).

[60]Laurie (2003, p. 94).

[61]Laurie (2004, p. 326).

[62]Schulte in den Baemen (2016, p. 77).

[63]Laurie (2004, p. 326), see also Article 21 of the Convention on Human Rights and Biomedicine, Council of Europe, Oviedo, 4 April 1997, [online]. Available at: https://rm.coe.int/168007cf98. Accessed 10 May 2019.

[64]Article 8 (a) of the International Declaration on Human Genetic Data (UNESCO Declaration).

Human Genome Declaration also proscribes that "the human genome in its natural state shall not give rise to financial gains."[65]

On the other hand, the debate of "ownership" rights in biological data has recently received influence and strong support from benefit-sharing models based on the concepts of equity and justice.[66] While the concept of benefit-sharing is not new and has been used in the context of genetic data in population studies for quite some time now, this model has been extended to focus on "ordinary" health data.[67] The benefit-sharing paradigm is based on the genetic fact that 99.9% of gene information is universally shared by everyone and our differences comes from only one in a thousand of the DNA pair bases. This scientific fact raises theoretical legal complications to the property paradigm as this makes it very difficult to delineate "ownership" rights in biological data. This is the reason why some scholars argued that this must remain within the "intellectual commons" as depicted above in the Ostrom common pool of resources paradigm.[68]

A good example to illustrate this classical divide was raised in the Canavan Disease Patent Case in the U.S.[69] This case concerned a recessive hereditary brain disease called Canavan, which manifests in early childhood. The disease leads to the loss of body control, blindness, poor growth and eventually death. It is very rare, occurring statistically in 1 of 6400 children, and mostly affects individuals of the Ashkenazi Jewish community. There is no cure.[70] This case, therefore, serve as a good example of a disease that affects a specific group of people.

The facts of the case were as follows: in the early 1980s, Daniel and Debbie Greenberg were the parents of two children (Jonathan and Amy) who were suffering from Canavan disease. In 1987, after the deaths of their two children, they contacted Dr. Reuben Matalon, a biochemical genetic researcher from the Miami Children's Hospital,[71] with the hope that he and his research team could develop a genetic test that could help future generations. Dr. Matalon agreed and with the help of 160 other affected families (the Greenberg group) carried genetic research over a period of 13 years.[72] The Greenberg group saw this research as a joint cooperative effort as they contributed not only post-mortem tissue and genetic data from their children but also invested time and financial resources ($100,000 as partial funding). They collected bodily materials (blood, urine, skin tissue)[73] and created a genetic database

[65] Article 4 of the Human Genome Declaration; see also El-Zein (2008, p. 326).

[66] Knoppers (2001, p. 114), see, also, generally, Hoppe (2016).

[67] Bovemberg (2006, p. 26).

[68] See, generally Davies and Naffine (2001, pp. 158–159, 165).

[69] *Greenberg et al v. Miami Children's Hospital Research Institute Inc.*, 208 F. Supp 2d 918 (2002), 264 F. Supp 2d. 1064 (2003), United States District Court, S. D. F. (United States).

[70] Greif and Merz (2007, p. 69), Lenk (2012, p. 86).

[71] Today called Nicklaus Children's Hospital.

[72] Greif and Merz (2007, p. 69), see also Dickenson et al. (2010, p. 67).

[73] Resnik (2004, p. 158).

together with the Miami Children's Hospital containing clinical and medical data about their families.[74]

Dr. Matalon and his research team were successful in identifying the cause of the problem. With all this data they managed to isolate the gene responsible for the Canavan disease. Then, without the knowledge and consent of the Greenberg group,[75] Dr. Matalon filed a patent application for the genetic sequence of the Canavan gene and successfully established a restrictive patent licensing program. Then, the Greenberg group, which had assumed that the benefits of Dr. Matalon's research would be in the public domain in order to foster future scientific research, sued the Miami Children's Hospital. The federal lawsuit was based on a number of legal grounds, such as lack of informed consent, breach of fiduciary duty, unjust enrichment, fraudulent concealment, and misappropriation of trade secrets. The Greenberg group also contended a claim for conversion on the grounds of property rights on the tissue and associated biological data. In the end, the Greenberg group lost the case.[76] The US District Court for the Southern District of Florida only accepted the claim for unjust enrichment and this claim was later resolved by a confidential settlement,[77] which granted a continued "royalty-based genetic testing" by some licensed laboratories and "royalty-free" research by doctors, scientists and institutions searching for a potential cure.[78]

This court decision set a precedent for determining "ownership" rights of donated detached tissue samples and its associated biological data. It also revealed that the property paradigm in biomedical research has often been misled by the old "gift" model. This usually implies the concept of a donation inspired in altruism and benevolence without properly delineating "ownership" rights. This is indeed what the court said; that one cannot own something that has been donated. In this sense, the gift model has been found to undermine the original "owners" of data, which, in this case, were the patients and family members from whom the genetic data were taken.[79] The Greenberg group also argued the lack of informed consent since they were not fully aware of the true intentions of Dr. Matalon and his research team as the patent application was certainly never discussed.[80]

In the context of medical treatment and genetic research, the issue of informed consent is considered to be a very sensitive and complex topic. This is because the definition varies from jurisdiction to jurisdiction and the way to express such consent also depends on the context.[81] By and large, it could be said that informed consent is not a single event, but a process that needs continuous communication between physicians and patients. Broadly speaking, the concept of informed consent partly

---

[74] McCabe and McCabe (2008, p. 154), Corrales Compagnucci (2010, pp. 7–8).

[75] Nwabueze (2016, p. 187).

[76] Papaioannou (2016, p. 199), Weir and Alick (2004, p. 191).

[77] Herder and Fernandez (2014, p. 425).

[78] Corrales Compagnucci (2010, pp. 7–8).

[79] See Laurie (2004, pp. 312–317), Corrales Compagnucci et al. (2009, p. 8).

[80] Singh (2015, p. 206), Minor (2015, p. 75).

[81] Edwards and Elwyn (2009, p. 89), see, also, generally, Healey and Marchese (2012).

depends on the institutional trust, such as a qualified doctor or a well-known hospital.[82] Informed consent is usually and traditionally given in writing,[83] but this should not be considered as a single act. Nowadays, one has to consider the continuous soft information and communication between all the parties involved.[84] This is consistent with the innovation intermediary services proposed in the context of this contractual framework. Cloud brokers can aid to keep and maintain continuous communication with patients and physicians. They can help to disclose information and the status of the contracted services regularly.

Investment companies and security houses are very good examples of facilitating this ongoing communication as a matter of good practice. They are continuously engaging with their customers and releasing the analysis information of their companies.[85] Regulations in the field of security and financial services can help to impose an obligation to disclose information regarding financial status and events,[86] however, this is not enough. Mutual trust could deteriorate if continuous communication channels are broken. The same is true if the communication between physicians and patients is interrupted. Maintaining a systematic, open and honest communication is also important because the quality of that service level, or medical treatment, or genetic research might dynamically change and/or improve through time.[87] Therefore, the role of cloud brokers has been identified as increasingly essential not only in bridging the interoperability legal gaps but also in providing a broader scope of value-added services such as maintaining the ongoing communication between the involved parties and acting as a trusted third party with fiduciary duties.[88]

Furthermore, it is also useful to think of cloud brokers in the context of *negligence* and fiduciary obligations. Using a medical example, patients contract with the hospital or clinic based on their track records and institutional trust. Here, again, we can see a triad relationship between patients, the hospital, and doctors. However, in reality, patients deal directly with doctors who practice medicine under the duties defined by a fiduciary relationship with their patients. If there is any malpractice or accident, the patients or family members always bring a lawsuit based on two grounds of reasoning: (i) breach of contract; or (ii) negligence. In many cases, the court finds it most appropriate to categorize the legal claim on the grounds of medical

[82]Kavaler and Spiegel (2003, p. 98).

[83]Schroeder (2009, p. 40).

[84]Nesbitt (2004, p. 256).

[85]See, generally, Tompkins (2004, p. 24).

[86]See, generally, Latimer and Maum (2015, pp. 232) et seq.; Pearson (2008, p. 156).

[87]Chen and Lin (2015, p. 881).

[88]Chulani et al. (2012, p. 23). See, also, generally, Nair et al. (2011).

negligence.[89] Brokers can reduce the uncertainties in the patient-physician relationship. While it is impossible to completely remove uncertainties, their role is to assure correct understanding and reduce the information gap between the involved parties.

From a practical point of view, the issue of negligence is very important not only in the context of health care and medical research, but also more generally in cloud computing and Big Data services. For example, if both cloud computing service providers and end-users face some difficulty, the end-users may claim some compensation for damages. From the perspective of the cloud providers, they can easily decide or consider whether there has been any breach in the contract or SLA. Nevertheless, if the court emphasizes the context of negligence, it is very difficult for cloud providers to defend themselves. This is because in the context of negligence, there is a very strong obligation to be careful in the same way a court may find it appropriate to place the burden on a physician regarding to his professional negligence in medical care. However, if brokers intervene and intermediate between the end-users and providers, the brokers play the role of ensuring a common understanding concerning the standard of care and carefulness between end-users and cloud providers. Brokers aim to make this understanding more explicit, since usually the understanding of both sides is very implicit.

Recent approaches involving "apps" for medical and genetic research are increasingly becoming popular as tools for helping researchers gather and analyze Big Data for clinical research studies.[90] The current technology allows medical researchers to run medical and research studies via mobile devices such as smartphones and tablet computers.[91] Some cloud services offer web-based apps or other interfaces that can be used to obtain and share information about hereditary diseases, such as in the Canavan disease case.[92]

Good examples of these data-driven technological trends are "Google Kit" and "Research Kit" recently launched by Google and Apple.[93] Consider the Research Kit's architecture for instance, which is an open-source cloud-based platform specifically designed to gather and analyze massive amounts of data for scientific research. It allows researchers to create applications for smartphone devices[94] and seamlessly share participants' data to improve the understanding and better treatment of human diseases.[95]

---

[89] In *Neade v. Portes* for instance, the widow of her late husband sued the physician for repeatedly failing to order an angiogram that would have found that her husband had a coronary artery problem. The Illinois Supreme Court accepted the claim only under the grounds of negligence and malpractice but rejected the claim of breach of fiduciary duty as they alleged the same operative facts and accepting both claims would be duplicative. See *Neade v. Portes*, 739 N.E.2d 496 (Ill. 2000).

[90] Von Jan and Albrecht (2016, p. 245).

[91] For example, the Lilly Oncology Pipeline App. See Colditz (2015, p. 395) (ed).

[92] Albrecht and Von Jan (2016, p. 227).

[93] Behrooz and Marsh (2016, p. 80).

[94] See Research Kit [online]. Available at: http://researchkit.org. Accessed May 10 2019.

[95] For example, Sage Bionetworks and its cloud-based platform called "Bridge." See Cessna and Balachandran (2016, p. 84).

Consumers from all over the world can now download apps for the research of Parkinson disease, diabetes, or even skin cancer. Using the camera, GPS systems and sensors, which are already embedded in the iPhone or Apple watch devices, one can easily gather data for additional insights.[96] This trend will revolutionize the way scientific research is done and how issues of informed consent will shift from a traditional written form to a more automated online cloud-based scenario.

To curb this tendency, I created a special template of an improved contractual framework that can help us to unlock the question of "ownership" rights of data. The proposed framework mainly focuses on the SLA and considers the various layers of cloud services (SaaS, PaaS and IaaS) . Although some of the cloud providers and cloud-based software vendors already have their own contract templates, I use the OPTIMIS software toolkit as an example to showcase a mechanism that clarifies "ownership" rights of data and databases that have been embedded in the toolkit programming model and SLA components.[97] The idea would be that cloud providers could use either this software and the template themselves, or they could copy the ideas behind this template as a model in order to improve their own contractual frameworks. This will grant participants of genetic research studies more control over their data.

In the context of biological data and scientific research, the OPTIMIS project runs a specific use case scenario in order to demonstrate how this toolkit could be implemented in real life. The use case scenario was part of the Programming Model (PM). This scenario sought to demonstrate the processing capabilities of the toolkit in genomic sequencing applications. This use case scenario can be deployed in hybrid cloud ecosystems in conjunction with a broker. Consider the hypothetical situation of various hospitals that want to make use of a genome DNA and protein database to detect a specific disease, such as in the Canavan disease case. This is one of the main focuses of current genomic activity using Big Data. The genomic application is part of the OPTIMIS toolkit and implements a workflow. This workflow performs an automatic gene detection based on a specific genomic analysis called "Genewise"[98] that is able to detect the gene patterns. The whole process involves several databases that run in the hospitals first and then in the cloud-based application.[99]

From a practical and legal point of view, the gist of the matter is who "owns" the data within cloud accessible databases. The problem is that these databases are currently being updated by users running this application, and thus new data is generated regularly. It is, therefore, mandatory to create a mechanism that allows all the parties involved to clarify "ownership" rights of data and even meta-data that accrue by using the programming tool. When several hospitals are working on a

---

[96]Garcia Wiley and Coulton (2009, p. 91).

[97]With regards to data protection and data security, see Forgó et al. (2013, p. 20).

[98]This analysis is based on algorithms that can predict accurate gene structures. See Birney et al. (2004, pp. 988–995).

[99]Chulani et al. (2012, pp. 27–28).

specific project together using their own private cloud, this situation could be solved by drafting a consortium agreement (CA).[100]

However, as hinted earlier, this is not as simple in cloud computing transformations where the involved parties do not know each other and there are many cloud providers involved. The following sections explain, in detail, the new contractual framework, which contains a unique template specifically designed to clarify "ownership" rights of data and databases taking into account the Big Data movement.

8.4 A Sui Generis Contractual Framework

This sui generis contractual model is based on an SLA and a service manifest, which establishes the relationship between the involved parties. The SLA and service manifest consist of different parts, including specific legal sections. The SLA template contains some mandatory legal tags. Furthermore, it also allows the possibility to attach framework contracts concluded by the parties. Framework contracts are additional agreements between the parties that may not be technically feasible to implement in the SLA and service manifest.[101] Yet, they could be added to the contractual framework by making reference to them in the SLA. This distinction is very important because it allows flexibility to the contractual framework in case any remaining legal issue needs to be additionally clarified. Nevertheless, a very important function of this unique framework is to emphasize that making decisions about "ownership" rights of data and databases should also be incorporated into the earlier stages of the architectural design.

As seen above, the arrival of cloud computing poses great challenges concerning the manipulation of data and databases, especially in hybrid clouds where end-users lack the knowledge and expertise to deal with all the complexities of cloud transactions. This section aims to explain in more detail the contractual framework that includes the clarification of "ownership" rights of data and databases. This is necessary for selecting the correct cloud provider for the outsourcing and sharing of data and databases in an automated fashion. Thus, the clarification of these rights may be seen as a legal constraint embedded in the software architecture as proposed by Lessig in the New Chicago School approach. In addition, this can also be framed as having improved choices as indicated by Thaler and Sunstein in the behavioral law and economics narrative. This sui generis contractual model can be checked in a machine-readable way in order to fully grasp the potential of cloud computing and Big Data. Therefore, I propose a mechanism where customers have more control when using cloud services. I also aim to provide them with the possibility of keeping their rights or waiving them depending on their location and specific needs by selecting the infrastructure provider, using a specific XML schema during the SLA negotiations.

[100]Chulani et al. (2012, p. 30).

[101]Chulani et al. (2012, p. 14).

This section takes into account previous work related to the OPTIMIS European funded project concerning the XML definition for data protection and security issues[102] and extends the work to include database rights and "ownership" rights of data. In the past, XML-based descriptions have been used mainly for the SLA definitions, but not in the pre-selection of infrastructure providers to match client needs. They usually refer only to how many resources one would get. Some SLAs have been extended with some textual input, but mainly from a contractual point of view (which is not machine-understandable and thus is a "take it or leave it" form of contract). Therefore, with this new approach, it is possible to *pre-filter* out cloud providers that do not meet the legal requirements based on the input of end-users.

An excerpt from the XML-based definition schema, which includes the clarification of "ownership" rights of data and databases, is shown in Fig. 8.1. This is just one section of the XML-code. More information on the described fields and process will be explained in the upcoming sections. Currently, there is no such automated procedure for checking whether "ownership" rights of data and databases are clearly defined and specified so that a broker can "on the fly" and automatically confirm the legal compliance.

```
<complexTypename="IntellectualComplianceType">
    <sequence>
        <elementname="DatabaseRights"type=tns:DatabaseRightsType"><element>
        <elementname="OwnershipRights"type="string"/>
        <elementname="Compliance"type="tns:ComplianceType"/>
    <sequence>
</complexType>
<complexTypename="DatabaseRightsType">
    <sequence>
        <elementname="Location">
            <simpleType>
                <restrictionbase="string">
                    <enumeration value="EU/EEU"/>
                    <enumeration value="Mexico"/>
                    <enumeration value="South Korea"/>
                    <enumeration value="Third Countries"/>
                </restriction>
            </simpleType>
        </element>
        <elementname="WaiveRights"type= "Boolean"/>
        <elementname="Clause"type="string"/>
    </sequence>
</complexType>
</schema>
```

Fig. 8.1 Sui generis contractual model (XML Fragment)

[102]See Barnitzke et al. (2011, pp. 51–55).

8.4.1 Automated Framework: The "Dead Man's Switch"

In order to attain the full potential offered by dynamic cloud transformations, a suitable declaration procedure that meets these legal requirements must be implemented. This will provide more flexibility and scalability while relaxing some of the cumbersome bureaucratic procedures such as the manual checking of contractual clauses. This section explains in detail the main features of the legal framework that must be embedded through a suitable XML schema. Within this framework, infrastructure providers should take the XML schema and fill it in with their own information, and then make it available to the public.[103] Therefore, cloud brokers can read this information during the selection of infrastructure providers procedures.

With this in mind, the infrastructure providers must enforce a mechanism that declares the locations of their data centers as this will establish the jurisdiction and, therefore, the applicable law. The information related to the location of data centers is possibly one of the most important factors. This information must be included and displayed by an infrastructure provider that needs to be suitably adapted into a machine-readable format so it can be processed in an automated fashion. This information is usually exposed for the infrastructure provider selection procedure in different group categories. Frequently, there is a legal information category that focuses on data protection and security issues. These related works emphasized data protection and security due to compliance issues with regards to the previous EU Data Protection Directive and the new European Data Protection Regulation (GDPR).[104] Therefore, this section aims at extending these capabilities to include "ownership" rights of data and databases.

The benefits of this automated and embedded system approach can be best explained by referring to the so-called "dead man's switch." The general principle behind the "dead man's switch," also known as "kill switch" or "dead man control," is to reduce the chances of making mistakes and having accidents. The Academic Press Dictionary of Science and Technology defines this term as follows: "a safety mechanism requiring constant pressure or manipulation by human operator; it stops a machine or vehicle automatically if the operator becomes incapacitated or inattentive."[105] They are frequently used in the operation of heavy machinery and electronic devices such as trains, roller coasters, ships, tread machines, tractors, lawnmowers, freight elevators, and many medical devices. The "kill switch" works automatically

[103]The XML schema was made in the Eclipse Integrated Development Environment (IDE), which is a graphical tool for creating code (and other things such as the xml example). By having the schema model file, an interested entity may import it in a programming environment such as the Eclipse IDE. See IDE and Tools—Eclipse, [online]. Available at: https://eclipse.org/ide/. Accessed May 10 2019. Based on the schema (also known as "xsd file" in reference to the file name extension ".xsd"), they can create an instance and populate the individual values (or select from value lists where this input is limited to a predefined selection). More detailed information on this process can be found in Vafiadis et al. (2012, pp. 27–31).

[104]Kousiouris et al. (2013, pp. 64–65).

[105]Morris (1992, p. 591).

in cases where the person becomes unable to drive or operate the machine such as through death, falling asleep, loss of consciousness, illness, poisoning, etc.[106]

This concept was originally applied to subway and railroad systems. A fatal accident occurred on 27 April 2010, when a driver operating a train in the US apparently suffered from a heart attack. When this happened, the "dead man's switch" kicked in. The train stopped immediately when the driver took his hands off the control system.[107] This concept was then adapted to other vehicles and machinery. For example, lawnmower machines need to be activated by pressing a secondary bar together with the main handle. If the person operating the machine releases the secondary handle, the mower blade stops spinning automatically. This mechanism may prevent potential accidents if the person cutting the grass stumbles or becomes incapacitated.[108] Treadmills at the gym are also good examples of a "dead man's switch." They often have a safety magnetic cord that the runner clips to his or her waist. If the runner moves too far away or is falling, the safety magnet will pull out away from the treadmill and the machine will stop immediately.[109]

The dead man's feature is now applied to other intangible software features. Perhaps a better term to characterize this in the software domain would be "enabling devices," as the term "dead-man switch" might send the wrong message.[110] Nevertheless, for the sake of an analogy and to understand the software features and SLA specifications, I will refer to the "dead man's switch" in a few examples in the remaining sections of this chapter. The point is that many of the legal requirements have been translated and embedded into the technical functions of the OPTIMIS toolkit and have been programmed to kick in automatically as in some of the abovementioned "dead man's switch" examples.

8.4.2 XML-Based Description Schema

The SLA and service manifest itself contains an XML-based Description Schema. Figures 8.2 and 8.3 show the graphical representation of this schema. The figures include a number of fields that are dictated by the relevant legal analysis and intellectual property compliance capabilities and are readily available and offered in the OPTIMIS platform via a Hypertext Transfer Protocol (HTTP) GET[111] interface (getCPdescription).[112] These are important as they indicate a set of capabilities of the cloud provider. The left columns show the high-level categories of legal aspects. For

---

[106] See, generally, Guastello (2014, p. 253), Brauer (2016, p. 172).

[107] Newman (2010).

[108] Ostroff (2011, pp. 10–12).

[109] Bayles (2014, p. 331).

[110] Nix (2011).

[111] An HTTP Get operation is a simple type of web service from which one can retrieve formatted information, similar to a request in a standard browser for a web page.

[112] Kousiouris et al. (2013, pp. 64–65).

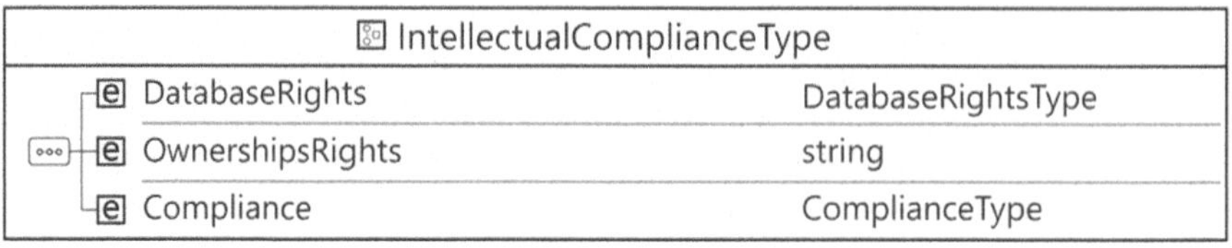

Fig. 8.2 Intellectual property compliance type

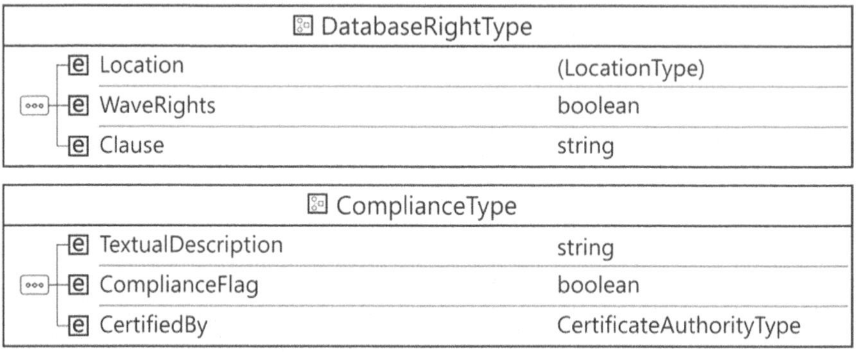

Fig. 8.3 Database right and compliance type section

each of these categories, new specialization types are defined in the right column, indicating specific fields or necessary information for each case.

What is of specific interest in the discussion of the present study is the "Intellectual Properties Compliance Type" section as depicted in more detail in Fig. 8.2. The "Intellectual Properties Compliance Type" section has been specifically implemented and expanded to address the research questions of this book. Some sections include "string" variables that allow, programmatically, the possibility to include legal text in plain language. Other sections are set out as "Boolean" data types. Booleans are data types that contain two values that are typically denoted as true or false. This section has been broken down into three main parts: (i) database rights, (ii) "ownership" rights, and (iii) compliance, as shown in Fig. 8.2.

The database rights section (DatabaseRightsType) is again divided into three parts as indicated in Fig. 8.3. This section includes the following: (i) a location constraint mechanism (LocationType), which allows the cloud provider to choose in which countries the databases are going to be located; (ii) a "Boolean" waiving system (WaiveRights boolean), whereby the cloud provider can choose to keep or waive database rights; (iii) a "string" field capability (Clause string), which allows the inclusion of contractual clauses written in plain English as defined by the provider on a case by case basis; and (iv) the "Compliance Type" section, which contains a "string" field variable that may also be validated by the respective Certification Authority. Moreover, this section also contains a "Compliance Flag" mechanism that will be activated immediately based on the geographic location restrictions according to end-user's criteria. This "Compliance Flag" is set to kick in automatically, like in the "dead man's switch" example.

8.4.3 Brokerage Workflow Process

As seen earlier, the broker is an entity positioned between customers and cloud providers who needs to find out which provider suits the demands requested in the SLA. Depending on the active role the broker takes during the brokerage process as a third party, he or she can act as a mere intermediate or can play an active role in the SLA negotiations and selection of the cloud providers. The complete process is graphically explained below in Fig. 8.4. In this hypothetical scenario, the main responsible actor is the broker located in the UK. The broker receives the legal requirements from the customer and must act accordingly. In any case, the broker must choose from a constellation of infrastructure providers (IPs) located either within the EU/EEA countries or outside of them. This will depend on the legal requirements selected by the cloud customer as a location constraint mechanism and other choices available. The complete process is as follows:

i. The cloud broker issues an XML template with the new available choices;
ii. The cloud providers use the template to create their description;

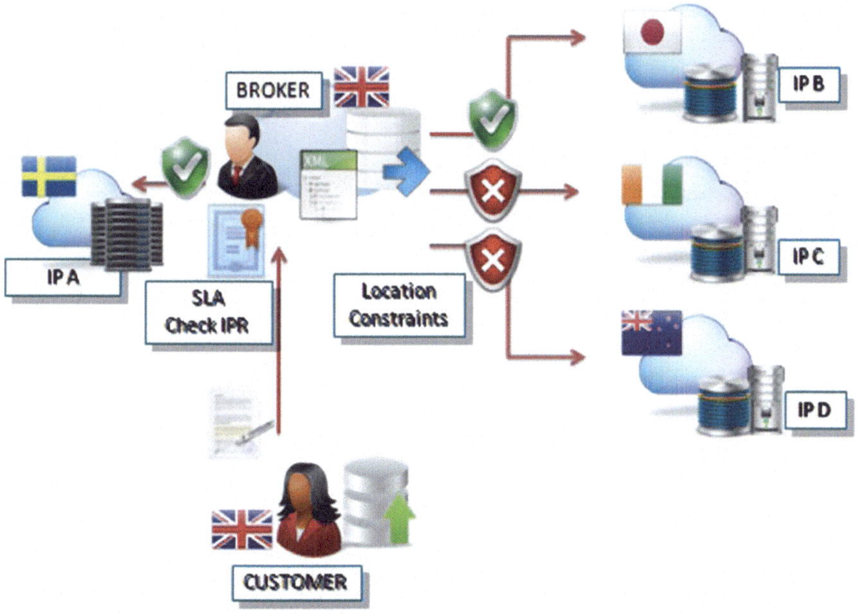

Fig. 8.4 Cloud service brokerage workflow process

iii. The user dictates which of the options they need activated. In order to do so, user input may be obtained from web forms that are automatically created from schema/template files through tools like the XML Schema Definition (XSD-Form)[113];
iv. The cloud broker compares the user requirements against the provider description.

The XML template is useful when defining the kind of input that is expected by a cloud provider and thus can be processed by the relevant software that implements the legal logic. For example, the LocationType field is an enumeration that can be limited to the defined values dictated by the template creator. In this case, the key areas are EU/EEA, Mexico, South Korea or any other third country as depicted on the right bottom corner of Fig. 8.5. This is because database rights exist in EU/EEA countries but also there are similar database rights in countries such as Mexico and South Korea.[114]

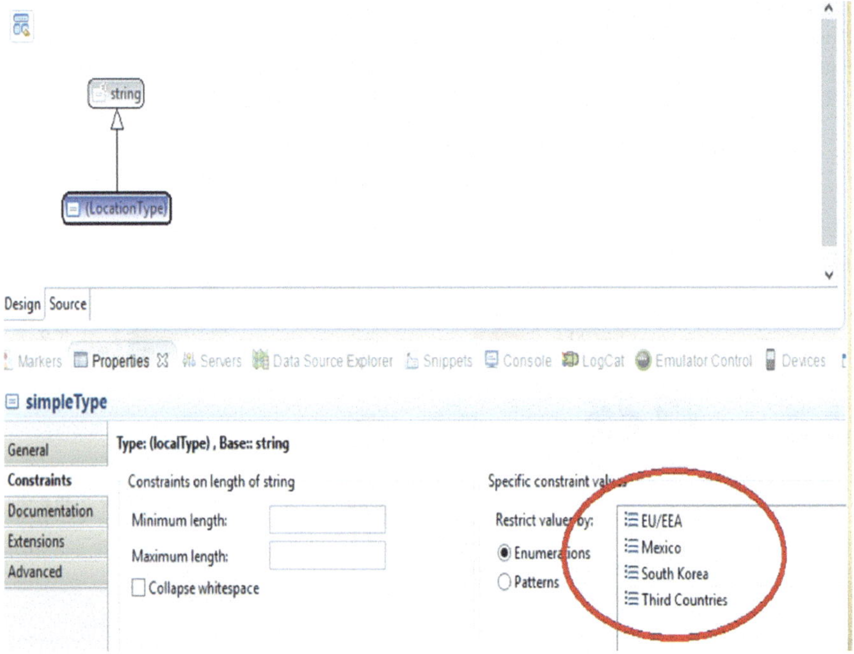

Fig. 8.5 Enumeration type for the cloud provider's data center location definition

[113]See Ilerian, XSD Form Features Overview [online]. Available at: https://ilerian.com/overview. Accessed May 10 2019.

[114]The database right in South Korea holds similar traits to its counterpart in Europe in various aspects in terms of both subject matter and substantive law; however, it contains unique features and some differences in comparison to the EU Database Directive. The raison d'être of this right both in the EU and South Korea is to protect the database "makers" (in the wording of the EU Directive) or "producers" (in the wording of the South Korean Copyright Act) who have invested in

As explained above, a cloud provider can dictate where their data centers are located and thus, in combination with the other options such as the database waiving rights option, decide through software logic if the specific provider can be legally selected.

"String" fields are free text entries, potentially useful for clarification using plain English language, while "Boolean" fields are binary state cases, in which the respective option may be "True" or "False." For example, in the Intellectual Compliance Type, the ComplianceFlag field is set to True if the provider has been certified by a respective Certification Authority or False if they have not. This authority could be any legal entity that is capable of issuing such certificates. In case no such formal entity exists, intermediate brokers could play this role, similar to the case of website verification agencies (like Verisign).[115]

This definition is performed by the cloud broker when they define the Cloud Provider Description Template (CPDT), in order to limit provider input. Figure 8.5 shows the process for creating an enumeration schema. It would be used by a cloud provider to select which values correspond to their cases (or by the broker acting on their behalf). The graphic is a screenshot of Eclipse, from which one can edit and define a list of specific values in defined enumerations. Enumerations are fields that can contain only values from a specific list (in this case the countries shown in the red circle). This enumeration can restrict the inserted information to specific list elements that are of use to specific concepts. This way the software behind the logical processing may directly compare user-selected input with the necessary textual concept.[116]

The OPTIMIS toolkit can be downloaded from the OPTIMIS website. It has been recently updated and expanded with an automated XML Description Model for clarifying "ownership" rights of data and databases. It can be used by the broker or by any of the parties depicted in the brokerage scenario. Thereafter, the content of the

---

the creation of the database. See Article 7 (1) and Recitals 7, 13, 14, 17 and 40 of the EU Database Directive; see also South Korean Copyright Act. For instance, one of the main differences is that in South Korea the term of protection is shorter as it only extends to 5 years (Article 95 (1) and (2) of the South Korean Copyright Act.) in comparison to the EU where database right subsists for 15 years (Article 10 (1) of the Database Directive). In both cases can be extended to another period provided that substantial changes have been made.

[115]See Verisign [online]. Available at: https://www.verisign.com. Accessed May 10 2019. Brokers (as depicted in the brokerage scenario) may also undertake a more active role following the negotiations, acting as "facilitators" and monitoring the enforcement of the SLA. This activity is similar to auditing and may involve all related aspects of SLA terms, from promised availability levels to location-based monitoring for the data and usage rights. In order to do so however, the broker needs to have the third party independent behavior, thus on the one hand abide by the rules set in the agreement, making sure that a violation is measured against the defined terms, and on the other hand, claim the according compensation from the provider acting on the cloud user's behalf.

[116]The "Minimum length," "Maximum length" and whitespaces shown on the left side are instructing how to behave with regard to the string fields. They set some constraints on the length for each string. For example, how many characters it may have if it is free to include any string. "Collapse whitespace" means that if someone inserts "EU/EEA" it would be stored as "EUEEA." But these options do not concern end-users since in this case they select from the pre-defined list in the right side of the graphic.

XML description may be checked directly by using the Data Manager in the OPTIMIS platform. This method collates the information published by the infrastructure provider with the user-specified requirements (i.e., location of provider or intellectual properties) and finally concludes the agreement if the target infrastructure provider meets the eligibility criteria of a specific service requested.[117]

To explain how this technical process works in simple words, we can refer to the "dead man's switch" analogy. The proposed SLA framework is based on a technology that enables the enforcement of specific legal requirements. This can be achieved by using a tag list of certain legal criteria that is automatically activated. Thus, the federation of data and databases does not take place if the target providers do not run their services based on the requirements of the end-users. To be more specific, if we take any of the "dead man's switch" examples, the federation will not proceed if one of the processors or sub-processors does not run their data centers within the specifications of the given SLA framework.

8.4.4 Unified Modeling Language and Pseudo-code

This section aims to propose an extension to the contractual framework which includes a selection tool that takes Unified Modeling Language (UML) models and exports their options through a Graphical User Interface (GUI) for end-users to select which options they need. UML is a "new general-purpose language for modeling object-oriented systems."[118] It became one of the de facto standard modeling languages that eases communication and mitigates confusion among project stakeholders. Just like architects have their own graphical standards for creating their technical drawings to document their design, software developers also need a common modeling language that everyone understands and that is also universally accepted.[119] Therefore, UML is ideally adapted to support the architectural design of software systems.[120] With regards to the user input and user interface, this could be done via web forms that directly accept schema files and create the necessary options. There are many tools for this.[121]

The UML schema will aid in the clarification of database and "ownership" rights of data *(and meta-data)*, which are necessary for choosing a cloud provider and outsourcing data in an automated fashion. This will also help to broaden the scope of SLAs in order to establish priorities and make the strategic choosing of cloud providers a global reality. This practical idea as an adjunct to the SLA framework and

[117] Kousiouris et al. (2013, p. 68).

[118] Overgaard (1999, p. 99).

[119] See, generally, Booch et al. (2005).

[120] Muresan (2009, p. 233).

[121] See, generally, Hennicker and Koch (2001, pp. 158–172).

data management was taken from the ARTIST project[122] and then extended to include the clarification of database rights and "ownership" rights of data. The ARTIST project includes a certification model that certifies whether the migrated software is compliant with the legal requirements. This feature is essential for increasing end-user confidence in software applications, taking into account certain parameters (categories) that will be evaluated.[123]

This is where framing questions based on nudge theory could be implemented effectively in a coordinated manner at different levels, especially if one follows a programming logic in which one can automatically check legal compliance. A set of questions and pre-defined options to answer such questions, such as "Yes"/"No"/"Configured in SLA," would nudge cloud providers to disclose information and make further modifications and clarifications in the SLAs and its underlying software. They are designed to be answered in an automated fashion. They could be answered by a human, who must check in a box. No free text should be allowed. This will enable the writing of computer code that has the ability to internally process the answers and produce a result. The major goal of the ARTIST certification model is to get the answers to a set of questions and then calculate some ratings for the used software (Bronze, Silver, Gold level).[124] Nevertheless, in the context of this work, the conclusion would be more straightforward to apply and would be of a "True" or "False" nature, to determine whether it is legally compliant or not.

Depending on the nature of the services required and the requests made by the concerned parties, some customers/businesses may also want to clarify the "ownership" of the product of any data processing (meta-data) that occurs on the provider's system. In my opinion, they should be informed first whether any data mining tools are running, and if so, they should be able to decide whether they still want to use the application. If not, they should be able to move to another service. For example, a pseudo-code has been created that allows the usage (or not) of data mining tools. A pseudo-code (also known as "program-design language") is the best way to *plan* a computer program before it is coded. According to Myler, a pseudo-code is "a simple, structured representation of a program sequence or algorithm that is not intended to be run on a machine."[125] It can also be loosely described as a "flowchart without the graphics."[126] While the word *pseudo* as a prefix here means that it is not the actual code but a synthetic expression of it, the code consists of the specific instructions written in the programming language itself. The pseudo-code can thus be implemented both in the preliminary and detailed architectural design stages.[127]

[122] Advanced Software-based Service Provisioning and Migration of Legacy Software (ARTIST). This project was partially funded by the European Commission under the Seventh (FP7-2007–2013) Framework Program for Research and Technological Development. For more details about the ARTIST project, see http://www.artist-project.eu/content/r12-certification-model#sthash.zpJSBZ9t.dpuf. Accessed 10 May 2019.

[123] ARTIST R12 Certification Model.

[124] ARTIST R12 Certification Model.

[125] Myler (1998, p. 37).

[126] Myler (1998, p. 37).

[127] Agarwal et al. (2010, p. 130).

While planning the pseudo-code, the software architect uses short English language phrases that follow a logical order. Phrases such as "If-Then-Else" and "End" are keywords used to structure the program-design language. Hyphens are used to link keywords to describe the control flow, while other English words are used to describe the processing actions.[128] The major advantages of following a straightforward pseudo-code approach are the following: (i) converting a pseudo-code into a source code is much easier to understand than that of a flowchart or table;[129] (ii) while writing a pseudo-code requires certain programming skills,[130] it takes less time and effort than developing any other programming tool; and (iii) developing a pseudo-code allows more flexibility since there are no strict rules. As a rule of thumb, the simpler the statements the better.[131]

8.4.5 Legal Questions for the Extraction of the Pseudo-code

In order to elicit a conclusion from the pseudo-code, one should first create a list of questions related to specific legal matters. A table of all the relevant legal questions has been included in Table 8.1. The table includes a set of 17 questions related to different legal issues including data protection, data security and intellectual property rights. This is mainly for two reasons. First, it is important to cover a wide range of legal problems. Second, in some cases, partial aspects of one question are overlapping and/or related to a previous question. This set of questions has been customized and extended to include the legal questions that refer specifically to "ownership" rights of data and databases. These questions are not only related to the SLA specifications, but also the general process or design of an application/usage of the underlying resources.

Following the legal analysis and programming code developed in the OPTIMIS project/toolkit,[132] a pseudo-code has been created as described below in Table 8.2. Following a pseudo-logic, a number of values have been assigned to each legal question. For example, question 1 is "L001," question 2 is "L002," etc. The pseudo-code has been broken down in categories in a logical linear manner and there is a specific category assigned to the legal compliance. The result of a legal analysis has been made explicitly clear and has a binary form of answering the questions: "Yes" or "No" (i.e., "legally compliant" or "not legally compliant"). Table 8.2 shows fragments of the pseudo-code.

The way this pseudo-code has been structured is to assume that it is legally compliant until one condition is broken. Therefore, the conditional formula uses the "If" function. For example, question 1 (L001) or question 2 (L002) are the conditions that

[128] Agarwal et al. (2010, p. 130).
[129] Ravichandran (2006, p. 177).
[130] Ravichandran (2006, p. 177).
[131] Myler (1998, p. 37).
[132] Chulani et al. (2012).

Table 8.1 Legal questions for the extraction of the pseudo-code

1. (L001) Does your SaaS application deal with sensitive/personal data?
2. (L002) Does your SaaS application support native encryption/protection of the data and authentication?
3. (L003) Does your SaaS application give the choice of EU-based data storage location?
4. (L004) Is your SaaS application dynamically configured for using IaaS/PaaS services?
5. (L005) Are the data or metadata "ownership" rights clearly defined and clarified in the contract/SLA?
6. (L006) Do you offer notifications in case you change the terms and conditions?
7. (L007) Do you offer notifications in case your underlying PaaS/IaaS provider changes the terms and conditions?
8. (L008) Do you offer the ability to the end-users to virtually be under more control over their own data ensuring data portability (i.e., migration, extraction and reuse of their data) and interoperability within the Cloud?
9. (L009) Do you offer the ability to the end-users the right to delete/eliminate their data (so-called "Right to be Forgotten") in the original used service?
10. (L010) Does your underlying PaaS/IaaS provider use Standard Contractual Clauses (SCC) with you and other parties?
11. (L011) Has your underlying PaaS/IaaS provider been certified for their Binding Corporate Rules (BCR) clauses by an EU DPA?
12. (L012) Do you take measures to prevent data loss (regular backups, replication, etc.)?
13. (L013) Are you using your own resources to run your application?
14. (L014) Are compilations of data (i.e., EU database rights) clearly defined in the contracts/SLA?
15. (L015) Does your SaaS application give the choice of waiving any kind of database rights?
16. (L016) Does your SaaS application give the choice of clarifying or waiving "ownership" rights of data?
17. (L017) Do you restrict access of data (without prior consent of the data subject) to third parties for specific purposes?

need to be checked. Then, the (Boolean) "True" or "False" values help to understand and check whether certain legal criteria are met or not. If the answer to one question is NO, then "Return LEGAL_COMPLIANCE;//stop legal analysis, final conclusion" is reached. If the answer to the question is YES, then there is no need to do anything else since the compliance is already set to be "True." Conditional logical formulas are used in various methods for testing one or more conditions. For example, accountants use this method in an Excel Worksheet to calculate the commissions and bonuses of each employee.[133] We also use conditional logical statements to calculate regular activities on a daily basis. The basic structure is as follows: If (condition, *true, false*). For example, let's say that the logical statement is If (it is the weekend, *stay in bed, get up and go to work*). The condition is "If" it is the weekend. If the condition is

[133]Blanc and Vento (2007, p. 192).

Table 8.2 Pseudo-code to check legal compliance

PROGRAM: "Check Legal Compliance"

```
//YES means that the answer to the question is either YES or Configurable in the SLA
//The symbol "//" implies a comment line, meaning the text after // does not affect execution,
//it is only used to explain the specific program line and enhance code readability
//The word "LEGAL_COMPLIANCE" is a variable, meaning a position in the memory
//structure of the computing system that holds the value (outcome of the analysis: true or //false for
being legally compliant)
//The symbol "=" is an assignment operator, meaning that the value at the right of the "=" //is stored
in the memory position that is indicated by the (variable) name on the left of the //"="
//The symbol "==" indicates equality between the elements (variables and/or values) to the //left and
right of the symbol
//The word "Return LEGAL_COMPLIANCE" means stop executing and return the value //of the
variable LEGAL_COMPLIANCE at that point

LEGAL_COMPLIANCE=True;
If((L002==NO)OR(L005==NO)OR(L008==NO)OR(L0012==NO)){
        LEGAL_COMPLIANCE=False;
        Return LEGAL_COMPLIANCE; //stop legal analysis, final conclusion is     reached
}
If(L001==YES){
        If((L005==NO)OR((L006==NO)OR(L007==NO)){
                LEGAL_COMPLIANCE=False;
                Return LEGAL_COMPLIANCE; //stop legal analysis, final conclusion
                is reached
        }
}
If (L003==NO){ //if not based in the EU, you need to be certified for BCR for EU usage
        If (L011==NO){
                LEGAL_COMPLIANCE=False;
                Return LEGAL_COMPLIANCE; //stop legal analysis, final conclusion
                is reached
}
If (L003==YES){// if based in the EU, you need to have specified DB "ownership" rights
        If (L014==NO){
                LEGAL_COMPLIANCE=False;
                Return LEGAL_COMPLIANCE; //stop legal analysis, final conclusion is
                reached
        }
}
If (L003==NO){ //if not based in the EU
        If (L015==YES){ //and you can waive DB rights
                If (L016==YES){ //and can waive/clarify "ownership" rights
                        //do nothing, legal compliance has been set to true before
                        }
        }else{
                LEGAL_COMPLIANCE=False;
                Return LEGAL_COMPLIANCE; //stop legal analysis, final conclusion
                is reached }
        }
```

(continued)

Table 8.2 (continued)

```
}
If (L003==YES){// if based in the EU,
        If (L009==YES){ //and you can offer the possibility to delete data
                //do nothing, legal compliance has been set to true before
                        }
        }else{
                LEGAL_COMPLIANCE=False;
                Return LEGAL_COMPLIANCE; //stop legal analysis, final conclusion is
                reached
        }
}
If (L003==NO){ //if not based in the EU
        If (L009==NO){ //and you don't offer the possibility to delete data
                //do nothing, legal compliance has been set to true before
                }
        }else{
                LEGAL_COMPLIANCE=False;
                Return LEGAL_COMPLIANCE; //stop legal analysis, final conclusion
                is reached
        }
}
If (L001==YES){ //if your SaaS application deals with sensitive/personal data
        If (L003==YES){// if based in the EU,
                If (L017=YES){ //if you restrict access of data to third parties for specific
                purposes
                //do nothing, legal compliance has been set to true before
                }
        }else{
                LEGAL_COMPLIANCE=False;
                Return LEGAL_COMPLIANCE; //stop legal analysis, final conclusion is
                reached
        }
}
If (L001==YES){ //if your SaaS application deals with sensitive/personal data
        If (L003==NO){// if not based in the EU,
                If (L017=NO){ //if you do not restrict access of data to third parties for
                specific purposes
                //do nothing, legal compliance has been set to true before
                }
        }else{
                LEGAL_COMPLIANCE=False;
                Return LEGAL_COMPLIANCE; //stop legal analysis, final conclusion is
                reached
        }
}
```

(continued)

Table 8.2 (continued)

```
Return LEGAL COMPLIANCE;
//continuous iteration section
If ((L004==YES)OR(L013==YES) { // Reiterate the code below continuously
        while (true){
                If (L003==NO { //you need to be either in white list with SCC or wherever
                with BCR
                        If ((Countries in White List==true)
                        AND((L010==YES))OR(L011==YES){
                        //do nothing since legal compliance is already set to True
        } else {
                LEGAL_COMPLIANCE=False;
                Return LEGAL_COMPLIANCE;
        }
}
```

"true," then you can *stay in bed*. If the condition is "false" (it is not the weekend), then you need *to get up and go to work*.[134]

Question 1: ***Does your SaaS application deal with sensitive/personal data?***

This question refers to sensitive and personal data. The purpose of this book is not to cover all legal aspects and from the beginning, it sets out to focus only on IPRs, and more specifically, database rights and "ownership" rights of data. However, since this questionnaire follows a pseudo-logic, this question is intertwined with other questions, especially when it comes to sensitive data such as health or genetic data. This is a very important data protection question that falls directly within the scope of the EU General Data Protection Regulation (GDPR) or other data protection regulations around the world. It is important to also include questions regarding protection and data security in order to follow an integrated and holistic approach. In this respect, the GDPR, for instance, urges data controllers and processors to implement data security measures to prevent unauthorized access and data loss. This involves legal requirements that relate to the encryption and anonymization of personal data and to take the necessary security measures to prevent the loss, disclosure, access or alteration of data.[135] However, such obligations are not enough. They must be implemented into technical standards. Therefore, the following question is more of a technical nature.

Question 2: ***Does your SaaS application support native encryption/protection of the data and authentication?***

This question also has a data protection scheme. Data protection regulations around the world are very different and they often urge cloud providers to implement data security measures to prevent unauthorized access and data loss. For example, the amendments of the PIPA Act in Japan expanded the scope of the definition for sensitive personal data and created restrictions to include biometric data such as fingerprints, face recognition and numeric identification codes. The PIPA Act also

[134]Weale (2001, p. 6).

[135]Barnitzke et al. (2011, pp. 51–55).

requires the data controller to keep complete books and records of data in reasonable detail and to take the necessary security measures to prevent the loss, disclosure or alteration of data.[136]

In Europe, according to Article 32 (1) (a) of the GDPR, "...the controller and the processor shall implement appropriate technical and organizational measures to ensure a level of security appropriate to the risk, including inter alia as appropriate: pseudonymization and encryption[137] of personal data."[138] This may include different authentication and encryption techniques during data transfer or storage with a range of strength options (i.e. bits used for the encryption) and/or security certification provided and validated by an external third party authority. It is important to note that the cloud provider does not need to publish the strategy itself, but must have the ability to comply with this legal and technical requirement.[139]

We often experience this when we use, for example, online banking systems from commercial banks. Most online banking services require their customers to change their passwords on a regular basis. Nevertheless, for security and practical reasons they use other techniques such as automatic password generators known as "tokens."[140] Some banks even distribute to their customers devices that look much like electronic calculators. These devices automatically generate a digital code, which must be used together with the username and password of the client. This method rules out the necessity of manually choosing a password every time, saving transaction and deliberation costs. With this new token system, the passcode changes automatically on a regular basis and helps to keep customers' data safe from malicious hackers.[141] This is also a good example of the Privacy by Design and Privacy by Default approach[142] set out in the GDPR.

Question 3: ***Does your SaaS application give the choice of an EU-based data storage location?***

This question was also originally designed to cope with data protection legislation in the EU, which sets out strict rules for the transferring of data to third countries outside of the EU. This means that some users would prefer to keep their data inside the jurisdiction of the EU. Nevertheless, this question is also relevant for database rights to establish the location of databases and to allow the location constraint mechanism. This question follows the Lessig approach, which refers to the architecture modality as a constraint. We may refer here again to the "dead man's switch" example. The

---

[136] Amended Act on the Protection of Personal Information (Tentative Translation), see also Winston and Strown (2015) Japan Updates Privacy Law [online]. Available at: http://www.winston.com/en/privacy-law-corner/japan-updates-privacy-law.html. Accessed May 10 2019.

[137] For further details with regard to encryption in the scope of the GDPR, see, e.g., Spindler and Schmechel (2016, pp. 163–177).

[138] See Article 32 (1) (a) of the GDPR; regarding these protective measures, see, also Recitals 74, 75, 76, 77 and 83 of the GDPR.

[139] Kousiouris et al. (2013, pp. 61–72).

[140] Caelli et al. (1989, p. 144).

[141] Williams (2007, p. 12).

[142] Hustinx (2010, pp. 253–255), Chulani et al. (2012, pp. 7–10).

automated SLA framework will kick in immediately and stop the processing of data and databases in case the cloud provider makes a mistake and attempts to make a transfer to a processor or sub-processor that is located in a different jurisdiction.

Question 4: ***Is your SaaS application dynamically configured for using IaaS/PaaS services?***

This question is more of a technical nature, which may have some legal consequences. It refers to the relationship between the software service provider (SaaS) and the infrastructure and platform providers (IaaS and PaaS). It could happen that during service provisioning, the SaaS provider may need to change or move to another cloud service (IaaS and PaaS) . Therefore, the SLA specifications should include a kind of dynamic rating certification scheme as this would imply re-applying the legal conclusion selection.

Question 5: ***Are the data or metadata "ownership" rights clearly defined in the contract/SLA?***

This question refers to the potential ability of cloud applications to generate new data out of data submitted to the cloud, such as data mining tools, AI, and data statistics. It is a common practice that some cloud services do not often specify "ownership" rights of such "derivative" data. Thus, this question would allow end-users to select other cloud providers in case they prefer a provider with a clear data "ownership" rights policy. This has been seen in some controversial Big Data cases, such as in the Suica Card Incident, where JR East attempted to use consumer data for other purposes. This question would allow end-users to choose not to allow the usage of data mining tools for marketing purposes.[143]

Question 6: ***Do you offer notifications in case you change the terms and conditions?***

Question 7: ***Do you offer notifications in case your underlying PaaS/IaaS provider changes the terms and conditions?***

Both questions refer to cases where some cloud providers do not notify consumers when they change their policies. Cloud providers often reserve the right to change the terms of service unilaterally, at will and at any time. This situation was found in all the terms and conditions surveyed by the Cloud Legal Guidelines Report of the OPTIMIS project. The most important thing to recognize is how efficiently cloud providers communicate these new changes to end-users. Some providers only mention this on their website, others prefer to notify their customers by email.[144] These policies need to be re-examined when they change, especially when this is related to the end-user's data.[145]

---

[143]Data aggregated from data would be considered as data again and probably not metadata. Metadata, on the other hand, is data used to describe and give context to data. It provides background information that allows data to be stored, preserved and accessed when it is needed. For example, an XML field: <age>18 The "age" tab is metadata, data is the "18." See Gartner (2016, p. 7).

[144]Forgó et al. (2013, p. 20).

[145]Pearson and Charlesworth (2009, p. 137).

Therefore, the aim of question 6 is to nudge cloud providers to include an automated mechanism that can clearly notify end-users about their change of policies. Once this has been clearly notified, end-users will have the choice to either accept the changes or terminate the contract and move to another service provider. Furthermore, cloud providers may also engage in federated scenarios with multiple other processors or sub-processors, which may be unknown to the end-users. This is often one of the main issues that spawns a lack of trust because the end-users have no control. They are unaware of these sub-processors' contracts and they cannot assess how compatible they are in terms of legal compliance.[146]

For this reason, assuming that a cloud provider would use another entity for the actual resources, question 7 considers how contracts between different layers of cloud services (SaaS and IaaS) notify end-users when there has been a change of the terms of services to their cloud customers. One humorous anecdotal example refers to the so-called "immortal soul clause", when, in 2010, a British on-line videogame retailer (GameStation) temporarily and playfully added a special clause to its terms and conditions.[147] The clause stated that customers granted GameStation the right to claim their "immortal soul". The clause was included in the terms and conditions on the 1st of April (April Fool's Day) as a joke.[148] The result was that the overwhelming majority of customers (88%) voluntarily agreed with the terms and conditions of this click-through agreement,[149] equaling seventy-five hundred souls "sold" (or "captured") on that single day.[150]

While this was obviously a joke, the company made a serious point: no one reads the fine print, especially if they are suddenly included in the terms and conditions of the contract without previous notification to the users.[151] Another interesting fact to point out in this anecdote is that the customers were given the choice to tick a box as an opt-out option. That is, the default rule was to automatically grant their "immortal souls" with an option to opt-out. Very few did and the company rewarded them with a £5 voucher. This is in line with the behavioral law and economics claim that "default rules tend to stick" as discussed in the previous chapter. At the end of the April Fool's Day, the company said that it would not be enforcing "ownership"

---

[146]Forgó et al. (2013, p. 14).

[147]House of Commons, Great Britain Parliament (2014, p. 21).

[148]The contract read: "By placing an order via this web site on the first day of the fourth month of the year 2010 Anno Domini, you agree to grant Us a non-transferable option to claim, for now and forever more, your immortal soul. Should We wish to exercise this option, you agree to surrender your immortal soul, and any claim you may have on it, within 5 (five) working days of receiving written notification from gamesation.co.uk or one of its duly authorized minions." See Fox News Tech, 7,500 Online Shoppers Unknowingly Sold Their Souls, (April 15 2010), [online]. Available at: https://www.foxnews.com/tech/7500-online-shoppers-unknowingly-sold-their-souls. Accessed May 10 2010.

[149]Lori (2012, p. 175).

[150]Lindstrom (2011, p. 225).

[151]Molinaro (2016, p. 35), Goodman (2015, p. 90).

rights (of their immortal souls), and planned to send an email to their customers revoking such rights.[152]

Question 8: ***Do you offer the ability to the user to migrate/extract and reuse their data without any specific and proprietary technology?***

This question refers to the data portability and availability issue. The problem is that most of the emphasis has been focused on strictly technical issues, with the hopes of increasing interoperability development. There is currently little guidance on how to resolve complex legal issues that arise with regards to data portability.[153] Before developing this criticism in more detail, consider the following hypothetical situation to illustrate this point further. Assuming a federated cloud scenario, there is one customer and one service provider both located in the U.K. and an array of infrastructure providers (IPA, IPB, IPC and IPD) located in different jurisdictions, each of which has its own legislation. Assume further that one of the infrastructure providers in which end-users' data is stored goes bankrupt. What are the chances that the end-user will recover his or her data if these kinds of circumstances have not been clarified in the contract and the state's legislation of the infrastructure provider in question is debtor friendly?

On a more theoretical level, this could be clarified in the contractual terms, such as that in cases of bankruptcy the cloud provider agrees to restore the client's data and agrees to facilitate the means for data migration to another provider. On a more practical level, however, SLAs do not allow much room for negotiation. If the contractual framework provided by the SLA is able to clarify data portability issues as a legal concept, as in the bankruptcy example, this will allow the customers to maximize the number of cloud providers. Another example would be the so-called "data hostage" clause, which requires the customer to pay a fee in cases where the contract is terminated if the customer wants his or her data to be returned.[154] This sort of clause essentially provides a risk of data lock-in and customers should be able to recover and migrate their data without further hindrances.

Question 9: ***Do you offer the end-users the right to delete/eliminate their data (so-called "Right to be Forgotten") in the original use service?***

This question refers to the deletion or removal of personal data, which is grounded in the provisions enshrined in the previous EU data protection scheme.[155] However, the GDPR explicitly includes the "Right to the Forgotten" as an important legal innovation and not only as codification of the existing law. In this sense, the GDPR refers to this new right as the data subject's right "to obtain from the controller the

[152]Luzak (2010); Rosenthal (2012).

[153]See, generally, Zanfir (2012, pp. 149–162).

[154]See, generally, Carpenter (2010, pp. 1–14).

[155]See *Google Spain SL, Google Inc. v Agencia Española de Protección de Datos (es), Mario Costeja González*, number C-131/12.

erasure of personal data concerning him or her without undue delay" and the data controller's obligation "to erase personal data without undue delay" under specific circumstances[156] as laid down in Article 17. The rationale behind this right is to enable individuals to request for the deletion or removal of any kind of personal data where there is no compelling reason for its continued processing. It is therefore not an absolute right and the GDPR provides a list of specific grounds for its removal/deletion.[157]

Reactions to this novel right vary from jurisdiction to jurisdiction, since the concept has not been fully harmonized yet. For example, in Japan, Japanese courts are dubious about recognizing the Right to be Forgotten. According to the decisions of the Saitama District Court, the Tokyo High Court, and the Japanese Supreme Court, the requirements and effects of the right to be forgotten remains unclear.[158] For this reason, the pseudo-code has been designed in a way that some jurisdictions outside of the EU may override this choice.

Question 10: ***Does your underlying PaaS/IaaS provider use Standard Contractual Clauses (SCCs) with you and other parties?***
Question 11: ***Has your underlying PaaS/IaaS provider been certified for their Binding Corporate Rules (BCR) clauses by an EU DPA?***
Question 13: ***Are you using your own resources to run your application?***

This set of questions refers to the transfer of data to third countries. The use of unmodified Standard Contractual Clauses (SCC)[159] and Binding Corporate Rules (BCR) are valuable legal requirements in the framework of the GDPR. Yet, the focus of this book is on IPR. Therefore, ideas underlying the principles behind the SCC and BCR could be extended and used for the clarification of "ownership" rights of data and databases. For instance, the BCR section allows programmatically for the inclusion of legal text as explained above in the "string" field. Therefore, I kept this set of questions as an example to showcase how the "ownership" rights section could also contain similar "string" capabilities. Incorporating such options in the SLA framework provides further evidence of an additional safeguard. The pseudo-code is, therefore, intended to check a specific instantiation of an SLA (meaning if a specific configuration with given options is legal) or to check if this option is configurable in the SLA. In order to check the instantiated SLA, the cloud provider should add a country/region field and include specific options in the SLA.

In this case, the pseudo-code urges cloud providers to allow for the inclusion of SCC and BCR as legal texts. The BCR, for instance, are internal rules (such as a Code of Conduct) adopted by a group of multinational companies who wish to transfer

---

156 See Article 17 of the GDPR.

157 See Article 17 (1) (2) (3) of the GDPR.

158 See, i.e., the decision of the Japanese Supreme Court of January 31, 2017 and the Tokyo High Court of July 12, 2016.

159 While writing this book, the CJEU was called to rule on the validity of the SCC.

data across different jurisdictions.[160] The automated SLA framework should be able to kick in immediately and stop the processing of data if the cloud provider makes a mistake and attempts to make a transfer to a processor or sub-processor that is located outside the group of companies. These checks may include the location of the federated infrastructure provider using a location constraint mechanism. If the target infrastructure provider is inside the jurisdiction of the EU/EEA Member States, then the outsourcing of data may be fulfilled with minimal intervention through the GDPR.[161] If the infrastructure provider is located outside the boundaries of any of the EU/EEA Member States, and, therefore, outside of the scope of the GDPR, then the federation cannot be performed if these checks are not in place in advance.

Many other data protection laws set some restrictions on the transfer of data to third countries. For example, one of the most significant changes in the Japanese PIPA Act has been the recent establishment of a new central government agency, the Personal Information Protection Commission ("PIPC"). The PIPC has replaced the former Specific Personal Information Protection Commission and operates as an independent authority. One of the underlying objectives of PIPC will be to ensure that personal data is lawfully processed when transferred to third countries. For instance, Article 24 of the amended Japanese Act imposes certain limitations on the transfer of personal information of Japanese citizens to foreign countries (any country or territory outside of the region of Japan), excluding countries possessing personal information protection systems recognized to be at the same level as Japan's in terms of protecting the rights and interests of individuals. This is also an attempt to bring the Japanese regulatory framework closer to the Members of the EU that have recently adopted the EU GDPR.[162] Then again, this set of questions is a good example of the so-called "Privacy by Design" approach that could be further extended to a more "IPR by Design" framework.

Question 12: ***Do you take measures to prevent data loss (regular backups, replication, etc.)?***

Data replication for backup purposes might be seen as one of the main benefits of the cloud as this prevents data loss in case of an accident. Even from a legal standpoint, this might be taken as beneficial if we were to consider data protection and data security issues. However, this also represents a hurdle if we have to consider data location and jurisdictional issues, assuming the customer is not fully aware of where the data has been replicated. In this case, the pseudo-code advocates for the inclusion of Data Management-specific (DM) technical options, such as replication rate, in the infrastructure. This would allow end-users to track back-up and replication jobs when the databases and Virtual Machines (VMs) grow too fast and may be quickly depleted by the target repository. This will provide greater control for end-users to monitor where their data is located in automated cloud environments.

---

[160] Kousiouris et al. (2013, p. 63).

[161] Corrales Compagnucci and Jurčys (2016).

[162] Corrales Compagnucci and Jurčys (2016).

Question 14: ***Are compilations of data (i.e., EU database rights) clearly defined in the contracts/SLA?***
Question 15: ***Does your SaaS application give the choice of waiving any kind of database rights?***
Question 16: ***Does your SaaS application give the choice of clarifying or waiving "ownership" rights of data?***

Questions 14, 15 and 16 refer directly to the research questions of this study. They have been implemented to nudge cloud providers to disclose information with regards to "ownership" rights of data and databases and make the necessary changes in their SLAs and overall architecture of their underlying resources. Questions 14 and 15 refer specifically to database rights in the EU. These two questions are also related to Question 3, which refers to the storage of data and databases in European countries. With this set of questions and the proposed template, brokers can find cloud providers willing and able to offer end-users the possibility to keep or waive database rights.

These checks may include the location of the federated infrastructure provider using a location constraint mechanism. If the target infrastructure provider is inside the jurisdiction of the EU/EEA Member States then the outsourcing of data and databases may be fulfilled with minimal intervention, taking into account that database rights exist within the jurisdiction of such countries and copyrights are somewhat harmonized.[163] If the infrastructure provider is located outside the boundaries of any of the EU/EEA Member States, and, therefore, outside of the scope of the Database Directive, then the federation cannot be performed if these checks are not in place in advance.

However, it is worth mentioning that, in Question 15, cloud customers can decide to waive their database rights in order to federate the databases outside the boundaries of these countries. As seen before, database rights are particularly problematic in the field of cloud computing as they could be potentially "exported" overseas to a jurisdiction without database rights. They should only be implemented in jurisdictions where this right exists and limited to a "geographic location" due to its territorial nature.

Question 16 refers to "ownership" rights of data more generally and not only to database rights. For example, this question could be used in the context of scientific data and databases. An "unconditional waiver" should be incorporated and with the "string" field capability end-users could put their data in the public domain as explained in the common pool of resources approach.[164] In any case, these options may be inserted as legal requirements from the user side and be used by the cloud broker during the selection process. This will help to clarify "ownership" rights of data at different levels and also empower end-users with more negotiating capabilities during SLA negotiations.

---

[163] Kousiouris et al. (2013, p. 63).

[164] The work and principles of the Creative Commons (CC) licenses. See, i.e., generally, Keller and Maracke (2007).

Question 17: ***Do you restrict access of data (without prior consent of the data subject) to third parties for specific purposes?***

Finally, this question has been set up to empower individuals with more control over their data since the question of "ownership" rights may be seen as a bundle of rights. Therefore, in some jurisdictions such as in the EU, the new GDPR allows individuals to restrict access of their data to third parties. However, in a jurisdiction where public healthcare insurance is prevailing, like Japan, patients should not conceal records from future hospitals and public healthcare insurance organizations. Therefore, in some jurisdictions, patients should not be able to conceal their health records. For this reason, similarly to Question 9, the pseudo-code has been designed in a way that some jurisdictions outside of the EU may be able to override this choice. This will allow flexibility and neutrality within the SLA and at the same time ensure the integrity of medical and healthcare records when society needs to keep public healthcare insurance well organized.

8.5 Summary and Interim Remarks

This chapter presented a sui generis contractual model that crystallizes the theoretical framework of Plan-like Architectures and shows how its practical (nudging) techniques have been implemented into a unique SLA template. This perspective emanates from the five core principles of law and economics, which suggest that individuals act rationally and that legal rules should be addressed proactively and efficiently. The interpretation of Coase's theory in the cloud suggests that "ownership" rights of data and databases, sometimes seen as negative externalities, need to be negotiated and clarified while keeping transaction costs very low. Therefore, the proposed template can turn these negative externalities into external benefits. This can be achieved by allowing end-users to choose different options and selecting cloud providers based on their own criteria. One of these options available now in the present template is the possibility of sharing data as depicted in the Ostrom common pool of resources approach, whereby everyone can get access to data and tap into it. This is perhaps a good alternative to foster scientific research and reap the benefits and full potential of Big Data.

References

Agarwal B, Tayal S, Gupta M (2010) Software engineering & testing: an introduction. Computer Science Series. Jones and Bartlett Publishers, Sudbury, p 130

Albrecht U, Von Jan U (2016) mHealth Apps and Their Risks—Taking Stock. In: Mantas J et al (eds) Unifying the applications and foundations of biomedical and health informatics. IOS Press, Amsterdam, p. 227

Andersen B (2006) If "Intellectual Property Right" is the Answer, What is the Question? Revisiting the patent controversy. In: Andersen B (ed) Intellectual property rights: innovation. Governance and the Institutional Environment. Edward Elgar Publishing, Cheltenham, pp 112–113

Anderson D (2015) A question of trust. Williams Lea Group, London, p. 159

Bakey P (2014) Big data means big benefits for retailers and consumers http://www.digitalistmag.com/industries/retail/2014/12/31/big-data-big-benefits-for-retailers-and-consumers-01972311. Accessed May 10 2019

Balboni P (2011) Data protection and data security issues related to cloud computing in the EU, p. 165. In: Pohlmann N, Reimer H, Schneider W (eds) *ISSE 2010* securing electronic business processes: highlights of the information security solutions, Europe 2010 Conference. Springer, Wiesbaden

Barnitzke et al (2011) Legal restraints and security requirements on personal data and their technical implementation in clouds. Workshop for E-contracting for Clouds, eChallenges, pp 51–55 http://www.optimis-project.eu/sites/default/files/content-files/document/echallenges2011-legal-restraints-security.pdf. Accessed May 10 2019

Bayles M (2014) Exercise testing. In: Swain D (ed) ACSM's Resource manual for guidelines for exercise testing and prescription, 7th edn. Wolters Kluwer (Lippincott Williams & Wilki), Philadelphia, p 331

Behrooz S, Marsh S (2016) A Trust-based framework for information sharing between mobile health care applications. In: Habib S et al (eds) Trust management X, 10th IFIP WG 11.11 international conference, IFIPTM 2016, Darmstadt, Germany, July 18–22, 2016, Proceedings. Springer, Cham, p 80

Berman (2013) Principles of big data: preparing, sharing, and analyzing complex information. Morgan Kaufmann (Elsevier), Waltham, pp 201–211

Birney E, Clamp M, Durbin R (2004) GeneWise and Genomewise. Genome Res 14(5):988–995

Blanc I, Vento C (2007) Performing with Microsoft Office 2007: Introductory. The Performing Series. Cengage Learning, Boston, p 192

Boniface G, Seymour A (2012) (eds) Using occupational therapy theory in practice. Wiley-Blackwell, Chichester

Booch G, Rumbaugh J, Jacobson I (2005) The unified modeling language user guide, Object Technology Series. Addison Wesley Longman, Reading

Borda G (1974) Manual de Contratos, 7th edn. Editorial Perrot, Buenos Aires, p 14

Borgman C (2015) Big data, little data, no data: scholarship in the networked world, p 73. The MIT Press, Cambridge

Bovemberg J (2006) Property rights in blood, genes and data: naturally yours? p 26. Martinus Nijhoff Publishers, Leiden

Bradshaw S, Millard C, Waelden I (2010) Contracts for clouds: comparison and analysis of the terms and conditions of cloud computing services, Queen Mary School of Law Legal Studies Research Paper No. 63/2010, pp 31–32 http://ssrn.com/abstract01662374. Accessed May 10 2019

Bragg S (2006) Outsourcing: a guide to selecting the correct business unit, negotiating the contract, maintaining control of the process, 2nd edn. Wiley, Hoboken, p 49

Brauer R (2016) Safety and health for engineers, 3rd edn. Wiley, Hoboken, p 172

Caelli V, Longley D, Shain M (1989) Information security for managers. Stockton Press, New York

Carpenter R (2010) Walking from cloud to cloud: the portability issue in cloud computing. Washington J Law Technol Arts 6(1):1–14

Carstensen J, Morgenthal J, Golden B (2012) Cloud computing: assessing the risks. IT Governance Publishing, Cambridgeshire, p. 244

Cessna E, Balachandran D (2016) Getting started with ResearchKit. Packt Publishing, Birmingham, p. 84

Chander A (2013) The electronic silk road: how the web binds the world together in commerce. Yale University Press, New Haven, pp 11, 16, 137, 143, 144, 145 and 169

Chen T, Lin C (2015) Study on partnering critical factors for construction industry in Taiwan. In: Sung W, Kao J (eds) Environment, energy and applied technology, Proceedings of the 2014

international conference of frontier of energy and environment engineering (ICFEEE 2014), Taiwan, December 6–7 2014. CRC Press, Boca Ratón, p 881
Chulani I et al (2012) Technical implementation of legal requirements, exploitation of the toolkit in use cases and component licenses, p 23, Cloud Legal Guidelines, OPTIMIS Deliverable 7.2.1.3 http://www.optimis-project.eu/sites/default/files/content-files/document/d7213-cloud-legal-guidelines.pdf. Accessed May 10 2019
Colditz G (2015) (ed) The SAGE Encyclopedia of cancer and society, 2nd edn. SAGE Publications, Los Angeles, p 395
Corrales Compagnucci M et al (2009) Analysis of the most important intellectual property issues resulting from the chosen ACGT architecture, p 8. ACGT Project, Deliverable 10.7
Corrales Compagnucci M (2010) Protecting patients' rights in clinical trial scenarios: the "bee metaphor" and the symbiotic relationship. In: Bottis M (ed) An information law for the 21st century, third international seminar on information law 2010. Nomiki Bibliothiki Group, Athens, pp 5–13
Corrales Compagnucci M, Jurčys P (2016) A new legal landscape for big data in Japan, Beck-Online, ZD-Aktuell 2016, No. 15, 05247 https://beckonline.beck.de/?vpath=bibdata%2Fzeits%2FZDAKTUELL%2F2016%2Fcont%2FZDAKTUELL.2016.05247.htm. Accessed May 10 2019
Crawford L (2015) JAPAN: New Amendments to Japanese Privacy Law http://blogs.dlapiper.com/privacymatters/new-amendments-to-japanese-privacy-law/. Accessed May 10 2019
Davenport T (2014) Big data at work: dispelling the myths, uncovering the opportunities. Harvard Business Review Press, Boston, p 167
Davies M, Naffine N (2001) Are persons property? Legal debates about property and personality, 165. Ashgate Publishing, Aldershot, pp 158–159
Davison M (2003) The legal protection of databases. Cambridge University Press, Cambridge
Derclaye E (2008) The legal protection of databases: a comparative analysis. Edgar Elgar Publishing, Cheltenham
Dickenson D, Huxtable R, Parker M (2010) The cambridge medical ethics workbook, 2nd edn. Cambridge University Press, Cambridge, p 67
Donaldson S, Siegel S (2001) Successful software development, 2nd edn. Prentice Hall, Upper Saddle River, p 144
Durham M (2016) Japan Updates Privacy Law http://www.winston.com/en/privacy-law-corner/japan-updates-privacy-law.html. Accessed May 10 2019
Edwards A, Elwyn G (2009) Shared decision-making in health care: achieving evidence-based patient choice, 2nd edn. Oxford University Press, Oxford, p 89
El-Zein S (2008) The regulation of human genetics by international soft law and international trade. In: Wüger D, Cottier T (eds) Genetic engineering and the world trade system: world trade forum. Cambridge University Press, Cambridge, p 326
Ezor J (1999) Clicking through: a survival guide for bringing your company online, 1st edn. Bloomberg Press, Princeton
Fisher T (2009) The data asset: how smart companies govern their data for business success. Wiley, Hoboken
Forgó N, Nwankwo S, Pfeiffenbring J (2013) Cloud Legal Guidelines Final Report, Deliverable 7.2.1.4, p. 20 http://www.optimis-project.eu/sites/default/files/content-files/document/optimis-public-deliverable-d7214-cloud-legal-guidelines-final-report.pdf. Accessed May 10 2019
Garcia Wiley C, Coulton P (2009) Persuasive mobile health applications. In: Weerasinghe D (ed) Electronic healthcare, first international conference, eHealth 2008, London UK, September 2008, Revised Selected Papers. Springer, Berlin, p 91
Gartner R (2016) Metadata: shaping knowledge from antiquity to the semantic Web. Springer, Cham, p 7
Gochfeld M, Burger J, Goldstein B (2001) Medical Care as a Common, Chapter 12 with further references. In: Burger J et al (eds) Protecting the commons: a framework for resource management in the Americas. Island Press, Washington D.C

Goodman M (2015) Future crimes: inside the digital underground and the battle for our connected world. Transworld Publishers (Bantam Press), London, p 90

Greif K, Merz J (2007) Current controversies in the biological sciences: case studies of policy challenges from new technologies. The MIT Press, Cambridge, p 69

Guastello S (2014) Human factors engineering and ergonomics: a systems approach, 2nd edn. CRC Press, Boca Ratón, p 253

Harney M (2002) Application service providers (ASPs): a manager's guide, 1st edn. Pearson Education, Upper Saddle River, p 126

Healey B, Marchese M (2012) Foundations of health care management: principles and methods. Jossey Bass (Wiley), San Francisco

Hennicker R, Koch N (2001) Modeling the user interface of web applications with UML. In: Evans A et al (eds) Practical UML-based rigorous development methods—countering or integrating the eXtremists, workshop of the pUML-Group at the UML 01, Toronto, Canada. Gesselschaft für Informatik. Köllen Druck-Verlag, Köllen, pp 158–172

Herder M, Fernandez C (2014) Cancer Genomics and Biobanking: Exploring Key Ethical and Legal Issues. In: Dellaire G, Berman J, Arceci R (eds) Cancer genomics: from bench to personalized medicine. Elsevier, Amsterdam, p. 425

Hoppe N (2016) Bioequity—Property and the Human Body. Routledge, London

House of Commons, Great Britain Parliament (2014) Responsible Use of Data. House of Commons, Science and Technology Committee, Fourth Report of Session 2014–15, p 2

Hustinx P (2010) Privacy by design: delivering the promises. Identity in the Information Society 3(2):253–255

Jin L, Machi-Raju V (2002) Analysis on service level agreement of web services, Technical Report HPL-2002–180, Software Technology Laboratories. HP Laboratories, Palo Alto http://www.hpl.hp.com/techreports/2002/HPL-2002-180.pdf. Accessed May 10 2019

Kavaler F, Spiegel A (2003) Risk management in health care institutions: a strategic approach, 2nd edn. Jones and Bartlett Publishers, Sudbury, p 98

Keller P, Maracke C (2007) Creative Commons, On the Treatment of the Sui Generis Rights in Version 3.0 of the Creative Commons Licenses http://wiki.creativecommons.org/images/f/f6/V3_Database_Rights.pdf. Accessed May 10 2019

King A, Squillante M (2005) Service level agreements for web hosting systems. In: Labbi A (ed) Handbook of integrated risk management for E-Business: measuring, modeling, and managing risk. J. Ross Publishing, Boca Ratón, pp 195 et seq

Kirkham T et al (2012) Risk-based SLA management in clouds: a legal perspective. In: IEEE internet technology and secured transactions, 2012 international conference for internet technology and secured transactions (ICITST-2012). Infonomics Society, s.l, pp 156–160

Knoppers B (2001) The human genome: individual property or common heritage? In Mattei J (ed) Ethical Eye: The Human Genome. Council of Europe Publishing, Strasbourg, p 114

Kousiouris G, Vafiadis G, Corrales Compagnucci M (2013) A cloud provider description schema for meeting legal requirements in cloud federation scenarios. In: Douligeris et al (eds) Collaborative, Trusted and Privacy-Aware e/m-Services, 12th IFIP WG 6.11 Conference on e-Business, e-Services, and e-Society, I3E 2013, Athens, Greece, April 25-26, 2013. Springer, Heidelberg, pp 61–72

Kunz C et al (2001) Click-through agreements: strategies for avoiding disputes on validity of assent 57(1) https://www.ssrn.com/abstract=1640196. Accessed May 10 2019

Latimer P, Maum P (2015) Promoting information in the marketplace for financial services: financial market regulation and international standards. Springer, Cham, p 232 et seq

Laurie G (2003) Privacy and property? Multi-level strategies for protecting personal interests in genetic material. In: Knoppers B, Scriver C (eds) Genomics, health and society: emerging issues for public policy. Policy Research Initiative, Ottawa

Laurie G (2004) Genetic privacy: a challenge to medico-legal norms. Cambridge University Press, Cambridge, p 326

Lenk C (2012) donors and users of human tissue for research purposes: conflict of interests and balancing of interests. In: Dabrock P, Taupitz J, Ried J (eds) Trust in Biobanking: dealing with ethical, legal and social issues in an emerging field of biotechnology. Springer, Berlin, p 86
Lindstrom M (2011) Brandwashed: tricks companies use to manipulate our minds and persuade us to buy, 1st edn. Crown Business, New York, p 225
Lipsey R, Chrystal A (2011) Economics, 12th Edition. Oxford University Press, Oxford, p 7
Lori A (2012) I know who you are and i saw what you did: social networks and the death of privacy. Free Press, New York, p 175
Luzak J (2010) One Click Could Save Your Soul, Recent Developments in European Consumer Law http://recent-ecl.blogspot.jp/2010/05/one-click-could-save-your-soul.html. Accessed May 10 2019
Maclean A (2009) Autonomy, informed consent and medical law: a relational challenge. Cambridge University Press, Cambridge, p 42
Mayer-Schoenberger V, Cukier K (2013) Big data: revolution that will transform how we live, work and think. John Murray (Publishers), London
McCabe L, McCabe E (2008) DNA: promise and Peril. University of California Press, Berkeley, p 154
McHugh S, Bannerman D (2010) Cognition: learning and memory: spatial. In: Koob G, Le Moal M, Thompson R (eds) Encyclopedia of behavioral neuroscience. Academic Press (Elsevier), London, p. 280
Matthews J, Gillespie M (2002) Service providers: ASPs, ISPs, MSPs, and WSPs: A Wiley Tech Brief. Wiley, New York, pp 143 et seq
Metcalfe J (2013) Japan railway company apologizes for selling IC card data. Wall Street J http://blogs.wsj.com/japanrealtime/2013/07/29/japan-railway-company-apologizes-for-selling-ic-card-data/. Accessed May 10 2019
Minor J (2015) Informed consent in predictive genetic testing: a revised model. Springer, Cham, p 75
Mitchell H (2005) The intellectual commons: toward an ecology of intellectual property. Lexington Books, Lanham, p 10
Molinaro V (2016) The leadership contract: the fine print to becoming an accountable leader. Wiley, Hoboken, p 35
Morabito V (2015) Big data and analytics: strategic and organizational impacts. Springer, Cham, p 75
Morris C (1992) The academic press dictionary of science and technology. Academic Press (Harcourt Brace Jovanovich Publishers), San Diego, p 591
Muresan G (2009) An integrated approach to interaction design and log analysis. In: Jansen B, Spink A, Taksa I (eds) Handbook of research on web log analysis. Information Science Reference (IGI Global), Hershey, p 233
Myler H (1998) Fundamentals of engineering programming with C and fortran. Cambridge University Press, Cambridge, p 37
Nair S et al (2011) Requirements and architecture of a cloud broker, OPTIMIS Work Package 6, Deliverable 6.4.1 http://www.optimis-project.eu/sites/default/files/content-files/document/requirements-and-architecture-cloud-broker.pdf. Accessed May 10 2019
Nesbitt L (2004) Clinical research: what it is and how it works. Jones and Bartlett Publishers, Sudbury, p 256
Newman A (2010) Not the First Time the "Dead-Man" Switch Did Its Job http://cityroom.blogs.nytimes.com/2010/05/07/not-the-first-time-the-dead-man-switch-did-its-job/?_r=0. Accessed May 10 2019
Nix D (2011) Why You Should Stop Using the Term "Deadman" http://machinerysafety101.com/2011/03/28/why-you-should-stop-using-the-term-deadman/. Accessed May 10 2019
Nwabueze R (2016) Biotechnology and the Challenge of Property: Property Rights in Dead Bodies, Body Parts, and Genetic Information. Routledge, London, p. 187
Ostroff E (2011) Universal design: an evolving paradigm. In: Preiser W (ed) Universal design handbook: building accessible and inclusive environments, 2nd edn. Advisory Committee on Accessibility (ACA) Access Design Subcommittee, Calgary, pp 10–12

Overgaard G (1999) A formal approach to collaborations in the unified modeling language. In: France R, Rumpe B (eds) UML'99—The unified Modeling language: beyond the standard, second international conference for collins, CO, USA, October 28–30, Proceedings. Springer, Berlin, p 99

Papaioannou T (2016) The limits to governance: the challenge of policy-making for the new life sciences, p 199. Routledge, London

Pearson G (2008) Financial services law and compliance in Australia. Cambridge University Press, Cambridge, p 156

Pearson S, Charlesworth A (2009) Accountability as a way forward for privacy protection in the cloud. In: Jaatun M, Zhao G, Rong C (eds) Cloud computing, 1st. international conference, CloudCom 2009, Beijing, China, December 2009, Proceedings. Springer, Berlin, p 137

Power M, Desouza K, Bonifazi C (2006) The outsourcing handbook: how to implement a successful outsourcing process. Kogan Page, London, p 84

Ravichandran D (2006) Introduction to computers and communication. Tata McGraw-Hill Publishing, New Delhi, p 177

Reed C (2010) Information "Ownership" in the Cloud, Legal Studies Research Paper No. 45/2010, pp 1–22 https://papers.ssrn.com/sol3/Data_Integrity_Notice.cfm?abid=1562461. Accessed May 10 2019

Reichman J, Uhlir P, Dedeurwaerdere T (2016) Governing digitally integrated genetic resources, data, and literature: global intellectual property strategies for a redesigned microbial research commons. Cambridge University Press, Cambridge, p 3

Resnik D (2004) Owning the genome: a moral analysis of DNA patenting. State University of New York Press, Albaby, p 158

Ron S, Aliko P (2001) Service level agreements. Internet NG. Internet NG project http://ing.ctit.utwente.nl/WU2/. Accessed May 10 2019

Rosenthal E (2012) I Disclose…Nothing, The New York Times http://www.nytimes.com/2012/01/22/sunday-review/hard-truths-about-disclosure.html?_r=0. Accessed May 10 2019

Shesshasaayee A, Swetha T (2016) SLA based utility analysis for improving QoS in cloud computing. In: Chandra C et al (eds) Information systems design and intelligent applications, Proceedings of the 3rd. International Conference, India 2016, Vol 3. Springer, New Delhi, p 574

Schroeder D (2009) Justice and benefit sharing. In: Wynberg R, Schroeder D, Chennells R (eds) Indigenous peoples, consent and benefit sharing: lessons from the San-Hoodia case. Springer, Dordrecht, p 40

Schulte in den Baeumen T (2016) International protection of human genetic data—The UNESCO declaration of human genetic data and the possible impact on genetic governance models. In: Lenk C, Hoppe N, Andorno R (eds) Ethics and law of intellectual property: current problems in politics, science and technology. Routledge, New York, p 77

Singh K (2015) Biotechnology and intellectual property rights: legal and social implications. Springer, New Delhi, p 206

Solis G, Gasteazoro R (1992) West's Spanish-English/English-Spanish Law Dictionary. West Group, Saint Paul, p 79

Spindler G, Schmechel P (2016) Personal data and encryption in the European general data protection regulation. JIPITEC 7:163–177

Stimmel C (2015) Big data analytics strategies for the smart grid. CRC Press, Boca Ratón, p 209

Sunstein (2015) Choose not to choose: understanding the value of choice. Oxford University Press, Oxford, pp 206 and 218

Svirskas B (2004) Dynamic management of business service quality in collaborative commerce systems. In: Mendes M, Suomi R, Passos C (eds) Digital communities in a networked society: e-Commerce, e-Business and e-Government. Kluwer Academic Publishers, New York, pp 96 et seq

Tompkins J (2004) Partnerships and the supply Chain. In: Tompkins J, Harmelink D (eds) The supply chain handbook. Tompkins Press, s. l, p 24

Tutton R (2004) Person, property and gift: exploring languages of tissue donation to biomedical research. In: Tutton R, Corrigan O (eds) Genetic databases: socio-ethical issues in the collection and Use of DNA. Routledge, Abingdon, p 30

Vafiadis G, Kousiouris G, Nair S (2012) Data manager (DM) User Guide, pp 27–31, OPTIMIS project, http://optimis-project.eu/sites/default/files/content-files/page/datamanageruserguide.pdf. Accessed May 10 2019
Van Alsenoy B et al (2015) From Social Media Service to Advertising Network: A Critical Analysis of Facebook's Revised Policies and Terms, Report, Draft Version 1.2., s.l
Veatch R (1997) Medical ethics, 2nd edn. Jones and Bartlett Publishers, Boston, pp 195 et seq
Verite L, Helberger N (2013) EU cloud computing expert group: discussion paper pre-contractual information requirements and cloud services [online]. Available at: https://dare.uva.nl/search?identifier=43f9e5e9-ab4a-43e6-8bcd-a40c7c2d58c6. Accessed May 10 2019
Von Jan U, Albrecht U (2016) Apps for research and research with apps—taking inventory. In: Mantas J et al (eds) unifying the applications and foundations of biomedical and health informatics. IOS Press, Amsterdam, p 245
Wall D (2014) The Sustainable Economics of Elinor Ostrom: Commons, Contestation and Craft. Routledge, London, p 80
Waschke M (2015) How clouds Hold IT together: integrating architecture with cloud deployment. CA Technologies APress, New York, p 122
Weale D (2001) The smart guide to excel 2000 further skills: a progressive course for more experienced users. Continuum, London, p 6
Weir R, Alick R (2004) The stored tissue issue: biomedical research, ethics, and law in the era of genomic medicine. Oxford University Press, Oxford, p 191
Williams G (2007) Online business security systems. Springer, New York, p 12
Winston & Strown LLP (2015) Japan Updates Privacy Law http://www.winston.com/en/privacy-law-corner/japan-updates-privacy-law.html. Accessed May 10 2019
Wrinkler V (2011) Cloud Computing: Negotiating Cloud Contracts, TechNet Magazine http://www.technet.microsoft.com/en-us/magazine/jj149022.aspx. Accessed May 10 2019
Wu L (2014) SLA-based Resource Provisioning for Management of Cloud-based Software-as-a-Service Applications, p. 20, Doctoral Thesis https://pdfs.semanticscholar.org/e2fd/7963dc422f6d8ae7de7a9246d85a0e30e427.pdf. Accessed May 10 2019
Zanfir G (2012) The Right to data portability in the context of the eu data protection reform. Int Data Privacy Law 2(3):149–162

Chapter 9
Towards a Legal Risk Assessment

> *"Life, risk and technology are getting more intimate than ever..."* (Ciborra 2007, p. 27).

9.1 Introduction

Before embarking on the generally known caveats regarding legal risks, I would like to point out what Claudio Ciborra, an information theorist, has explained in his writings on information systems and risk management.[1] In what he called the "duality of risk,"[2] he reminds us that it is not just that our society is becoming increasingly dependent on mobile phones and computers as the primary means of communication, it is not about business transactions processed through electronic networks, it is not even about jobs being fully automated or human reasoning being replaced by human-like artificial intelligence that emulates the decision-making of human experts.[3] Looking ahead and reflecting on the next generation of ICT platforms and risk management, it goes beyond those electronic devices that we use in our daily lifes. The challenge is that "our life (project) becomes simultaneously conditioned, constrained or enabled by grid technologies. The technology is already there, albeit in an indirect and hidden form..."[4] The duality of risk here refers to the hidden infrastructure and the electronic devices that we use.

---

[1] The work of Claudio Ciborra, see Gutwirth and Hildebrandt (2010, p. 33).

[2] See, generally, Ciborra (2005).

[3] For details about artificial intelligence (AI) and expert systems, see Jackson (1998).

[4] Ciborra (2007, p. 27).

M. Corrales Compagnucci, *Big Data, Databases and "Ownership" Rights in the Cloud*, Perspectives in Law, Business and Innovation,
https://doi.org/10.1007/978-981-15-0349-8_9

Ciborra wrote the above lines more than ten years ago and since then, grid technologies have evolved into different models.[5] Cloud computing is a kind of grid computing which focuses on QoS and reliability problems.[6] The cloud differs from the grid essentially in the implementation details.[7] According to Ciborra, change and innovation bring the emergence of new risks, however his vision goes beyond that to suggest that risks are often the source of innovation[8] and a new order.[9] As such, risk is not, in itself, a bad thing; rather, it is essential for accelerating progress.[10] This chapter aims to widen the lens through which we view risk and analyze particular kinds of legal risk connected to the design and deployment of grid and cloud computing infrastructures in brokerage scenarios.[11] This chapter presents an SLA brokering framework that includes innovative risk-aware assessment techniques which facilitate the clarification of database and "ownership" rights of data and evaluate the probability of SLA failure. It uses the web service agreement specification (WS-Agreement)[12] as a template and extends prior work on risk metrics from the OPTIMIS project to facilitate SLA creation between service consumers and providers within typical cloud brokerage scenarios. However, since the WS-Agreement allows for an automated mechanism between only two parties and does not cover the use of an intermediary within the agreement process, I use the specific work carried out in the AssessGrid project that includes a brokerage mechanism and pays considerable attention to addressing a risk assessment.[13]

SLAs are facilitators for increasing the commercial uptake of cloud computing services. They provide clear-cut rules concerning expectations and obligations between service consumers and providers.[14] Current frameworks, however, fail to provide flexibility[15] and there is no global standard that clarifies database rights and, more generally, "ownership" rights of data. Therefore, it is always advisable to thoroughly check cloud SLAs before being legally bound by the terms of contracts. Furthermore, without the ability to evaluate the probability that an SLA might fail, market growth will be limited, since neither party will be willing to agree. By introducing a database and "ownership" rights risk assessment alongside automated SLA creation

[5]For details about the evolution of grid infrastructure technologies, see Jones and Bird (2013, pp. 160) et seq.

[6]Kasemsap and Sunandha (2015, p. 33).

[7]Teng and Magoules (2010, p. 126).

[8]Shantz (2005, p. 511).

[9]Ciborra (2009, p. 78).

[10]Drissi et al. (2013, p. 143).

[11]See Gourlay et al. (2008, pp. 437–443).

[12]See Andrieux et al. (2007), Gourlay et al. (2008, p. 438). More specifically, for negotiating and creating SLAs, I use the WSAG4 J framework developed at Fraunhofer Institute SCAI. The WSAG4 J is a tool that helps to create and manage SLAs in distributed systems and has been fully implemented as part of the Open Grid Forum (OGF) WS-Agreement standard.

[13]The Advanced Risk Assessment and Management for Trustable Grids project (AssessGrid), was founded by the EU Commission under the FP6 IST framework (contract no. 031772).

[14]Djemame et al. (2011a, p. 1558).

[15]See Kirkham et al. (2012a, p. 1063).

and negotiation processes, end-users can uncover high-risk areas to attenuate such risks and eliminate those cloud providers that will not promote their needs.

This chapter is divided into 10 sections. Section 9.2 briefly reviews the extant literature with regards to risk assessment in the cloud. It also explains the motivation and justification for deepening and expanding research into other areas of law such as database rights and "ownership" rights of data. Section 9.3 is concerned with the methodology used for this study, namely a risk-based approach through the whole service lifecycle. Section 9.4 presents an overview of the legal risks involved and how a risk mitigation strategy will enhance legal interoperability. Section 9.5 delves into detail concerning database and "ownership" rights of data, focusing on the three key themes that create risk in cloud computing and Big Data projects. Section 9.6 begins by offering a glimpse of the main actors involved and then goes on to explain the two general use cases being considered. Finally, it explains the brokering mechanism and risk assessment techniques using the WS-Agreement, which facilitates the creation of risk-aware SLAs between end-users and cloud providers. Section 9.7 presents the risk inventory within the system architecture design. It includes an updated and customized risk inventory focused on the legal areas considered to present the highest risks and constraints. Section 9.8 explains step-by-step the different stages of the risk assessment process in cloud brokerage scenarios. In Sect. 9.9, two hypothetical scenarios are considered to showcase how risk assessment can be effectively applied in real cases. Finally, Sect. 9.10 concludes.

9.2 Risk Assessment: Literature Review, Motivation and Justification

As the realization of cloud-based services and infrastructures advance[16] from one single private cloud infrastructure towards more complex migrations in dynamic federated scenarios consisting of several coexisting public or hybrid clouds, there are increasing high-level concerns. These concerns include issues of risk, trust and legal considerations that establish solid foundations for the non-functional requirements[17] of the ecosystem. Cloud migrations have reached a high level of development, yet the management of cloud services entails a loss of control over the data being processed. This also impairs the trustworthiness in cloud computing technology because end-users are not entirely confident in using the cloud.[18]

[16] Mahmood (2014) (ed).

[17] Non-functional requirements present a systematic approach that provides quality to the software system. They define the criteria used in the system operation, which is specified in the system architecture. For a comprehensive explanation of non-functional requirements. See, generally, Chung et al. (2000), Chung and Sampaio do Prado Leite (2009).

[18] Li and Singh (2014, p. 670).

There are many legal risks involved that have been amplified by the Big Data movement to the cloud. The American Heritage Dictionary defines risk as "the possibility of suffering harm or loss; danger. A factor, thing, element, or course involving uncertain danger; a hazard."[19] Similarly, the Black's Law Dictionary defines risk as "the uncertainty of a result. Happening or loss; the chance of injury, damage or loss; esp., the existence and extent of the possibility of harm."[20] Therefore, the term "risk" can be loosely described as exposing oneself to an activity or event that can lead to the possibility of damage, harm or loss.

Risk assessment is fundamental for widespread commercial adoption, and risk management tools need to be integrated into the emerging cloud paradigm.[21] While a variety of definitions of the term "risk management" have been suggested, in this work I adopt the definition given by the International Standards Organization (ISO) as follows: "risk management refers to a coordinated set of activities and methods that is used to direct an organization and to control the many risks that can affect its ability to achieve objectives."[22] This definition is close to the Black's Law Dictionary definition that refers to risk management as "the activity of identifying, estimating and evaluating the probability of harm associated with an activity and determining an acceptable level of risk."[23] The underlying concepts of risk assessment and risk management aim to improve the confidence level between a provider and end-user in order to sign an SLA.[24]

A risk assessment must be proactively introduced into the SLA framework to allow the end-users and cloud providers to automatically recognize critical PoF and to propose corrective actions that would reduce the risks at specific points of the contract in order to avoid soaring transaction costs and prevent future issues. This precautionary approach is meant to fill in the gaps in the current SLA frameworks, and to imbue a risk management culture among cloud providers.[25]

Although many generic risk management assessment standards exist today, such as the ISO 31000:2009,[26] one major difficulty that might arise in the implementation of this requirement is the lack of specific guidelines.[27] The ISO 31000:2009 stipulates the detection and identification of emerging risks. Nevertheless, a standard risk assessment methodology for database rights and "ownership" rights of data is still

---

[19]For this definition, see American Heritage Dictionary.

[20]Garner (2014, p. 1524).

[21]See Gourlay et al. (2009, p. 36).

[22]Plain English ISO 31000:2018, Risk Management Dictionary [online]. Available at: http://www.praxiom.com/iso-31000-terms.htm. Accessed May 10 2019.

[23]Garner (2014, p. 1525) (ed).

[24]Sangrasi et al. (2012, pp. 445–452).

[25]See Nwankwo (2014).

[26]See ISO 31000:2009 risk management standard sets out the principles and guidelines on risk management that can be applied to any type of risk in any field of industry or sector [online]. Available at: https://www.iso.org/obp/ui/#iso:std:43170:en. Accessed May10 2019.

[27]See, generally, Lund et al. (2011).

missing. A well-known standard risk assessment methodology like OCTAVE (Operationally Critical Threat, Asset, and Vulnerability Evaluation)[28] provides a systemic and asset-driven mitigation strategy approach, however it focuses mainly on security aspects and does not address how risk assessment results shall be updated on a regular basis.[29] Moreover, most risk assessments have been devoted to other areas of law such as privacy, data protection and data security; these include[30] the ISO 22307:2008[31] privacy impact assessment (PIA)[32] for financial services and banking management, the ISO/IEC WD 29134 PIA methodology,[33] the ISO/IEC 29101:2013 for information technology security techniques and privacy architecture framework,[34] and the ISO/IEC NP 19086–4 for cloud computing SLA framework.[35]

The European Network and Information Security Agency (ENISA) released at the end of 2012, an updated version of its 2009 cloud security risk assessment. The risks are classified into three categories: (a) Policy and Organizational, (b) Technical, and (c) Legal. It contains a list of 23 risks. One of these risks refers to intellectual property issues, which is a good indicator that the perceptions of associated risks of cloud computing have put IPRs under the radar.[36] However, this is described, in my view, too broadly and focuses mainly on the copyrights of original work such as new applications and software, while other aspects of IPRs such as database rights are not mentioned. As with all the IPRs described in the ENISA recommendations, database rights and other issues related to "ownership" rights of data must be clarified by the adequate contractual clauses and within the service manifest of the SLA, otherwise this might be at risk.

Until now, no systematic investigation has adequately explained database rights and "ownership" rights of data in relation to the cloud and Big Data phenomenon. In this regard, the present study is the first to undertake a specific risk analysis in this domain and aims to contribute to this growing area of research. Understanding the link between Big Data, database rights and "ownership" rights of data, will help

---

[28] For details, see also the 2007 OCTAVE Allegro version. See Caralli (2007).

[29] See, generally, Lund et al. (2011).

[30] Cattedu and Hogben (2009) (eds).

[31] ISO 22307:2008 is a privacy impact assessment for financial services and banking management tools. It recognizes the importance to mitigate risks associated to consumer data utilizing automated and networked systems [online]. Available at: https://www.iso.org/standard/40897.html. Accessed May 10 2019.

[32] See Corrales (2012); see, also, generally, Wright and De Hert (2012) (eds), Pearson and Yee (2013) (eds).

[33] ISO/IEC WD 29134 PIA methodology [online]. Available at: https://www.iso.org/iso/home/store/catalogue_tc/catalogue_detail.htm?csnumber=62289. Accessed May 10 2019.

[34] ISO/IEC 29101:2013 Information Technology—Security Techniques—Privacy Architecture Framework [online]. Available at: https://www.iso.org/standard/45124.html. Accessed May 10 2019.

[35] ISO/IEC NP 19086–4 (2019) Information Technology—Cloud Computing—Service Level Agreement (SLA) framework and technology—Part 4 Security and Privacy [online]. Available at: https://www.iso.org/standard/68242.html. Accessed May 10 2019.

[36] ENISA has played a crucial role in providing stakeholders an overview of the main risks involved in cloud computing. See Cattedu and Hogben (2009).

to reduce the legal uncertainties and risks involved in the cloud and Big Data. Thus, the broadening of the scope of the risk assessment methods followed hitherto is accordingly designed and advocated in order to establish priorities and make the strategic choosing of cloud providers a global reality.

Incorporating risk assessment techniques into cloud brokerage scenarios and including database rights and "ownership" rights of data during SLA negotiations and service operation will aid the decision-making process regarding contractual agreements. Currently, there is a lack of confidence and trust in terms of the uncertainties involved with the SLA level of quality.[37] This is one of the most important barriers to the adoption of cloud computing. In order to improve confidence and create more trust in cloud transactions, it is necessary to improve control over the resources available. The design of cloud architecture related to application deployment seems to be the best route to achieve this. This will also create more optimized and transparent resources.[38]

It is important to bear in mind that it is not possible to reduce all the risks down to zero. Nevertheless, mitigation strategies may at least increase the confidence of end-users and lead to reliable productivity and a cost-effective solution for cloud service providers. In this research, confidence is defined as "the expectation of a successful fulfillment of SLA agreed between a cloud service consumer and a cloud service provider,"[39] and the notion of cost-effective and reliable productivity as a "providers capability of fulfilling an SLA through the entire lifecycle of the service provision and at the same time realizing its own business level objectives."[40] In other words, it is important to capitalize and mak a certain amount of profit, while optimizing the efficacy of infrastructure provider resources.[41]

Based on the framework of the OPTIMIS and AssessGrid software toolkits, as a basic risk factor mechanism, the main contributions of this research are the design and effective implementation of a risk assessment framework tailored to database rights and "ownership" rights of data with an eye towards Big Data and other future similar movements. This can be efficiently implemented into other high-level cloud management and control software systems for both service providers and infrastructure providers. Although a specific risk assessment is the main focus of this chapter, I also consider the decision-making process of how to implement corresponding mitigation strategies that may involve other high-level considerations such as cost-efficiency and trust.[42]

[37] Djemame et al. (2011b, p. 119).

[38] Kirkham et al. (2013, p. 7).

[39] Djemame et al. (2011b, p. 119).

[40] Djemame et al. (2011b, p. 119).

[41] Djemame et al. (2011b, p. 119).

[42] Djemame et al. (2011b, p. 119).

9.3 Risk Assessment Methodology

Risk analysis can be examined at various stages of cloud interactions. Each of the actors involved in the cloud will have their own concerns and points of view towards others in terms of trust, risks and legal issues.[43] They might have specific legal demands that need to be taken into consideration. For example, how to reconcile the "ownership" of data that may accrue from the use of cloud computing technology. New data can be potentially created out of the data derived from the usage of various tools such as data mining, analytics, AI, etc. The concept of "ownership" in this context implies that the owner can control how the data will be regulated.[44] Events like this and their impact need to be assessed in order to compute the overall probability of an SLA violation, which requires a detailed analysis. This assessment will also depend on the cloud deployment scenario—bursting, federated, hybrid, etc.[45] In this research, I will consider a cloud brokerage scenario since the broker can participate as an intermediary in any of these scenarios.

These legal concerns can also be refined to consider the different stages of the cloud lifecycle as follows: (i) the service deployment stage for initial placement of services on cloud providers, taking into account the legal issues as a gauge for cloud provider selection, and (ii) the service operation, where cloud resources and databases are managed by the cloud provider for the attainment of all the service-level objectives (SLO), including the legal ones. During these two stages, legal risks need to be continuously and systematically monitored in order to avert any additional transaction costs that will be incurred by the end-users and cloud providers.[46] Figure 9.1 describes the risk assessment steps during service deployment and service operation.

A number of stages have been identified with the aim of performing a complete risk assessment on cloud platforms. Each iteration is used to parse, in real-time, a

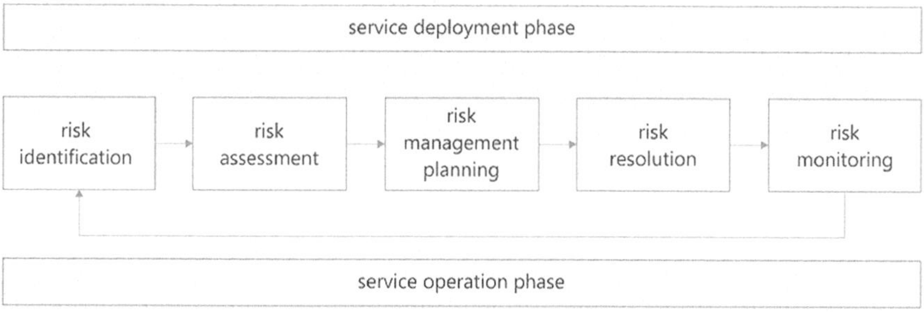

Fig. 9.1 Risk assessment life cycle during service deployment and operation

---

[43] Khan et al. (2012, p. 122).

[44] Djemame et al. (2013, p. 3).

[45] Khan et al. (2012, p. 122).

[46] Khan et al. (2012, p. 122).

core risk assessment and helps us to better understand the process. The constituent parts of this approach and their relationships are further explained below.[47]

9.3.1 High Level Analysis of the System

A primary high-level analysis of the different deployment scenarios aids in identifying the actions and assets involved at the different stages of the risk assessment process. This helps to effectively identify the vulnerable parts of each asset and how they can change through time. As a general rule, legal concerns need to be assessed before the service deployment phase if the SLA demands specific expectations be met. In the service operation phase, the legal issues involved are constantly monitored throughout the service execution.[48]

9.3.2 Identifying the Assets Involved

Various assets need to be protected from specific threats during service deployment and operation phases. From a legal perspective, the focus here is on data, databases and the terms specified in the SLA.[49]

9.3.3 Identifying the Threats in Each Cloud Deployment Scenario

The risk assessment model adopts a systemic approach through which threats and vulnerabilities can be identified. The risk analysis methodology is linked to a threat and vulnerability assessment tool. This approach is particularly helpful because it contains a threat model that ensures synergies with distributed systems and software in general. This model has been adapted to cloud applications using the CORAS[50] risk modeling language technique, which is an open-source risk-modeling tool.[51]

[47] Khan et al. (2012, p. 122).
[48] Khan et al. (2012, p. 122).
[49] Khan et al. (2012, p. 122).
[50] See Vraalsen et al. (2005, pp. 45–60).
[51] Khan et al. (2012, p. 123), Djemame et al. (2013, p. 12).

9.4 Embracing Legal Risks and Enhancing Legal Interoperability

Richard Susskind, in his book *The Future of Law*, under the sub-heading, *From legal problem solving to legal risk management*, anticipated a paradigm shift in the approach to legal problems. While legal problems will still need to be addressed in the future, they will be substantially mitigated with proactive legal risk management tools and services that will pre-empt the conventional reactive legal method.[52] There is an increasing interest in the adoption of risk management methods borrowed from other disciplines that can be effectively adapted for use in the legal domain. Therefore, the proposed software-based risk assessment tools seem a reasonable preventive route for amending the legislative gaps and finding a solution for the many shortcomings of the rigid and, oftentimes, unrealistic constraints of traditional black-letter laws.[53]

Preliminary work on legal risk management was undertaken as an approach to providing legal services in various areas of the IT industry and this continues to be an active area of research. However, these generic methods have not yet reached a high level of sophistication or been fully implemented.[54] Current software process optimized models do not properly address the legal implications for each phase of the software development lifecycle. The lack of systematic and organized standards in this domain provides only scattered references to legal aspects. This means that legal risks are managed reactively instead of proactively before damage or loss occurs.

Drawing on software projects, Rejas-Muslera et al. presented a significant analysis and discussion on the subject. The authors identified that legal audits are closely related to *planning* activities. In line with the Plan-like Architectures theoretical framework of this book, the authors recognized that legal activities (and other measures) must be planned in advance and invoked as time goes by across the entire lifecycle of the product or project in order to avoid or reduce negative legal impacts on the achieved objectives. While their study covers many aspects of law inter alia copyright, registration and user rights, data protection, and trading standards,[55] the core interest of this book lies in the risks associated with managing databases.

The main goal is not to deny these risks and their overall implications but to create a smart strategy that can deal with this trade-off. In the following sections and subsections, I discuss these legal aspects in the context of Big Data and cloud computing. Legal issues are present at each phase of the whole outsourcing lifecycle

---

[52]Susskind (1998, p. 290). According to Susskind: "While legal problem solving will not be eliminated in tomorrow's legal paradigm, it will nonetheless diminish markedly in significance. The emphasis will shift towards legal risk management supported by proactive facilities, which will be available in the form of legal information services and procedures. As citizens learn to seek legal guidance more regularly and far earlier than in the past, many potential legal difficulties will be dissolved before needing to be resolved. Where legal problems of today are often symptomatic of delayed legal input, earlier consultation should result in users understanding and identifying their risks and controlling them before any questions of escalation."

[53]Wahlgren (2007, p. 91).

[54]Burnett (2005, pp. 61–67).

[55]Rejas-Muslera et al. (2007, pp. 118–124).

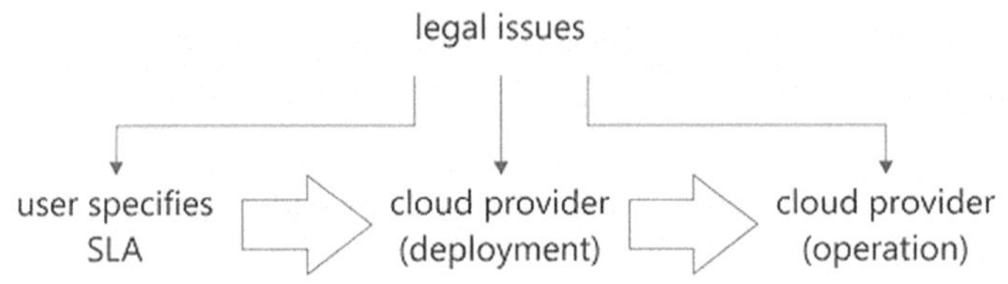

Fig. 9.2 Legal issues and service lifecycle stages

of a cloud service. Figure 9.2 shows a graphical depiction of the overall model from a high-level perspective.

In the initial contractual agreement stage, the end-user may specify legal clauses regarding certain service requirements and how such databases must be handled. While large companies and institutions may have more resources to bargain and negotiate specific contractual clauses with, the standard nature of the SLAs does not allow much room for single users and SMEs to negotiate the contract.[56] However, an XML automated schema has been specifically crafted as explained in the previous chapter. This will provide more flexibility for smaller companies and individuals so they can clarify database rights and "ownership" rights of data, and all parties involved can be better off. Nevertheless, the point to bear in mind for the moment is that even though end-users can negotiate the terms of the contract, these contracts are legally binding. The cloud provider must fulfill all the requirements and ensure that all clauses conform to legal rules before deploying the service. Otherwise, they will be at risk of facing liability issues should there be any breach of the contract. Therefore, there should be monitoring strategies for legal risks throughout the operation phase.[57]

This framework will improve the legal interoperability among providers on a global scale. According to the GEO Data Sharing Task Force, legal interoperability among multiple datasets from different sources occurs when "the legal rights, terms, and conditions of databases from two or more sources are compatible and the data may be combined by any user without compromising the legal rights of any of the data sources used."[58] This definition is important when applying the following conditions:[59]

i. The conditions to use data are clear and readily determinable for each dataset[60];
ii. The legal conditions granted to use each data set permits the creation and use of "combined and derivative products"[61]; and

---

[56] Bradshaw et al. (2010, pp. 31–32).

[57] Batre et al. (2007, p. 193).

[58] Draft White Paper on Legal Options for the Exchange of Data through the GEOSS Data-CORE (2011). Group on Earth Observations [online]. Available at: https://www.earthobservations.org/documents/dsp/draft_white_paper_geoss_legal_interoperability_30_october_2011.pdf. Accessed May 10 2019.

[59] White Paper, Mechanisms to Share Data as Part of GEOSS Data-CORE, p. 3.

[60] White Paper, Mechanisms to Share Data as Part of GEOSS Data-CORE, p. 3.

[61] White Paper, Mechanisms to Share Data as Part of GEOSS Data-CORE, p. 3.

iii. End-users may lawfully get access and use each dataset without seeking permission from data creators.[62]

Legal interoperability is a bottleneck in cloud computing and Big Data transformations where many resources are available and data is used, re-combined and then derivative data is re-disseminated. This might also prove a great hindrance to public research. The protectionist mentality underlying database rights is, however, very dangerous because it automatically frames access to data as a threat. Within this mindset, there is a risk of databases being locked in. As we shall soon see, the sui generis right creates serious problems for the Big Data movement, which does not understand the protection of databases in the same way as the protectionist mentality. The quest for Big Data invites the researcher or entrepreneur to a place where information can lead to innovation and productivity. There should be an equitable trade-off between the protection of databases and access to data that is in the public domain.

The term public domain has come to be used to refer to "information that is: (a) not subject to copyright or related rights (including database rights), and; (b) not subject to conditions on reuse imposed by other means."[63] This approach could raise and promote social welfare as well as the goals intended by the Big Data movement by making datasets available to end-users. In a free-market economy, individuals should be allowed to obtain unrestricted use and re-dissemination of data. This market competition process may help to correct behavioral market problems. The public domain status may be formally created through laws and policies that exempt certain categories of data and information from database protection. However, this could also be achieved through contractual private agreements among parties.[64]

For many scholars, the database right is considered unsuccessful. Detractors of the EU Database Directive have often expressed criticism that this could raise hurdles against innovation and free development in various areas of the industry.[65] Another objection to database rights is that they may lock up data and information, which can negatively affect research and academic communities that rely on the availability of data and information to carry on their business or research. Finally, opponents of these rights argue that this form of protection is too narrow in scope and fails to address other relevant issues for the database industry.[66] These arguments clearly show the negative perception among some scholars, which prompts worries about its potential negative effects.

I think all these arguments are legitimate and that sui generis rights could eventually lock up data to the detriment of the scientific and academic communities as well

[62] White Paper, Mechanisms to Share Data as Part of GEOSS Data-CORE, p. 3.

[63] Summary White Paper, Legal Options for the Exchange of Data through the GEOSS Data-CORE, p. 2, Data Sharing Task Force, Group on Earth Observations.

[64] Summary White Paper, Legal Options for the Exchange of Data through the GEOSS Data-CORE, p. 19.

[65] Sundara Rajan (2011, p. 286).

[66] DG Internal Market and Services Working Paper, First Evaluation of Directive 96/9/EC on the Legal Protection of Databases, p. 4.

as other areas of industry. It yields much greater protection to databases, yet with a certain degree of uncertainty that may fall foul of prior intellectual property law principles by placing strong, exclusive property rights on investment instead of creativity and innovation. Still, I find it possible to argue for a more balanced approach that is more flexible and less objectionable than database rights. In order to respond to the critics of sui generis rights, the proposal of this book follows the core principles and guidelines of best practices through which legal interoperability and a right balance between the transferability of conventional databases and the availability of Big Data can be achieved.

9.5 Conventional Databases Versus Big Data: Striking the Right Balance

As seen in Chap. 2, the sui generis right is a well-established IPR protected under the umbrella of the EU Database Directive. This right stems from the necessity to foster the database industry in the EU in a time when databases needed an extra scope of protection. However, this right caused some concerns among legal experts, mainly due to its failure to come to terms with new technological advances of the Internet and with the onset of cloud computing services along with the Big Data movement, which may undermine and hamper scientific research activities.

The Database Directive is still clinging to old fashioned ideas of conventional databases that have a fixed structure on which one accumulates and stores data. Another defining factor is the ubiquitous nature of the cloud that often obscures the physical location of databases. The ability of cloud providers to transfer databases through VMs across multiple countries represents the problem of dealing with different legal jurisdictions. This situation can be exacerbated when the legislations of those countries do not cover database rights. Therefore, the first problem that should be addressed in the SLAs is that database rights should only be implemented in jurisdictions where this right exists and limited to a geographic location due to its territorial nature.

This represents a good starting point. However, if we only follow this approach, this debate continues to be stuck in the old paradigm. In view of the immense influence of the Big Data phenomenon, the real issue lies elsewhere. If our aim is the empowerment of end-users so they can take initiative and make decisions in the face of the Big Data movement, then database rights seem entirely counterproductive. The exponential growth[67] and breadth of reach of Big Data has expanded so much that it has surpassed the traditional logistics of storing, processing, or analyzing data.[68] It touches upon almost every corner of the digitized world and its benefits encompass all aspects of human life.[69]

[67] Majkic (2014), preface.

[68] Dean (2014, p. 10).

[69] Ridley (2015, p. 79).

Nevertheless, this comes hand-in-hand with various risks and opens the door for litigation.[70] Big Data in the cloud refers not only to the storage and accumulation of large amounts of data but also to how to organize and label such data in a variety of different and useful ways[71] (structured, unstructured,[72] semi-structured,[73] etc.). Big Data generally slices and dices information. This breakdown process implies a systematic reduction of information into smaller pieces that can be arranged in such a way that will yield new information. This includes machine-generated data from automated sensors, nuclear plants, X-ray and scanning machines, airplane engines, consumer interaction from businesses,[74] mobiles and social media.[75] If this information is exploited properly it will revolutionize the decision-making process—entrusting more on data analysis instead of intuition and experience. This being said, individuals and institutions need to consider not only the best means to generate and exploit data but also how to protect and manage their data. This raises challenging questions about policies and practices that have direct implications on our lives.[76]

The vexing question is how to strike the right balance between the transferability of conventional databases and the availability of Big Data. This book attempts to answer some of these lingering questions and fill a long-held gap in the scientific literature. In line with the principle of free and open access to data,[77] the proposed framework endows end-users and cloud providers with a flexible mechanism through which the cloud broker can ensure freedom of contract. This interpretation gleaned from the aforementioned principles and ideas can be best treated under three headings: (i) Territorial scope of protection; (ii) "Ownership" rights of new data generated by Big Data; and (iii) Lack of international legal and contractual standards.

9.5.1 Territorial Scope of Protection

This problem relates to the ubiquitous nature of the cloud and the territorial scope of protection of database rights that create legal hurdles. One of the most contentious provisions of the EU Database Directive which is relevant to our discussion regarding cloud computing and Big Data, is Article 11 which establishes territorial constraints on who may obtain database rights. In principle, the right extends only to makers

[70] Ridley (2015, p. 79).

[71] See, generally, Sakr and Gaber (2014) (eds).

[72] Unstructured data is the subset of information. For example: text mining in the medical field. See Holzinger et al. (2013, p. 13).

[73] Semi-structured data such as XML. See Ishikawa (2015), preface. See, also, generally, Kitchin (2014).

[74] Krishnan (2013, p. 5).

[75] Vashist (2015, p. 1).

[76] Lohr (2015).

[77] See, generally, OECD (2007) Principles and Guidelines for Access to Research Data from Public Funding [online]. Available at: http://www.oecd.org/sti/inno/38500813.pdf. Accessed May 10 2019.

or rights holders who are nationals or habitual residents of an EU/EEA Member State. This is further explained in Article 11 (2) and includes companies or firms that have their principal place of business or central administration within the EU.[78] This is a controversial and anachronistic provision in the context of cloud computing and Big Data due to its essentially pervasive nature. In view of the fact that servers can be located in different countries outside of the EU, and that databases can be easily reproduced in VM, there is a risk of potential future controversies between the involved parties.

If a database qualifies for protection, and it is stored on a server within the jurisdiction of the EU/EEA Member States, then there is no doubt that it will be protected. However, it is crucial to determine whether the jurisdiction applies to the place where the database has been created, or where the database has been recorded. This distinction will fundamentally affect database protection in cloud transactions, as there are no database rights in other countries outside of the EU.[79]

Currently, there is no such automated procedure for checking whether database rights are clearly defined and specified so that a broker can "on the fly" confirm legal compliance. As explained in the previous chapter, these checks may include the location of the federated infrastructure provider using a location constraint mechanism. If the target infrastructure provider is inside the jurisdiction of the EU/EEA Member States then the outsourcing of data and databases may be fulfilled with minimal intervention.[80]

However, cloud customers can decide to waive their database rights in order to federate databases outside the boundaries of the EU/EEA Member States. As seen earlier, databases represent the risk of being potentially "exported" overseas to a jurisdiction without database rights. Therefore, they should only be implemented in jurisdictions where this right exists and limited to a "geographic location" due to its territorial nature. For this reason, the legal "glocalizational" solution suggested in the previous chapter—which includes an unconditional waiver as an alternative for scientific databases and/or for databases transferred across different jurisdictions outside the EU/EEA countries—could be a good way to mitigate this risk.

9.5.2 "Ownership" Rights of New Data Generated by Big Data

As hinted above, the exponential growth of data, both structured and unstructured, and the booming of Big Data trends can create new information from the data submitted to the cloud. This newly created data has value for both end-users and cloud providers.

---

[78]Davison (2003, p. 97).

[79]With the exception of Mexico, South Korea and Russia.

[80]See Kousiouris et al. (2013, pp. 61–72). In this work, the authors refer mainly to data protection issues, however, the same principles and ideas underlying the geographic location and data transfers may apply to database rights.

This means that some of the provisions enshrined in the EU Database Directive are becoming obsolete. Furthermore, there seems to be a lack of an international legal standard that defines "ownership" rights of data accruing from scientific research and Big Data analyses. There is a sort of prevailing "global norm" where the person or company who collects the data "owns" it. This problem seems to bring conflicting arguments between the involved parties.[81] Therefore, there is a need for an efficient and automated procedure during the negotiation of SLAs which aims to establish a clear and effective procedure to layout early in the contract who "owns" the data and define the conditions as to whether data will be shared or not among, for example, cloud providers and end-users.

9.5.3 *Lack of International Legal and Contractual Standards*

The third problem is the lack of a common international contractual framework to mitigate these legal risks. This leads to a lack of interoperability at the global scale that prevents cloud computing and Big Data markets from thriving. Cloud customers are facing difficulties in choosing the right cloud provider that best fits their needs. The lack of a structure or frame supporting the clarification of such rights creates tension between the stakeholders involved. Customers using cloud computing services are no longer satisfied with dealing with these uncertainties post facto. They need clear guidelines at the time they enter into a cloud and Big Data service.

As a corollary, due to the lack of an efficient and automatic procedure for the clarification of database rights and "ownership" rights of data in the cloud, end-users have to cope with the uncertainties and intricacies of the decision-making. Currently, the cloud market only allows for a limited category of static and non-negotiable click-through SLAs (usually ranked as gold, silver, or bronze).[82] The manual selection of cloud providers in order to meet their functional requirements (i.e., storage capabilities, number and size of servers, etc.) and non-functional capabilities (i.e., legal) has been perceived as imposing transaction costs. End-users must go through the cumbersome procedure of manually visiting the websites of cloud providers to compare their quality of services and legal policies.[83]

In short, what this framework attempts to achieve is a flexible and automated SLA that includes two things. The first is the possibility to keep databases (and as a consequence database rights) within the EU jurisdiction.[84] This would be the case when an end-user does not want to share data, but still keep database rights and enjoy the benefits of the EU Directive. If so, databases should stay within the EU jurisdiction. The second is the possibility to clarify who "owns" the processed and derivate data.

---

[81] See, generally, Jentzsch (2007, p. 27).

[82] See ARTIST R12 Certification Model.

[83] See Wu et al. (2013, pp. 235–244), Jrad (2014, p. 4).

[84] Or in countries such as Mexico, South Korea and Russia as these countries have also database rights similar the EU Database Directive.

This would be the case of Big Data projects/applications, such as those using data mining tool techniques, statistics, analytics or AI, where there is potentially valuable information for both the end-users and cloud providers. The contract should be able to clarify who "owns" this new data. This situation is between end-users and providers, or potentially among end-users working in the same project, like a research project using genetic, geographic or spatial data. It goes without saying that all these legal issues could be clarified via a consortium agreement (CA). In a realistic cloud computing scenario, however, what we need to avoid are manual negotiations. Therefore, this capability should be carried out automatically, and a waiving mechanism should be included, by which end-users may relinquish their database rights and "ownership" rights of data. This would be the case of a Big Data collaborative project where, for example, many countries are involved.[85] This way databases would remain open and everyone could access and tap into them. On the one hand, most research is conducted by joint efforts of public as well as private institutions in interdisciplinary and international contexts. On the other, competition in a behaviorally imperfect market is inevitable, and the possibility of waiving database rights does not mean that competition has to be curtailed. Providing more information and warning signals can offer end-users more choices and grant them more control over their data.

9.6 Risk Assessment Techniques and Typical Actors Involved in Brokering WS-Agreements

9.6.1 Typical Actors Involved

This section focuses on explaining in more detail the brokering mechanism, which facilitates the creation of risk-aware SLAs between the typical actors involved in cloud computing transactions. Three actors exist in the architecture of a typical cloud brokerage scenario: end-user, broker and provider. An end-user is an individual or a company who wants to use the cloud in order to perform certain tasks consisting of one or more services. The end-user must explicitly specify the tasks and associated requirements within an SLA template. In the preamble of this process, the end-user needs to make informed and risk-aware decisions about the SLA quotes. In order to make this risk assessment more practical, I consider two broad typical brokerage scenarios that provide ideal use cases. In both situations, resources are dynamically allocated and redistributed. These scenarios are as follows:

[85] See GEOSS-data Core project.

9.6.1.1 Broker as Mediator

In this case, the broker performs a risk assessment on behalf of the end-user in order to find the most suitable cloud provider and bring the parties together. It follows a four-step process. First, the end-user sends an SLA request to the broker. Then, the broker forwards the SLA quotes to a pool of suitable cloud providers. Once all the SLA quotes are received from the providers, the broker performs an independent risk assessment of each provider. Then, the broker creates a ranked list according to their PoF. Finally, the end-user is then free to choose and commit to an SLA quote by engaging directly with the selected provider.[86]

9.6.1.2 Broker as Contractor

In this case, the broker takes a more active role and offers its own SLA to end-users. The risk assessment works in the same way as the previous scenario. However, the main difference here is that the broker takes full responsibility for the SLA and performs the role of a "virtual" provider. Therefore, an end-user contracts directly with a broker instead of with the cloud provider. The broker agrees to the terms and conditions of the SLA between itself and each cloud provider.[87]

9.6.2 Risk Assessment Techniques

This brokerage mechanism will be used as a technical framework to include database and "ownership" rights of data risk assessment techniques. It is in the best interest of both sides. It increases the selection of cloud providers by comparing SLA quotes that match the expectations of the end-users, and it generates a larger user pool base of end-users and attempts to reduce deliberation costs in deciding upon which SLA requests to accept. From a provider's perspective, accepting an SLA implies the potential risk of paying a penalty if such commitment cannot be met.[88]

It is important to bear in mind the limitations of this framework. The introduction of a broker alone will not remove all uncertainties before the SLA is signed. Nonetheless, the implementation of a risk-aware brokering mechanism provides the means to formally evaluate the probability and expected impact of potential adverse events. Without such knowledge, end-users and cloud providers cannot make the

[86] Djemame et al. (2011a, p. 1561).

[87] Djemame et al. (2011a, p. 1561).

[88] Djemame et al. (2011a, p. 1561).

right decisions with regards to costs and benefits. In a nutshell, this is a win-win situation[89] and in agreement with the theories of law and economics that suggest reducing transaction costs and solving coordination problems.[90]

Nevertheless, the crucial question that still remains is whether the cloud brokers are poised to offer a viable and transparent alternative route for end-users and cloud providers.[91] To some extent, the cloud broker-enabling technology should improve the available choices by providing the means for control and transparency to make effective and proactive data-driven decision-making. From the perspective of end-users, the broker should be seen as a trusted advisor that aids them in making better decisions.[92]

For this reason, a relevant aspect of this framework is the implementation of a software component, or confidence service, designed to perform an independent and objective assessment of the reliability of cloud providers in relation to the SLA PoF. Cloud providers usually run their own risk assessment. However, this can be too optimistic and overlook some of the important facts that are relevant to end-users. Therefore, the confidence service component provides more transparency and additional risk information to enhance the SLA decision-making process of end-users.[93]

9.7 Risk Inventory Design for the Identification of Legal Risks

The design of a risk inventory depends on the purpose and area in which they are applied. It has to be contextualized and take into account all the parties involved. As explained above, in the use case scenarios, these actors are end-users, cloud providers and the broker who can acquire different roles (mediator or contractor).[94] The risk inventory may also have different categories. In the case of the OPTIMIS risk assessor component, there are four broad categories such as general, technical, policy and legal.[95] A risk inventory must be tailored and refined to fit a specific purpose. For the implementation of this framework, a set of processes has been identified as follows[96]:

---

[89] Djemame et al. (2011a, pp. 1559–1560).

[90] See, generally, Stone (2005, p. 14).

[91] Fellows (2013), Gourlay et al. (2008, p. 438).

[92] Fellows (2013), Gourlay et al. (2008, p. 438), Fellows (2014).

[93] Djemame et al. (2011a, pp. 1559–1560).

[94] Djemame et al. (2011a, p. 1561).

[95] Djemame et al. (2011b, p. 122).

[96] Djemame et al. (2012, pp. 9–10).

i. *Use Cases*: determine precisely which use case scenario to focus on. In this case, a cloud brokerage scenario[97];
ii. *Levels of Interaction*: establish the areas of interaction in the cloud. Interactions may involve various levels in the cloud. In this case, two levels should be considered: (a) end-user to service provider; and (b) service provider to infrastructure provider. During each of these levels, particular aspects of the SLA need to be agreed upon and its fulfillment monitored[98];
iii. *Assets*: it is necessary to identify what is the asset being protected. In this case, database and "ownership" rights (and their characteristics) and SLAs. Risk events will be assessed and protected taking into account external or internal dangers (risks)[99];
iv. *Incidents/Risks Scenarios*: it is necessary to describe any event, condition or a blend of both that has the potential to diminish the capacity or availability of an asset. These consist of the vulnerabilities and threats the assets may face during the service operation. This includes the "adaptive capacity," which is the specific description of the mitigation strategy to be carried out for each risk scenario and its asset[100];
v. *Triggering Factor*: it is necessary to identify the factors that lead to an activated risk. Risks may also be dynamic. This means they can change and continually fluctuate over time as they are directly exposed to changes in the cloud ecosystem, such as regulatory requirements, changes in policies and contractual clauses, transactions, etc. The implementation of monitoring strategies may help to mitigate them during cloud service deployment and operation phases.[101]

The risk inventory designed within the scope of the OPTIMIS project has been integrated as a rule-based legal risk[102] modeling component and an integral part of the risk assessment software tool (Fig. 9.3). The risk assessment tool is a "self-contained independent functional model," which means that it is a completely independent component that enables customization and is able to work as a "plug-in."[103] This allows the addition of specific features to the existing software application. In the context of the OPTIMIS toolkit, the risk assessment tool has been implemented as two coexisting but independent components as follows: (i) the service provider risk

[97]Djemame et al. (2012, pp. 9–10).

[98]Djemame et al. (2012, pp. 9–10).

[99]Djemame et al. (2012, pp. 9–10).

[100]Djemame et al. (2012, pp. 9–10).

[101]Djemame et al. (2012, pp. 9–10).

[102]In computer science and software development, rule-based systems (also known as "expert-systems") are used to store and analyze information in useful ways that tell you what to do in different situations. They are often used as the basis for AI programing and systems to find answers to various problems. See, generally, Grosan and Abraham (2011, pp. 149–185), Toosizadeh and Farshchi (2011).

[103]Plug-in, add-in or add-on extensions are all synonyms for software components.

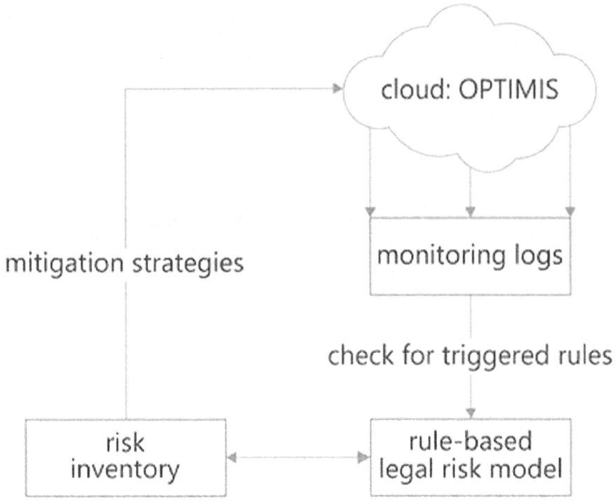

Fig. 9.3 Risk inventory for the identification of legal risks in the cloud architecture

assessment tool (SPRAT); and (ii) the infrastructure provider risk assessment tool (IPRAT).[104]

9.8 Different Stages of Risk Assessment in Cloud Brokerage Scenarios (CBS)

As explained earlier, in a typical CBS there are three main parties involved. These are the end-users, the broker and the cloud provider. The cloud provider could be a service provider or an infrastructure provider (i.e., VM provider). From a service and infrastructure provider perspective, data management services are supplied by the broker to co-ordinate and provide services or infrastructure in terms of data processing and quality of service. Figure 9.4 shows the document flow for creating an SLA and the different stages where the risk assessment can take place.

This procedure takes part during the life-span of the whole service (establishment, deployment and execution phase).[105] To make it easier for the layperson, this process can be split into five consecutive steps as follows:

i. At stage number 1, the SLA request is sent to various infrastructure providers (i.e., IP A, IP B, and IP C). At this stage, the broker wants to know which provider can run a service based on the end-user's request (see blue arrows in Fig. 9.4). Prior to making this contact, the broker should be able to assess the end-user's requirements and "filter" from its list of infrastructure providers those that may be able to make an SLA offer. Note that upon receiving an SLA request the

[104] Djemame et al. (2011b, pp. 121–122).
[105] Kirkham et al. (2012a, p. 1067).

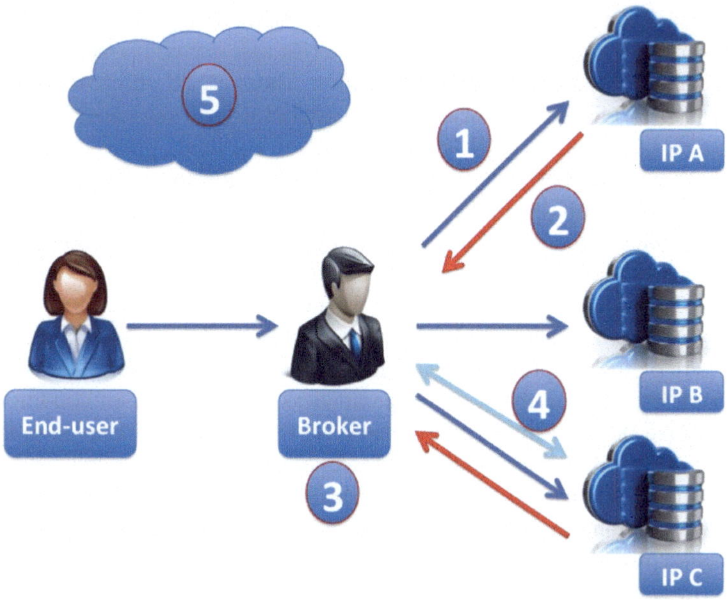

Fig. 9.4 Different stages of risk assessment in cloud brokerage scenarios

infrastructure provider can selectively choose to accept (and consequently the SLA needs to be fulfilled at service operation) or reject it;

ii. At stage number 2, the broker receives a reply from the infrastructure provider in the form of an SLA offer. It may happen that the broker will receive several replies from different infrastructure providers. In Fig. 9.4, the broker receives an SLA offer from IP A and IP C (see red arrows).

iii. At stage number 3, the broker filters all the offers received from the infrastructure providers who can run the service. At this stage, the broker can see which offer is more favorable to the end-user by ranking them.

iv. At stage number 4, the broker selects the most suitable infrastructure provider among all the SLA offers and contracts with one of them. At this stage, the SLA is bound between the infrastructure provider and the broker (see light blue arrow).

v. At stage number 5, the service is in operation. At this stage, the broker has chosen and told the infrastructure provider to run the cloud service.

Risk can occur at any time. That is, at stage 1, risk can take place before sending an SLA request to the infrastructure provider. In this case, the risk assessment is going to assess the risk of dealing with various infrastructure providers. This will work as a kind of "pre-assessment" when the broker is about to choose the provider. After this first screening procedure, the broker can then discard the providers that do not comply with the end-user's requirements. At stage 3, the broker filters the provider's offer. In this case, the risk assessor component can "look" inside the shortlisted SLA offers and can assess the risk of accepting the SLA. At stage 5, the infrastructure provider is running the service. Therefore, the risk assessor component assesses the risk of the SLA failing during service operation. These are all different kinds of risk assessments. In addition, the risk assessment applies to both sides as it can be run by the broker on behalf of the end-user and by the infrastructure provider. In the latter case, the infrastructure provider might have the same questions, including: What is the risk of dealing with this broker? What is the risk of accepting this SLA request? And, finally, what is the risk of the SLA failing during service operation?[106]

The question arises, however, what does this have to do with databases and the "ownership" rights of data? The answer for this question is that all of the above could be tailored to database rights and "ownership" rights of data. It could be an integral part of the equation, such as part of the SLA negotiations. A key point of this book is to extend the scope of parameters and the range of conditions that can be understood, measured and evaluated. This needs to be included in the risk assessor model as an extension to the legal category. Database rights and "ownership" rights of data can be part of the "policy," "legal," "technical," or "general" criteria to be considered and evaluated. For instance, what is the risk of dealing with an infrastructure provider considering database rights? To answer this question, one may look at different criteria that can be assessed quantitatively or qualitatively. These criteria can refer to different areas that have been filtered from the ISO standards[107] and ENISA guidelines, such as back SLA performance, business stability, general security practices, privacy practices, certification standards, geographic location of the infrastructure providers and general infrastructure practices (i.e., information about back-up, history, machine).[108]

A *quantitative* risk assessment provides a numerical expression of probabilities.[109] It is based on the track record of the broker dealing with the infrastructure provider. It is a reputation-based mechanism that classifies information based on past SLA performance. A risk level numerical estimation can be used to represent the probability of a risk that a specific harm will result from the occurrence of a particular event. For example, consider a 10-point rating scale. If the infrastructure provider fails 1 time out of 10, the score is 9 out of 10.[110] Travel and accommodation websites such as Trip Advisor and Airbnb are clear examples of this kind of ranking system. They often provide a forum where previous travelers can share their opinions and experiences.[111]

The data is analyzed within the inherent reputation engine of the risk assessor model using algorithms and statistical analyses. This score is then translated into risk. The highest score represents a high risk and the lowest score a very low risk. This forms part of the "confidence service" that has been developed as part of the

[106] Djemame et al. (2011b, p. 125).

[107] See ISO 31000:2009; ISO 27000 standards; ISO Guide 73:2009.

[108] Cattedu and Hogben (2009).

[109] Summer et al. (2004, p. 6).

[110] Djemame et al. (2011a, p. 1570).

[111] Leber and Hermann (2013, p. 406).

risk assessment model.[112] The only downside to a quantitative reputation-based risk assessment is when there are no track records (i.e., when there is no past-SLA information). In this case, the information has to be garnered from scratch. Stages number 1 and 3 in Fig. 9.4 are relatively easy as they refer to existing data (data that has already been collected).

Stage number 5, however, is more difficult to calculate, as this data has to be interpreted semantically and needs to be collected when the service is running during the service operation. At this stage, the approach of any risk assessment must be *qualitative*. This method relies upon prior expert knowledge based on non-numeric values.[113] This means that the information or data that needs to be collected are expressed in verbal form instead of numbers or quantities as in the case of the quantitative method.[114] Therefore, the risk inventory must be extended to support database rights and "ownership" rights of data either as a new category or as part of the legal risk criteria. The qualitative risk assessment model needs data to be monitored based on the vulnerabilities and threats attached to it. This becomes one more component at the moment of assessing the overall risk of the SLA failing at the service operation phase (i.e., the risk of a computer system or VM failing in cases of natural disasters such as earthquakes, floods, etc.).

9.9 Use Case Scenarios: Examples

In this section, two hypothetical scenarios are considered to showcase how the risk assessment can be effectively applied in real cases with emphasis on the different threats and vulnerabilities identified in the risk assessment process. To address these legal issues, we need to envisage hypothetical scenarios where database rights and "ownership" rights of data are breached or likely to be breached. For example, if the right to access a database has been granted, what are the inherent risks of that happening? Or, if database rights have not been granted, what are the results of this happening? In other words, we need to identify the specific *threats* and *vulnerabilities* related to database rights and "ownership" rights of data. Note that a threat is "a potential cause of an unwanted incident"[115] which may cause harm to a system or organization,[116] whereas a vulnerability is "a weakness, flaw or deficiency that opens for, or may be exploited by, a threat to cause harm to or reduce the value of an asset,"[117] i.e., the database and the right to access it. It is only when the obvious gaps are realized and the risk assessment model acquires its full value, that we will have a better understanding of the concrete data that we need to assess, measure and

[112]Djemame (2016, pp. 265–278).

[113]Taubenberger (2011, p. 260).

[114]Sharif and Basri (2011, p. 222).

[115]Lund et al. (2011, p. 131).

[116]Luiijf (2016, p. 69).

[117]Grossman and Seehusen (2015, p. 23), Lund et al. (2011, p. 137).

Table 9.1 Risk exposure rating

Likelihood	Impact				
	Negligible	**Minor**	**Moderate**	**Major**	**Extreme**
Rare	Low	Low	Low	Medium	Medium
Unlikely	Low	Medium	Medium	Medium	High
Possible	Low	Medium	Medium	High	High
Likely	Medium	Medium	High	High	Very high
Almost certain	Medium	High	High	Very high	Very high

monitor in those situations and convert into a specific risk analysis, with risk being "the likelihood of an unwanted incident (an event) and its consequence (impact) for a specific asset."[118]

"Several consequence descriptors may apply to a single risk. The most serious/significant of these should be used to determine the risk exposure rating. The likelihood and impact levels are then cross tabulated to give a risk exposure rating."[119] This calculates whether a risk is categorized as red, amber, yellow or green (Table 9.1).[120] Use of color-coding enables rapid communication and understanding of risks. This ranking of risks that are assigned the same risk exposure rating is determined by examining the strength of the control measures in place for these risks. For instance, "a *high* rated risk could have effective control measures in place that cannot be improved upon, whereas a *medium* rated risk may not have any control measures in place, and this is the risk that should be prioritized for action."[121]

This research focuses on two different scenarios targeting broad sectors within the scope of a globalized world. These scenarios are, cloud services in business transactions and cloud services in scientific research. While the first refers to a corporate form usually found in the so-called "personal cloud"[122] where end-users and SMEs contract a cloud provider to better run their day-to-day businesses, the second refers to a research form that is typically found in transnational research such as genetic research projects within clinical trials. These two scenarios provide two completely different ideal use cases. In this context, the risk assessment model is combined with

[118]Beckers (2015, p. 457).

[119]Lund et al. (2011, p. 137).

[120]Lund et al. (2011, p. 137). This figure has been taken from the risk management of HAI and slightly adapted by the author.

[121]Lund et al. (2011, p. 137).

[122]Many people are already using the so-called "personal cloud" like Apple's iCloud or Dropbox or Amazon Cloud Storage or Evernote. This also includes the employees of a company or an organization who use these applications to manage their daily work activities. See Radizeski (2012, p. 22). In this sense, a "personal cloud" system is also readily available for everyone to use it.

an adaptive and flexible SLA with a data-centric monitoring infrastructure. The main focus is to expand the range of SLAs to cover cross-border activities similar to the use cases depicted below. The overall aim is to equip the involved parties with a tool that can offer more choices to satisfy the legal requirements in cloud computing and Big Data transformations.

9.9.1 Use Case 1: Cloud Services in Business Transactions

This is the typical scenario where individuals or companies of all sizes specifically SMEs from different geographic areas (local, regional, international), contract a cloud computing service for a specific purpose in order to operate a particular kind of business. By way of an example, we refer to the classical scenario in the webserver scope.[123] Consider the situation of an SME that sells products on-line like smartphone products or books. If a company hosts its website on a single server, the website could get overloaded and overrun at some point of the year such as Christmas or Valentine's Day, which are the periods of the year when customers buy more products. If this situation occurred, the company's website might not be able to sufficiently process and store its customers' information. Nevertheless, if the company hosted its website "in the cloud," a constellation of services are available since the servers are interconnected and so the processing, memory and storage capabilities are enhanced and shared.[124]

This cluster or network of computers which are "in the cloud" can handle more data during peak load times than a single server. This scenario refers to a very general form of cloud services that involve cross-border transactions at least when it comes to offering products and services worldwide. From an end-user perspective, these kinds of scenarios prevent the investment of substantial amounts of capital in terms of hardware, software, and other services. If we consider this scenario, it may be noticed that resources can be scaled up or down depending on processing or storage needs.[125] This also means cost savings for the company by only paying high costs during such peak load times, instead of having to pay for all the equipment and extra servers to cover the potential demand if this were to happen during a busy time of the year. Therefore, instead of buying extra powerful servers, they can be rented for a lower cost. As databases are moved to the cloud and distributed across different servers, cloud computing also enables a high degree of redundancy, which offers users the capability to backup. This means that if one server is down for any reason, such as a shortage of power supply, there is usually enough data replicated on another server, which avoids the problem of data loss.[126]

---

[123]This example was mentioned in Chap. 2 of this book.

[124]See Griffith (2012), Chaps. 1 and 2 with further references.

[125]Barnatt (2010, p. 11), Rosenberg and Mateos (2011, p. 5).

[126]See, generally, Smoot and Tan (2012), introduction.

Table 9.2 Example of policy category

• RISK CATEGORY: Policy
• ASSET IDENTIFIED: SLA
• VULNERABILITY OF ASSET: Lack of jurisdiction information
• THREAT TO ASSET: Database rights
• RISK LIKELIHOOD: Almost certain
• RISK IMPACT: Major
• RESULTING RISK LEVEL: Product of risk likelihood and risk impact = Very high
• RISK EVENT: This risk takes place at step number 5 (see Fig. 9.4) during service operation when the cloud provider attempts to federate the databases. This redeployment of databases may lead to changes in jurisdiction and thus the applicable law
• RESULTING RISK MITIGATION: Check monitoring logs: this threat needs to be monitored by traversing the logs that record where the databases are moved during the whole cloud computing life cycle

From a legal standpoint, due to the intrinsic characteristics of cloud computing, legal risks have grown more acute. End-users are now forced to navigate through a veritable mosaic of countless jurisdictions. As seen earlier, in most jurisdictions, no statutory law provides a specific definition of "ownership" rights of data, and database rights are only applicable to EU Member States. Very few other countries (i.e., Mexico and South Korea) have similar database rights provisions comparable to the EU. The risk model in this research will be applied to assess some of these legal risks that will fall under four general categories: (i) policy; (ii) legal; (iii) general; and (iv) technical. An example of the first category ("policy") is illustrated in Table 9.2.[127]

In this case, the threat of moving databases to jurisdictions other than the ones selected by end-users can be detected by using monitoring log files that can constantly document the movement of databases. This can be achieved by repeatedly checking the files using the following rule:[128] *if* (location == 'unknown_IP_address') *then*, *Check* risk inventory *where* 'Asset == Database', *output* 'Impact Level of Risk.'[129] This level of risk can be communicated to the cloud brokers, who can then decide upon the best mitigation strategy, and whether to accept the risk if the impact level is low, or shut down certain processes if the impact level is deemed to be too high.[130]

Since there is no direct link between end-users and infrastructure providers, the ability to get informed explicit consent from end-users is not always feasible. Therefore, assurances and a best-effort approach from cloud brokers offer a good alternative to achieve legal compliance.[131] In the example above, the asset identified is the SLA, which consists of specific requirements adapted from the end-user's request. The SLA can include Data Management (DM) specific technical options, such as

[127]For details of the risk model, see Djemame et al. (2011b, pp. 119–126).

[128]Djemame et al. (2012, pp. 11–12).

[129]Djemame et al. (2012, pp. 11–12).

[130]Djemame et al. (2012, pp. 11–12).

[131]See Kirkham et al. (2012a, pp. 1063–1069), Alhadeff et al. (2010, pp. 1–122).

replication rate, in the infrastructure. This risk assessment allows end-users to track back-up and replication jobs when the databases and VMs grow too fast and may be quickly depleted on the target repository. This will provide greater control for end-users to monitor where their databases are located in automated cloud environments. The steps described above were implemented in the OPTIMIS toolkit.[132]

Coming back to the different stages of the risk assessment (Fig. 9.4), at stage number 1 the initial risk assessment is done based on the end-user's explicit consent for certain forms of data processing. The broker uses this risk assessment to determine the matching capabilities and filters them from the list of cloud providers. The compliance data from this first screening procedure is retrieved from the DM using the XML Provider Description Template depicted above in Chap. 8. This is why the XML improved template is fundamental; it contains critical information with regards to the setup and management of the infrastructure provider. At stage 2, the IP receives the SLA and carries out its own risk assessment in the infrastructure in order to make sure it can fulfill the SLA requirements. Next, a third risk assessment is completed in stage 3. This assessment is carried out by the broker. They will use the XML in order to investigate business-oriented risks including more technical and legal data such as jurisdictional issues. If all these assessments go through, a re-evaluation of the SLA risk is performed. This is done in case the infrastructure provider changed any parameter during its own risk assessment.[133]

Finally, once the SLA is agreed between the broker and infrastructure provider, the service operation and execution phase starts. During this last stage, the broker may act as a trusted third party and carry out a continuous risk assessment service in order to monitor that the SLA is never breached. This can be assured by a report from the DM that produces an XML view based on the current status of the data processed by the infrastructure provider. The DM exposes two interfaces. The first one consists of an XML update report that is used to monitor location information and storage resources. This report includes the used replication factor as well as the location of the storage nodes. Then the specific component within the risk assessment tool (the "IPRAT")[134] collects the relevant information and performs the risk assessment accordingly. The second interface refers to the ability of the IPRAT to suggest actions to reduce the risk levels. The suggested actions include: (i) enablement of federation; (ii) addition/removal of storage services; (iii) increase/decrease in the number of resources; and (iv) increase of replication. This set of actions can be largely grouped into mandatory and voluntary actions. The mandatory actions should always be followed. The option to federate data, however, belongs to the voluntary category as it can be explicitly stated by end-users in the SLA that they do not want to transfer data outside their own jurisdiction under any given circumstance.[135]

---

[132] Kirkham et al. (2012b, pp. 156–160).

[133] Kirkham et al. (2012b, pp. 156–160).

[134] Kirkham et al. (2012b, pp. 156–160). The results of this risk assessment are carried out using different formulas. For example, the results of the risk calculation are ranked using the Euclidean Distance norm.

[135] Kirkham et al. (2012b, pp. 156–160).

Furthermore, as in the "immortal soul" example explained in the previous chapter,[136] certain situations exist where the cloud provider wishes to unilaterally modify some of the contractual terms or service levels of the original agreement. It is expected that the quality of that service must dynamically change through time. Nevertheless, this situation might undermine the general interest of end-users and could be detrimental to the balanced relationship between end-users and cloud providers. SLAs should be managed in such a way as to safeguard the correct balance between the involved parties. The SLA should include a risk-aware mechanism based on which contractual terms would be regularly monitored in order to remedy an unbalanced contractual relationship. In this situation, the risk assessment tool will trigger a warning signal in order to correct or restore the effects of any detrimental clause to the end-user. An example of the second category ("legal") is illustrated in Table 9.3.

In this case, the broker will make a systematic *re-assessment* of the contractual terms of the SLA. Even if this re-assessment suggests no substantial changes, it is beneficial for the end-users of cloud computing services as they cannot assess the SLAs themselves. This will also allow them to make the best use of competition in the market as changing the provider may put end-users at a cost-disadvantage; leaving the cloud provider can turn out to be more expensive in the end. In such a case, the re-assessment can substitute the end-user's choice according to market competition.

Table 9.3 Example of legal category

• RISK CATEGORY: Legal
• ASSET IDENTIFIED: SLA
• VULNERABILITY OF ASSET: New clauses unilaterally and arbitrarily included in the SLA by the cloud provider
• THREAT TO ASSET: New clauses may create an imbalance between the contractual parties. This may also undermine the general interests of end-users
• RISK LIKELIHOOD: Possible
• RISK IMPACT: Moderate
• RESULTING RISK LEVEL: Product of risk likelihood and risk impact = Medium
• RISK EVENT: This risk takes place at step number 5 (see Fig. 9.4) during service operation. That is, when the cloud provider is running the service and suddenly changes/up- dates the SLA (Terms and Conditions) without prior notification to end-users
• RESULTING RISK MITIGATION: Audit SLAs: The SLA should include a risk-aware mechanism to constantly monitor its terms

[136]See Chap. 8 of this book.

9.9.2 Use Case 2: Genetic Research Projects Within Clinical Trials Scenarios

Genetic research projects within clinical trial scenarios frequently collect biological and genetic data from patients/participants. This data is then stored in a hospital's databases for future research purposes. Genetic data is regarded to be unique and very sensitive as it has the potential of revealing personal, scientific and medical information of each patient, including the family members of the data subject.[137] For this reason, genetic research projects typically handle anonymized data using advanced encryption tools in order to safeguard patients' privacy rights and be in compliance with data protection laws. Once the data has become entirely anonymous, it is ready to be used by the research community.[138] It is not the purpose of this chapter to discuss data protection matters; rather this section focuses on answering the question, who has the "ownership" rights of such data and databases? Or, who is allowed to use and get access to such data for scientific research purposes? In other words, it is more about the controllability of data and databases, and will point to some general features of the SLA that, in tandem with the risk assessment tool, may help to clarify and mitigate some of the uncertainties around these questions.

For this reason, the role of the broker in this type of use case scenario is very important as it can take on a fiduciary nature as a trusted third-party and audit such compliance. The broker can intervene and be in charge of engaging and establishing continuous communication with end-users. At the same time, some of the brokers may correct the complaints or requests of the end-users and serve as a gateway to information that is necessary to clarify and rectify the contractual terms of the SLA. This provides an opportunity to expand its assistance as a mere agent considerably beyond the model for what has already been established and cover various use case scenarios within an international framework. Tables 9.4 and 9.5 illustrate some of the risk assessment features that fall within the "policy" and "legal" categories.

Finally, when the researchers and doctors use a cloud computing service to store and process patient data, they are particularly concerned about the confidentiality and integrity of such data. These two aspects are integral parts of the security infrastructure, but so is the *availability* of such data during a time of crisis. While confidentiality refers to the property of data or information not being made available or disclosed to unauthorized persons,[139] integrity means that the information must be accurate (i.e., not allowing data to be modified).[140] Availability, on the other hand, is concerned with ensuring that data and services are accessible where and when they are needed with the proviso that they are consistent with the SLA legal framework.[141]

[137] See Article 29 Data Protection Working Party, Working Document on Genetic Data. Adopted on March 17, 2004, pp. 1–14, [online]. Available at: https://iapp.org/media/pdf/knowledge_center/wp91_Genetic-Data_03-2004.pdf. Accessed May 10 2019.

[138] See Forgó et al. (2010).

[139] Gough and Nettleton (2010, p. 149).

[140] Kattan et al. (2011, p. 199).

[141] Williams (2013, p. 187), Bonewell (2006, p. 1178).

Table 9.4 Example of policy/legal category

• RISK CATEGORY: Policy/Legal
• ASSET IDENTIFIED: Data ("ownership" rights of new data generated by Big Data applications)
• VULNERABILITY OF ASSET: Lack of clarification within the SLA of who is allowed to use and access the new data generated in the cloud
• THREAT TO ASSET: SLA
• RISK LIKELIHOOD: Possible
• RISK IMPACT: Extreme
• RESULTING RISK LEVEL: Product of risk likelihood and risk impact = High
• RISK EVENT: Negligence. This risk takes place at steps number 1 and 3 (see Fig. 9.4). That is, when the broker sends the SLA request to various cloud providers and then filters the offers received. In this case, the broker must choose the provider according to end-user's criteria
• RESULTING RISK MITIGATION: Include a *string* field capability within the SLA, which allows the inclusion of contractual clauses that can clarify who is allowed to use this data for scientific research

Table 9.5 Example of legal category

• RISK CATEGORY: Legal
• ASSET IDENTIFIED: Databases
• VULNERABILITY OF ASSET: Database rights may create some constraints for scientific research
• THREAT TO ASSET: Database rights
• RISK LIKELIHOOD: Possible
• RISK IMPACT: Major
• RESULTING RISK LEVEL: High
• RISK EVENT: Negligence. This risk takes place at steps number 1 and 3 (see Fig. 9.4). That is, when the broker sends the SLA request to various cloud providers and then filters the offers received. In this case, the broker must choose the provider according to end-user's criteria
• RESULTING RISK MITIGATION: Clearly define database rights within the SLA through the XML Description Schema and add a Boolean "waiving" system whereby the cloud provider can choose to *keep* or *waive* database rights based on end-user's input

In the event of any disaster (i.e., earthquake, floods, etc.), the risk assessment framework through the CBS may help to fix the situation immediately and fill the gap in emergency situations. According to the ISO 27001, availability is "a characteristic that applies to assets. An asset is available if it is accessible and usable when needed by an authorized entity". Within the context of this ISO standard, "assets include things like information, systems, facilities, networks, and computers."[142] From a legal perspective, "availability" is strongly related to "ownership" rights of data as this also refers to the legal ability to control and make good use of data.

[142]For this term see ISO 27000 definitions [online]. Available at: https://www.praxiom.com/iso-27000-definitions.htm. Accessed 10 May 2019.

Table 9.6 Example of technical/general category

• RISK CATEGORY: Technical/General
• ASSET IDENTIFIED: Availability of data and databases
• VULNERABILITY OF ASSET: Lack of maintenance
• THREAT TO ASSET: Database server failure
• RISK LIKELIHOOD: Rare
• RISK IMPACT: Moderate
• RESULTING RISK LEVEL: Product of risk likelihood and risk impact = Low
• RISK EVENT: Unavailability of data due to server failure. This risk takes place at step number 5 (see Fig. 9.4) during service operation. That is, when the cloud provider is running the service and unexpectedly there is a server failure, i.e., one or more VMs stop running
• RESULTING RISK MITIGATION: Fault-tolerance solutions provision

Table 9.7 Example of technical/general category

RISK CATEGORY: Technical/General
• ASSET IDENTIFIED: Availability of data and databases
• VULNERABILITY OF ASSET: Data center infrastructure (servers)
• THREAT TO ASSET: Force majeure (such as floods, earthquakes, etc.)
• RISK LIKELIHOOD: Rare
• RISK IMPACT: Major
• RESULTING RISK LEVEL: Product of risk likelihood and risk impact = Medium
• RISK EVENT: Unavailability of data due to server failure: This risk takes place at step number 5 (see Fig. 9.4) during service operation. That is, when the cloud provider is running the service and unexpectedly there is an event of force majeure
• RESULTING RISK MITIGATION: Redundancy and use of back-up servers located in different places (cities). Data should be constantly replicated with databases and back-up solutions during the whole cloud computing service lifecycle

The threat analysis suggests that the risk ratings belonging to availability were identified and classified as medium in comparison to confidentiality (high) and integrity (low). This is because the end-users (or patients in this case) are more concerned with their privacy. Therefore, confidentiality has a stronger effect on trust and the provider's reputation. Integrity can be compromised by accidental software and user errors, equipment failure and/or deliberate alteration of data by third parties. It is relatively low, however, because the impact is much lower in comparison to the availability of data. Loss of availability is classified as medium since end-users and enterprises are better off using cloud computing provider resources rather than deploying their own infrastructure considering the cost benefits[143] (Tables 9.6 and 9.7).

[143] Khan et al. (2012, p. 124).

9.10 Summary and Interim Remarks

Increasing interest in the use of SLAs to govern interactions in cloud computing and Big Data has gained momentum. While such agreements are vital in ensuring a successful relationship between end-users and cloud providers, they are limited in scope and coverage. Such limitations may give rise to considerable exposure to risks not only for end-users, but also for service providers. Therefore, a risk assessment component has been fully implemented in the OPTIMIS software toolkit which aligns with the SLA framework in the context of grid and cloud resource brokers. This model provides a solution as to how to express these requirements on a technical level in the SLAs and the data management system. It has also been equipped with a monitoring tool as well as the requirements of an inherent legal risk inventory, which provides an additional layer of legal protection. This enables very fine-grained and continuous control over the data and databases thus allowing for the identification actions that are needed to reduce and mitigate such risks. Crucially, this new framework attempts not only to raise collective awareness of the risks entailed in a neglected area of research but also at increasing confidence levels, prompting the involved parties to trust each other to a greater extent than is currently the case.

References

Alhadeff J et al (2010) Requirements: privacy, governance and contractual options, pp 1–122, TAS3 Deliverable, WP6, D6.1, Version 3.0 http://cordis.europa.eu/docs/projects/cnect/7/216287/080/deliverables/002-TAS3D06p1Privacyre-quirementsv3p0.pdf. Accessed May 10, 2019

Andrieux A et al (2007) Web Services Agreement Specification (WS-Agreement), Global Forum American Heritage Dictionary https://www.ahdictionary.com/word/search.html?q=risk&submit.x=872&submit.y=. Accessed May 10, 2019

Barnatt C (2010) A brief guide to cloud computing: an essential guide to the next computing revolution. Kindle Edition, s.l, p 11

Batre D et al (2007) Gaining Users' Trust by Publishing Failure Probabilities. Security and Privacy in Communications Networks and the Workshops, SecureComm 2007. Proceedings of the Third International Conference on Security and Privacy in Communication Networks, Nice, p 193

Beckers K (2015) Pattern and security requirements: engineering-based establishment of security standards. Springer, Cham, p 457

Bonewell D (2006) Security and privacy for data warehouses: opportunity or threat? In: Tipton H, Krause M (eds) Information security management handbook, 5th edn. Auerbach Publications, Boca Ratón, p 1178

Bradshaw S, Millard C, Waelden I (2010) Contracts for Clouds: Comparison and Analysis of the Terms and Conditions of Cloud Computing Services, Queen Mary School of Law Legal Studies Research Paper No. 63/2010, pp. 31–32 http://ssrn.com/abstract01662374. Accessed May 10, 2019

Burnett R (2005) Legal risk management for the it industry. Comput Law Secur Report 21(1):61–67

Caralli R et al (2007) Introducing OCTAVE Allegro: Improving the Information Security Risk Assessment Process, Technical Report. Software Engineering Institute, Carnegie Mellon, s.l

Cattedu D, Hogben G (2009) Cloud Computing: Benefits, Risks and Recommendations for Information Security, ENISA (European Network and Information Security Agency) http://

www.enisa.europa.eu/act/rm/files/deliverables/cloud-computing-risk-assessment/at_down-load/fullReport. Accessed May 10 2019
Chung L et al (2000) Non-functional requirements in software engineering. Springer, New York
Chung L, Sampaio do Prado Leite J (2009) On non-functional requirements in software engineering. In: Borgida A et al (eds) Conceptual modeling: foundations and applications, Essays in Honor of John Mylopoulos, Lecture Notes in Computer Science/Information Systems and Applications, incl. Internet/Web, and HCI (Book 5600). Springer, Berlin
Ciborra C (2005) Digital Technologies and the Duality of Risk, Centre for Analysis of Risk and Regulation. London School of Economics and Political Science, London
Ciborra C (2007) Digital technologies and risk: a critical review. In: Hanseth O, Ciborra C (eds) Risk, complexity and ICT. Edgar Elgar Publishing, Cheltenham, p 27
Ciborra C (2009) Imbrication of representations: risks and digital technologies. In: Avgerou C, Lanzara F, Willcocks L (eds) Bricolage, care and information systems: Claudio Ciborra's legacy in information systems research. Palgrave MacMillan, New York, p 78
Corrales M (2012) Privacy risk impact assessment: a new requirement for safer clouds. Beck-Online, ZD-Aktuell, p 03036
Davison M (2003) The legal protection of databases. Cambridge University Press, Cambridge, p. 97
Dean J (2014) Big data, data mining and machine learning: value creation for business leaders and practitioners. Wiley, Hoboken, p 10
Djemame K et al (2011a) Brokering of risk-aware service level agreements in grids. Concurr Comput: Pract Exp 23(13):1558–1582
Djemame K et al (2011b) A risk assessment framework and software toolkit for cloud service ecosystems, The Second International Conference on Cloud Computing, GRIDs, and Virtualization, p 119 http://www.optimis-project.eu/content/risk-assessment-framework-and-software-toolkit-cloud-service-ecosystems. Accessed May 10, 2019
Djemame K et al (2012) Legal issues in the cloud: towards a risk inventory. Philos Trans R Soc A 371(1983)
Djemame K et al (2013) Legal issues in clouds: towards a risk inventory. Phil Trans R Soc A 371(1983) https://royalsocietypublishing.org/doi/full/10.1098/rsta.2012.0075. Accessed May 10, 2019
Djemame K (2016) A risk assessment framework for cloud computing. IEEE Trans Cloud Comput 4(3):265–278
Drissi S, Houmani H, Medromi H (2013) Survey: risk assessment for cloud computing. Int J Adv Comput Sci Appl (IJACSA) 4(12):143–148
Fellows W (2013) Cloud Brokers: Now Seeking Ready-to-Pay Customers, 451 Research https://451research.com/report-long?icid=2666. Accessed May 10, 2019
Fellows W (2014) Cloud Brokers: Making ITaaS a Practical Reality? 451 Research https://451research.com/images/Marketing/451_CloudBrokers_2014_ExecOverview.pdf. Accessed May 10, 2019
Forgó N et al (2010) Ethical and legal requirements for transnational genetic research. Beck, Munich
Garner B (ed) (2014) Black's Law dictionary, 10th edn. Thomson Reuters, St. Paul
Gouch J, Nettleton D (2010) Managing the documentation maze: answers to questions you didn't even know. Wiley, Hoboken, p 149
Gough J, Nettleton D (2010) Managing the documentation maze: answers to questions you didn't even know. Wiley, Hoboken
Gourlay I et al (2008) Reliability and risk in grid resource brokering. In: Second IEEE International Conference on Digital Ecosystems and Technologies (IEEE DEST 2008)
Gourlay I, Djemame J, Padgett J (2009) Evaluating provider reliability in grid resource brokering. In: 11th IEEE international conference on high performance computing and communications, p 36 https://ieeexplore.ieee.org/document/5166974. Accessed May 10, 2019
Griffith R (2012) A short introduction to cloud computing: everything you need to know in around 1000 Words, locs. 21 and 29. Kindle Edition

Grosan C, Abraham A (2011) Ruled-Based Expert Systems. In: Grosan C, Abraham C (eds) Intelligent systems: a modern approach, intelligent systems reference library, vol 17. Springer, Berlin, pp 149–185
Grossman J, Seehusen F (2015) Combining security risk assessment and security testing based on standards. In: Seehusen F et al (eds) Risk assessment and risk-driven testing, third international workshop, RISK 2015, Berlin Germany. Springer, Cham, p 23
Gutwirth S, Hildebrandt M (2010) Some caveats on profiling. In: Gutwirth S, Poullet Y, Paul de Hert P (eds) Data Protection in a Profiled World. Springer, Dordrecht, p 33
Holzinger A et al (2013) Combining HCI, natural language processing, and knowledge discovery—potential of ibm content analytics as an assistive technology in the biomedical field. In: Holzinger A, Pasi G (eds) Human computer interaction and knowledge discovery in complex, unstructured, big data, third international workshop, HCI-KDD 2013, Maribor, Slovenia, July 2013, Proceedings. Springer, Heidelberg, p 13
Ishikawa H (2015) Social big data mining. CRC Press, Boca Ratón
Jackson P (1998) Introduction to expert systems, 3rd edn. Addison-Wesley, Harlow
Jentzsch N (2007) Financial privacy: an international comparison of credit reporting systems, 2nd edn. Springer, Berlin, p 27
Jones B, Bird I (2013) Data-intensive production grids. In: Critchlow T, Kleese van Dam K (eds) Data-intensive science. Chapman & Hall (CRC Press), Boca Ratón, pp 160 et seq
Jrad F (2014) A service broker for intercloud computing, Doctoral Thesis, Karlsruhe Institute of Technology, KIT, p 4 http://d-nb.info/1054989486/34. Accessed May 10, 2019
Kasemsap K, Sunandha S (2015) The role of cloud computing adoption in global business. In: Chang V, Walter R, Wills G (eds) Delivery and adoption of cloud computing services in contemporary organizations. Information Science Reference (IGI Global), Hershey, p 33
Kattan I, Nunu A, Saleh K (2011) A stochastic model for improving information security in supply chain systems. In: Wang J (ed) Supply chain optimization, management and integration: emerging applications. Business Science Reference, Hershey, p 199
Khan A et al (2012) Security risks and their management in cloud computing. In: 2012 IEEE 4th international conference on cloud computing technology and science, IEEE computer society, p 122 https://ieeexplore.ieee.org/document/6427574. Accessed May 10, 2019
Kirkham T et al (2012a) Assuring data privacy in cloud transformations, trust, security and privacy in computing and communications (TrustCom). In: 2012 IEEE 11th international conference on digital object identifier, pp 1063–1069 https://ieeexplore.ieee.org/iel5/6294581/6295938/06296092.pdf. Accessed May 10, 2019
Kirkham T et al (2012b) Risk based SLA management in clouds: a legal perspective, The 7th International Conference for Internet Technology and Secured Transactions, IEEE (ICITST 2012), pp 156–160 https://ieeexplore.ieee.org/document/6470934. Accessed May 10, 2019
Kirkham T et al (2013) Richer requirements for better clouds. In: 2013 IEEE international conference on cloud computing technology and science. IEEE Computer Society, p 7. https://ieeexplore.ieee.org/document/6735388?section=abstract. Accessed May 10, 2019
Kitchin R (2014) The data revolution: big data, open data. Data Infrastructures & Their Consequences. Sage Publications Ltd., Los Angeles
Kousiouris G et al (2013) A cloud provider description schema for meeting legal requirements in cloud federation scenarios. In: Douligeris et al (eds) Collaborative, Trusted and Privacy-Aware e/m-Services, 12th IFIP WG 6.11 conference on e-business, e-services, and esociety, I3E 2013, Athens, Greece, Apr 25–26 2013, Proceedings. Springer, Heidelberg
Krishnan K (2013) Data warehousing in the age of big data. Elsevier, Amsterdam, p 5
Li T, Singh M (2014) Hybrid trust framework for loss of control in cloud management. In: Jeong H et al (eds) Advances in computer science and its applications: CSA 2013. Springer, Heidelberg, p 670
Leber D, Hermann J (2013) Decision analysis methods for selecting consumer services with attribute value uncertainty. In: Lee M et al (eds) Risk assessment and evaluation of predictions. Springer, New York, p 406

Lohr S (2015) Data-ism: the revolution transforming decision making, consumer behavior, and almost everything else. HarperCollins Publishers, New York
Lund M, Solhaug B, Stolen K (2011) Model-driven risk analysis: the CORAS approach. Springer, Heidelberg, p 131 et seq
Luiijf E (2016) Threats in industrial control systems. In: Colbert E, Kott A (eds) Cybersecurity of SCADA and other industrial control systems. Springer, Cham, p 69
Mckelvey N et al (2015) Cloud computing and security in the future. In: Zhu S, Hill R. Trovati M (eds) Guide to security assurance for cloud computing. Springer, Cham, p 100
Mahmood Z (2014) (ed) Continued rise of the cloud: advances and trends in cloud computing. Springer, London
Majkic Z (2014) Big data integration theory: theory and methods of database mappings, programming languages, and semantics. Springer, Cham
Nwankwo S (2014) Developing a Risk Assessment Methodology for Data Protection, IRI Blog https://blog.iri.uni-hannover.de/index.php/2014/12/17/developing-a-risk-assessment-methodology-for-data-protection/. Accessed May 10, 2019
Pearson S, Yee G (2013) (eds) Privacy and security for cloud computing, computer communications and networks series. Springer, London
Radizeski P (2012) Sellecom 2: selling cloud services, Rad-Info, Inc. Lulu.com, p 22
Rejas-Muslera R, Cuadraro-Gallego J, Rodriguez D (2007) Defining a legal risk management strategy: process, legal risk and lifecycle. In: Abrahamsson P et al (eds) Software process improvement, vol 2007. Lecture Notes in Computer Science, Programming and Software Engineering, Proceeding of the 14th European Software Process Improvement Conference, EuroSPI 2007, Potsdam, Germany, September. Springer, Berlin, pp 118–124
Ridley E (2015) Big data and risk assessment. In: Kalyvas J, Overly M (eds) Big data: a business and legal guide. CRC Press, Boca Ratón, p 79
Rosenberg J, Mateos A (2011) The cloud at your service: the when, how, and why of enterprise cloud computing. Manning Publications Co., Greenwich, p 1
Sakr S, Gaber M (2014) (eds) Large scale and big data: processing and management. CRC Press, Boca Ratón
Sangrasi A, Djemame K, Jokhio I (2012) Aggregating Node Level Risk Assessment in Grids Using an R-out-of-N Model. In: Chowdhry B et al (eds) Emerging trends and applications in information communication technologies: second international multi topic conference, IMTIC 2012, Jamshoro, Pakistan, March 2012, proceedings, communications in computer and information science, vol 281. Springer, Heidelberg, pp 445–452
Shantz J (2005) Beyond risk and boredom: reflections on claudio ciborra and sociology. Eur J Inf Syst 14:510–514
Sharif A, Basri S (2011) Software risk assessment: a review on small and medium software projects. In: Zain J, Mohd W, El-Qawasmeh E (eds) Software engineering and computer systems, Second International Conference ICSECS 2011, Kuantan, Pahang, Malaysia, June 2011, Proceedings Part 2. Springer, Heidelberg, p 222
Smoot S, Tan N (2012) Private cloud computing: consolidation, virtualization, and service-oriented infrastructure. Elsevier, Waltham
Stone R (2005) The modern law of contract, 6th edn. Cavendish Publishing, London, p 14
Summer J, Ross T, Ababouchi L (2004) Application of risk assessment in the fish industry, FAO Fisheries Technical Paper No. 442, Part 1, p 6
Sundara Rajan M (2011) Moral rights: principles, practice and new technology. Oxford University Press, Oxford, p 286
Susskind R (1998) The future of law. Oxford University Press, Oxford, p 290
Taubenberger S (2011) Problem analysis of traditional it-security risk assessment methods—an experience report from the insurance and auditing domain. In: Camensich J et al (eds) future challenges in security and privacy for academia and industry, 26th IFIP TC 11 international information security conference, SEC 2011, Lucerne Switzerland, June 2011, Proceedings. Springer, Heidelberg, p 260

Teng F, Magoules F (2010) Future of grids resources management. In: Frederic Magoules (ed) Fundamentals of grid computing: theory, algorithms and technologies. Chapman and Hall (CRC Press), Boca Ratón, p 126
Toosizadeh S, Farshchi R (2011) Ruled-based programming for building expert systems: how do you create an expert system? LAP Lambert Academic Publishing, s.l
Vashist R (2015) Cloud Computing infrastructure for massive data: a gigantic task ahead. In: Hassanien A et al (eds) Big data in complex systems: challenges and opportunities, studies in big data, Vol 9. Springer, Cham, p 1
Vraalsen F et al (2005) Specifying legal risk scenarios using the CORAS threat modeling language: experiences and the way forward. In: Herrmann P, Issarny V, Shiu S (eds) Trust management, third international conference, iTrust 2005, Paris, France, May 23–26, 2005. Proceedings, Series Vol 3477. Springer, Berlin, pp 45–60
Wahlgren P (2007) Legislative Techniques, p. 91, In: Wintgens L (ed) Legislation in Context: Essays in Legisprudence, Applied Legal Philosophy. Ashgate Pub Co., Hampshire
Williams P (2013) Information security governance: a risk assessment approach to health information systems protection. In: Hovenga E, Grain H (eds) Health information governance in a digital environment. IOS Press, Amsterdam, p 187
Wright D, De Hert P (2012) (eds) Privacy impact assessment, law, governance and technology series, vol 6. Springer, Dordrecht
Wu L et al (2013) Automated SLA negotiation framework for cloud computing. In: Cluster, cloud and grid computing (CCGrid), 2013 13th IEEE/ACM international symposium, May 2013, pp 235–244 https://ieeexplore.ieee.org/document/6546098. Accessed May 10, 2019

Chapter 10
Conclusion—Main Findings and Contributions to the Current Knowledge

10.1 Theoretical Contribution

This book taps into two main streams of the economic analysis of law and advances the proposition that cloud computing architectures will benefit from making use of both strands of thoughts. The purpose is to take some of the key tenets of the traditional school of law and economics, but give greater weight to the new behavioral insights within the reach of cloud computing and Big Data transformations. The theoretical framework of this work draws from different paradigms and lies not only in conceptual and abstract thoughts but suggests a change with significant legal and pragmatic implications. In many instances, this framework critically outlines existing theories and extends them to construct an archetype that can better describe the research questions under study and relates them to the broader field of electronic contracts and SLAs.[1]

This theoretical framework crystallizes and solidifies in what I call "Plan-like Architectures," by which cloud end-users are in a better position to negotiate the "ownership" rights of their data and databases. As the current cloud computing and Big Data markets limit the scope of SLAs and pose technically complex issues for individual customers and SMEs, the role of innovation intermediaries (or brokers) can help to translate these intricacies during the negotiation process. Cloud brokers are hubs in this supple communication network. They can elicit the requirements of end-users and pursue the cloud providers that best reflect their needs. The promise of this book lays in the assumption that cloud brokers are in a better position to steer and coordinate some of the perils that rest in the ubiquitous and global nature of the cloud.

This is where Plan-like Architectures and its planning agency model comes to the forefront. Within this approach, expressing the true *intention* of individuals is fundamental. Intentions are "plan states" that constrain our thinking. They do what

---

[1] See, generally, Swanson (2013, pp. 5–73).

M. Corrales Compagnucci, *Big Data, Databases and "Ownership" Rights in the Cloud*, Perspectives in Law, Business and Innovation,
https://doi.org/10.1007/978-981-15-0349-8_10

Bratman calls "filter multiple options." The cloud broker's role is to combine legal analysis and technical knowledge in order to automate the process and "filter" the selection of multiple providers. This will reduce deliberation and bargaining costs. Furthermore, the role of the cloud broker is to ensure that the two parties (end users and cloud providers) are in line with their legal requirements and reach a mutual agreement that will be beneficial and clear for both sides.

The systematic theoretical framework presented here incorporates a general set of ideas that better explains and understands the cloud and Big Data phenomena from a legal point of view. A higher caliber of analysis will indeed be needed in future works for this to qualify as a fully-fledged theory. Therefore, I do not claim that Plan-like Architectures will capture all the complexities surrounding cloud and Big Data transformations. Nevertheless, the void may be filled by other legal sources and we can always adjust the contours of this framework given the continually changing world that encompasses the cloud. Even if cloud computing and Big Data services undergo a disruptive change as technological advances are made, this general conceptualization, seen from a high-level perspective, is hardly likely to be altered.

10.2 Scientific Contribution

"Big Data" has been identified as a "gold mine"[2] and as Meglena Kuneva, the former European Consumer Commissioner said in her speech in March 2009, "...data is the new oil of the Internet and the new currency of the digital world."[3] This is particularly true since raw data flow through the Internet and becomes information when it is presented in a meaningful and useful context.[4] As historian of information, James Gleick moves this discussion further along to say "information is what our world runs on: the blood and the fuel, the vital principle. It pervades the science from top to bottom transforming every branch of knowledge."[5] Indeed, information will ultimately turn into knowledge,[6] and knowledge is quintessentially a human creation.[7] Against this backdrop, databases are valuable tools used to gather, store and present information. They play a key role in cloud computing and Big Data services and they are at the core of business transactions, representing one of the main assets an organization might have.

As with any intellectual property matter, the European Database Directive was designed to counterbalance two opposite forces. In the words of Maurer et al.,

[2]Raley (2013, p. 123). For Marshall, "Big Data is surely the Gold Rush of the Information Age." See Marshall (2012, p. 1).

[3]Kuneva (2009).

[4]Liu et al. (2002) (eds), Raman (2007, p. 197).

[5]Gleick (2010, p. 20).

[6]Onifade et al. (2010, p. 234).

[7]Knox (2007, p. 681).

"database protection was like the big mongrel dog that nobody wanted to wake."[8] Database protection is indeed an instrument that may foster innovation and investment within the database industry. On the opposing end, stringent laws such as database rights may also create a monopoly of information. Notably, statistics have shown that about 50% of all legal suits have been raised by a scarce minority of companies that own telephone directories, sport betting fixtures, concert events, and broadcast schedules.[9] Ironically, what these companies have in common is that they do not collect data from the outside world. They create it through events organized by themselves. This sort of data is known as "synthetic" data.[10]

The CJEU has ruled out that compilations of "synthetic" data require database protection unless some additional "substantial investment" is made in presenting and verifying the content of such "sole-source" databases. This interpretation is very important in preventing the emergence of a monopoly being established in the area of information. Nevertheless, circumventing the "substantial investment" test would not be very difficult to achieve and database makers of "sole-source" databases should already be aware of this.[11] In addition, even though scientists do not often use synthetic data resources like geospatial information (earth, soil and climate), the acquisition of these data are hardly going to be funded again. Many scientists and organizations have expressed their concerns about how private companies might further control and monopolize information.[12]

At the present time, the biggest challenge is undoubtedly the emergence of the Big Data movement along with scientific databases such as those containing biological and genetic data. Big Data is often collected from different sources as the premise is to gather as much data as possible. Then, with the use of data mining, artificial intelligence and analytical tools, new data is created and presented in a summary form. This is also known as "data aggregation" and is used for purposes such as statistical analysis.[13] When it comes to "owning" genetic data, people tend to react emotionally. The underlying data sets or the new data generated in the cloud could create some problems when it comes to apportioning "ownership" rights of such data.

This being said, the European Database Directive might have turned out to be like a double-edged sword that could challenge scientific progress. It's archaic protective mentality may also slow down the cloud market and obstruct businesses from flourishing. This book aims at filling the gap in the current debates. The solution I submit in this work advocates for the establishment of clear language concerning "ownership" rights of data and databases seeking to prevent ex-ante future controversies. In addition, this quest should no longer be exclusively anchored inside domestic or regional legal orders, but rather the search for legal certainty should be oriented in

[8] Maurer et al. (2001, p. 789).

[9] Maurer (2008, pp. 13–14 and 13–80).

[10] Maurer et al. (2001, pp. 789–790).

[11] Hugentholtz (2005, pp. 203–219).

[12] Maurer et al. (2001, pp. 789–790).

[13] Maurer et al. (2001, pp. 789–790), see, also, generally, Karthick and Kalarani (2014, pp. 28–32).

a multi-jurisdictional environment that takes into account the trans-border nature of the cloud.

This implies that there is an increasing interest in the planning of clear-cut rules at the early stages of SLA negotiations. At the upper end of the spectrum, I propose the development of a contractual framework to assign and clarify "ownership" rights of data and databases. At the other end of the scale, I have developed a new contractual model for thinking about the sharing of information (Big Data) on a global scale. Using key insights from law, economics, psychology, sociology, philosophy, and IT, this book advocates for a more balanced and transparent process during negotiation (and re-negotiation) of SLAs in the cloud.

This book provides cloud brokerage services with a new template, which has been embedded in a computer software. This toolkit deals specifically with these legal issues and can be implemented as an adjunct to other SLA offerings. I argue that the cloud broker can release end-users from the tedious task of selecting the right cloud provider and help them to negotiate the contractual terms more effectively and successfully on an equal basis. Thus, "ownership" rights of data and database may be checked in a machine-readable way in order to fully grasp the potential of cloud computing and Big Data in dynamic cloud scenarios. If cloud providers were able to recognize and implement an SLA framework that has an established method which clarifies data and databases "ownership" rights in an automated and efficient fashion, and, if there were agreement among the parties involved in every cloud computing transaction, this would serve as a vehicle to reduce transaction costs and lead to more legal certainty.

In light of the above, it can be concluded that this work takes theory to practice. From a pragmatic point of view, one of the main disadvantages is that data and databases are managed by a third party. Therefore, issues of mutual trust and control are strongly associated with some legal implications. Once the databases leave the physical environment of an organization there are several risks related to data and databases. The concept of "risk" should not only be construed in the negative sense, but it should also be thought of as having a positive impact (a "reward"). Using the words of Eric Schou, they constitute the "yin and yang" of business and organizations that want to embrace the advantages of cloud computing and Big Data. The risk element of this is surrounded by the volatile nature of cloud computing and Big Data environments where end-users need to relinquish physical control of their data and deal with the uncertainties of giving up the management of one's own databases and computing infrastructure to a cloud provider.[14]

Even though the concept of trust has been defined in many different ways, most authors seem to agree that trust is inextricably linked to risk.[15] In situations involving trust, it seems natural to find a strong correlation between risk and trust.[16] Therefore, the approach stressed in this book allows end-users to have more awareness and control over the specific risks to which they are exposed. Therefore, adopting a

[14]Schou (2011).

[15]Klijn and Eshuis (2013), Chap. 5 with further references.

[16]Almlund et al. (2011, p. 81).

multi-layered and multi-dimensional construct to trust, when combined with a strong risk management framework, provides a choice that can be more flexible and create competitive cost advantages for cloud businesses. For this reason, the risk assessment framework will be an indispensable tool for developing or adapting the trust management framework.

In sum, if Plan-like Architectures, along with the family of theories and the contractual framework submitted herein, is put into practice, then substantial effects will be observed in both the European and global economy because cloud customers will be able to assert or even relinquish their "ownership" rights of data and databases according to their special needs. This can also be implemented as an international business model where cloud brokerage services can act as a clearinghouse for "ownership" rights of data and databases. This approach will reduce risks and create a more trustworthy cloud environment, yielding significant results for electronic transactions across the globe.

References

Almlund M et al (2011) Personality, psychology and economics. In: Hanushek E, Machin S, Woessmann L (eds) Handbook of the economics of education, vol 4, Elsevier, Waltham, p 81

Gleick J (2010) The information: a history, a theory, a flood. Pantheon Books, New York, p 20

Hugentholtz B (2005) Abuse of database right sole-source information banks under the EU Database Directive. In: Lévêque F, Shelanski H (eds) Antitrust, patents and copyright: EU and US perspectives. New horizons in competition law and economics. Edward Elgar Publishing, Cheltenham, pp 203–219

Karthick N, Kalarani X (2014) A survey on data aggregation in big data and cloud computing. Int J Comput Trends Technol (IJCTT) 7(1):28–32

Klijn E, Eshuis J (2013) Trust and networks, Part I. In: Llewellyn S, Brookes S, Mahon A (eds) Trust and confidence in government and public services. Routledge, New York

Knox K (2007) The various and conflicting notions of information. In: Cohen E (ed) Information and beyond: Part II. Journal of issues in informing science and information technology, vol 4. Informing Science Press, Santa Rosa, p 681

Kuneva M (2009) Press Release, Speech/09/156, European Commission Database. http://europa.eu/rapid/press-release_SPEECH-09-156_en.htm. Accessed May 10, 2019

Liu et al (eds) (2002) Organizational semiotics: evolving a science of information systems. In: IFIP TC8/WG8.1 working conference on organizational semiotics: evolving a science of information systems, July 23–25, 2001, Montreal, Quebec, Canada. Springer, New York

Marshall C (2012) Big data, the crowd, and me. https://www.semanticscholar.org/paper/Big-Data%2C-the-crowd-and-me-Marshall/1c8fba5bdc52ee125ce8ec79880a0dec9dbff468. Accessed 10 May 2019

Maurer S (2008) Across two worlds: database protection in the United States and Europe. In: Putnam J (ed) Intellectual property and innovation in the knowledge-based economy, conference proceedings, 23–24 May 2001, Toronto, ON, Canada. University of Calgary Press, Calgary, pp 13–14 and 13–80

Maurer S, Hugenholtz B, Onsrud H (2001) Europe's database experiment. Science 294(5543):789–790

Onifade O et al (2010) Fuzzontology: resolving information mining ambiguity in economic intelligent process. In: Prasad S et al (eds) Proceedings of the 4th international conference on information systems, technology and management, ICISTM 2010, Bangkok, Thailand, March 2010. Springer, Berlin, p 234

Raley R (2013) Dataveillance and countervailance. In: Gitelman L (ed) Raw data is an oxymoron. The MIT Press, Cambridge, p 123

Raman A (2007) knowledge management: a resource book. Excel Books, New Delhi, p 197

Schou E (2011) Database protection from a cloud computing and virtual environment perspective. SecurityWeek Network. https://www.securityweek.com/database-protection-cloud-computing-and-virtual-environment-perspective. Accessed 10 May 2019

Swanson R (2013) Theory building in applied disciplines. Berrett-Koehler Publishers, San Francisco, pp 5–73

Index

M. Corrales Compagnucci, *Big Data, Databases and "Ownership" Rights in the Cloud*, Perspectives in Law, Business and Innovation,
https://doi.org/10.1007/978-981-15-0349-8

D